# When My Mother was a Mountain

# When My Mother was a Mountain

By Regina Strongheart

Forest Circles

Published by Forest Circles

http://forestcircles.com/

ISBN: 979-8-9882014-0-3

This book is memoir and memory is subjective. It reflects the author's present recollections of experiences over time. Some names have been changed and some dialogue has been recreated. This work depicts actual events in the life of the author as truthfully and respectfully as recollection permits.

Cover painting by Kat Logan

Cover and Book Design by Clif Graves of Hinterlandspress.com

## Dedication

This is for Linda, who always believed in me

# Acknowledgments

I extend a huge thank you to the staff at the Topsham Public Library who provided a welcoming space and computer guidance over the last six years.

I want to thank John Eickert who, seven years ago, held my hand and encouraged me to write about my mystical adventures. Thank you Sarah Arnold for our late night dinners and listening as I read my latest chapters. My gratitude to Jack Collins, Anne Berry, and Rick Wile and his Writers Group for their encouragement when I first imagined I could write. To Emma J. Gibbon and Nancy Collins who generously read and reread my pieces and made me feel competent. To Chief Oscar Mokeme, Brian Spirit Bear, Josie Conte DO, and Susan Fekety NP, who shared their expertise for some sections. My thanks to my sister-in-law Dolly and to Paul LaFrance who were willing to journey back with me to the 70's and relive some difficult times. To my dear friends, Elizabeth Morrill, Beth Thompson, and Barbara MacNamee, who read the manuscript and loved it. Janet LaBelle, my life long devoted friend and valuable critic, thank you. Special thanks to Kat Logan who painted Bear Butte after a not so subtle nudge from Spirit.

And most of all deep gratitude to my dedicated and loyal friend who, for nearly seven years, spent countless hours scanning and making suggestions for my work. Linda Jacobs, your faith and patience in me made this possible.

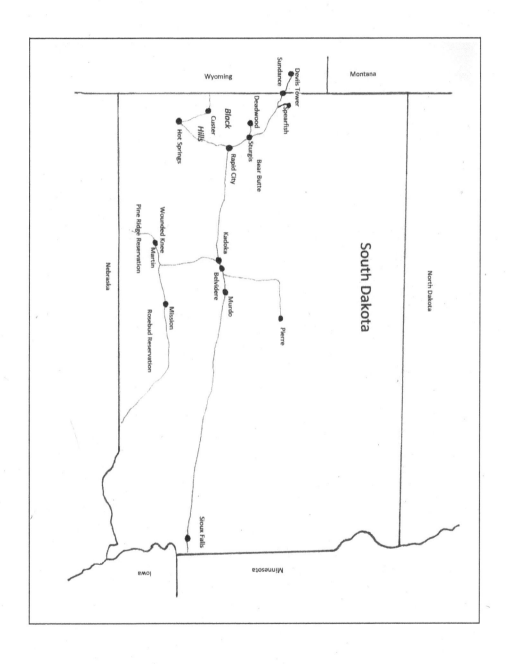

# 1: The Direction of Fate

## Up, down, and sideways

Whap-whap-whap joggles my foggy brain. My eyes pop open as a flash of lightning floods the trembling tent walls. The wind growls. The rain hammers. Wake up? Nooo. Snug in my little dome tent, I turn over to find my wristwatch. It's 2 a.m. I squirm my tall, athletic body deeper into my sleeping bag, fluff my pillow, and drift back to sleep.

But not for long. Barking, eerie and faint, cuts through the wind and jolts me awake. Doug's upset. *Damn. Better check on him.* I unzip the tent and stick my head out into an angry, ghost-like cloud. No one's happy tonight.

I pull my head back inside, swipe my short hair, then zip up the tent. I pat down my gear to find the flashlight, then shove my hand inside the nylon travel bag searching for the rubbery feel of my poncho. It's a man's medium, so even sitting, it's easy to put on. Hands shaking, I lace my hiking boots then crawl out the door and sink into the soaked ground. When I stand up, wind and rain whip up, down, and sideways pushing against me, making it hard to breathe. *What the hell!*

I tug my poncho drawstrings and leave just enough slack to see through. As another streak of lightning zigzags across the sky, I squint my eyes and turn to look for the other tents that were here yesterday but the place is deserted. My jaw tightens, I lean forward, then follow the flashlight beam into the storm. A powerful current fights me, but I've dealt with worse so I charge ahead to rescue Doug.

Ten yards away, through the gray haze, I spot my hundred-pound German shepherd standing on the ground at the rear of my car. He keeps barking as he looks towards me and then off into the murkiness. Even though he's wet and frazzled, when I get close, he quiets and jumps back into the opened rear of the station wagon. I wipe him down with the edge of his car blanket and give him a few pats. He wags his bushy tail, drops to his blanket, and curls up. I pull down the hatchback to keep him safe inside.

As I turn away from the car, a figure approaches out of the mist. When she's close enough, I realize it's one of the campground owners. The wind's roar is so loud we have to stand almost nose to nose to hear each other.

She yells, "The sheriff called. I've been trying to rouse you off and on for a half hour. I was afraid of your dog. The sheriff said we're going to get violent winds, heavy rain, and dangerous lightning. You need to take down your tent and find shelter!" I thank her. *Find shelter? Where? I'm in a remote prairie in South Dakota. Oh well, I've been duly warned.* It's my first time out here so storms like this are new to me.

Even with her warning I know there's no way I'm taking down my tent, not in this weather. It'd make a lovely sail and who knows where I'd end up. *Stupid idea.* I check on Doug again, give him another pat, and close the back. Tucked inside his little compartment, he seems unfazed.

I push back into the tempest and, thank goodness, my tent's intact. The storm's still furious and, even though I've always had a serious fear of high winds, for some reason, I feel safe and comfortable inside my little shelter.

My sleeping bag's plush cotton both cushions and calms me and when I turn over onto my back, I collapse further into it and my body softens. *I'm safe. Doug is safe. We made it through the ruckus.* I came here for an adventure, to visit Wounded Knee and the Black Hills, and to learn more about our Indigenous people. I never imagined this.

Soon, the sounds of fluttering walls and roaring wind begin to unnerve me again. *Are the tent stakes deep enough to hold it down?* My determined-to-be-independent-at-all-costs Virgo self requires twenty minutes to realize I need to find cover. As much as I dread going outside, I sit up, put my poncho back on, and trudge to the car.

*Thank goodness, I made it.* Dry and safe, I'll wait out the storm inside here with Doug.

At this point, it's not so much that I'm afraid, it's just that this seems like the logical thing to do. After forty-eight daunting years, I'm pretty good at masking my fears.

## 2: Strength Is a Verb

### You're so goddamn independent

The storm continues its slow creep across the prairie as staccato groans rock my vehicle like a dinghy tossed by ocean swells. But, nestled inside my car, I'm safe for the moment. Condensation coats the windows and it smells of dog and musty floor mats. I scan the interior with its drained color and little definition. It's a drab world inside and out. I try taking a deep breath to settle myself but it comes out shallow and jerky.

*Getting nervous Regina? Think.* I start the car, turn the defroster fan on high, and the windows begin to clear. With my neck craned over the steering wheel, I look out and gasp at the mess of swirling gray outside. My headlights jet out through loops of wind and pelting rain that smack the hood and windshield. But I'm sealed safe inside with Doug.

Closed off from the unpredictable outside world, in a strange way, my situation feels familiar. My world in here is limited, with easily defined boundaries, and a quiet vacancy. I like that. It's comforting like being in a library cubicle, my tent, or a hospital bed.

In 1954 at age six, I was hospitalized for seven months with a mild case of polio. It wasn't an unpleasant experience because I felt encouraged by the nurses, and I liked the anticipated structure of each day. In reality, most of my stay was fun and the kind nurses even gave us birthday parties. A couple of us kids, who couldn't sit or stand during our long convalescence, even had stretcher races down the hallways. I was lucky I made a full recovery.

During that time, I don't remember missing my four siblings or parents. I have no memory of my mother being there... *interesting*. But I do remember family friends visiting.

The hospital in Hanover, NH was a teaching hospital so interns did rounds with the doctors. One day a male intern came into my room alone and said he wanted to check on my progress. He came to my bedside, pulled the sheet back from my feet, and began to palpate my legs. But he didn't stop there. He moved up to my privates and briefly fondled me then left right after.

Even though I'd been invaded, at first I only felt surprised. Within minutes, I began to process what happened and my little six-year-old-self decided that was not cool. I made a plan for what I'd do if he returned.

A few days later, the intern came back to my room. When he walked up to the side of my bed and said hello, I was ready for him. In my best little warrior voice I yelled, "If you do that again I'll tell the nurse." His jaw dropped then he beat it out of my room. I never saw him again.

For thirty-two years I never told anyone. I felt neither traumatized nor ashamed, so I didn't feel the need. My "Little Regina" self had dealt with it. I was a confident and resourceful young girl but those qualities seemed to annoy my exasperated mother. I can remember her saying, "You are so goddamn independent."

I was confused. I knew I was a good girl, but, according to my mom, something about me was off. And it stayed with me, the feeling that something wasn't quite right, not just with me, but also with my mother and me.

—w—

As the prairie storm rages on, I grasp the steering wheel, pull myself forward straining to see more of the outside. My headlights expose even wilder swirls of rain and, now, grass flying in circles. The storm is building and I can feel my shoulders tighten and curl inward. With a vice-grip hold on the steering wheel and my heart racing, I realize it's time for Doug and me to find shelter. *But where?*

I lean back and try picturing what the bustling campground looked like yesterday when I arrived. I remember acre after acre of treeless grassland and the ten or so occupied tent sites were so large I could hear just snippets of my neighbors' chatter. I recall a small bathhouse on the other side of the campground. *I'll go there.*

I muster all my navigational instincts and turn right then do a tentative slow roll forward. The storm persists, rocking the car and slamming it with sheets of wind and rain. Lightning flashes expose empty campsites and the deserted, dirt car path in front of me. It's a gloomy and unyielding world out there.

Soldiering on, I struggle to keep my fear at bay and after a few minutes, I see the corner of a building. With its shallow-pitched roof and cinder block walls, the bathhouse looks stoic and dull. My grip on the steering wheel softens as I circle the building then park close to one side out of the wind. *There, made it.* I let out a sigh. *I'm protected.*

I turn off the car and settle into my seat to wait out this craziness. But, after a long few minutes, something feels amiss. My journal, another trusted companion, was in the tent.

Blocking out my fear, and with the headlights pointing the way, I head out to rescue it. *Curious, I still don't see any campers from yesterday.*

There in the hazy distance is my tent. *Thank God, it's still standing.*

I park a few feet away then take a minute to plot my dreaded opening of the door. I'm hoping the wind blasts let up, but after a couple minutes, they don't. I have no other choice; I have to go for it and hope the wind doesn't buckle the door off its hinges.

When I do commit, wind gushes in and nearly takes my breath away. I brace my feet and pull hard on the handle to shut it. In my rear view mirror I see Doug sitting up looking at me. He knows something's up and this doesn't help my nerves.

I lean back, settle myself, then catapult myself outside with my head down and my flashlight beam leading the way to the tent. When a giant blast comes up, I plant my feet on the ground, turn to face it, then let it have its way with me. Its determination is invigorating and in this moment I feel part of the commotion, not a victim of it. *One with the commotion; that's a new one.* Once the blast lessens, I get a few seconds of calm, and enter my tent.

The air inside is dry and still. The flailing walls and wind sounds are still here, but it's a nice reprieve from outside. For a minute, I'm tempted to stay, but I remember why I came. I use my flashlight to search the tent floor for my journal. My heart sinks. *What if it's wet and ruined?* I entertain the thought for a second then shush it away. *Focus on your goal, Regina: find the journal.*

And here it is, tucked and dry in my backpack. I stuff it down inside the waistband of my shorts under my raincoat then head back to the car. I stick it in the glove compartment, just in case.

After another harrowing drive back to the bathhouse, I park in the same spot, turn off the engine, and prepare to wait out the storm.

There's no Doug in my rear view mirror so that's a good sign. *He must be curled up and asleep.* If he was the least bit nervous, he'd be sitting up ready to engage. I'm happy to have one less thing to worry about.

The storm keeps on. The wind and rain conspire to shoot huge torrents off the rusted roof that slam the top and sides of my car. I begin to allow reality in; I am at the mercy of this menace and there's nothing more I can do to escape it. Fear starts to take over.

But, I don't like this being-afraid business. I've had enough fright in my life. So now, with no alternative but to stay terrorized, I decide to objectify my situation. *It's just a wind storm and it's temporary.* I say a prayer asking to be kept safe. Imprisoned in my car, an inexplicable sense of freedom fills me. I begin to conceptualize fear as more than a feeling. Its form seems finite and neutral so I don't have to let it limit me. I decide I am the overseer of this situation, my situation. Reality begins to shift. I am present but detached. I begin to feel at peace.

Also, I start to think about how alone I am. Family and friends know I'm tenting in South Dakota but no one, I mean no one, knows exactly where I am or has made any plans to check in on me. But this has been my norm, chugging along in life, often times alone, from one adventure to another. I'm probably a little off center from the status quo, diving in the way I do to new life challenges.

Internal silence warms me even more. I accept my circumstance, settle in and become one with it. What the hell, what's the worst that could happen? Sure, I could die but I have little control over that. And once again, I give myself over to whatever fate, or the Universe, has in store for me.

# 3: Some Houses Are Not Homes

## Home was like a habit I returned to

By 4:30 the storm has moved on leaving a drab, ashen dawn. After two hours hunkered down in the car, my back and legs ache for a good stretch. It's tight quarters but I bend and flex my lanky body at some weird angles and get relief. I pull myself forward on the steering wheel then make an extra wide yawn releasing some anxiety. Slumping deep into my seat again, I look around. Everything, including me, is damp, stinky, and worn out.

It's a little lighter outside so I can see more of the bathhouse and the campground with its limp, faded grasses. When I roll down the window and turn on the ignition, Doug pops up in my rear view mirror. He thumps his tail on the window, and if dogs smile, he does. All is well. I steer the car onto the gravel path and, except for the hum of the motor, outside is still and dead silent.

It's a surreal time of the morning, just before sunrise when I imagine Earth stirs, pauses, and considers whether or not to wake. My car's hesitant, too, and robotic like me, as it rolls back to my campsite. *Damn. That storm was wild.* All the other campers must have left last night or gotten blown away.

I pull up to the site and am relieved my tent's still standing. *See, the authorities aren't always right.* When I turn off the ignition, my world stops too. I've read about this kind of listless post-traumatic space. It's like I'm in some sort of empty vessel of stillness. I remember how meditating helps calm me so I take a big breath and sink deeper into my body. *Regina, it's over, the storm is done.*

More daylight marches in, takes over. A few birds, tiny

shadows of what's to come, flutter by and I'm pulled back to my regular world.

The eastern sky is contorting, organizing itself after a long, tough night. Disheveled, fast-moving, and massive cloud clusters fold into each other. Enthralled, I lean over the passenger seat to see more and am audience to the birthing of majestic cathedrals of dull, puffy clouds. They billow upward, form themselves into ghostly heights, hold their form just long enough for me to notice, then gently collapse and disperse into the drier air. Their power and size both delight and unnerve me. This exhibition doesn't seem possible. Then from some unknown source, I hear inside me, *Welcome.*

—⟋⟍—

In 1962, we lived in a huge fourteen-room house my dad had a contractor build for our family of seven. Home was like a habit I returned to. It was predictable in its physical structure but fraught with emotional turmoil and confusion. Our interpersonal foundations were fragile. Raised in difficult environments it was hard for my parents to give us something they'd never gotten.

But our house was also a gathering place. Townsfolk would drop in unannounced and were welcomed. My attractive parents, "Pat and Betty," always one with the other, were a fixture in town. They loved to entertain and hosted lots of parties and huge family festivities. They welcomed my dad's siblings to live with us once they left the mountain farm while on their way to pursuing their adult lives. People were always coming and going at our house. I saw relatives and friends sharing and loving it and each other and I know it gave my parents great joy to be able to share what they had.

When our house was being built, each of us kids, five at the time, got to choose our own bedroom. I was second oldest and picked a big space. I loved my antique spool bed once used by my great-grandparents then my parents. When I came home from school, finished my chores, and fed my many pets, I'd hurry upstairs to my room, to that place that felt like my very own oasis, and close the door. I'd stack a few 45s on my record player's turntable then plop down on the bed and with the help of Bobby Vinton and Neil Sedaka drift away with my imaginary boyfriend. My bedroom was my sanctuary.

In the early '60s, my father's grandmother, Josephine Proulx, made the rounds visiting our family a few times each year. I felt special when she took the time to sit and teach me to cook and sew by hand. I got to share my bed with her and she would get up with us kids in the morning and make us oatmeal. It was a treat because, even when Grammy was not there, my mom always slept in and we made our own breakfast.

Because my parents grew up in challenging circumstances, I always thought they wanted us kids to have what they hadn't. My father worked hard and built a successful plumbing and heating business. My mom showered us with so many gifts at Christmas I felt uncomfortable and, perhaps, embarrassed because to me, the presents didn't seem to come with any parental love or approval.

My dad grew up on a mountain farm in Bath, NH and lived there until he married my mom in 1947. Dad's biological father left when he was three and he never saw him again. My dad's mother remarried an abusive man, and had six more children. My dad suffered chronic physical and emotional abuse at the hands of his stepfather. Dirt poor, my father described his school lunch as a chunk of bread with a lump of lard on top. Needed on the farm, my dad got as far as grade six. His mother, Delia, was a spiritual rock and it's why my dad and his siblings turned out to be such good people.

My mom was adopted and very much ashamed of that fact. She and her two adopted sisters were raised by a wealthy Irish Catholic couple in Boston. My mom recounted to us how, when she was very young, her family would travel in their limo to the White Mountains in NH for vacations. My grandfather died of a heart attack after losing all his money in the stock market crash of 1929. My mom and her two sisters were schooled by the harsh and unwavering nuns at Mission Hill Catholic School. My mom's angry and sickly mother lost both legs to diabetes and died when I was an infant.

I know my mother loved her home, her husband, friends, and, in her own way, her children. I think she loved us kids more when we were young and fewer in number. She once told us she wanted just one child. But as a practicing Catholic, I guess birth control was not an option.

I don't remember experiencing a loving touch or intimate attention from my mother. Maybe it happened, it's possible. Sadness and anger can distort a person's memory.

So, I guess our big house was *sort of* a home to me, in that I could depend on it being there. But while vibrant, spacious, and comfortable, it wasn't *home* the way I made my own to be: a peaceful, safe place to land at the end of the day, where my kids and I sat playing Candy Land at night, where I helped them with their homework, where we snuggled together for a bedtime story, where

9

we planned fishing adventures. My siblings and I deserved something physical like a hug, a pat on the back, or, God-forbid, a kiss on the cheek, things so necessary to a child's development. We kids got most of the material things we desired but not enough emotional support. A simple "I love you," would have been nice.

What we did get, though, was plenty of time with animals and rich experiences with our pets. With the help of townsfolk and the 4H club, my sister and I learned how to raise and show our horses. We learned how to teach ourselves. My siblings and I became confident adults. These wonderful traits were modeled by my father, and both my parents supported us in our adventures. The same attributes are evident in the generations that have followed.

I also learned about nature and science, and grew to be independent. I became the town's young budding naturalist, hanging around dairy farms, assisting the local vet, and fishing anywhere I could drop a line in water.

—m—

One cold winter's night when I was around fifteen I was on another solo walk across the huge field behind our house. The crescent moon had slid behind the horizon revealing a gazillion stars and ahead of me the tops of Mt. Moosilauke and Black Mt. looked like they'd been drizzled with white frosting. With each step in the deep, fresh snow, I fluffed up a cloud of glittery, diamond dust. It was easy going. I remember feeling, not so much thinking: *Oh, to hold this moment, take it with me, wear it, and have it feed me forever.* The land gave me something in that serene moment and I was nourished and reassured. Nothing in my surroundings interrupted the flow of land's mothering and I felt valued and loved. To this day, that memory has stayed with me.

I've spent a lot of my life stalking the feelings I had that night. That is, my heart stalked them. In nature, I found what I was looking for. It was there my whole body found home. My brain and soul and heart all came together and felt fulfilled. When I was young, without realizing it, I went to the hay fields, the pasture streams, the pine forests, and took long bike expeditions to find my nurturing. And that instinct never left. Because I found mothering in nature, I didn't realize something at home was missing.

# 4: Pissy Sheets

## Her back was to her kids

One morning when I was eleven, I bounced down the stairs from my bedroom. I'd been listening to Paul Anka's "Put Your Head on My Shoulder" on my record player and it always put me in a dreamy mood.

I skipped down the hallway then turned into the kitchen. It was filled with top-of-the-line new appliances and two rows of custom-made cupboards. The space was huge to accommodate our large family and was the focal point of our home. It also had what seemed a constant stream of visitors so when I rounded the hallway corner, I was prepared for almost anything.

Stepping into the kitchen I stopped short. To my right on the floor in front of the washer and dryer sat three sheet-covered mounds. They looked like camel humps but imprisoned inside were my three younger siblings. Lorraine was nine, giggly, and had big brown eyes. At seven, Linda was perky and cute as a button. Eight-year-old Pat was an all-around happy little guy. My mom, dressed in her plaid cotton dress, was at her usual perch, slouched on her stool at the end of the kitchen peninsula. Between drags on her Winston's she sipped tea and nibbled a cookie. Her back was to her kids on the floor.

Closer to the sheets, I heard whispers. Then I got a whiff. My siblings were bed-wetters and sitting under what my mom called "pissy sheets" was their punishment. My older brother, John, and I, trained at an early age, were spared this humiliation.

She just sat there, never looking up from her tea and cigarette, while I froze. I wanted to cry a little, for them. But, young me, I worried the whole world might see my spunky, sometimes annoying little sisters and brother cramped inside their urine-dampened tents. I clenched my fists and willed as hard as I could that no one would come through the kitchen door. What would they think about our family? To an outsider the scene would be shocking; to my siblings and me it was not that unusual. We were used to our mom turning away whenever we needed comfort or encouragement.

Looking down at the three little humps, I heard giggles then, "Linda, stop! Mom, Linda's sticking her finger at me!" squealed Pat. Between the sheet flaps I saw Linda's slight finger poking through a hole in her sheet. She was tickling Pat's head.

When the giggles under the sheets got louder, my mom lost it. She swirled on her stool and said, "If you three keep it up, you can stay there all day."

A second later someone knocked at the door and my mom's friend, Nancy, let herself in. She smiled, said hello to my mother and me, and looked at the sheets, then at my mother. Whatever my mother said to her turned Nancy's face red. She said nothing then sat down next to my mom. Head down, I slipped into the kitchen past my mother and Nancy, opened the cupboard door, and helped myself to a row of Oreos. I stuffed them in my jacket then, once outside, I jumped on my bike and went for an extra-long ride.

Now, in S.D., traversing this beloved continent, it seems I'm on another quest to find home. I don't know how to explain it or if anyone could. This trek is leading me to the Black Hills where sacred sites I've read about have touched my core. Finding home also means finding people who revere the Earth and Spirit like I do. People like the Lakota.

# 5: Jay's Land

## Years ago humanity's touch just nibbled at Earth's hem

The morning before the storm, I'd left Sioux Falls, South Dakota at eight. Strong prairie headwinds fought me the whole two-hundred-thirty-mile drive to the campground in Belvidere. The blistering sun and temps in the high 90s made me irritable, Doug restless, and my car, an older Subaru wagon, overheat. I turned off the air conditioner, stayed under fifty-five, and added more coolant to the radiator. It helped, a little. And, with all the windows rolled down, it was more than just a little breezy.

The persistent grasslands pushed-out forever. And like the repeating notes of a lullaby, their smooth undulations rocked and soothed as if singing; *Keep drifting, keep drifting forward.*

Well into my drive and out of the blue, a shy subtle something, like a whisper, settled into my chest. My brain didn't understand but gave in, so I listened. Many times over the years I'd been inspired to write and when I'd read it later, I'd wonder whose words they were. They hadn't come from me; with my science training, my mind didn't work like that. The words came from outside of me, I'm sure, and I've always wondered how and why.

I felt a stirring to write in my journal like I'd been doing since leaving Maine. But this felt different so I thought it best to just listen and trust the words that came as I had trusted whatever brought me on this adventure.

I first imagined visiting the Black Hills during a meditation. I didn't know why but I'd been excited to go. My plan was to follow my intuitive heart, visit Wounded Knee, and explore these lands for as long as it felt right. In the process I hoped to grow myself.

13

As I drove down the long, deserted stretch of hot prairie, subtle vibrations seemed to flow out from the land. Like a lament forming in my mind, I heard: *We're holding on, barely... too much farming... too much hunting. .. We're not being replenished... Where are the buffalo?* It felt like I was hearing memories in the land.

I gazed out into the vast landscape and imagined great herds of bison streaming over the grassy rolls and charging into the horizon. Long ago, in sync, life forms melded into each other: symbiosis. I imagine it formed a beautiful, invisible web of energy over the globe. Like the web formed by a loving family, it was created out of shared experiences, need, and appreciation for each other. Back then humanity's touch, a nibble at Earth's hem, was hardly noticed. Humans were insignificant, maybe just tolerated.

At 2:00 p.m., after six hours on the road, I was baked and exhausted when I pulled into the KOA campground. Right off the main road, it was dead center in the middle of the sweeping grasslands. *What a relief.*

After I checked in, I scoped the grounds for a site and opted for one far from the entrance road and office. I pitched my tent near a large cottonwood tree. It was close to the banks of a small pond where gangs of red-winged blackbirds dive-bombed through the rushes lining it. Their squeaky songs were relentless so my tired spirit had no choice but to be revived.

Compared to my torturous drive, setting up the tent, organizing my gear, walking, then settling Doug in was easy. After that, all I wanted to do was stretch out in my tent and relax.

Later in the afternoon I sat in my folding chair in the shade of the cottonwood tree. Doug, hitched to the rear of the car, began to bark. I looked over and saw a wiry, teenage Indigenous boy heading towards me. He had on dusty jeans, a heavy-metal t-shirt, and cowboy boots. He gave me a big smile as he invited himself into my campsite. It happened so fast I had no chance to react.

"Hi, I'm James Little Bear. People call me Jay. I work here at the campground." Down in my short-legged chair, I used my hand to block out the sun from one eye so I could get a good look at him. He appeared normal.

I introduced myself and right away he asked where I was from. "I'm from Maine and I'm traveling through the Black Hills area for a few weeks with my dog." He raised his eyebrows.

Having had minimal contact with people in my four-day drive here, I was a little tongue-tied but after thinking it through, I formed what I hoped was a cohesive sentence. "I'm wondering where I can get some water to cool down my dog." *What do I say to the kid?* I'm not a chatty person.

He twisted his body then pointed to a small cinder-block building fifty yards away. "The bathhouse has an outside faucet and hose you can use." I smiled and thanked him.

A friendly kid, maybe fifteenish, he gave me another toothy smile then nodded to my car and asked about Doug. "Oh, that's Doug," I said. Doug, who had stopped barking and was standing on the ground hitched to his long lead, was staring at us. Before I could say another word, Jay headed over to the car, knelt down, and started patting Doug. I held my breath.

When Doug's hitched, he thinks he's on duty to protect me. But his tail was wagging so I stayed put; however, I was ready to spring over there if need be. After a couple minutes, I got up my nerve, and as nonchalantly as possible, so Doug didn't sense my nervousness, I picked up my chair and walked over to the car.

Even though I was still nervous, I wanted to pick the kid's brain so I moved my chair near him and got ready to question my first Native American. "I like your name. Can you tell me about it?"

"The medicine man gave me my name in a sweat lodge when I was a baby. I am one hundred percent Sioux!" He gave me a proud smile. I knew from my studies the Lakota are a branch of the Sioux nation and inhabit this area.

Enamored by Jay's culture, I plowed ahead and asked him about sweat lodges and vision quests. Later I was ashamed when I realized it would be like someone I didn't know quizzing me on being raised Catholic and what I thought of communion and confessions. *Good God, you just met the kid, Regina.*

Years later, some of my American Indian friends told me it's disturbing to see nonnatives copy their customs without permission and use American Indian stereotypes as mascots or symbols. When I think back to my conversations with Jay, I feel embarrassed at how I was more focused on what enamored me about the culture than the friendly kid next to me. Maybe I wanted to boost my ego by being part of traditions I valued more than my own. Maybe I felt entitled to know about a private and sacred part of his religion, a part he had not offered to share with me. So began my real-life education in cultural appropriation. And it would be a lifetime of lessons.

"My parents are into that New Age stuff but I'm into modern stuff like CDs, computers, and music videos," he added.

He paused for a second then looked at me curious-like and asked, "Do you know the Calhouns? They're two women from Maine and are into that 'Save the Earth' and Native American spiritual stuff. They moved to Iowa a little while ago because people around here wouldn't accept differences in people."

I shifted in my chair guessing they were lesbians like me.

I saw my opening. "Do you know people who are into New Age spiritual stuff?"

"I don't know about any. The Sioux ceremonies are very much closed." The door was slammed shut. My potential "in" with the Sioux community evaporated.

As we continued talking, Jay stayed focused on Doug, patting his head and back. At the same time, I peppered the youngster with even more questions about the Lakota. Again, I heard my words. I sounded like the stereotypical American Indian wannabe that makes me cringe. I'd even elevated this boy to some sort of lofty position based on his birth. It took me years to forgive myself for being so insensitive.

A short while later, I took out one of my travel maps and asked Jay about places he'd recommend I visit. He looked up from my Black Hills map and named some of his favorites: The Badlands, the Needles, and the Grasslands Reserve. He told me his dream was to buy a motorcycle and race it through the Needles, a hilly, narrow road flanked by clusters of giant, vertical, granite outcroppings in the Black Hills. I smiled, "That sounds like a wild ride." It sounded like something my son, Jake, would do with his motorcycle.

For a minute, I missed my seventeen-year-old. Then I remembered how much he looks forward to spending summers with his father and all the adventures they have. *How lucky am I, mother of three, able to go off like this?* I thought of my daughters and how I've never worried much about them. *Should I have?* Then I reminded myself that they inherited my family's self-confidence. Jenny has a job she loves, a good guy in her life, and enjoys her city life. Jessie is a counselor in Outward Bound working out of Florida, Maine, and Maryland. She's also a gifted runner.

My inappropriate imagination was still running wild. I wondered if he'd agree to be my guide. I conjured up an image of a tall white woman who had solicited a young Indigenous kid to teach her about the sacred Black Hills, the very lands my culture stole from him. And right away I felt humiliated that I'd even thought that. A short time later Jay said goodbye to Doug and me and left. I hoped he come back to visit while I was there.

Jay did come back. He came by twice the next day to visit Doug. I learned from the camp owners they've become his unofficial adoptive parents as his home life on the reservation was not so good.

After Jay left, I gave Doug his cool shower at the bathhouse then slipped into my tent for another rest. Stretched out on my sleeping bag, I broke into a smile reflecting on every minute of Jay's visit. I was in South Dakota, Jay was the real deal, and my dream was coming true.

I felt comforted by the merry blended songs of my feathered neighbors. A warm breeze came up and the lazy flapping of tent walls lulled me into a dreamy daze. I closed my eyes, sank into my body, and from somewhere deep inside, words came quickly. *You're not here to investigate or venerate Native American culture. Your intention is to learn how to follow your heart, your spiritual compass.*

So I reminded myself to take one step at a time into my emerging adventure. And I began to understand that my path will be created as I settle into my essence and follow its subtle urges.

I remembered something that happened while driving through Ohio, Indiana, Wisconsin, and Minnesota. Rock music was playing on the radio but all I could hear were Native American drums and chanting. It felt a little weird to me but those voices seemed encouraging. For some reason, I guessed they were Chippewa, Cree, and Sioux songs. My later research suggested I was right. It was easy for me to believe the singers knew I was there and approved.

In 1971 when *Bury My Heart at Wounded Knee* by Dee Brown came out, I inhaled my copy. The book is a history of the West during the last part of the nineteenth century but from the American Indian perspective. Part of it tells of the massacre by the US Army of hundreds of Sioux at Wounded Knee. Over the years I've read numerous accounts of the tragedy and for some reason find the event strangely familiar. I never imagined I would be here, let alone get to visit Wounded Knee, but I planned to go there.

Earlier, the campground owners told me there's a powwow at Mission happening tomorrow. Mission is a community on the Rosebud Reservation, one of the most poverty stricken of all the reservations. I prepared myself for what I might see if I attended and I was determined to do so.

Late in the afternoon, after Jay's visit, larger swarms of red-winged blackbirds joined me at my campsite. Their chatter and constant flitting back and forth between the cattail clusters and tall spiky grasses rubbed off making me giddy. *I'm so happy to be here and solo.* My plan was to visit Wounded Knee on the Pine Ridge Reservation and now, the powwow at Mission. For that afternoon, my first day on the prairie, life was perfect.

# 6: Three Ladies at the Prom

## How grand to be the real you inside your body

Judy walked up to my desk after school one afternoon in 1996: "Ms. Boudreault, I want to go to the Prom."
I looked up from my papers and smiled, "That's great."
"With Sarah." She giggled.

—⋘—

By the time Judy approached me, it had been several years since I'd realized I was a lesbian. In 1989 I was teaching at a local high school and made friends with my coworker, Naomi. After a few months it hit me: I had a major crush on her. It was Naomi's self-assurance and wisdom that attracted me at first. Also, like my PE teacher stereotype, she was physically fit and direct with her words. I felt like a love-struck teenager when I was near her. Because of my feminist college friends, it was easy to accept that I could be a lesbian. But in my gut there were questions gnawing at me. *What will happen to the old me? What about my three kids?* In the midst of only fleeting internal concern I kept reminding myself of the oath I'd made years before, *"I will always live my truth."* And after years of therapy, I was determined to do just that so my questioning lasted less than a day.

I asked Naomi if we could meet in her office after school to talk. She smiled and agreed. I think she knew what was up. After school let out, the door to her office was open so I walked in and sat down. A minute later Naomi came in and sat opposite me and to the side of her desk. I slid my hands under my thighs and leaned forward urging courage to flood up inside me.

Naomi smiled. The room felt too quiet like it was waiting on me, so I blurted out "Thank you for meeting. I just have to tell you something because it's a new feeling for me. I don't want a romantic relationship, I just want to speak my truth. I'm attracted to you."

Poor Naomi, at that moment, the tall confident woman I knew looked uneasy. But then after a short pause and a knowing smile, she rebounded. "You know I'm in a new relationship, right?"

I nodded that I did and smiled back still afraid she might think I wanted to be with her. Then she said, "Your courage, telling me like this, just about knocked my socks off." Then with a bigger smile, we both stood up, and she gave me a long hug. My whole body exhaled.

Naomi was a few years older than me, had been "out" for decades, so I knew she understood what I was going through. Our friendship grew and I began to idolize her. Days after our meeting she introduced me to a gregarious group of athletic, professional women. I remember the first day I stepped onto that tennis court and discovered a dozen other women like me, the me I never knew existed. Naomi's compassion and integrity are something I will always be grateful for. At forty, I began my new life.

—∭—

In the spring of '93, along with a million others, I participated in the Gay Pride March in Washington, DC. The largest of its kind, it became a catalyst for key gay rights legislation. Two lesbian friends and I joined the masses of people in what was the most exhilarating experience of communal joy I could imagine. I didn't want it to end. The March inspired me to become more involved in the gay rights movement and, later that year, I joined a couple of local LGBT organizations.

The weekend of the Pride March, my son, Jake, age twelve, was in DC on a class trip. I had not come out to him but I sensed he knew. When my friends and I arrived at our DC hotel room, I looked out the window and was startled to see the bus from Jake's school parked across the street at another hotel. What were the chances? I saw it as a sign; it was time to have "the talk" with him.

Back home, three days later, Jake sat reading in the loft above our kitchen. I was downstairs with my hands in warm, soapy, dishwater. My head was down and I felt my heart thump-thump in my chest because I knew it was time to tell him. I hollered up, "You know the March in Washington last weekend?

"Were you in it Mom?"

"Yup... I marched with all the other gay women."

"Cool. Mom, what's for lunch?"

That was it. It was that simple. He seemed fine with my announcement and I was relieved.

I had come out to my daughters a couple years before when they were older teenagers. I asked them not to tell Jake thinking he might be too young to handle it. When I told my more worldly daughter, Jenny, she smiled and said, "Whatever makes you happy, Mom." I guessed she probably knew all along. My more innocent daughter, Jessie, asked, "Why don't you want to be with men, and what about the sex?" Shocked by her explicit question, I decided to tell her what being attracted to a woman was for me. "It isn't a sexual attraction; it's something much bigger than that. I mostly feel it in my heart. It's like finding my very best friend and someone a lot like me." I think she accepted it but didn't quite understand, either.

A week after the Pride March and April vacation, I was back at school, still jazzed, and feeling invincible after my weekend. I thought I owed it to myself and my students to be more comfortable with my lifestyle so I decided to be more "out" at school.

But I'd take baby steps, so on my first day back, I wore a miniature rainbow pin on my blouse. That was as brave as I could be. It was a long day, wearing that tiny emblem advertising I was gay. But thank goodness no one noticed, that is, until the last three minutes of the day. That's when a rowdy, young girl piped up, "Ms. Boudreault, what's that pin on your shirt?"

My face got hot, I gulped, then took a deep breath, and said, "It's a rainbow pin."

Wide eyed, she stared at me and asked, "Were *you* at the March in Washington?"

For some reason I'd forgotten that my students watch TV. *I've been found out.*

"Yes," I said. All of a sudden I realized I had come out at school. For some reason I'd thought wearing the pin, even if no one saw it, was advancing gay rights.

"Really? Wow," she said.

The room chatter stopped and with mild interest, all twenty students looked at me. I waited for the infamous other shoe to drop, and then in the very next second, the room intercom buzzed. The office announced, "Ms. Boudreault?"

"Yes," I said.

"The superintendent would like to see you in her office right after school." *I've been found out. That didn't take long.*

I stopped breathing and for a second I felt like some sort of deviant. But I didn't waffle. I remained standing next to my desk and two minutes later the final bell rang. My students gathered up their gear and filed out of the room as if it was another ordinary day. As for me, I readied myself for the nerve-wracking walk to the central office and the censure that was sure to follow.

The superintendent, a petite, gay woman, was all business. She was also very closeted so I couldn't imagine showing off my rainbow pin. Once I stepped into her office, she smiled, shook my hand, and even though I towered over her, I felt small. She gestured for me to sit and like a good Catholic girl I sat and waited for my penance. But the pin, now hidden in my classroom desk drawer, was never brought up. The reason for the meeting eludes me now; I think I was too nervous to retain much. Then after a brief conversation, we stood, and she reached up to pat me on the shoulder. *I must have done something right.*

After that day, things at school went well for me. My progressive and liberal school district took pride in promoting social change. I worked to be more out at school, never shying away in conversations and at staff meetings from the fact I was gay.

Soon a couple of lesbian students began stopping by my classroom for short visits before or after school. My room was becoming a safe oasis. A couple months later, the principal gave me permission to offer an alternative lunch space in my classroom for gay students. The word spread and a couple more students trickled in. As they entered the room, it was heartwarming to watch them shed some of their emotional armor and relax into their authentic selves. The two gay boys sat tall and polite in their seats. Two young lesbians sat backwards in their chairs, sometimes with their legs slung over the desktops. I chuckled at the wonderful scene. How grand to be the real you inside your body.

At any given lunchtime around six students showed up in my room. A couple times unaware straight students knocked at my door and asked to join us. I always answered yes. Once seated, they'd look around then soon find a reason to leave. Nevertheless, in the end, all were welcome.

On that afternoon in '94 when Judy told me she wanted to go to the Prom, it caught me by surprise. Even though the school had been supportive of our gay lunchroom, I wasn't sure how this would go over. After thinking about it, I thought the school needed to stretch its inclusiveness a little more.

Judy was short, toned, and cute as a button. Her baseball cap, boyish shirt, and pants made it hard for me to imagine her in a prom dress but I wanted to help her.

When she asked me about the Prom, I must have looked confused and I was, for a minute. Then from somewhere a spontaneous idea popped into my head. "If you want to go, I'll go too."

Her cherub face lit up, "You will?"

"Absolutely,"

21

Judy left my room and skipped up the stairs to buy the Prom tickets from the teacher in charge. A few minutes later she was back, grinning. "Ms. Boudreault, when I told Mr. Miller I wanted to buy two tickets to the Prom he said okay. Then he asked me who I was going with. I told him, Sarah. Then he said no, who are you going with? I told him, Sarah. Ms. Boudreault, his face got really, really red." We both started laughing. Then after a few minutes talking Prom business, Judy walked out beaming with the tickets in her hand.

In order to keep my promise, I forced myself to do one of my least favorite things: clothes shopping. I found an acceptable, black pantsuit and some decent, black, oxford shoes to go with it. I was all set for the big night. Excited? No. Worried I might resemble a Johnny Cash lookalike? Yes.

The fancy ballroom, alive with loud rock music, was a sea of beautiful, expensive gowns and handsome suits and tuxedos. I scanned the room hoping for a vacant chair at one of the teachers' tables and found one near the entrance. After sitting down, I realized I was surrounded by administrators and their wives. I smiled at them and got some nods and curious looks. *I bet they're wondering why I'm here.*

I craned my neck trying to spot Judy and Sarah and it didn't take long. I think they saw me first. They walked over to the table and my back stiffened. It was one thing to fight for equality amidst a multitude of others, but working for ground-level change in everyday situations was risky. I was nervous and to be honest, maybe a little embarrassed for the girls because they stood out. But at the same time I was proud of them and it was their courage that inspired me, for the first time, to be a big, bold lesbian around my administration. Now I hoped to be courageous enough to handle any derogatory issues associated with my lifestyle.

Judy and Sarah looked awfully cute, like twin knickknacks in their matching tuxedos, glowing faces, and busting-out smiles. As they stood hand in hand by the table, the adult conversation stopped, and the atmosphere staled. *Oh, well.* I stood up, gave the girls a big hug, excused myself from the adults, then we three "ladies in black" walked out of the ballroom

Once in the lobby I asked, "How's it going?"

Judy said, "We heard a few wisecracks like, 'You've got to be kidding me.' But some of the kids said, 'Way to go!' and 'You guys look great!'"

Overall, it seemed most everyone was civil. Most importantly the girls were having fun. I was thrilled.

The following year Judy was in real trouble, academically and emotionally. She was suicidal and had been hospitalized with severe depression. She was a senior and way behind in her classes. The school called in a group of specialists to do an educational triage for her. A meeting was scheduled and I was asked to attend. I was curious as to why I was invited because I was not one of her teachers. Later I surmised her special education teacher saw me as Judy's mentor.

On the day of the meeting, I stepped into the school's large conference room. At a giant rectangular table sat the specialists: a guidance counselor, special education people, therapists, and administration. Judy's parents and Judy were there too. My heart sank when I saw Judy scrunched down at one end of the long table with her baseball cap yanked down over her eyebrows. *This is not the spunky munchkin I know.*

After introductions were made, the meeting began. Educational expertise was flaunted, clinical observations shared, and Judy's test scores circled the table while Judy slid lower and lower into her chair.

I knew we were here to help Judy but the little person at the end of the table was being ignored.

My insides churned, I was beginning to boil. Why was I there? How could these people ignore the obvious?

For almost an hour the experts and Judy's parents talked to themselves. I kept my eyes on Judy. Then I raised my hand.

When I got the nod from the Director of Special Ed to speak, I said, "Maybe the real issue here is Judy's lifestyle."

After a long pause, heads turned and all eyes were on me. Finally, Judy's Special Ed teacher, a good woman and colleague friend of mine, spoke up. "I think Judy wants her parents to accept her lifestyle." The air in the room softened as did everyone, including Judy and her parents. The track of conversations shifted away from test scores and clinical notes. They asked Judy what she wanted in her future. In a short amount of time, a new plan was drawn up to help Judy complete her work so she could graduate. And plans were made to heal her relationship with her parents.

From that day forward, Judy's life improved. She had the usual ups and downs of any average teenager but overall, she was happy and became a successful student.

At graduation, after receiving her diploma, Judy turned away from the principal and dignitaries, looked into the crowd of a couple thousand, and found me. I was at floor level with the other teachers seated near the front of the gymnasium. The ceremony paused as she walked over to me, and with a big smile she shook my hand and said, "Thank you."

I dared to live authentically and, now, Judy was living her truth, too.

# 7: Beautiful Freedom

## This is the place where childlike joy and dreams exist

After a long nap, splayed out in my tent, I crawl out half-awake and stagger upright. The perky sun smiles, looks innocent, maybe unaware of last night's tempest, maybe pretending. My hair's a mass of wild spikes and I'm wrinkled and clammy. As I walk over to check on Doug, I notice the air smells different, fresh and renewed, kind of like how I feel after "getting something off my chest." Doug's in his car bed and when he sees me coming, he raises his big head and flip flops his wolf tail on the floor. After a few pats I look into his adoring eyes and say, "Good morning Doug. We made it didn't we." He closes his eyes, drops his head, and slips back to dreamland. A part of me envies him and another part wants to get on with this new day.

Sitting at my picnic table, I scope the campground and what I'd guessed earlier is confirmed; the storm cleared out the place. But, last night's bombastic sky has now morphed into a storybook blue, with a smattering of wispy clouds flitting about. It's a typical summer sky after a cold front has moved through. Though ragged and tired, I too am at peace, a surrendered peace.

Even though it's way past my breakfast time, I'm not hungry. But, being a creature of habit, I'll eat. The usual bowl of oatmeal is too much work, so it'll be a couple of granola bars and some range coffee.

I set my mini propane stove on top of the picnic table then heat up a pan of water. When the water boils, I turn off the gas, throw in a small handful of ground coffee and wait for the desired hue. Ten minutes later, the dark brew gets poured into my cup and the steamy, pungent, liquid with waterlogged grounds on the bottom makes for my perfect morning wake-me-up.

Wearing a fresh t-shirt, shorts, hiking boots, and safari hat I hunch over the table finishing yesterday's journal entry. It feels great to be alone with no one else to tend to but my dog. I start thinking about last night when a sensory kind of idea, if there's such a thing, comes to mind. It seemed like Earth took a turbulent inhale and exhale and the storm cleared a tangled mess of energy and, after it finished, the land was left peaceful. I imagine I was a part of that breath and I got tossed about inside that maze. But now, the storm's done with me and I'm at peace too.

The sun feels like a warm balm on my arms and legs and after another sip of coffee and a bite of my granola bar, my fruitful imagination kicks in. I feel a little Hemingway-ish, writing my narrative from the front lines after a grand skirmish. I want to absorb it all so I take a deep breath, spin on my seat, and welcome the tonic of cool morning air into my chest. Alone in these expansive grasslands, I'm invigorated and I have everything I need.

After more work on my journal, more coffee, and another granola bar, I'm still writing about last night's storm. I hadn't planned to document my trip but before I left Maine, my daughter, Jennifer, gave me a lovely journal with a feather on the cover. I started it a couple days before leaving home and now I write every morning, sometimes at night, and enjoy reflecting on my travels. As I write, I begin to notice the mysticism in my journey. Months ago I had a vision where I journeyed to the Black Hills and now here I am, almost there. Following some sort of internal instinct, I intend to meander from one location to another as my adventure unfolds. I trust I will know where to go, what to do, and when it's time to go home.

When I look up from my journal then to my car, I don't see Doug. *He must be still sleeping.* It's time for his breakfast so I head to the car. When I get there, I notice the portable car phone sitting on the console of the front seat. One of my friends insisted I bring one along. I'll use it only for emergencies. Funny, I forgot about it last night.

On the car's back seat is a cardboard box with a bag of peanuts, some apples, and a dozen granola bars inside. I positioned the box so snacks are easy to grab while I'm driving. It also holds my Quaker Oats, a bag of brown rice, half a dozen potatoes, a couple cans of baked beans, two cans of string beans, and a box of raisins. On the floor are a half-gallon plastic jug of drinking water and a cooler with a quart of plain yogurt on ice. Doug goes off his dry food on long trips so there are a few cans of smelly wet food for him. When I'm driving, my backpack sits on the front seat holding my camera, AAA trip maps, and guide books.

When we're at home, I fill Doug's bowl with a week's worth of dry food and he rations himself eating only what he needs each day. His grandmother, Mandy, was a husky-wolf mix and I've always thought his wolf genes explained some of his interesting traits.

Doug is still asleep, so I leave his bowl of food on the ground near him and smile looking over at my big, handsome buddy. He's always game for an adventure, be it running for miles with me as I mountain bike or hiking off-leash in the forests near home. Ever aware of my whereabouts, he'll run ahead then always circle back to check on me. Protector, friend, and placid partner, even as a pup people would ask, "Is he a puppy or an adult?" He was that easygoing.

Doug can be a handful though. He loves people but he follows some strict canine hierarchical rules. He sees himself as second in charge of our pack of two and he can't be on guard if he's eating. When I entertain at home, he waits until my guests have left to eat the supper sitting in his bowl. If my dinner guests stay well past Doug's dinner time, he goes to each person at the table and, while wagging his tail, one at a time, he sets his big head into each person's lap. He's asking them to leave. Everyone laughs and gives him a good pat. After my guests depart, Doug finally eats his dinner.

My house sentry will not let in anyone he doesn't know unless he's sure I can see the person. Once he sees a joyful expression on my face, he welcomes the visitor. Many times I've had to greet the propane man or local politician with an over-the-top gushy hello so as to calm Doug and safely open the door.

With exemplary dog manners, he's never climbed on my furniture. The one exception was when Kate, a woman I met a year before my trip, was visiting. She's one of those people you meet whom you're sure you've known before. The first time she came to visit, Doug jumped up, all one hundred pounds of him, onto my couch, and into her lap. It was the first and only time he's done that. I think he felt the same familiarity with this new friend that I did. Soon after, Kate would become an important part of my life.

With my breakfast and journaling done, I get up from the table and, for lack of any burning compulsion, go sit in the car. Once I open all the windows and stretch out, I start to feel restless. *Sleep, read, walk; what do I want to do?* Too exhausted to decide, I just sit. After a few minutes slumped in my seat and a little bored, I turn, look out the window, and am captivated. The sky begins to fill with bulky clusters of bright white clouds that merge then morph into magnificent thunderheads. *What, more drama?* Too worn out to care, I get out of the car and head back to my tent to rest and the sky settles down too.

When I roll over inside the tent, I realize an inch of rainwater has collected between the floor and the ground tarp underneath. I'm on a comfy waterbed and no matter how much I search; I can't find a single drop of water inside my tent. You've got to love LL Bean gear.

For the rest of the morning Doug and I nap. When I finally climb out of the tent, I'm rested and eager to explore. The small pond nearby is fringed with cattails and home to edgy red-winged blackbirds and swarms of hyper dragonflies. The delightful little ecosystem seems so overwhelmed with life, it's like they just have to dance. It makes me smile and I try to breathe in its magic.

The cottonwood tree on the bank is a husky one. I take down the tent's wet rainfly and string it up on the tree branches along with my clothes and sleeping bag. It's always good to air things out after wet weather.

Oh, these dragonflies! Dozens of them dart in circles, like tiny dive-bombers foraging for mosquitoes. This naturalist is amazed; I've never seen so many! According to mystical lore, dragonflies mean magic is in the works. *I'll take that.*

Standing on the pond's bank, with my gear dangling from the tree branches, I look up and whisper, "Oh, big sky, you are so blue. You make me smile." Temps are in the mid-'80s, the sun is high, and the faithful little breeze caresses me.

Now, with my energy restored, I'm ready to drive into the grasslands and find something to photograph. My vintage 35-millimeter Canon camera is a beauty and has rewarded my family and me with dozens of memorable shots. I've been told I have a good eye and I plan to document my trip.

Doug and I get in the car and head east, out deeper into the grassy plains. In every direction stretching to the skyline is nothing but rolling, suntanned prairie. It's so new to me, I feel I'm in a beautiful dream. Maybe I am.

Out here, I'm used to being the only car on the road. This pristine asphalt town route is unlike the pitted, hilly roads in Maine. Totally free, I could be at the beginning of an intriguing escapade. *Prairie, are you inviting me to fly? I'm ready.*

A dozen miles in, I find a spot wide enough to pull off the road and park. I open up the back so Doug stays cool then look out and see an unending sea of grasses swelling in the breeze. Still no traffic, we're alone. Even after the four-day trip from Maine and the big storm, something inside me says, *you haven't seen anything yet.*

My legs feel tingly and light as I walk thirty yards into the knee-high grass. The sun looks down on me like a proud parent, encouraging me to continue with my whims. The tepid breeze feathers my face as waves of skinny grasses greet me. Like a mother, Earth carries me a little ways with her. Then, the land invites me to participate in its dance.

Because of my years of meditation, it happens quickly, I accept with a single thought, *yes*. Then a shift occurs and I feel abuzz and giddy. I imagine it's the feeling one experiences reading the perfect poem, singing in a rocking church choir, or listening to an exquisite musical performance. It's when mystical realities replace the usual day-to-day doldrums and a more whimsical and nourishing reality seems possible and indeed desirable. This is the exhilarating place where childlike joy and dreams exist. This is where I want to live.

Having left the campground's manicured lawns, groomed paths, and tailored campsites behind, I become conscious that I'm on land not maligned by civilization. Then all of a sudden, a huge cloud of hundreds of frenzied dragonflies swarms me. Like daring fighter pilots on a mission in an old WWI movie, they dart around me. With my arms spread out from my sides, I feel like I'm the lead in a Western love story and ready to burst into song. I'm glad no one's here to see me.

I let the rippling, yellow-blossomed strands brush up against me and pamper me, as they sweep outward in all directions for as far as I can see: shimmery blankets of life, like the great coiling masses of seaweed in the tranquil Sargasso Sea. These are permanent things if we let them be. And this place, radiant with sunlight, is charmed even more by dozens of tiny darting birds. Magic *is* real.

My hunger to explore is renewed and grows. After a short pause to give thanks for every little bit of this, I do my best to get some good camera shots but I know it's impossible to capture anything close to what I've just experienced.

Back in the car, I head to the Pierre National Grasslands. It's a sixty-mile drive but feels like five. As I sail along on the road, I'm excited to get on with my day and after a long while, I pull over, and as before, there's no traffic. Click, click, click. I try again, but I know the pictures will fall short. All my senses are alive. Revved up and surrounded by cheerful swarms of tiny birds and dragonflies, I become like my spunky, young self again.

# 8: More than just a Bunny

## Unaware of the trauma we were inflicting

One day when I was eleven, my dad accidentally disturbed a nest of baby rabbits at his work site. He jumped off his backhoe, scooped up one of the babies, and wrapped it in an old shirt. He then did something unusual for him, he left work and drove all the way home.

I was surprised to see him walk into the kitchen at that time of the day. He handed me the bundle and, when I peeled away the shirt layers, I was surprised. It was the cutest little ball of fluff I'd ever seen. It had brown eyes, soft warm fur, and its translucent ears hugged the sides of its tiny, round head. With a wide smile stretched across my face, I was oblivious to the frightened eyes bulging out in a blank stare. He could have fit in a sugar bowl. I decided it was a boy.

After my dad smiled and told me how he caught him, he said, "It's a 'coony' rabbit, a kind of miniature cottontail." Confident in my abilities to care for it, he went back to work.

My ten-year-old sister, Lorraine, came into the kitchen. The two of us giggled as we took turns cuddling the little fur-ball. Probably scared out of his wits, the baby did the typical rabbit thing and tucked his head into his chest, and froze. We didn't know any better so poor little bunny had to suffer our snuggles. After a few minutes and having survived our introductions, he lifted his head, wriggled his nose, and looked around. Lorraine and I, unaware of the trauma we were inflicting, kept passing him back and forth.

Making a little cage for him was no big deal; we had a menagerie of caged pets at the time: ducks, rabbits, guinea pigs, and chickens. I assembled a simple, little wooden box with a screen cover, stuffed it with fresh hay, and set in a dish of water and some rabbit pellets. Then I put him in a peaceful spot in the basement till he got used to his new environment.

I took good care of my little pet and after a few days, moved his cage to a shady area behind our garage. I loved him so much I couldn't imagine letting him loose but, in the back of my mind, I knew he deserved his freedom and planned to let him go when he was old enough. Adorable, he was easy to love but, I suspect, I cherished him because my dad had given him to me.

One day, after returning from a bike ride, I walked into the house and Lorraine looked at me sheepishly and said, "Tiny bunny is gone."

My heart sank and I glared at her. "What do you mean he's gone?"

"I took him out and put him on the back steps so I could take a picture of him and he ran away,"

I bolted out the kitchen door and charged into the backyard. Panicked, I raced around the garage poking and peeking into every possible hiding place in the weeds and lumber pile looking for my pet. But he was gone. *This did not happen, it just couldn't. Dad gave him to me!*

I ran back into the house and screamed at Lorraine, "How could you? Who gave you permission to take him out?" She put her hands up to her face and cried then ran into the other room. My mom was there, heard it all, and said nothing. Nothing...

I ran upstairs, threw myself face down on my bed, and heaved and sobbed like never before. I wept because I'd lost my sweet pet, something I loved more than anything and, even though I didn't know it then, I wept because no one cared. No one came to comfort me or my poor sister and soon I realized no one would. No one, not even my dad, said anything about it. I began to sense that feeling sad and vulnerable was a liability, like exposing myself to even more pain. It might be that this was when I began to hide my heart.

# 9: Did I Just See That?

## If it is of beauty or love, it is real enough

After the long drive, I stop in Phillips for a snack and a break. The town looks like what I think an old prairie settlement would look like, with a scattering of tiny, modest houses and sagging barns. There's a grocery store and next to it is a '50s gas station. But, maybe I'm just on the outskirts of the town proper. Maybe I've lived much of my life on the outskirts of something.

I'm feeling incognito in my safari hat, "Maine" t-shirt, and hiking boots. My hat belonged to my dear brother, Pat, who died suddenly of a brain aneurysm. His wife gave me his hat and it means a lot to me. Gentle Pat was a fellow nature lover and had many adventures in his short forty-one years. I've brought him along with me and I can feel his encouragement and his shared joy.

Once I situate the car in the shade of some trees, I open the hatchback, fill Doug's water bowl then give him a pat. It was a long ride so it feels good to stretch before walking to the gas station parking lot and the store. The lot is hard, oil-packed dirt probably from years of traffic and leaked car fluids. Civilization is unsettling.

I walk up a couple steps to the storefront, turn the knob on what looks like someone's front door, and enter. Two older guys, in Maine we'd call them townies, turn and look at me. They seem surprised at what they see. I'm a little surprised at how I feel, *Katherine Hepburn in hiking boots, maybe?* I smile and giggle. My little fantasy makes me feel a bit taller because no one here knows me. I can have any history I want and be anyone I choose. What fun.

After pulling out of my little daydream, I browse the snacks and tourist trinkets. Then in a darkened far corner, I see something that doesn't seem real. Two intriguing feminine shapes sit in a rounded huddle of dark hair and wrapped robes. I'm baffled, these lovelies are so out of place in this rundown store. *What are they doing here?* Then like an enticing little secret, their image draws me in. I walk to the back and when I get close, they turn their heads, and with shy, warm smiles they acknowledge me. They have caramel, porcelain skin and their long, black hair glides down their backs. Captivated by their hypnotic dark eyes, high cheekbones, and angular jawlines, it's hard not to stare. They are two of the most beautiful humans I have ever seen. Standing here, in my grubby outfit, gawking at these exquisite beauties, I feel out of place and awkward. Not quite believing what I see, I'm rattled and can't even smile at them so I turn away and walk back to the front of the store.

*They're real, right?* Honestly, I'm not sure because I've never seen women so stunning. Over the years I've romanticized American Indians, so I think that maybe it's just my imagination creating something I want to see. Then I stop thinking and decide to accept they are real but something my rational mind doesn't understand. Their beauty captivated me and at the same time seemed out of place in the dark corner of the store. Maybe they don't seem real because I feel it in a part of me that's been walled off for a very long time. Maybe I don't feel it because I don't trust my emotional self.

Once I accept I can't comprehend what I've seen, I continue walking to the front of the store and back to my conventional reality. I buy an ice cream sandwich, chips, and soda. It's my much-used rationale; junk food helps to ground me after a strange experience like this.

Back at the car, I let Doug out for a stretch then get in and feast on my ice cream and slip back into my normal self. *I can't wait to write about those women in my journal.*

The route back to camp takes me through Hayes and Midland which are even smaller settlements. I wonder about the towns' histories and the folks who live there. I wonder what their days are like and if they like their life. Tucked away inside vast redundant grasslands and sparse patches of willowy trees, it's so different from the composite little northern New England towns with their pristine colonial homes, ever-present hills, and lush vegetation. *Are prairie lives interesting? How can a person thrive in such an unvarying landscape?*

On the long loop back to the campground, I see three hawks in the distance. Two are circling overhead and one is perched on a fence post. About thirty feet past the one on the fence, I stop the car, get out, and use my binoculars for a good look. I can see its white belly feathers but I'm not sure if it's a red-tailed hawk, my favorite. A few seconds later the hawk takes flight and, just as I mouth, "Are you a red-tailed?" it tips for me to see the sunlit tail of its bright red feathers. I'm overwhelmed with emotion and tears flow down my cheeks. I'm confused. A minute later it hits me. I'm crying because out here alone in thousands of acres of desolate plains, to some small degree, I feel acknowledged.

Echoes of childhood flood in; I often felt insignificant, unnoticed. Maybe I'm being reminded to acknowledge an overlooked mystery, the mystery of sight and perception. What happened in the store did something to me; it reminded me to trust my experiences, even if no one understands or believes me. If it is of beauty or love, it is real enough. So, it might be this simple; we are here to know and appreciate our simple selves and our experiences within the context of being fully alive.

Back in the car, I drive a few hundred yards further and pass what looks like another large hawk sitting on a fence post. I pull over, fifty feet past it and park. I get out of the car and focus in on the bird with my binoculars. But it's a giant lark. I can't believe it; I was sure it was some sort of hawk. I keep looking through my binoculars. *Yes, it's definitely a lark.* I get back in my car then drive back to get a closer look. I use my binoculars again. *Yup, still looks like a large lark.* I pull down my binoculars then look through them again. I can't believe it. It's another large red-tailed hawk! The bird morphed right before me.

*You better think through what just happened.* I turn, touch my car, look at Doug, and stamp the tar road under my feet. I've read about morphing phenomena so maybe the bird changed from a hawk to a lark and back to a hawk or maybe it was just my overactive imagination kicking in and making it happen. Nevertheless, I thank the day for giving me these gifts and leave it at that.

On the way back to camp I keep thinking about the hawks and the two women. I've studied how unusual animal sightings and synchronicities can help us understand what's about to transpire in our lives. *In some Indigenous traditions, hawk says to be observant as messages from Creator are being sent to help us understand our life's higher purpose.*

In the couple of months leading up to my trip here, along the side of a road I traveled daily, I found a total of three hawks and three owls, all dead. None were disfigured in any way and they had died recently. I had never found any before nor have since. Because I had been studying Indigenous traditions and mythologies, I began to think the hawks and owls might be real messengers encouraging my spiritual development. *Again, I wonder what the Universe has in store for me.*

# 10: Bullet Holes in My Fantasy

## I imagine they must have begun to die inside

A good night's sleep and the warm, breezy morning with its cloudless sky revive me. One full day after the storm, Doug and I are on our way to the settlement of Mission on the Rosebud Reservation. It's only a half-hour drive and I'm excited to get some info on the powwow.

Fifteen minutes into the trip, vibrant prairie changes into sun-bleached, parched grasses, blotches of unremarkable shrubs, and neglected barbed wire fences. *Did I cross some sort of boundary?* Ahead, a worn-out road sign says, "Entering the Rosebud Reservation" and my enthusiasm fades even more. *Just what are you expecting, Regina?*

Further down the road, I count eight red-tailed hawks: a couple perch on fence posts, some on telephone poles, and a few float in the sky ahead of me. Then a huge one circles about thirty feet above my car so I pull off the road to get a better look. I focus my binoculars and whisper, "Show me a sign." Right then it tips sideways and poops, making me chuckle. I wonder if I'm being told to lighten up. I've been told I can be a little intense. *I wonder what messages hawk is sending.*

A few miles further I come to the outskirts of Mission with its scattering of tiny faded homes and house trailers. Ahead, in what looks like the town center, stand six humble, little stores. I'm not sure what I'd expected but it wasn't a sad scene like this. My heart stops; I feel like a foreigner in a strange land. Well, truth be told, I am.

I drive at a snail's pace down the main street and try to absorb it all because that's what I imagined I'd do once I got here. But, it's hard to take in because it seems so desolate. I thought, at the very least, the town would feel alive.

In front of one store, two men with dark, sun-baked skin, slump over benches. It's too hot for their long-sleeved shirts and their ill-fitting pants that are twisted by a belt into a thick fold at the top. A third man, sitting on the ground in an alley, is propped up against the side of a building. His head droops onto his chest and he looks asleep but I suspect he's passed-out drunk. At first, these depressing scenes bother me but I make myself ignore them. *After all, I'm here for the powwow.*

A sign at the far end of the street jumps out at me like a desert oasis: "Gift Shop." I roll down the street then pull over and park near the store. I'll have to make it quick since the migrant sun is going to ruin Doug's shade. When I step onto the street, the land feels muted, lacking the subtle aliveness I felt on yesterday's drive. The town is silent and aside from the men, the streets are empty. *Where is everyone?*

I collect myself, remember why I'm here, and am so eager walking up the shop steps, I nearly smash into the front door. As I enter I am revived when a warm smile greets me. The young woman looks to be in her early twenties and wears a loose-fitting white blouse, slacks, and trendy rimless glasses. A pastel scarf holds back her wavy black hair. She says, "Hello," and her cheerful eyes make the cute shop even more welcoming. I assume she is Lakota; she needs to be to fit my fantasy. It feels good to be in here, away from the depressing street.

This tidy, small store reminds me of some little antique shops in Maine: quaint and chock full of surprises. Near the door and checkout counter are shelves and glass cases filled with Native, beaded crafts: baskets, carved wooden objects, and feathers. My pulse quickens. *I can hardly believe I'm here and I'm the only customer.* The young woman is sitting on a stool behind the counter and I sneak a peek at her. She looks like she's engrossed in some sort of textbook. I wonder what she's reading. *Is she in college? Is there even a college around here?* From what I've seen, I can't imagine there is.

While I'm perusing the crafts I look up and notice another room. As I step inside I see bookshelves along one wall with seventy to eighty books for sale. I begin scanning them. They're all Native American titles and right away one jumps out at me so I slide it off the shelf and open it to a picture. The caption says it's of Black Hawk, a Lakota medicine man. He's standing next to what looks like an old-fashioned keyhole or the opening of a birth canal. It's called Wind Cave, is four-feet tall, two-and-a-half-feet wide, and is located in a sacred location in the Black Hills. For thousands of years, Indians have visited it to be energized by Mother Earth. It's believed to be a place where humans were birthed. As I read, chills run up and down my arms and legs. Of the many books I've read on American Indian cultures, I've never heard of Wind Cave. *Interesting.*

I slide the book back on the shelf then walk over to the front counter to visit with the young woman and get some powwow info.

She looks up and smiles when I approach. I take this as an invitation to talk. "Hi, I'm staying in Belvidere at the campground and I heard about the powwow here this weekend. I was wondering if you could tell me about it."

"Oh, the powwow is next weekend and you're welcome to come. It's intertribal so anyone can attend."

"Oh, next weekend, really? I'm not sure I'll be around next week but maybe. I'm heading to Wounded Knee, after that I'm not sure where I'll be."

She peppers me with questions about my trip and asks about living in Maine. I tell her about driving west and just a little about my home because it seems so ordinary compared to this place. What I want to talk about is her life, if the opportunity is presented. *Don't get too eager or be rude, Regina.*

She starts talking about what she calls, "the old ways," how things in her community have changed, and how their traditional religion is disappearing. The sad reality of life here begins to register and her words sting me. I think of those poor men on the street and I'm embarrassed about how easily I dismissed them. She explains how poverty and misery have taken root in the hearts and minds of many of her people and my giddiness at being on an actual reservation fades. These are real people who are going through hell. It's time I released those idealized images I have of all of them: dressed in feathered regalia, dancing in circles to a drum beat, and living in harmony with Earth.

As I prepare to leave, I'm halfway out the door when she calls to me, "Oh, you should visit Wind Cave." Chills cover me again. I hadn't mentioned the book or anything about Wind Cave to her. *For sure, hawk's telling me I'll be visiting Wind Cave.*

We exchange goodbyes then I head back to the car. I look in and smile at Doug all curled up and comfy in the back. He's so easy, always willing to wait for me. After driving ten hours each of the four days on the way here, I'd rent a motel room for the night. Once I checked in, I'd take Doug for a walk, then tell him I was leaving him in the room while I went to get dinner. Undaunted, he'd curl up and nap without a peep. Our relationship is built on respect and trust. *Respect and trust. Huh. This town, these poor people could have used some of that from our government.*

Slumped down in my seat outside the gift shop, I try to process the last half hour. What I've seen, including those poor souls on the street, makes me appreciate my treasured sense of hope and sovereignty. I know I can tailor much of my life as I see fit. Then a couple minutes later, the depressing energy of this place hits me again and harder. These people have lost so much. *Do I even deserve my joy today?* But, life moves us along whether we are ready or not so I start up the car and leave Mission, confused.

It's a ninety-three-mile drive to Wounded Knee on the Pine Ridge Reservation but, again, the driving out here feels effortless. Thirty miles from Mission, the pristine tarred road ahead looks like an endless airport runway that's piercing the horizon. Surrounded by a dried-up landscape with hardly any green, it's a stark contrast to the verdant grasslands on the public land in Belvidere.

I begin thinking how the European settlers destroyed the hunting grounds and cultures of these First Nations. They moved them to places like this and tried to turn once predominately nomadic hunters into farmers. On this land! Confined, no longer allowed to hunt or even roam, there was no need to communicate with nature to find their sustenance. I imagine they must have begun to die inside. *Were connections to Earth broken then?* Maybe that's why this land seems silent, inert.

Far ahead on the road, that is, I'm hoping it's far ahead, some serious storm clouds are filling the horizon. I stop the car, get out my field compass, and check the storm's orientation. It's heading northeast. *Thank goodness, I'm heading west.*

As I drive further, my chest tightens, and I feel a raw sadness inside. It's like how I sometimes feel when I meditate and my heart begins to swell. Waves of compassion for these poor mistreated people make me weep so I have to stop the car. Then, like a lament from some faraway place, words form, tumble into my chest, and I feel them. *This land holds great sorrow.* I thought I might feel some unusual things on my trip but not this deep emotional stuff. *What's happening?*

After a few minutes, the sensations disappear and I regain my composure enough to continue down the road. *Maybe I'm starting to get it: these new feelings must be prayer.* In real prayer we don't just recite words, we open ourselves to both the love we have for others and to their sorrows. Maybe it's like reading the perfect prose, with its perfect words, at the perfect time. That's when a soul is receptive and empathy is stirred. It dawns on me that empathy might be prayer.

I feel better. Then three miles later, I turn off Route 18 and go down a dusty dirt road leading to the village. I see a giant, green metal sign on the side of the road, Wounded Knee. Its twenty bullet holes make for a pretty dramatic message. A short way further another green sign, "Oglala Sioux, War Chief Crazy Horse, 1840-1877," is also riddled with bullet holes. Reality yanks me back even further from my preconceived Indigenous American dream world.

# 11: Two Tepees Show the Way

## Peaceful family energy feels awfully nice

The road ahead flows down through fawn-colored prairie with thin clusters of pine. It then dips into a large ravine that cups a small village. The few dozen modest buildings at Wounded Knee are scattered haphazardly near the main street. The words, "post office," on my map make me think this is a real town. On a knoll just outside the village I see a tiny white chapel and the little white cross at its peak is making a sad stretch up to heaven. The map suggests it's not far from the cemetery and massacre monument. When I look, I'm a little surprised because this sparse, faded land is beginning to appeal to me.

I'm not sure why, but it feels right to go slow. As I approach the center of the settlement, I pass two men shuffling along the side of the road heading towards town. They're wearing jeans, plaid cowboy shirts and hats. Heads down in what seems like conversation, they look like they're on a mission. My mind is at it again. *Who are these guys, where are they headed, and what are their days like?*

My car moves at a snail's pace as I wonder if the village has a retail section. Then in the village center, I slow to a stop. A few yards to my left, at a storefront, sits a tall man and there's something about his soiled, long-sleeved shirt that disturbs me. When he sees my car, he uncoils from his bench and approaches me. Six feet away, he bends down and stares at me through my open window. He has a dark, beet-red, wrinkled face and I can't remember ever being this frightened of anyone. I cringe, push on the accelerator, and escape. *Here's a poor withered soul and all you think to do is drive away?* I leave him in the street and head to the cemetery. My fantasy of another community is again shattered. These people are living desperate lives. *But, my god, I've had enough sadness today.*

The burial ground sits on a knoll, a short mile past the village next to the monument marking the site of the horrific massacre. On a bitter December day in 1890 a small band of Lakota Sioux, starving, exhausted, and many dressed only in rags, arrived in this ravine. They had walked here from Canada and had been promised safe harbor. They came to surrender, give up their way of life, and live on a reservation as ordered by the US government. After a small scuffle with the Seventh Cavalry, the mostly unarmed Sioux, were mowed down with rapid-fire Hotchkiss canons. Many of the women and children were hunted then shot dead by troops on horseback. Some bodies were found as far away as three miles. Several days later the soldiers gathered the approximately 300 bodies of the dead Sioux and dumped them in a mass grave, the present-day cemetery. No one knows exactly what prompted the annihilation but it may have been revenge because the Sioux and Cheyenne had wiped out that same cavalry at the Little Bighorn just fourteen years earlier.

I sit in my car at the foot of the small hill that leads to the graveyard for a couple minutes to take it all in. I've been dreaming about this for months. *Yup, I'm finally here.* But something's missing. The place feels empty. It's not like the historic sites I've visited in New England where I can often feel the history of the place and sometimes even the essence of the former inhabitants. Come to think of it, with the massacre and all, that might be a good thing.

Two other cars are parked at the top near the cemetery's archway and a few visitors are milling around near there. I put my car into gear and wind my way up a short, cratered road of hardened mud to the monument.

Once I turn off the car, I open the door, lean out, and nature attacks: wind and rain, unbelievable wind and rain, again. It feels like it's blowing sixty miles an hour as visitors race to their cars and vehicles scatter. I curl back into mine, close the door, and roll up the windows. The distant storm I saw earlier must have made a turn. After a few dizzying minutes, I compose myself, start the car, and slip-slide down the now muddied road to the bottom. I park but the car is rocking. *Is it going to tip over?*

*Didn't I pay my dues, thrashed around by last night's storm?* Now, all I can think to do is drive in mini circles. After a few laps, the interior windows fog up so I blast the AC then peek outside: Déjà vu. There is no cover, no protection.

I can't stay here. I need to find shelter so I drive down the dirt road leading away from town. The car is rocking, my hands are like vice-grips on the steering wheel, and the windshield wipers do their best to show the way but it looks like I'm heading into oblivion.

I cut through the whirlwind until two white tepees appear in the distance. Lurched forward in my seat I struggle to see enough to stay on the road as the car inches forward. I make it up to where the tepees sit at the bottom of a muddy driveway. At the top is a pint-sized, pale-blue house. Nearby, a small garage or shed leans into the wind. The house reminds me of a modest lakeside camp back home.

My car, thank goodness, with its all-wheel-drive charges up the hill. At the top I coast to the house and pull up opposite the side door. Rattled, I'm afraid to open my door and when I do, it blows all the way open then takes all my strength to pull it shut. In that short time I notice an adult and two little ones peeking out at me on the other side of a screen door. I roll my window down halfway, prepare to do battle with the deafening wind, and yell, "Can I come in?"

The adult yells back a flat, "Yes."

I sag into my seat and sigh. Once the wind lessens, I push open the door and scramble out of the car leaving Doug in the back. *I'm sure he'll be fine.* So says my selective reasoning. This is the best I can do because taking him into a new house with strangers, he'd sense my nervousness and it wouldn't be pretty.

When I charge through the open screen door, the woman gestures to me and I follow her into the kitchen. For a second, I wonder what she might be thinking having a shaggy, wet, white woman just burst into her house. But, all I can think about is my safety so at this moment I can't care what she thinks.

The kitchen is off to the left of the doorway and opposite it is the living room where three adults sit watching television. My guess is the single-story house has four small rooms, and measures maybe twenty by thirty feet, *Tiny for so many people.*

I settle myself into a small wooden chair at the kitchen table. It's next to one of three windows that make for a bright little space. The rustic room has white plaster walls and a well-worn plywood floor. The tidy interior is welcoming and the air's fresh in spite of the lit cigarettes. The smoke must escape through the gaps along the window frames. When I notice movement in the living room, I lean from my seat and make a quick mental tally. I think there are seven people in here: a boy and girl, each about four or five, a teenage boy and girl, a man and woman in their thirties, and a grandmother.

Grandma comes into the kitchen and sits down opposite me at the table. She's a tall, robust woman with a full midsection, maybe in her late 70s. She's wearing an apron over her flowery cotton dress, has white hair, and faded skin tones. She reminds me a little of my Gram, my dad's mother. The younger woman is thin, has dyed red hair, and is pivoting a half-finished cigarette between two fingers. Every couple minutes she pops into the kitchen offering me a warm smile. *She must be the young mother of the house.* Tipping my head towards the living room I see a man, I guess is her husband, sprawled out on a recliner watching TV and holding his own cigarette. The teenagers make a brief stroll into the kitchen, survey me, say nothing, then return to the living room. The two youngest ones roam from room to room curious about their visitor.

I'm still a bit on edge, worried about Doug and, of course, feeling like an intruder. The storm continues its crazy ruckus while the interior of this house is filled with peaceful family energy that feels awfully nice.

# 12: Grandma's Words

## Crazy Rules for Everything

Grandma and I sit at the kitchen table while the adorable little boy stands close by staring up at me. The chipper little girl waltzes in holding a tiny puppy inside her red knit sweater. Her pup, sleepy-eyed and content in his swaddling, has on what looks like a doll's flowery, cotton jacket. The cherub-faced little girl has two yellow barrettes holding back her black hair and she's wearing a cotton blouse embroidered with butterflies. With onyx eyes she gazes up at me and says, "His name is Jake." I perk up.

"My son's name is Jake," I say. Not impressed, she stands motionless near my chair and looks up at me with eyes like her puppy.

I'm hoping the little boy is chatty. He has on shorts and a Mickey Mouse t-shirt, flip flops, and has the same coal eyes. It's my chance to engage so I say, "Do you like Mickey Mouse?"

He says, "Yes, and I'm going to Disney World someday and ride all the rides." He makes me smile.

We talk about Mickey, Minnie, and other Disney characters then I run out of questions, look up and take another stab at it. I venture into, of all things, a conversation about the broken spring on the screen door. "What happened to the door? Did the wind break it? Is it going to get fixed?"

He responds with a blank look. He's so young and my attempt to fill the desolate spaces between me and these people is pathetic. No one else seems interested in talking which makes me feel even more like an intruder.

The two little ones drift into the living room. *I can't sit here for long, alone with Grandma stationed across the table from me.* She's an imposing figure and I'm not used to being with such nonverbal people for this length of time. And on their turf. I've learned through my studies and limited experiences with Indigenous friends, most are reserved people. But experiencing it like this, scared for my safety, and stranded in a home of strangers, is, well, unsettling.

Rather than sitting here feeling invisible, I decide to initiate some sort of exchange. To get up my courage, I take a deep breath, then look at Grandma and say, "Do you get many storms like this?"

Nothing. She takes one last drag on her cigarette, grinds it into the half-filled ashtray, then looks out the window.

I sigh, force a half-assed grin, and look at her across the table. "I thought my car was going to blow back to Maine. I'm from Maine. I hope your house holds up." Except for the wailing winds that muffle most of the TV sounds, the kitchen is silent.

At this point it's hailing and the wind's blowing sideways. I can see the rain pushing its way inside around the window frames. *My God, how do they survive winters here?* I remember reading about the brutal South Dakota weather then stop because I can't go there. The image is too disturbing. *But, how do these people endure?*

The little boy comes back into the kitchen and he and I start playing peekaboo over the edge of the table. I look over at Grandma but she still seems oblivious to me. My feeble attempt to converse failed and she's making no eye contact. She smiles as she pats the heads of the two little ones.

My stomach's tied up in knots so I need to do something. I say, "I saw the tepees at the end of your driveway."

She stiffens, turns to me, and with a slight scowl says, "My nephew made them. They're not being taken care of, the poles keep breaking. It's hard to get poles since the Whites took over and make us follow rules about cutting our own trees. Crazy rules for everything."

I slink further in my chair, look away, and think better of encouraging more conversation. My romantic thoughts about their way of life crumble even more.

After a very long twenty minutes or so, the storm begins to let up. I whisper, "Thank you" to Grandma then stand up and ease myself toward the doorway.

I poke my head into the living room and the four folks look up from the TV. "Thanks for letting me in." The dad and the young man each lift a hand off the arm of their chair in a noncommittal flag. The mom and teenage woman look into my eyes and smile. No words needed.

Before I open the screen door, the two little ones appear at my feet. I say my goodbyes and their sunny smiles are like a pat on my back.

When I step outside, the misty air whisks up against my face. The thick blanket of low-hanging clouds is dissolving, and the sun's poking through. I'm revived too. I hope Doug understands and forgives me for leaving him. He always has.

The car is fine, all is well. When I open the door and look inside, Doug greets me with hard tail thumps on the back side window. Thinking he deserves some love, I open the back hatch and hug him around the neck, give him a bunch of strokes down his back. "What a gooood boy." He plops down on his blanket, curls up, and appears to resume whatever he was doing in my absence. Easy-going friend and courageous guardian, I know I sometimes take him for granted. I don't realize how much I love him until he passes some seven years later at the age of thirteen and a half.

When I journal about this day, I'm struck again by this family's kindness in giving me shelter. I'm reminded of the many aboriginal tribes who offered the same to the Europeans only to be cheated and robbed of their lands. Today's generosity is a cultural norm I've experienced time and time again. Though some of my ways were not embraced, and despite my nerves, I felt respected and safe in that little house.

# 13: Infatuated with a Stunt-double

## A girlish smile plasters my face

Before climbing back into the car I stand outside the little house checking out the long, muddy driveway. The car is fine, Doug is fine, and I'm a little more mature, I hope.

Back at the wheel, I slip-slide down the pudding driveway then stop at the end. A little flicker in my gut signals there's something more to do. I reach to the back seat and grab the camera from my backpack. I stretch out the car window, and snap a picture of the white tepees with the little blue house in the background at the top of the frame. When I look up from my camera, everything feels different. Innocent breezes, flung in from away, wipe out old upheavals and the blue sky and insistent sun reassure me that all's well. I loosen up. Nature's tantrum is over and the air is renewed. *What a storm!*

The road to the memorial is pocked with huge puddles but my miniature rhino-on-wheels plows through with ease. I pull off the road to read a metal plaque with a summary of the massacre. It tells how during the terrifying onslaught, many of the Indians ran over two hundred yards north of this spot seeking safety from the soldiers. Today, nearly two hundred yards north of here is the house where I took refuge. Without warning, it feels like there's a lead weight in my stomach so heavy it makes me double over. I try to embrace this strange new feeling and not over analyze it. I know my body is telling me something.

Over the years I've come to believe, like many others, that land holds memory of trauma just like one's body. Standing on the massacre site, my body feels something, maybe confusion. Then it gets clearer; I am heartbroken and ashamed of my race and my government. I get back into my car and hope I can disappear.

The Native's dream of prosperity continues, I've read about some communities organizing social programs to advance education, mental health, and important cultural traditions. Yes, but I believe it's veiled in empty promises by the US government. Even with lawful protests by its residents, our government allows big business to mine and build fuel pipelines here. *How could anything or anyone thrive on this land?*

I slide down into my seat and remember bouncing along like a kid at camp on my prairie adventure. Before I left home, I hoped to be able to feel the memory this land is holding. Now, as I sit, I feel its sadness. Protected parts inside me crack open and I feel exposed but also a little more alive. When I start to embrace this feeling, I have a good cry for everything and everyone here, now, and before. It's not logical, it's visceral and so my feelings are real.

A few minutes later and feeling exhausted, I pull myself up in the seat. When I look down the road, I see some sort of mini structure across from the monument. I don't remember noticing it when I came through. Well, how could I have noticed it, hell-bent on running for shelter?

Closer to the memorial I pull off the road. It looks like a lean-to, something like the ramadas I've seen in Arizona deserts. Whatever it is, it's a welcome distraction from my grief. I pull in closer to the structure then take Doug out for a short walk. Even with all the drama, my cheerful boy bounces back into the car when we're done. And here, the ground's energy feels softer and the fickle, impish breezes invite me to stay in this peaceful spot.

Apparently a victim of the windstorm, the ramada, which is about the size of my car, has partially collapsed. Three young people and a gray-haired older woman seem to glide in out of nowhere and start propping it back up. Its flat roof, made of about twenty long pine poles, is held up by a seven-foot-tall pole at each of the four corners. It's silent, tranquil work.

I walk over to the curious form, scan the young people, smile, and then give an optimistic hello. The teenage girl looks up from the corner pole she's wedging into a hole in the ground and returns a kind smile. A thin strip of red fabric, stretched round the top of her head, holds back her beautiful, long, black hair. She has on jeans and scuffed-up white sneakers. *Oh my, she has a stain on her blouse.* In my imagination she would be pristine, modest in dress but pristine. *You live in a dream world, Regina.*

She keeps looking at me, flashes an even bigger smile, and says, "Want to buy a dream-catcher?"

Her miniature dream-catchers dangle from a rickety repurposed picture frame propped up on a table. Swaying in the delicate breeze, the fascinating and fanciful crafts catch my eye. I've made dream-catchers myself from local materials. I've read that traditional ones are made from a thin willow branch, wrapped in leather braids, and curled into a hoop shape. Woven in the center is a symmetrical rawhide web and, hanging from the bottom of the hoop, are six thin strips of leather, adorned with tiny beads and feathers. It's believed that when hung near sleeping children, dream-catchers snare the bad dreams and usher in the good ones.

Further inside the enchanting little structure are two older teenage guys struggling to prop up the corner poles and fix the roof. There's something cheery and innocent about these young people. Then I remember this structure is temporary which is customary for these once semi-nomadic people. A part of me wants to lend a hand, offer suggestions for making it sturdier, with more longevity. But I also sense there's an accepted impermanence to this thing so I hold back. Nothing is permanent and that's something that has always troubled me.

—◊—

Back in the 60s, I couldn't wait for our town's biggest annual event, the tiny North Haverhill Fair. The two food stands, run by the VFW and the Woman's Club, served the best French fries, hamburgers, hot dogs, homemade coleslaw, and pies ever—even to this day. At the far end of the grounds was a giant ring for the tractor and horse pulling contests. The fairgrounds had two barns for the cattle and our elementary school was filled with 4-H exhibits. And, of course, there was a midway with the customary four rides of the day: Ferris-wheel, merry-go-round, tilt-a-whirl, and the swings. The rides and the six game booths were run by foreign-looking carnival guys called "carnies."

We lived just down the street from the fairgrounds, and in those days it was safe for kids to be on their own for the whole day, and I was, for most of its three days and nights. It was mysterious and exciting, like my first visit to a foreign country. By the end of the last day, I knew every inch of the track and had developed a crush on a handsome carnie.

Monday morning, after the fair left town, I'd roam the grounds alone, with my heart aching. I'd pass the battened-up food stalls and the blighted squares of once grassy spots where the game stalls had stood. I'd conjure up the heartwarming smells and intriguing sounds of the late-night magic that had been. Strolling down the length of the cattle barns, I'd delight in the memory of pungent animal smells and sounds so familiar in our farm community. When I kicked up sawdust remnants left behind, I felt a little empty and forgotten. The dusty midway with its crumbled ride tickets, cheap plastic prizes, and barely recognizable pieces of French fries was evidence of a mini invasion.

To my young eyes, it was proof that magic and mystery did exist and that's where I wanted to live.

Back inside the ramada at Wounded Knee, I introduce myself to the girl and she asks about my travels. When I'm done telling her about where I've been, she quizzes me about my knowledge of the monument and my response is a bare-bones rundown. After hearing my words it dawns on me: How much of what I've read is true?

She says, "My great, great grandfather was at the massacre and owned the cemetery area and beyond. He was a great gardener and well loved." She continues, telling me about the infant, Lost Bird, who was found alive under her mother's dead body four days after the massacre. The baby was then adopted by a soldier and his wife, and had a terrible life fraught with neglect and abuse. "Lost Bird is buried to the right as you go up to the site," she points. The tale she tells feels old and tired, maybe run down after so much telling.

Thank goodness our buoyant chat resumes and I ramble on asking about her village and she seems happy to fill me in. "The unemployment rate is 53%. My boyfriend is here helping me out." She points to him and he looks up and flashes me a perfect, toothy smile. He's handsome enough to be a model and around nineteen. He has short, shiny, black hair held back by a black and white bandana. His monogrammed t-shirt, baggy white shorts, and high-top sneakers remind me of a hip-hop city kid.

As we continue chatting, I realize I'm glowing. It feels good to be listened to again. After I tell her more about my camping, she suggests I might be able to tent nearby, and points down the road to the chapel I passed when I arrived.

"The young pastor probably would be okay with that," she says. For a minute, I'm tempted. *Wow, camping at Wounded Knee.* Then my good senses kick in. This place holds way too many eerie memories and with the high rate of alcoholism, it's not a good idea.

Her cousin, another striking young man, joins our conversation. His shiny black hair flows down to the middle of his bare back. He has classic, indigenous facial features, and warm dark eyes. His blue jeans and cowboy boots complete what I judge to be the standard Indian cowboy look. Without looking up from his pole-bracing work, he tells me, "I was stepped on by a bull a little while ago. I'm into rodeos, big time." Despite all the scars on his neck and chest from rodeo riding mishaps, he exudes kindness.

I'm stunned when he starts talking about being in the *Crazy Horse* movie, shot in Rapid City last year. Unimpressed, he says, "I wish I hadn't done all those stunts without pads. I was Crazy Horse's double and I had to fall off horses and carry people around. But, the money was good." He looks up and smiles. My cheeks feel hot as a girlish smile plasters my face. I am forty-eight years old and I am enamored.

*I can't help it; he's talking about Crazy Horse, the icon I idolize.* I blurt out, "What did you wear. How did it feel?" He answers with a shy smile that tells me I've asked enough questions, so I stop.

"The movie's on TV tonight. Are you going to watch it?" he asks. "Everybody in the village is going to." Evidently it's the first showing of the movie, anywhere, and I happen to be here on the opening day talking with Crazy Horse's movie double. *Amazing.*

Feeling giddy, I answer, "I would love to watch it but I'm camping so I'll have to wait and see it some other time."

For an hour the four of us chat about Maine's dense forests and my camping adventures but they hardly measure up to their tales of riding horses across the plains. I want to ask what it's like to live here, what their hopes and dreams are. But my silent time with Grandma at her house is still fresh so I resist asking, for now at least.

Quick to smile and laugh, their male confidence and verve vaporize my maturity. *I have found my people.*

With my mental filter off, I jump in again and bluster, "Do you believe in past lives?"

The stunt-double kid looks up and gives me a deadpan answer, "No."

I continue with my deluge, "I think I was one of you guys in another lifetime." The two guys look up from their work and give me a polite chuckle.

Oblivious to my foolishness, I persist, "Do you think about the old days, like how they used to hunt, and ride, and eat what they hunted?"

With sparkling eyes and a mischievous smile, the hip-hop boyfriend locks eyes with me and says, "Yes, and tepee-peeking."

I must have looked puzzled. "You sneak out late at night and lift up the bottom flaps of tepees to check out the girls." Stifled by what at first seems like a cheeky response I pause before chuckling along with the other two. As much as this feminist has always taken offense to the phrase, "boys will be boys," it does fit here and I surprise myself.

As if on cue, the young woman's aunt, who had been on the outskirts of the ramada, hikes up each side of her long cotton skirt, steps over a wood crate, and stands near me. When she extends her hand, we shake and I smile as one of her gray braids tumbles onto her chest. Maybe my newly practiced reticence is noticed and maybe it signals I want to listen because she begins talking about life here. She explains how this

49

land is home to her people and she seems resigned to her history, telling me about an incident that happened not too long ago.

Buddy Lamont, a well-respected member of the Oglala Lakota tribe, was thirty-one when he joined the Wounded Knee standoff in 1973. US government troops surrounded the town while a large group of militant Indians protested conditions after decades of terrible poverty and corruption in local tribal government.

"An FBI sharpshooter shot Buddy as he was leaving his tear-gassed bunker. He died soon after. He became a martyr to the cause." She raises her head and looks out into the distance as her attention and words fade away.

I remember reading something from a book about a great Lakota medicine man. The author said, "I notice how the older ones seem to drift off in conversations like these and look into the hills, not staying long in your eyes or coming words." I imagine this strong, intelligent woman is resigned to her way of life, even though it's an abbreviated way of life with a crumbling culture and lost traditions. However, these are friendly people and I feel welcomed.

A thin white woman ducks her head down then walks into the ramada. Her tiny white shorts, hair-sprayed, blonde hair, and long black fingernails make me cringe. *You don't belong here—with us.* Her elbow pivots on her hip and she cradles a serious 35mm camera that makes her look like a professional. What intrigues me about her is that she looks a lot like two of my sisters. I keep sneaking sideways peeks, seeing the likeness of one sister then the other. *I wonder what this means. It must mean something, right? Synchronicities and all?* Then again maybe I want it to mean something or maybe there really is something mystical afoot. I can't imagine what my family has to do with this.

The camera lady steps up to me and, in stark contrast to these reserved people, she looks me squarely in the eyes and I feel pressured into conversation. She announces she's from Florida and is camping and traveling alone. Besides exploring the West she is here hoping to heal some family issues. It's interesting: she resembles my sisters, I'm open to personal healing on my trip and, God knows, my family could use some. About fifteen minutes into our chat, we say our goodbyes and agree to try and meet up on Sunday in Rapid City at the powwow. It's the first I've heard of it and I'm psyched... about the powwow, that is.

I buy two dream catchers, one with a sinew web and red leather on the hoop, the other is all white leather. Later, I give the red one to a friend. The white one would hang on my car's rear-view mirror for sixteen years, a constant reminder of this day, these people, and how their generous ways began to change me.

# 14: Just Leap

## Confinement can do that to us

I turn to my Lakota friends and thank them for our visit then jump into the car and drive to the cemetery. Though I could have stayed longer, I think I've embarrassed myself enough today.

I drive to the monument parking area, stop at the foot of the hill, and then hike up the path to the top. Even though I'm grateful to be the single soul here, the eerie silence is unsettling. The land's life force might have been obliterated or maybe it just left. Waves of sadness and loss sober me.

At the top of the hill, the unkempt, brown grasses and the chain-link fence circling the mass grave are grim reminders of this genocide. But it's the twenty or so small tombstones that make me stop and offer prayers for peace. What a pitiful resting place for these three hundred slaughtered souls. I had expected to sense some sort of revelation but all I feel is empty and confused.

I know that chronic and/or severe trauma can cause emotional and physical ailments in one's body. I stop to think about this. Did the suffering that occurred here seep into the land leaving its vitality scattered and out of balance?

I became aware of this phenomenon hiking in New England. Sensing unsettled energy in a location, sometimes I'd find out later it was the site of an accidental death, a battle, clear-cutting of a forest, or some other trauma.

A few minutes later a cool little breeze signals it's time, so I turn to leave. I walk through the archway entrance with its tall brick columns on each side. I bend down and slip a heart-shaped stone into the hole at the base of a magnificent tall pole flying red flags. It's something I'd planned, a gesture to show I'm here and I care what happened. I say a few more goodbyes to these poor people, unknown to most of our country, then start my faltering retreat back to the car and Doug.

For months I'd prepared myself for this and, even though I don't admit it, I probably expected to be wowed by a paranormal experience or two. The reality is, my time here has been ordinary yet profound. Just like the land and these people.

When I leave Wounded Knee, it's late afternoon. As I drive back to the campground, I revisit today's adventures: the Rosebud Reservation, the second wind storm, refuge with the kind family, my ramada friends, and the cemetery visit. *So much to digest in just one day.* There can't be room for more.

Back at the campground, I check my tourist map and plan my next destination. Once I pack up my things, I drive to the town of Hot Springs. My brochure says it's the site of a massive archaeological dig where fossilized animal bones from the Ice Age were found. On the way I see two red-tailed hawks on a fence post. My spirit messengers are now commonplace and no longer thrill me the way they did days ago but I appreciate the company and their reassurance that I'm on a good path.

I stop and park the car to take a picture of the hawks. As I lean into the back seat for my camera, Doug vaults off the back window frame then sails out through the open window. Once he hits the ground, he dives between the bottom two spans of a barbed wire fence, then into a small herd of serious beef cattle. *Holy shit!*

He's never, ever, done anything like this before. He always waits for a signal from me to jump out of the car.

My heart's in my throat as I catapult myself out of the car and bolt to the expected dog/cow brawl. The six muscle-bound beef cattle, their heads lowered, stand their ground and stare Doug down.

Then, without a bark, a wine, or a whimper, he turns, unfazed, and with his tail held neutral, trots back under the fence, brushes by me, jumps back through the window, and into his bed. After I collect myself, I start the car and we proceed down the road as if nothing just happened. Who knows, after the events of today, maybe nothing did.

My new campsite is at the KOA Camp Ground in Hot Springs and right next to a cow pasture. *Oh, goodie.* Set at the foot of the southernmost tip of the Black Hills, it's a busy but, thankfully, cheery campground.

In the evening I write in my journal: *"Today at the ramada, for a moment I felt like I was sliding back in time, maybe to one of my previous lives. I could feel something in my body, maybe it was stored memories. Not fantasies but memories of other times with the newborn prairie mornings, stretched-out horizons, my intimate relationship with Earth, and my strong agile body. And,*

*I missed my devotion to my community. I wish I could return to those simple ways of honoring each day and each precious moment of each day."* I stop to wipe away some tears. *Are these words coming from my mind or am I dreaming?* I am fine with either.

A little later I think about how Doug had acted on impulse. He charged out then thought better as reality revealed itself more clearly. I suspect he enjoyed his leap through the air and the thrill of facing the herd of beasts especially after so many hours confined in the car. Confinement can do that to us.

Today I leaped too, into the lives of others. And after that, I was gently spun back by what felt like a considerate otherworldly force, back into my ordinary world. For now, I'm thankful for my mundane life here in my sleeping bag. Even though I'm exhausted, I delight in this day's adventures which are too many to think about let alone understand.

# 15: The Leaving Begins

## Sadly, it became a family pattern

Tonight it's good to be alone, sealed up inside my tent, away from the outside world. My mind flashbacks to this day which feels more like three. These memories swirl inside my head, the teacher in me wants to make sense of them. *I search for the day's theme. There must be a theme; there usually is, right?*

Once I stop thinking, I slip into a sleepy, dreamlike place, and whispered words wander in; *Today was about family.* I start thinking about my grandmother.

—∭—

Even though I didn't get to see her often enough, I felt a very close bond with my paternal grandmother, Delia Proulx. Gram was tall for her generation, big-boned, and attractive. Quick to giggle at her own silly jokes, she always had a few to lighten our visit. Along with her joking attitude she had a spiritual faith and resilience which got both her and me through many hard times.

Gram's first husband, my grandfather, Patrick, abandoned her and their four young children in 1931. Gram's parents took them in even though they still had five teenagers living at home. But times were tough, and a year later the crowded house of three adults, five teenagers, and four children became too much for everyone. Gram was pressured to leave. With no alternative, she was only days away from putting her children in foster care when a local man offered her a house to rent. To support herself, the kind man found her work doing laundry for area families.

54

After my father's father left, my grandmother remarried, had six more children and lived on a remote mountain farm in northern NH. My family told me her new husband was a terrible man who abused Gram and most of the kids especially his four stepchildren. After he died, Gram had twenty peaceful years living alone in her pretty little home at the foot of the same mountain where she raised her family.

A religious woman, once her second husband died, she was thrilled to be able to attend mass again. Gram pursued her love of sewing and her Raggedy Ann and Andy dolls became family favorites. She even sewed my Prom dress, from scratch, without a pattern. The white, cotton dress had a modest A-line style and short sleeves. It was about as exciting as my Prom but I loved that she made it for me.

I remember one of the times I visited Gram. It was winter and a few years before my trip to South Dakota. When I walked in, the generous sunlight and Gram's warm heart flooded the insides of her dollhouse-of-a-home. The hearty aroma of her soup cooking on the wood stove made me recall when we used to visit her on the farm. It seemed she was always cooking something for someone. This little kitchen was what my mom called, "busy" with dozens of knickknacks and pictures of her huge family. The simple scents of her wood stove, fried bacon, and warm homemade bread filled and nourished my empty parts. *What a perfect life Gram has.*

I sat up close to Gram at her kitchen table which took up almost half the room. She handed me a cup of coffee and one of her delicious but dense donuts the family loved to joke about. As a child, I thought she had a hidden stash somewhere because she always had some to give us. As we sat catching up, Gram kept reaching over to touch my hand and tell me how happy she was to see me. Her words and touch were a soft salve of approval and even though I'd never known that sort of tenderness at home, she made me feel deserving of it.

After enough catch-up-talk, I asked Gram about our family history. She began talking about her parents, Joseph and Josephine, and some more distant relatives. Then she stumbled a bit when she mentioned Lydia. I asked her to tell me more.

"Well" she said, "Lydia was an Indian. No one talked about it but we all knew. In those days to have an Indian in your family was something to be ashamed of."

I perked up. Since I was a little girl I'd dreamed about what it must have been like to live like an American Indian. "Really, Gram? What do you know about her?" She sent me to the desk in her living room and told me to find a large black and white photograph of a group of people. I found it and took it back to the kitchen table.

There were eight adults in the photo, four sitting and four standing. A woman in the front row was holding an infant. Gram said the baby was her father, Joseph. From their clothing, I guessed the photo was taken in the late 1800s and that would fit because I knew Gram's mother, Josephine, was born in 1885. An old man sat on the far right of the photo. She said he was ninety-three and the great grandfather to the baby. It took a minute for it to sink in. I had a beautifully preserved photograph of my relatives taken over a hundred years ago and going back six generations.

Gram pointed to the woman holding the baby. "That there is Lydia, yes, that's her. She was Micmac." Gram stopped talking and we sat there in silence for a bit. I bent over to get a closer look searching Lydia's face for some familiar or indigenous features but her image was small, gray, and a little grainy. Her dress looked like many I'd seen in photos of the 1880s. It was long, black, and had a full skirt with what I imagined were layers of petticoats underneath. The tight-fitting waist and tall collar looked constrictive and probably explained her rigid face. Her gray hair was pulled back tight on her head, and she might have had a bun in the back. She looked a lot shorter than the others. I wondered if that's where two of my sisters got their stature.

Excited, I didn't know what to say. As she told me the names of all the people, I penciled them in on the back. I asked her if I could borrow it to make a copy. She said yes but made me promise to return it. I assured her I would and I did. It is one of my most treasured pieces of family history.

Even if the old guy in the picture was ninety-three at the time, he looked robust for his age. That also means he was born in the 18th century. I had a photo of grandparents going back as far as my fourth great grandfather, and some evidence that at least one of my relatives was American Indian. I was excited. The idea that I had some Indigenous genes made me feel different, more complex and interesting than the ordinary white person I was.

My father's father was devilishly handsome. In one photo he stands posed like a model with his head cocked and one hand in the vest of his stylish three-piece suit. At a family reunion in 1992, I sat in a circle with six eighty-something-year-old women who had known my grandfather when they were young. I asked them what they remembered about him. They straightened in their seats and their eyes twinkled. One lady volunteered, "Oh, that Patrick with his gold tooth; when he came into town all us girls were smitten." I had to chuckle.

From what I'd learned over the years, when Grandfather Patrick was married to Gram, he found it hard to stay put and would leave his little ones and Gram and go to New York City for work. At that time, they lived with Gram's parents. Their house was near a busy railroad route in northern NH so I imagined it was easy for him to travel. We were told my grandfather was a construction worker who walked the iron beams used to build skyscrapers including the Empire State Building. I'd like to think this is true, lending something positive to his life story.

But, bottom line, my grandfather was a restless man who loved traveling, gambling, drinking, and the ladies.

One of the saddest stories Gram told me, and she shared it with me a few times, was about the day my grandfather left. After Gram's father told him to go, Patrick drifted down the sprawling fields, continued up over the side of a small mountain, and disappeared. As she related this tale, a small tear formed in her eye. "You know, he never looked back, not once." She never saw him again. Unfortunately, it became a family pattern that would play out in future generations.

Tonight, lying here in my tent I think about how hard it must have been on Gram. But she and I shared a spiritual faith and resilience which got us through similar hard times.

# 16: Stories Are More than Tales

## I could change the role I have in my family.

My granddaughter, Grace, reminds me of myself. We have a very close bond. In her twenty-two years she's had some major ups and downs but they've molded her into an independent and confident young woman.

From when she was a toddler, till the family moved away ten years later, she took turns with her younger twin brothers spending one weekend a month with me. They were the best of times.

When Grace was four I took her frog hunting at a friend's tiny pond. Before we headed down to the water I told her we had to ask my friend, Deb, for permission to go there. I made it a bit of a big deal, telling Grace, "You always have to ask." Then, like a child much older, she approached Deb and said, "Deb, can we have permission go to your pond and look for frogs?" Deb giggled and said, "Yes, of course."

I'd brought along a butterfly net and a five-gallon bucket for our catch. I said, "Grace, you are in charge of the net. You are the "frog catcher." She looked up at me, grinned and, I swear, stood a little taller.

Grace charged at a full gallop down the grassy field towards the pond's shoreline. Even as a toddler, she'd always had perfect balance. Now that I think about it, she hardly ever fell. She had a way with gravity.

Now another memory rushes in, something I haven't thought of in years. When Grace was about ten months old, I took her for a walk in her stroller. We stopped at the edge of a tiny swamp near where she lived. It was a beautiful summer day, the sapphire sky was stunning but it was the bull frogs who commanded my attention. Their unremitting singing was loud and sounded like a chorus of one hundred. I stopped to tell little Grace, reclining inside her stroller, it was frogs we were hearing. But, before I could say a word, she uttered, "Hello. Hello, hello." I melted. She didn't need me to explain how to connect with nature; she hadn't thought otherwise.

At the shoreline of Deb's pond, Grace got right to work. She took off her sneakers and waded into the thick spread of enormous lily pads. I cringed at the thought of blood suckers and crayfish near her tiny toes but the child had no fear.

The pond was loaded with giant bull frogs, the largest I'd ever seen and so easy to detect. I stepped back allowing Grace to make her own discoveries, sort of how my dad and mom let us kids make our own way.

It didn't take me long to spot a huge shiny green head with its bulging set of eyes floating nearby. And she saw it too. "Grandma, I see one. Can we get him?"

"You can try, step over here, I'll show you how I do it." I picked up the net and stalked the slippery bugger, swung the net in from his rear, and scooped him up." Grace yelled, "Yay Grandma, you got 'im. Good job."

The beast was so big, Grace had to use two hands to take it out of the net. I showed her how to hold him tight, under his arms but gently. Its long, limp legs hung down for more than a foot. I wanted a picture of the two of them so I told her to hold it up in front of her. In the developed picture, Grace and her massive frog had the very same broad smile.

I took lots of pictures that day. Many are included in a storybook I made about Grace and me hunting for frogs at Deb's beautiful pond.

In 1985, I attended a workshop and learned some fascinating theories about family dynamics. One premise suggested certain roles played out in a family will repeat themselves in every generation. And each of us takes on a specific familiar role. This is how "family stories" are created and the same narrative is repeated until someone changes his or her role. I think Gram and I had similar roles. Maybe
Grace does too.

Presently, I wonder what stories the Lakota told before the colonists came and what are told now. It's possible the best ones were lost like ones shared to help hold a family, clan, and tribe together. I've read about indigenous fables and remember how they elevated me out of my Catholic way of thinking about what it means to be a human. Indigenous American legends taught me our planet is as alive as we are and how plants and animals can communicate with us. I remember how it comforted me to read what I'd felt since childhood but had no words for;

I am part of a great family of living things sharing this planet. The concept is not just a pretty metaphor; it has become the foundation for all of my beliefs.

Before there were scientific words for it, Indigenous peoples spoke of fantastic things. They told of real-life connections between all forms of life including Earth. The old ones spoke of the great mysteries of life and offered a guide for navigating it.

Dr. Charles Eastman, born in 1858 and a graduate of Dartmouth College, was a Sioux physician and author. His books are about how he was raised in the traditional way on this very land. He was the only physician to care for the injured at the Wounded Knee massacre. He explains how their ancient fables were meant to help people understand life and deal with its challenges. The stories were meant to teach values and stir wonder in their spiritual existence. Some of the narratives reminded me of the few biblical tales I could remember.

After a long while in my little tent, reality slips in and shakes me up. I accept that many, maybe most, of the original indigenous stories are probably gone, erased by the atrocities inflicted on these people: stealing their children, outlawing their religious practices, and forcing them to live on reservations. When I think that they were forbidden to share their legends and forced to adopt the white man's Bible, it hits me hard and I'm furious.

How can a culture thrive without passing on their histories through myths? I think about my own life, where scripture challenged me to be in good favor with a revengeful God, the works of transcendentalists like Hawthorne and Thoreau telling us that nature and God are one, and indigenous legends that inspired me to explore nature and what it takes to be a good human. As I grew into adulthood it wasn't hard to leave my catechism behind.

Years after my trip, I learned the importance of sharing personal history from a Native American physician and psychologist who travels the world teaching about its healing power. The indigenous folklore he shared made me think differently about my life, my family, and my role in both. His programs not only enriched my interest in Aboriginal spiritualism, but they made me realize I could change my role in my family as well as my life. And even though I didn't realize it at the time, I came to understand how excruciating but freeing it can be to "speak."

In modern culture, history comes alive through literature and the arts. I am reminded daily of the importance of sharing our stories. Every once in a while I send one of these chapters to Grace, to get her opinion but, mostly, to share our family's past with her. When she responds with, 'Wow, I didn't know that. Thanks for telling me, Grandma. Can you tell me more?" I feel like I'm doing my part."

# 17: Myra's Magic Wand

## Why do I have to drag this big body around?

The KOA campground in Hot Springs is fine, nothing fancy, but it's peaceful and after my rousing visit to Mission and Wounded Knee, that's huge. Before today, I never realized how much solitude I need, how my alone time restores me. When I slip into my tent tonight, I'm home.

Once my journal entry's done, I wiggle deeper into my sleeping bag to read. Before starting, I pause to take it all in. Everything about this evening is revitalizing, like a tall, cool drink after a daylong thirst. The still air is fresh and dry and even the chorus of crickets is muted and comforting. I might be self-absorbed but this night feels like my gift after a stormy twenty hours.

I open my book hoping it'll lull me into sleep, but it doesn't. I keep thinking about a commitment I made to myself years ago: *I want to live to my highest spiritual potential.* The words feel sort of like a personal oath made in a moment of contemplation and a soothing prayer I repeat often. I let the phrase roll about in my head like a ticker tape and after a little time sleep finally takes over. For hours, I'm dead to the world.

Just after dawn and before the day gets a grip on me, I wake. *I have absolutely no one to answer to and nothing on my agenda.* The newborn day's silky softness makes me limp. My warm sleeping bag is all I need. My life is perfect.

My logical brain's sluggish, not quite ready to fire up so my fertile imagination takes over. I stare up at the translucent ceiling and notice how it filters out certain color hues but allows others through. I think about the land and people at Mission and Wounded Knee. *What if*

61

*something could filter out the sadness held in that land and in those people? Where did that crazy thought come from?* At first, I think I'm being *loopy*, again, but then I go easy on myself and realize it's my empathetic imagination at work. If I didn't care...

And now, even after a good night's sleep, I'm still wiped out. It's like I have an emotional hangover. But it's a brand new day in my adventure, so I crawl out of the tent and force my stiff self upright amidst a few new aches and pains. When the ebullient sun greets me I recoil and shade my eyes before plodding over to check on Doug. He lifts his massive black head and smiles with his eyes. After giving me a tail thump, he stretches out onto his blanket and sinks back into dreamland. Lucky Doug gets to sleep.

The campground bathhouse calls to me. I hate the thought of it, but a cold wash might jolt me awake, so I head over for a quick face spritz. It helps a little and when I get back to the car, I dig through my backseat provisions. I'm more tired than hungry but I know I should eat something. It might perk me up. All I can handle is a few raisins and granola in yogurt. Coffee is too much trouble, so after finishing my concoction, I duck back into the tent, hoping to sleep some more.

The impish sun tries to bake my tent's innards but the gentle wind is relentlessly loyal, sputtering the door flaps as it drifts in and moderates the sun's attempt.

By mid-morning, I've endured three hours of tossing and turning. Then, without intending to, I slip into a dreamy-awake place. My mind quiets, my body feels slightly heavier and slight breezes flowing through the tent make me feel like I'm floating. Seconds later I drift into that in-between place just before we drop into sleep. My busy mind stills but my body's tuned into everything inside and outside of it. Now it extends outward and merges with the surroundings. I know my reality is informed not just by my sensory organs but by my whole physical form. *My body is one huge sensory organ.* And now it feels much bigger, more expansive than before, not in an ego sort of way, but in a more-alive way. The peace I feel is indescribably tender. All is well. It feels great to be in my wonderful body, a body I've not always appreciated.

Something happened years ago during a session I had with an energy healer. Myra, in my mind, was the stereotypic "granola" bodyworker. Short, pudgy, and in her fifties, she had the kindest heart and I totally trusted her even though I didn't understand how she worked her magic. I'm sure I puzzled her too. I once complained, "Why do I have to drag this big body around?" I remember the shocked look on her face, "How could you not love your body?"

As she began her work, she reminded me that our bodies are pure energy and that our feelings alter that energy. Emotions affect the body like a pebble dropped into a puddle of water causing ripples to move through it, changing our body's chemistry. If our feelings are negative and not released through expression, they can get buried inside and cause physical as well as emotional problems. I wondered if there was a connection between my chronic neck and back pain and some of my difficult experiences.

Well into Myra's ninety-minute session, something weird happened. Lying on my back, fully clothed on her table, I was dreamy-eyed after she'd gently massaged my arms, legs, and head. It was wonderful to be touched in such a loving way. She whispered, "Open your eyes." I was surprised to see her holding a wand with a tiny tangle of sparkly ribbons on the end. She waved it slowly over my hips and asked, "Have you ever been sexually abused?" Startled at the question, I took a breath then told her about the hospital intern. Myra closed her eyes, paused, and then said she sensed I had dealt with that perfectly. She said that because I yelled at the guy, my body was not holding trauma of the assault anymore. At the time I didn't completely understand what she meant, but I had faith in her intuitive gifts.

Then she asked me if there was abuse at another time. I lay there wracking my brain for what felt a few minutes. All I could think of was one of my relatives. "I had an uncle who always made me feel uncomfortable. He didn't do anything more than that, though."

Myra bent down near my face as she waved her wand with the glittery ribbon over my pelvic area and gently asked, "Did he feel creepy to you?"

The man was a nice person and everyone liked him, but creepy? I told her, "No, he was a nice guy."

I watched the wand still waving and she persisted, "Take yourself back to that time. How did you feel around him? Was it creepy?"

At first, I thought she was trying to brainwash me into feeling something I didn't but when I began to imagine being near him, old memories came up and yes, I did feel creeped out. I think she sensed that too because she insisted, "Say it. He was creepy. Have those memories and feelings one last time and release them from your precious body. Send them into the sunlight."

I closed my eyes, imagined the disturbing feelings in my belly, and imagined them flowing out of me into the sun. I was surprised at how real it felt. "He was creepy!" When I opened my eyes Myra's little wand was bouncing over my forehead and her loving face was radiant.

After that session, the chronic stiffness in my lower back was much better. I was happy for the relief but mostly I remembered how that creepy uncle had made me feel and how my poor body had suffered holding on to that memory.

My times with Myra changed me, and not just physically. Her treatments and her words made me think differently. I realized my body is truly alive and not just a lump of tissue. It's a mass of trillions of cells, each with its own unique job and energy. I learned that by being more aware of how it feels, I could better understand how to help it heal.

I also began to appreciate that my body is not just a vehicle for maintaining life; it's also a monitor for understanding and navigating it. After a time, I would learn to use my body to move energy as Myra did, but I'd never use a wand.

—◊◊◊—

Stretched out in my tent this morning, I begin feeling a little heavier and my brain begins to wake up. I've had unusual experiences like this before so it's easy to shift back into my normal gear. Now, resigned to the fact sleep is not coming, I get up to begin my day.

I give Doug his breakfast then we take a long walk through the grounds. Afterwards I head to the bathhouse building to do laundry. While I wait for the clothes in the dryer, I mail a bunch of postcards home to friends, my house sitter, and my three kids. I gather the clean clothes then walk back to my site and go into the tent to read.

Early in the afternoon, I feel a vague, familiar tingle on the outside of my skin and my body begins to feel lighter and lighter. I put down my book and go with the feelings. After that, my tranquil and somewhat wilted body nestles into my bedding and a drugged-like sleep consumes me. Three hours later, I wake up refreshed, a brand new person.

# 18: When Plans Take a Detour

## I wave the feather back and forth in front of the sun

After my nap, I make an exploratory trip to Hot Springs and Wind Cave National Park. I plan to investigate them in detail tomorrow. As I circle the outer boundary of Wind Cave Park, I see my first bison, a lone bull curled up on the ground near the entrance gate.

Buffalo reminds us to maintain an intimate connection with Earth and to help others with the powerful energy of prayer. Myra's healing comes to mind.

Back at the campground, I need some exercise so I put Doug on his leash, load a blanket and camera in my backpack, and we head out. It's about a quarter mile to the campground boundary near the foot of the Black Hills. I remember reading that the hills got their name because, from a distance, the bark on the pine trees looks as dark as midnight. I wonder what the hills look like up close.

Ten minutes into our walk, Doug and I begin to wind our way through a sparse cluster of tall Ponderosa pine. Then we stroll into wide waves of prairie that reach out to touch the dark base of the mountains. I gasp. I never dreamed they'd be so stunning.

Looking at these enigmatic hills is like looking at a magnificent black stallion; there's something about their power and darkness that says, 'Be careful.' So I turn away, look up at the bright blue sky, and we wander out further onto the range.

Doug is fidgety; he knows what's coming. It's hard to be patient with him as he springs like a Pogo stick three feet in the air. For a minute I fear he might pull my arm off, but, when I tell him to sit, he complies. Set free, he's off like a bullet getting in his first good run in days. His unbounded joy makes me smile. He's so dedicated to me, I don't worry about him taking off.

A little ways ahead, I see a foot-long turkey feather with wide horizontal white and gray stripes lying on the ground. Wobbly like an excited kid, I pick it up, set my backpack down, and take out my camera. I lean the feather upright on the ground against my pack then step back to take a picture with the mountains in the background. Suddenly, I feel a lump in my throat. I've seen this exact scene of the feather with the Black Hills before. Seeing it now, in this place, brings on a wave of tears.

—∿—

For months in '95, my close friends, April, Karen, Jo, and Paula, met at my home where we were learning how to meditate. First, we'd catch up on our lives then go into my new healing room, one of several new things in my life. I had sold the house and land where my children grew up and moved into a cute, little cape in another town.

The five of us, two couples and me, had been friends for years and we'd thought it interesting that we were now all living in the same area. The science sleuth in me felt a nagging need, actually a strange compulsion, to investigate why. I used a ruler to draw straight lines on a map connecting the exact locations of our three houses. It formed a perfect equilateral triangle and was exactly three miles on each side.

Still intrigued, I researched some more and found that in many metaphysical traditions, three is a powerful number. It represents divine completeness and perfection. I also learned that the three-sided figure is the simplest spatial shape and that three is the smallest number needed to create a pattern. This made my puzzle even more fascinating. I shared my findings with my friends and we wondered if there was something significant about the alignment of our houses. Three of us were science teachers and two were energy healers. In our own way we were fascinated with the synchronicity.

So the five of us met at my house every week or so to learn about meditation and various types of mysticism. In some ways we were like kids on a treasure hunt. We'd sit on the floor in my healing room with our backs against the wall and with eyes closed we'd listen to Paula, who was the most adept, lead the meditation. With her hushed voice she'd help us relax our bodies, concentrate on our breathing, then imagine we were slipping into the ground. We caught on quickly and after just a few weeks we began experiencing some fascinating phenomena.

We saw images as metaphors representing our relationships with each other and the planet. What I saw looked like abstract paintings and our little group said they often felt emotional connections to their imagery. We discovered that some of the vibrant colors symbolized our personality types and spiritual gifts. Karen, with her strong connection to the angelic realm, was violet which represents the crown chakra or energy center and has the highest vibrations. Jo was the most down to earth and resonated with a beautiful red color which represents the root chakra, the one associated with feeling grounded. My friends saw green around me. It represents the heart chakra which I'd read is associated with inner wisdom and compassion. It struck me as funny because my favorite color is green.

It was great fun but a couple times we were jarred when we saw a dark area on one of us. It represented a trauma or confusion. With Paula's guidance we learned to trust the physical sensations in our bodies as well as our intuition to interpret what we saw. We also discovered how to use imagery to dissolve dark areas by flooding it with white light. We were learning to trust our intuition and the enormous power of intention. But the most important step was what we did before starting. We said a prayer out loud asking our angels and guides to help us and do what was best for the highest good. When we finished, we talked about what happened and tried to make sense of it. It was the high-point of my week.

After a couple months, our meditations became more like paranormal journeys. We sometimes felt transported to places beyond the room. Enthralled, at times we were bewildered. But, because we'd set positive intentions, we trusted the process. Each meditation gave us some wonderful insight into our lives and we shared and laughed and postulated about what it all meant. At the same time we continued to wonder why it was all happening to us.

It was at the beginning of May in '96 that something curious happened. Spontaneously, without a suggestion from anyone, the exact same image of a turkey feather standing upright with the Black Hills in the background, began to show up in each person's vision. We intuitively knew it was the Black Hills. Excited about the anomaly, we wondered what it meant. After a couple weeks of discussion, we thought it might mean we should travel there. So we began to plan for a group road trip to the Black Hills that summer.

In our meditation a few weeks before our planned trip, I got another clear vision like in a vivid dream. I saw Doug and me in my car heading west, but alone. I was confused so when the meditation ended, I hoped my friends would help me make sense of it. When I shared the imagery Jo, Karen, and April looked confused and at a loss for what it meant. Red-faced, Paula stared at me and said, "Oh, so you don't want to spend all that time in the car with me?"

Surprised, I said, "No. That's not it. I'm just telling you what I saw."

Paula looked furious and I didn't know why. The others remained silent.

Over the following weeks I stayed excited about our upcoming adventure. I remained my usual naïve self, oblivious to the group's inclinations, and continued making trip plans.

Then, one after another, and eventually all four, told me they were not going. They gave no reason and, uncomfortable with what I perceived would be confrontational, I didn't ask for one. I was disappointed but mostly I was surprised. Just three months earlier, April, Jo and I had spent a week camping in Arizona and we'd had a great time.

The powerful pull to go to South Dakota helped me ignore the disappointment I felt in my friends. I knew I'd go because like a surfer who'd caught a perfect wave, I had to ride it and let it take me where it would.

—⚏—

Buffalo also symbolizes "walking alone" as you share what you have and who you are. The five of us planned to travel together, but the Universe had a different idea. Now I'm delighted to be alone, to have all this time to contemplate what my journey is about and who I might become.

I settle cross-legged on my blanket, surrounded by an ocean of grass. I look out over the hills then wave the turkey feather back and forth in front of the sun. I whisper, "Creator, please help these sacred hills and this land to release their sorrow." When I look at the mountains again, I become nervous because I get a strong feeling they might erupt but, thank goodness, it's a fleeting thought. I go back to praying for peace in those hills as well as in my heart.

This land feels welcoming, like home to me. It's something I know I could never explain to anyone so I just take it in and know I can revisit these moments at any time.

A couple minutes later, about thirty yards away, two mule deer pop their heads up from the tall grass. Doug, who's a bit ahead of me, sees them too. He turns, looks at me, but stays put. Years ago, Doug's grandmother, a wolf/husky mix named Mandy, and I were walking down the dirt road by my house. Mandy was off leash when we came upon two deer ahead of us on the road. She stopped then sat down at my feet. I knelt down and put my arm on her back and we watched the deer together, interested but detached. It lasted a nice long time.

In some indigenous traditions, deer represents innocence, letting go of fear. One legend tells of a monster who lived at the top of a mountain. No human or animal dared climb the mountain for fear of being eaten. Deer had not heard this story so one day she began grazing up the side of that same mountain. When she made it to the top, the monster jumped out at her in all his customary ferociousness. Deer lifted her sleek neck and with her beautiful, warm eyes, she gazed at the monster. She didn't see a terrible beast; she saw the creature's docile heart spinning in place trying to find peace. How she reacted to what she saw changed the monster. He became his true, kind self. The monster disappeared forever because he did not exist in the mind of deer and he had felt it.

When Doug dove out the window into the cow pasture, when he accepted Jay's presence, and when he, like Mandy, saw a deer, I'd expected a commotion. However, the opposite happened. Both dogs were interested but remained detached. It makes me wonder if animals have an innate respect for each other. Perhaps they are far more civilized than humans.

# 19: Wrapped in Red Flannel

## It was sold to us by a Lakota man so he could buy food for his family.

My achy body and the noisy camp make for a less than restful night. Up at six, I feed Doug then we walk the grounds. Next, I put together my usual breakfast, with range coffee this time, then settle into my camp chair outside the tent for a good long read. A few pages into the book the author suggests our planet is a living entity and it's a plausible concept for this nature girl.

After a couple hours reading, I do another quick wash-up at the bath house then with all the windows open, Doug and I sprint down the road towards Hot Springs. He stands in the back looking at me and, through the squall of airborne dust, papers, and food crumbs, he starts sneezing. In spite of the commotion, I'm tickled. The sky's a pastel blue, the air's cooler, and even the sun seems reticent. The high-pitched notes of Lakota singers and drumming pour from my cassette player and fill me like a sugary tonic. *It's good to be alive.*

I start to think how we tend to section our days into blocks of time: some we struggle to get through while others we savor and wish would last longer. Going through a day can be like exploring a cave. You find the entrance, step in, imagine the exit, and then let the current of your adventure carry you through the middle. And here on my prairie drift, I am exactly where I want to be at what feels like the entrance to my adventure. There are no road blocks in my day.

The ride northwest is easy and a few miles in, a diffuse cloud cover seems to soften everything outside. I pull over, park near a convenience store, then take Doug out for a stroll. Back in the car it's time for lunch: two apples, a couple handfuls of peanuts, and a big bag of corn chips. After a few more minutes on the road again, I see two enormous billboards featuring pictures of mammoths with giant, sloping tusks. This is something no self-respecting science teacher can resist.

The town of Hot Springs, population 4,000, is home to the Mammoth Site. In 1974 a piece of land was being bulldozed for construction when some curious old bones and teeth were discovered. They were in a sink hole which had developed after the last Ice Age, about 18,000 years ago.

After six years of scientific investigation, the site was declared a National Natural Landmark. A modern and expansive museum was constructed over the site where archaeological study is ongoing.

My tour inside the huge structure is spectacular with more exhibits and information than I can take in. The tour guide points out that scientists find it interesting that almost all of the mammoths found in the pit were adolescent males. *I'm not surprised knowing how impulsive teenage boys can be.* I imagine the curious, inexperienced mammoths leaning over the odd holes and falling in. Besides all the mammal bones, artifacts of the Clovis and Folsom nomadic people who lived in the area 6,000 to 13,000 years ago have also been unearthed. *Humans have been here for thirteen thousand years!*

Two hours at the Mammoth Site reminds me of how much I love scientific investigation and I'm ready to explore some more so I drive towards downtown Hot Springs to check it out. A dozen western-movie-style storefronts line the main street. From the roof of one, a decrepit carved sign hangs down and reads, "Old Guns and Indian and Western Americana." I can't believe my luck. I'm sure they've got some cool treasures.

I find a cool spot to park then walk inside. In the center of the large room stands a handsome man with a beard and hair pulled back into a ponytail. When I approach him, he looks up and gives me a weak hello so I make mine faint, too. Like a commander of the place, he fills the store. *He must be the owner.*

The pawn shop's interior is a tad dusty and tired but I don't care because it's jammed full of contemporary and antique American Indian items: bead-work, feathers, knives, tomahawks, ceremonial objects, jewelry. Everywhere I look, I imagine swirls of stories embedded in these old treasures. Then, suddenly, I quiver a little because the place feels heavy with memory.

But this is no time for melancholy so I shush away the sad feelings then bounce from counter to counter, glass display case to feathered displays, and on to the beaded wall hangings. When I remember it's a pawn shop and these trinkets and treasures were surrendered, my excitement starts to fade. *Some of these might have been someone's cherished valuables.* And now, I'm not sure how I should feel being here.

71

After making a couple laps inside the store, something inside a glass case stops me. Spread out on a piece of red cloth is a large bone choker. Ancient, regal, and so big, it would hang half way down my chest. A young American Indian girl with dainty pink glasses walks over to me. Her black hair is in one long braid and hangs forward over her shoulder. Her two delicate, beaded bracelets catch my eye. Standing on the other side of the counter, for some reason, she looks happy to see me. "Can I help you with anything?"

I smile back then point to the choker and ask, "Yes. Can I handle it, that choker, the large one in the middle?"

Cheery and, I assume, unaware of the troubling past I'm feeling right now, she takes the choker from the case. I notice her reverence as she picks it up and handles it like it's a sacred object. I slowly and gently inspect it while she beams. Nothing in this scene makes any sense to me because this perky, pretty girl is helping me in this somber old store amid all these upsetting relics.

She says the choker is made of thin elk bones. They are off-white and pitted with brown spots from age. There's a bead at the tapered end of each bone and they're strung together with rawhide strips. A wide piece of rawhide runs down the middle of the choker and suspended at the bottom center are two enormous bear claws. The thing feels virile and wild so a brief touch is enough for me. *There's something cantankerous in these bones.* The energy is so strong it's almost disturbing so I grip only the leather ties to study it.

Out of the blue, the girl proudly announces she is Cherokee then asks me about my trip. I give her a short overview then change the subject and ask if the choker is old. She says, "It was restrung and sold to us by a Lakota man so he could buy food for his family. It was his grandmother's." My heart sinks and once again, I'm jolted back to the real world, their world.

I purchase the beautiful choker, wrap it in some red flannel as is customary for sacred objects, and pack it away in my gear. When I return to Maine, I plan to give it to a lovely friend with a "Native" heart who, I know, will be happy to share in my journey.

Later in the evening my sinuses are killing me. *Was it the dusty pawn shop, the stuff flying around inside the car, the Mammoth Site?* I realize the air inside the Mammoth Site building was filled with fine dust particles and the delightful two hours wandering inside has left me feeling horrible.

# 20: His Cone-shaped Hat

### The land and our ancestors have something to tell humans

About a year before my South Dakota trip, my friend, Michael Spirit Bear, called. We'd first met at a local powwow and, with his friendly, easygoing ways, I liked him immediately. He belongs to the Micmac or Mi'kmag tribe who are an Indigenous people native to northern Maine and eastern Canada. Ever since my grandmother had told me my second great-grandmother was Mi'kmag I'd been passionate about everything American Indian so I delighted in Michael's friendship. Most importantly, Michael was a kind man and I loved the afternoons we spent at my home talking about local Indigenous history and culture.

Michael lived on his family's land in the coastal town of York, in southern Maine. Legend has it a sachem, a Mi'kmag spiritual leader named Chief Asbinquid, was martyred there in 1696. The burial site was said to be at the summit of Mt. Agamenticus, a small mountain on a thirty-thousand-acre public reserve. The forested parcel bordered Michael's family land.

On the phone Michael said, "Hello friend! Hey, you wanna go on a hike?" This was so typical of him; he was a man of few words and was always up for an adventure.

"Hi Michael."

"Remember what I told you about my family's land in York?"

"Yup, I remember."

"Well, with your connections, I mean being able to see into the spirit world and all, I was wondering if you wanted to go up there and see if we can find the sachem's grave site."

After a gulp and some goose bumps on my arms, I said, "That sounds awesome!"

We made a plan to meet in York the following week. My only hesitation was Michael's health. He was forty-something, heavy, and asthmatic. Even with his inhaler, I was concerned about him hiking. He assured me he knew his limit.

On hike day I drove south down coastal Rt.1 to York and met Michael at the Mt. Agamenticus park entrance. He got into my car and we babbled like two hyped-up kids all the way up the crumbly tar road to the summit.

I parked at the top and we got out to scout the area. The summit was a half-acre of mostly flat, exposed bedrock. It was dotted with a couple long-dead campfires, a rickety picnic table, and two rusted-out, metal trash cans. The fire tower stood like a scout in the center of the bedrock. It was sixty-five feet of severely weathered wood. On our walk to the tower I dodged a few low-bush blueberry bushes that had found cover and sustenance in the bedrock cleavages. That classic New England fall day with its crispy-clean air and cloudless sky was like a mini shot of adrenaline to me. My child-like heart was aflutter. *Let the search begin.*

The battered fire tower and abutting fire-warden's cabin impressed me. After decades of ocean storms and ice and humans, they were still tall. We scouted the summit for a few minutes to get our bearings before starting our search, and then walked back over to the fire tower. On our sketchy climb up the decrepit steps to the lookout platform, I kept sneaking peeks down at Michael to monitor his breathing. He looked okay.

At the top, even though the 360-degree view was familiar, it made me catch my breath. To the east, the slate blue Atlantic Ocean stretched from north to south along the entire eastern horizon. In the thousands of acres of flat coastal plains, loopy-edged bodies of water broke the textured monotony of forests. Off to the northwest flat lands turned into hills then beyond that into the White Mountains of NH. The most distant, Mt. Washington, sprinkled in confectionery white, hinted at the coming season. *Earth's majesty; there are no words.*

When we stepped down from the tower, I noticed that Michael's face was red and his respiration was much faster. I reminded myself: *Regina, he's not your kid and he's a grown man.* He looked over at me, said nothing, then we both beamed with excitement. We knew we were about to start our search. His breathing would have to take a back seat to our mission.

The sachem's grave site was said to be near the summit so we began there. Michael headed for the boundary of the summit clearing, down where the old pine forest began and where old stone walls sat, moss covered and crumbling. It was where he'd once discovered remnants of an old farmhouse.

74

At the fire tower I felt a quickening in my chest. I sank into my core and said a little prayer out loud asking for help in my search. After a few deep breaths, I began to walk where my body felt gently pulled to go. It took me a short distance down the sloped ocean-side of the tower's base, then with well-planted baby steps, I descended the steep slope. A short way into the sparse pine forest, tree branches scattered the sunlight struggling to make it to the ground. I breathed in the familiar cologne of pine needles. Serene and welcoming like a mythical forest, the spot seemed enchanted.

A couple minutes later, the air around my body felt different. Then I sensed threads of subtle energy in the area just beyond me. I was in my investigator mode so I walked back and forth a few times in that area. Then I felt a presence. It was off to the left, a little behind me, and nearer the tower. At first it was just a feeling that something was there. Once I turned and stepped in that direction, it took form. What looked like a dusty cloud condensed into a human shape and I jumped back, afraid, with my insides in a knot. Then, like I was watching from a distance, my fear turned into curiosity.

About fifteen feet from me, a seven-foot tall male figure stood staring at me. Its energy was intense but unemotional. It felt male. His heavy long-sleeved coat, made of a dark, brown material, hung down to his ankles. His tall, cone-shaped hat with its thick, woven fabric was pulled down to the tops of his ears. The blunt tip of his hat bent towards his face. He had thick slipper-like shoes. I'd never seen attire like that before. He resembled a giant fairytale sorcerer.

His demanding gaze grabbed me; he wanted my attention so I couldn't look away. But, it was his mouth that frightened me. It was stretched out, opened wide, and it looked like a dark, deep hole. When I focused on his insistent eyes, they softened. Nevertheless, his mouth drew me in, made me stare at it, and I was even more disturbed. The strange, scary image, was something my mind could not make sense of but, at the same time, I couldn't look away. It was like looking at a provocative Salvatore Dali piece; magnetic but unsettling.

Only a few seconds later, my body actually felt his silent words and, like a prayer, I heard his plea, *"The land and our ancestors have something to tell humans. Listen to the land, to the stories and the traditions of the Indigenous people. Return the land to how it was when Earth and all life were honored."*

Then he disappeared. I'd communicated with "angels" before so it was pretty easy to shift back to my ordinary reality. But this being, with his intense male energy and staggering appearance, left me shaken. After a few deep breaths I said a prayer to Creator giving thanks for the experience. I didn't know why he appeared to me but I trusted there was a reason. I twist in place to gather myself until my nerves felt more settled. I walked over to where my visitor had appeared. I searched for any evidence like a footprint or disturbed pine needles. There was nothing.

As I climbed back up to the summit area, I thought about the messenger and his message. I knew the experience was real but I couldn't imagine how I could help.

I noticed things I hadn't noticed before: beer bottles strewn about a water-logged campfire and paper wrappers flitting along the ground pushed by an erratic sea breeze. This defiling of the landscape made his words find a sad place deep inside me. It was a call to do something about all this but I was still rattled.

I hiked across the parking lot into the forest to find Michael. I wasn't sure how to explain what I'd seen because I wasn't sure I understood enough to tell anyone.

He was easy to spot in the thick stand of old pines. "Michael, I had a visitor."

He looked up from studying the stone wall he was sitting on, gave me a sly smile, and said, "Oh, really? You don't say?" I already knew that he would believe me.

"I was over by the fire tower and a man, a very tall man, spooked me. He was in spirit form and he began telling me things about protecting the Earth and listening to our ancestors."

When I described the man's clothing, Michael's eyes lit up and he broke into a wide smile. "I'm not surprised. I wonder if it was the sachem, Asbinquid?"

"I have so much to tell you and so many questions. Have you found anything?"

"No, nothing yet, but we can keep looking if you want to and, yup, we'll talk about your friend later."

Michael and I canvassed the forested area for signs of a grave site and after my visitation, we were pretty confident we'd find something. After almost two hours traversing the hilly forest crisscrossed with tumbledown rock walls, huge decaying pine logs, and fern-filled ravines, we stopped. We'd found nothing and Michael was sweaty and wheezing. I was nervous so we decided to call it quits.

On our drive down the mountain to his car, as was customary for my friend, he said very little. On the other hand I was bursting with questions about what I'd seen and what he thought. In the end we agreed we'd had a good day, had made a few discoveries, and I spent the next week periodically unnerved by my visitor's image. We never did have the long drawn out conversation about what happened. At first I was disappointed then I accepted the fact that this was Michael's family history, not mine.

A few months after our hike, and before Google, I found a book with images of Original Peoples of New England. It had a picture of the outfit, or regalia, I'd seen on the mountain. It was nothing I'd ever seen before. The text said the long, droopy-coned hat is called a peaked hat. It is characteristic of the Mi'kmag tribe. I got chills.

The energy of the entity felt very male so I assumed it might be the regalia a sachem might wear. Maybe I wanted it to be a man. After my research I learned the peaked hat is worn by women, not men. It may have been a woman with prominent male energy or maybe it was a sachem disguised as a woman who was trying to teach me something. Maybe it was about honoring my own male energy.

Out of the blue, in 2018, while writing this chapter, Michael Spirit Bear contacted me. He told me the grave of Aspinquid had been discovered on Mt. Agamenticus. We plan to meet again soon to catch up and, of course, to talk about the sachem.

I knew the communication wasn't just for me. Anyone plugged intuitively into nature would understand. I began to think this might explain why I'm drawn to Native American culture; it's their relationship to the Earth. And, right then, the tiny tickle of an idea began to form. I was going to find a way to spread the entity's words.

# 21: The Lost Souls of Wind Cave

## The breeze picks up and feels like a whispered question

It's a short drive from Hot Springs to Wind Cave National Park and the overcast sky brings cooler temps so Doug will be comfy in the car. The brochure says there are man-made cave entrances for tourists. I wonder if I'll have to do a tour in order to see the natural cave opening, the one I saw in the book at Mission.

When I arrive, I circle the parking lot then have to slow down for the huge crowds near the Visitor's Center. *Damn, it's looking touristy.* I'm determined to see the sacred cave entrance so, in case it gets sunny, I find a shady place for the car and settle Doug.

The Center's entrance opens to a modern interior. Seriously waxed floors, high ceilings, and a blast of air conditioning give it a cold, hard feel making me miss my bucolic campsite.

The crowds inside are sparse compared to outside, so it's easy to find a park guide. He has on a soft green and tan uniform and stands against a wall, smiling. When I ask about the tours he says, "The tours take you deep into the cave system. You'll be crawling through some small spaces, some only two feet in diameter." I envision a nightmarish scenario: crawling through stifling, dank air with a herd of excitable, sweaty tourists, while squeezing my not-so-flexible body through tight tunnels.

I give him a fake smile and a fib. "Oh, that sounds interesting but I'm not a good hiker. What I really want to see is the natural entrance to the cave."

"You can walk around to the backside of the Visitor's Center, to where the natural entrance is, without paying. Just follow the path that circles the building." *OMG! I just won the frickin' lottery.* I head outside, a giant smile plastered on my face.

The Center is partially tucked into one side of a broad grassy hill and on the other side is the cave's natural entrance. As I walk through the immaculate grounds, my feet almost glide over the stone path. The place is beautiful with what looks like original, native landscaping. I can't believe I'm here, alone, and about to explore the sacred site.

About thirty yards down the path, I spot it. The four-foot tall rock opening is to my left and recessed into the hillside. It looks smaller than I imagined it would, but matches the picture in the book. And lucky me, the place is deserted.

I close my eyes and try to absorb the enchanting solitude of this spot. I remember reading sixty-mile-an-hour winds once gushed out of the cave. I wish I could have been here then. No wonder this place was honored. Unfortunately, with construction inside the center, the winds are no more.

Revered for hundreds, maybe thousands of years, I imagine how those mighty winds must have awed the people. It seems logical for humans to rely on myth and religion to explain inexplicable forces of nature like this.

Once I leave my daydream, I look for a place to sit, hike up a grassy slope leading to the vast plains, and settle down on the sun-warmed turf overlooking the cave entrance. The fickle, flitting breeze and the prairie, my unwavering companions, invite me to stay. Behind me stand a tiny ponderosa pine and a lonely purple thistle. Thistle signifies strength and protection and reminds us to maintain pride in who we are. *Be proud of who I am? But, who am I? And, what the heck am I doing here?* Sitting near this venerated site, it takes me two seconds to decide that my insecurities don't belong here so I wave them away with my hand.

Like the replenished pause after a long exhale, the air gets still. Then the breeze picks up and it feels like a whispered question found someone who'd answer. My deep breaths nourish my insides, my body softens and seems to slump into the ground. *What a peaceful moment.*

Then, surfacing out of nowhere like a rousing memory, words form and I pause to feel the resonance of each. *Thank you, angels, for helping me to be here.* I feel so full of love for Earth, a warm tear slides down my cheek. I feel lighter but the air on my arms and legs feels slightly denser. *Wow, that was some sort of prayer.*

A couple minutes later, and with my eyes still closed, I begin to perceive five or six wispy human shapes milling about near the cave opening. The cloudy American Indian forms have robes pulled up over their drooping heads. I feel like I'm in an awake-dream, but the dream is

79

not a real dream. I keep my eyes closed, slip further into my center, and ask Spirit if this is real. I feel the answer. *It's real.* So I relax a little.

What disturbs me is they're shuffling and it seems perpetual and it's been going on for a very long time. *Are they stuck? Are they waiting for something?* When these questions form in my mind, the answer bubbles up inside me. *They are confused.*

Now I'm even more puzzled because what I see resembles an old movie-short on repeat: shuffling and shuffling, again and again. After a couple more minutes, something inside me wants to connect energetically with them and, when I do, I feel their anxiety and confusion and it distresses me. I want to help but I know that in order to help, I must stay focused.

Similar to when I meditate, I sink deep into my heart. But this time strong waves of compassion turn into prayers I send to the beings below. *Dear ones, you can leave and move into the Light. This place is at peace. From now on, for those who seek it, this will be a site for spiritual renewal.* I know that intention is powerful; I've seen how it can change things, so I'm confident my words will help, at least a little.

I muster as much empathy and warrior-like confidence as I can. And while pausing to fully feel the meaning of each word, in little more than a whisper I say, "May all those who visit this park learn to know their hearts better, love our planet more, and dare to live their divine essence."

Once I finish, I think about what I've said and I'm embarrassed. *Who do I think I am, some sort of priest or mystic?* After a long pause, I remind myself we all have the right to wish blessings for others. *It's no big deal. Why am I making it a big deal? Maybe it's because not everyone does this?* For years, as a child, I read my Catholic Missal and also made up my own long list of nightly prayers for my family and friends. Praying has always made me feel like I belong to something much bigger than I can understand. I feel peaceful when I pray; maybe it's because I believe someone is listening.

Sitting on the welcoming slope, I continue: *Please Creator, move all sadness, along with those confused beings, into the Light. I ask that this area is honored again, but in a modern way. I am grateful to be here. Amen.*

When I open my eyes and look down at the cave, nothing has changed. But, when I close my eyes and look at it in my mind, the spirits are gone and the area seems peaceful. I'm not exactly sure what happened, but it feels like whatever it was helped, and that is enough.

As I walk back to the car, the ground feels softer than I remembered. It seems to reach up to meet each of my steps and a very big wave of contentment splashes over me.

By the time I make it across the huge parking lot, something changes. I'm suddenly angry. I turn to face the Visitor's Center and realize there's not one plaque designating this as a religious or historic site. It's been designated as a unique geologic curiosity, that's it. There's nothing in the museum, the brochures, and no mention of this from the park guide. As I drive back to the campground, I'm steaming. *How much Indigenous history and how many of their sacred sites have been erased by the white man?*

Later in the night, my sinuses need TLC so I take some aspirin and drink a couple extra cups of water for the pain. Bedded down in my tent and after a few hours of tossing and turning, I give up my attempts to read and begin to pray for some restful sleep. But, racked with head and body aches, I dream of the planet's troubled history and the upheavals in its crust.

# 22: "Nituwe So?" Means Who Are You?

## She felt like long-lost family

O n a winter day, a year before my trip, I joined ten other athletic women, in their thirties and early forties, for a day of
cross-country skiing. We met monthly and this day's plan was to circum-
navigate beautiful Sebago Lake in southern Maine. The crisp air was like
a taste of pure spring water and the deep, new snow glistened with wind-
scattered glitter. Surrounded by that dynamic group, I felt almost giddy
and probably sparkled, too.

The six-mile trail was mostly flat and forested. Halfway on the
well-groomed trail our leader, Kate, a gifted athlete and teacher, signaled
our line of skiers to stop for a break.

Ahead, I watched the procession flow into a forest clearing then
release boots from skis. One after another, they flipped their ski poles
into the air so the pointy-ends stabbed the snowbank. All their tops were
leaning together.

I followed suit then turned to head to where the group had
gathered. But, something I'd seen tugged at me so I pivoted to look at the
hodgepodge of poles. Their configuration mesmerized me. I turned away
but was drawn back to look again and again. *What is going on?* The
appealing image seemed strangely familiar, like an old family photo taken
on a special day. The sensation stayed with me for the rest of that
afternoon.

We topped off the day with our customary potluck dinner. This
time it was at Kate's house, a rustic cape nestled in a forest. As our group
settled into boisterous chitchat and eating, Kate and I joked and jostled
with each other in her kitchen. Today had been the first time we'd met
but we acted like old friends. It was wild. She felt like long lost family and

I was confused but those women were so much fun, I just went along with the curious encounter. In addition, whatever was happening, I could tell by Kate's laughter, the feeling was mutual.

Kate seemed like a dear, favorite sister and more. Even though it didn't feel like a romantic attraction, I feared rejection so I tried to deny how I felt. After three fretful days, though, I finally got up the courage to call and invite her to a small gathering. At the end of the evening a friend confirmed what I'd felt. It was obvious Kate and I had a connection.

A week later, I invited Kate to dinner for just the two of us. I served my usual forgettable meal but we were both teachers, loved the outdoors, and Native American spirituality so our conversation flowed like that of an old couple in their slow waltz. Everything about being with Kate was easy. Doug seemed to recognize her too. When he jumped into her lap on the couch, I knew he approved.

Before leaving, Kate handed me a cassette tape and said, "Here, I made you a tape of my ten favorite songs."

Surprised, I thanked her. *Wow, we just met and you did this for me? That must have taken a good chunk of time.* After she left, I looked at the cassette cover where she'd scribbled her own title, "Nituwe So?" On the back she wrote the translation for those Lakota words: "Who Are You?" She signed it, "Love, Kate." Emotionally wasted after a long day of teaching and our dinner, I was only mildly curious about the cassette so I set it on my kitchen counter and went to bed.

The next morning, I picked up the cassette and smiled when I read, "Nituwe So?" For a year, without knowing why, I'd been fascinated with Deadwood, South Dakota where Crazy Horse had been captured. I loved doing research and enjoyed my little obsession learning about him and Sioux history. So, I climbed into my car, tossed the cassette onto the passenger seat, and headed down the road towards school.

After a few minutes of listening to the radio deejay's banter, I noticed the cassette on the seat. *What had she recorded?* I popped the tape into the cassette player and heard a woman singing about Deadwood, South Dakota and the killing of Crazy Horse. The words hit me hard. It felt like the saddest movie of all time was playing inside my chest. I began to sob. *My god, what is happening?*

Overwhelmed, I pulled off to the side of the road and sat tears running down my cheeks. It was like the words in the song bypassed my brain and landed in some raw memories inside me. And the sounds of my crying shocked me.

I reached over and turned off the cassette player. *Troublemaker.* After blowing my nose and wiping my face, I waited a couple minutes before driving again. Once I was back on the road, still curious or just stubborn, I turned on the cassette player and fast-forwarded to the next song.

Indigenous women were singing and I started crying again so I had to pull the car over once more. I tried two more songs and broke down with each. Finally, I turned it off for good. Thank goodness I had a long day of teaching ahead so I could force-feed my brain with lesson plans. I also hoped for a return to sanity.

My reaction to the songs shocked me. It was unlike any emotional meltdown I'd ever had, second only to losing my brother. It seemed some very old, sad memories had surfaced. It took me years to make sense of my fascination with Crazy Horse and the Sioux and to understand my reaction to the cassette. For the next few years, Kate and I remained close friends spending time on outdoor adventures and participating in a women's spiritual group. We never talked about the cassette or our possible past life connection, but it was always there messing with my head and heart.

—ᵐ—

The image of the ski poles still comforts me and years later I may have learned why. Scientific research has found that all our experiences get encoded on our DNA and can be passed on to the DNA of our progeny. Experiments done with lab rats and wild animals have supported this theory. When rats are shown a picture of a certain flower then stimulated with a mild shock, they will pass on that reaction to their offspring. The babies, who were never shocked, will react to the same picture as if shocked. It makes sense that this phenomenon happens in humans and it might explain why we are attracted to some people but repelled by others and may also suggest the effects of cultural trauma might be inherited.

I wondered if my body recognized the pattern of ski poles in the snowbank. Maybe it remembered something, but that "something" was still unclear. Maybe generations ago Kate and I were related.

On my first day in South Dakota I stopped at a rest area that had a touristy tepee. When I stepped inside it, my eyes were drawn to the smoke hole. Poles were sticking out every which way just like the ski poles in the snowbank. As I stood staring at them, I choked up. I had long imagined that I'd lived before and probably had a special relationship with someone. I began to think I had the answer to my lingering questions: *Who are you, Kate, and have we met before?*

# 23: One Beam of Sunlight

**What matters is how it makes me feel, not what my mind thinks**

The sun wakes me this beautiful South Dakota morning and I give it a big I'm-happy-to-be-alive smile. My headache is gone, sinuses are better, and after a couple cups of extra strong range coffee, I get back on the road.

The high-pitched sounds and drumming of powwow songs from my speakers are like thumping heartbeats and energize me like another cup of coffee. In the distance, the majestic peaks of the Black Hills help fade memories of somber Wind Cave and the annoying tourists.

Custer State Park is a seventy-thousand-acre reserve only ten miles from Wind Cave. As I drive into the park, there are small herds of antelope and mule deer just yards from the road. Grazing in the tall grass, they bob their heads up and down then scan the terrain, graze, then scan again. It's a picture-perfect fluid postcard.

The action is catching because I whip my head back and forth scanning the land for buffalo. But when I see Doug in my rearview mirror, I stop. Upright and rigid with his nose jammed into the window's sliver of an opening, he's intrigued by the new animal scents so I grip the steering wheel and brace for some car-rocking commotion. When Doug barks inside the car, he puts his whole body into it and it scares the bejesus out of me. *Just keep driving; if he smells your fear, it'll only make it worse.* Thank goodness my silent chant works and after a couple melodramatic miles, Doug is down again, and I unwind.

The road sign indicates the summit of Mount Coolidge is a few miles ahead so I pull over to check my brochure. It says you can see Mount Rushmore, the Crazy Horse Monument, the Needles, and on a clear day the Badlands, which is about sixty miles away. Prospects look good, and with no other plans today, I take the road.

At the summit, the dirt road ends in a parking lot near an impressive stone lookout tower. And, once again, I'm the only one here. It's a good place for Doug to run loose so I let him go and his puppy-like cavorting through the grounds makes me giggle. Minutes later, a weighty, damp overcast floats in and the countryside becomes still and subdued. I put Doug on his leash and we walk to the fire tower that looks like it belongs in an old western fort and is made of huge blocks of pinkish granite cemented together. In front of me, happy Doug bounces up the tall rock steps.

At the top I have an unobstructed view of the huge reserve. A dozen or more clusters of grayish, majestic rock spires spring up from broad mountain tops. The brochure says they're the Needles and each is ten to twenty stories tall. The pine, spruce, and oak forests with their drab tapestry of muted greens and grays blanket everything. Other than the spires, it's a little dull and disappointing because the landscape boundaries are blurred. It makes for a heavy scene. How can the land breathe shrouded in such gloomy greenery? I'm confused. *Why does this trouble me?* The question jabs at me, but I don't know what to do with it, so for once, I stop thinking about it.

Still hoping for a pleasant experience, I grab the binoculars from my backpack and search the topography. I focus in on what was there all along but couldn't be seen with my naked eye: the magnificent, rounded lumps of mottled bedrock, small clusters of jagged, stony peaks, twisty trails, and a few small bodies of water. Doug's lying at my feet and, as if he too wants something more interesting, lets out a disgruntled sigh. I look again and, streaming down through the quilted, gray cloud cover, is a narrow shaft of sunlight, the only one, illuminating a spot. Through my binoculars, I can make out a face and head carved from the side of a mountain. It's the Crazy Horse Monument. In the middle of thousands of acres of dull terrain, the beam of sunlight lands on that one place. Chills race up and down my legs.

I linger, wondering if the sighting is some sort of sign. I can't imagine it is so I chalk it up to just chance. As I head down the tower steps and back to the car, I mumble a quick thank you for the surprise. In my seat, I turn and stare out the car window at the tower. *What did that mean? Am I romanticizing again, making a mountain out of a molehill?* My insides say the sighting was unusual and interesting, and for now, that's good enough.

But later, riding in the car, I'm still thinking about it. As usual, my mind seeks a logical explanation but, like observing the spirits at Wind

Cave, it's not logical. I decide that the illumination of the Crazy Horse Monument was like admiring a piece of art. What matters is how it makes me feel, not what my mind thinks. *Or something like that. Right?*

I leave the mountain then drive into the town of Custer. I read that only a few miles from town is French Creek, where gold was discovered during an expedition in 1847. Lieutenant Colonel George Custer led the expedition searching for a possible fort location, a route to the southwest, and gold. Treaties between the US government and the Sioux had promised the Sioux protection from settlements in the Black Hills. After gold was discovered, however, the stampede of white settlers into the sacred lands went on unimpeded.

There's a sign for French Creek and a ways down the road, beside a gentle slope, is the famous creek. A little further is a sign indicating where Custer's army camped and where word was sent to Washington about the gold. The traffic is light so I can poke along in the car and be open to the land's energy. It feels exploited and dismissed. *You're just imaging this, Regina, because you know its history.* Then in the exact moment I think this, from Kate's cassette I hear Nancy Griffin singing about Crazy Horse's death and the discovery of gold in the Black Hills. The sad words thump me so hard I have to pull off to the side of the road. I curl up in my seat and cry. It's not logical, this sorrow; my mind can't fathom what's happening. Sad, sad old, formless sensations bubble up inside my chest. *But, why me?*

Later in the afternoon I search for the KOA campground in the area and luckily it's easy to find. I settle Doug in at our new site, set up my gear, and then make dinner. A little later every part of my body feels exhausted and I have a bad headache. I'm prone to sinus infections and this feels like another one. Sick with a fever, I put myself to bed at 8:30.

# 24: Two Speckled Fawns

## A confluence in the making

The one book I brought along on my trip, Buffalo Woman Comes Singing by Brooke Medicine Eagle, is my daily read. Brooke's autobiographical stories both encourage and affirm me. I relate to her traumatic upbringing and her numerous mystical experiences. Oftentimes when I'm reading in the evening, the book will mention a place I inadvertently visited earlier the same day. Along with the author's life stories, the book includes some American Indian history, ceremonial practices, and the spiritual significance of certain sites. The stories in her book make me feel guided like someone knows I'm here. Other than exploring the Black Hills, I'm beginning to think there are more reasons for my trip.

Reading the history in her book reminds me of all the research I did on Crazy Horse before my trip. He was of the Oglala Lakota tribe. Simply put, the Oglala are a branch of the Lakota and the Lakota are a branch of the Sioux. I devoured a half dozen biographies and every documentary I could find about the man. There was something familiar about him and I was enamored by his personality.

The great warrior was born at Bear Butte, South Dakota in 1840. Described as "Our Strange Man," by his people, he was an odd fellow, a loner, and a man of few words. For days at a time, he would separate from the tribe finding solitude in a cave or hollow. He was devoted to his people and was a great spiritual force for the tribe but he shunned certain religious traditions like the sundance. With a pale complexion, light brown hair, and sub-average stature, he stood out. He dedicated his life trying to help his tribe find a way to return to the old ways of following the herds of buffalo and practicing their religion as passed down to them for millennia. His tribe also revered him for his commitment to the care of the young and old and for never conceding to the white man's domination.

His skills and bravery in battle were legendary but, because he was a humble man, he never wore a headdress. In his hair he wore one single feather from a red-tailed hawk. Before battle he painted white zigzags on his face to represent lightning, the "Thunder Beings," that brought powerful storms and were said to be magnificent celebrations of life. He also thumb-printed white dots on his body to represent hail. The hawks and dots would become significant messages in my own life.

In 1877, Crazy Horse died, as he had prophesied from a dream, at the hands of a tribal member while being apprehended by the US Army. It's unclear if he had made this arrangement in the event of looming death or if it was because of a personal conflict with that other man. Some say his parents carried his body far out into the prairie near Mission, South Dakota and buried him in an unmarked grave.

I admire how he did not conform, held tight to his values, cared for his people, and mostly I love his devotion to Spirit. I identify with his ethos.

Synchronicities and confluences abound and even before my trip I noticed these phenomena. Suddenly red-tailed hawks started appearing in my meditations and in my physical world. Because of the frequency and uniqueness of the sightings, I began to believe they were omens for me and my upcoming journey. I trusted they'd appeared to encourage me to continue planning my adventure.

One day while walking in the forest behind my house, something compelled me to stop. I looked down to where I would have planted my next step and there, curled up on the ground, was a newborn fawn. It was a ball of soft fur with white dots scattered over its back. I froze, felt a shiver, and immediately thought of Crazy Horse's white hail spots.

Two days later while walking in a different section of the same forest, I looked down at the broad-leafed plants covering the ground. *I wonder who lives in here?* Just before my next step, another white-spotted fawn jumped up and bounded away. The image of Crazy Horse came again. I choked up, wiped a tear away, and then continued my hike.

It felt like another affirmation of something, maybe a mystical confluence in the making. I'd placed my feet on my beloved New England soil and never imagined I would someday leave my own footprints behind in the Black Hills.

# 25: Words with a Mountain

## We really are all connected

Even though I'm feeling better when I wake, my swollen sinuses force me back to bed for a late morning nap. *I'll take it easy today, won't do anything too heroic, ha ha.*

After I feed Doug and we take our walk, I decide to ignore my symptoms and set out for the day. The Crazy Horse Monument is only four miles from here and I don't know if it's my grogginess or what the brochure said but I have low expectations about the place. It reads like just another tourist attraction. When I drive up the entrance road, my suspicions are confirmed; it's crawling with people. *Ugh.*

Because it's Crazy Horse, mystic warrior, and my idol, I feel compelled to check it out. I settle Doug in the car in the woodsy shade with the tailgate open then head across the parking lot. Almost immediately a large swarm of tourists pulls me in and lumps me in with them. Head achy and irritated, I feel a little superior and a bit snarky. *Here's another homogeneous mob of humans seeking one more form of titillation.* It takes me a minute to stifle my hostilities and when I do, I let the crowd's momentum buoy me toward the entrance.

I plan a short visit, just long enough to pay my respects to Crazy Horse's memory. After paying the entrance fee I pass through another modern-monstrosity-of-a-visitors-center. The two-acre layout ahead of me sports gift shops, restaurants, the Native American Cultural Center, information kiosks, and an Indian Museum. Maze-like walkways connect the buildings that have glossy, pine-board siding and slick, green, metal roofs. It's a weird, artificial homage to the magnificent stone-faced warrior whose head is poking out like a hood ornament from the side of the mountain. Standing in the center court I feel disoriented. *This is just another frickin' tourist attraction.*

I make a beeline to the construction site that's beyond the far end of the center. Its giant cranes, scaffolding, and small mountains of blasting debris make it easy to find. I remember reading it was begun in 1948, the same year I was begun. And, also, like me it isn't finished yet. I love synchronicities like this. But, unlike me, it's only a quarter complete. When done, the statue will have the warrior sitting astride a horse with one arm stretched out pointing to the sacred Black Hills. Except for a tourist or two, I'm alone at the statue's base. I look up and a couple hundred feet above me is Crazy Horse's chiseled chin, Roman nose, and high cheekbones. I want to feel something, but I don't. *Such a letdown. What a waste of their money and effort.* Then I think about the herds of people I need to plow through to make my way back and it makes me cranky again. It doesn't even feel like a normal mountain. It should exude something wild and natural but it seems dull.

Then I remind myself that I'm at a construction site and it's not the majestic, spotlighted Crazy Horse I saw from Coolidge Mountain. But, something else bothers me. This land feels jumbled and unwelcoming like one might feel walking into a room where there's been a huge disturbance.

I've learned all terrestrial forms, both animate and inanimate, are surrounded by an aura or sphere of energy that extends up into the heavens and down into the ground. But this monument's aura feels contorted.

A couple of deep breaths help me to settle down and I try to stay immune to the distortions I'm feeling. I know the developers intend to honor a great warrior and were sanctioned by some Sioux leaders, but I wonder how they prepared the area. Also, there are too many people sampling tidbits of the warrior's legend and oblivious to his mystical life. I wonder if they leave a gift of gratitude, like a prayer or a trinket as is the Indigenous custom. I wonder what all this does to the land. But most importantly, I wonder how the land feels about what's been constructed here. *Land, I leave you with thoughts of peace.*

Disappointed, I head back to the car and the campground. I so wanted my visit to be profound but now, like most of the tourists, I leave feeling not much of anything.

The land at camp feels far more alive and it helps. But, as Doug and I poke about investigating the grounds, I'm still a little unsettled. When I realize my fixation on the monument is getting me nowhere, I stop trying to make sense of my jumbled thoughts and just leave them that way, jumbled.

After our walk I stretch out in the tent and snack on chips while combing through my little collection of maps and brochures. One says the Willow Creek trail is just a short walk from the campground. It's a two-and-a-half-mile trek that's easy to moderate in difficulty and near Harney Peak, the highest peak in the Black Hills. After today's disappointment, this might be just what I need.

Willow Creek's trailhead opens to a wide dirt path bordered by a thin, mature pine forest. It's easy walking and this late in the afternoon the trail's nearly deserted. I haven't been on a good hike for a couple weeks and, after days scrunched up in the car, it feels good to work some forgotten muscles. Blessed with another comfortable, sunny day, I pause, look skyward, and say, Thanks. Inside me I hear, "Don't take this for granted." I wonder what it means.

Doug is on his long leash and I'm trying to keep up with him as he lopes back and forth from one side of the trail to the other investigating all the new smells. I wish he could run free but, here, dogs have to be leashed. Never one to complain, he's his agreeable self.

Near the end of the trail, we walk up to the base of a good-sized hill with a twenty-foot shelf of layered rock protruding from the top. Doug seems to know where I want to go, so I unsnap his leash and with one very long leap, he stretches up the steep grade, sinks his front claws into the top of the rocky cliff, then pulls himself up. I look up and see him looking down at me, panting. His stare and wagging tail tell me it's my turn but lacking his spring and grace, I crawl like a baby up over the rock face while Doug watches me. Once I make it to the top, he rewards me with a sloppy lap on my face. What a friend.

He leans into me as we sit side by side on the outcrop like two hiking buddies. I take a long drink of water from my canteen then pour some into Doug's plastic travel bowl. His long tongue whips water out of the bowl and I get doused again. Hydrated and feeling the best I've felt all day, I wiggle my bottom to get comfy on my rock seat. I massage my calves then give my dusty, long legs a good stretch. Boy, they could use a shave...What a glorious day!

Doug sits like an Egyptian demigod on his rock throne and together we scan the distant mountainous terrain. It's a contrast to the softer-looking forests in New England. The trees here are angular, sharp, and stand proud. Maybe they seem that way because this geography's new to me but I don't know. Straight ahead, I notice a bold, jagged mountain that looks like it's been plunked down in front of me. I check my map and discover it's Harney Peak and is about two miles away even though it looks much closer. I remember reading something about it in a book about the Lakota medicine man, Black Elk, but I can't remember the details.

My lofty seat entices me to lie back and close my eyes and, when I do, my body relaxes and I absorb even more ambiance of this exquisite spot. But, after a few minutes, out of the blue, I feel something strange, like Harney Peak is sending out vibrations. Flustered, I open my eyes to check the mountain and Doug. They both look normal so I give Doug who's lying down now, a pat on the back, close my eyes, and slip back into my sleepy place. Once more it feels like subtle vibrations are streaming towards me. They feel male and strong, but not threatening. I'm reminded of Doug.

Then I realize the vibrations feel jumbled, like at the monument. Resting with Doug on the rock shelf, the mountain begins to send out even more sensations. In turn I start to speak out loud and my words are spontaneous and, even though I'm alone, I feel weird. The words are curious. "Dear mountain, stay strong and erect for everyone to see. I pray you return to perfect balance, with perfect connections to all that is." As I speak, the mountain seems to soften and maybe my words soften too. *I'm not sure what I'm doing and this is one of the strangest moments ever!* But, it feels real. Very strange, but real.

Later when trying to understand what happened I think about being in the classroom. Usually, all a confident and caring teacher needs to do in order to calm a noisy classroom is to stand, hold her power, while remembering her devotion to her students. Most students will feel the teacher's energy and respond while passing on their calmness to the others. I think of this when I remember communicating with the mountain. We really are all connected and the more we embrace our strength and resilience the more we can help others to do the same.

Years later, Harney Peak was renamed Black Elk Peak by the US Board on Geographic Names. The change was in honor of Nicholas Black Elk and to acknowledge the significance of the summit to Indigenous Americans, especially the Sioux. It was upon this peak towering over the Sioux Nation that a young Black Elk experienced a vision. Many years later, as a respected elder and medicine man, he recounted that vision publicly. In his biography of Black Elk, Neihardt recorded the great man's words about his vision: "I was standing on the highest mountain of them all, and round about beneath me was the whole hoop of the world. And while I stood there, I saw more than I can tell and I understood more than I saw; for I was seeing in a sacred manner the shapes of all things in the Spirit, and the shape of all shapes as they must live together like one being."

I wish I had read that book before my trip. It probably would have been even more spectacular knowing I was near where Black Elk had his mystical revelations.

# 26: Biker Dude

## All those hours alone, what's that like?

After exploring Wind Cave, Harney Peak, and the Crazy Horse Monument, I need a tranquil evening so I start a chapter about Bear Butte in Buffalo Woman Comes Singing. I find out it's a small, near-naked mountain that jets out from the prairie and has been a sacred ceremonial site for the Lakota, Cheyenne, and Arapaho for hundreds, maybe thousands, of years. I remember learning it's where Crazy Horse was born and where artifacts over eleven thousand years old have been found. Even older Lakota origin stories tell about giant lizards, tiny horses, and cats with huge teeth that stalked buffalo on the land. Thousands of Indians gathered near Bear Butte before the Battle of the Little Big Horn and it's where great warriors and chiefs including Red Cloud, Sitting Bull, and Crazy Horse did their vision quests.

In a vision quest, the seeker goes out on the land for three to four days without food, water, or shelter seeking spiritual insight and healing. They are said to be *crying for a vision* and American Indian biographies are loaded with accounts of spectacular visions. The seekers, under the supervision of a teacher, prepare for their quest by participating in an Inipi, Lakota for "to live again," and what some non-Natives call a sweat lodge ceremony. To many Indigenous people, sweat lodge is a derogatory term, another example of the appropriation of their culture. In this super-hot, sacred sauna, the seeker prays to be purified of all human weakness, to gain humility, and to be returned to his or her otherworldly origins. Modern-day seekers commonly include women which was not the case years ago.

Even though my book is fascinating, I drift off after a short time and get a good night's sleep. Come morning, I wake up refreshed and can't wait to get on the road, again. Doug gets a short, fast walk and I give myself a quick wash-up before breakfast. Back in the car, I unfold my map and there it is: Bear Butte. For some reason, I like how it sounds. *Bear Butte.*

Driving down another seemingly endless stretch of road, the nice allure of prairie grass perfumes the air, the sun flirts with me, and once again I feel a little like a kid on an expedition. Nearing the town of Sturgis I have few expectations; as usual, we'll see what we see.

Dozens of braggadocious billboards advertise the annual Motorcycle Rally. They make the town of six thousand easy to find and much larger than it actually is. The event attracts hundreds of thousands of bikers from all over the country. Thank goodness, I'll miss that onslaught of motorcycles. It reminds me of the thousands of Indian ponies that once gathered in this area and I hope some of those joyful memories linger in this land. And then the memory of a certain biker pops into my head.

—m—

A few days before leaving Maine, I was troubled. All the trip arrangements had been made but I had a gnawing feeling it was a crazy idea. Other than visiting Wounded Knee, why was I going? To connect with Earth? Was that enough of a reason if, in fact, that was my goal? Was I trying to prove something to myself, to others? I felt a strong internal pull to go but my logical mind wondered why. Silently, I asked for a sign my trip was a good idea.

I was still a bit anxious about the trip as I walked into an old convenience store in town. I bought some snacks then stepped outside. In my path at the bottom of the rickety wooden stairs was a biker dude dismounting his impressive Harley. His leather jacket, long stringy hair, and beefy beard put me on edge, and I was already on edge. *Is he in a biker gang?*

Then, from under his leather jacket I saw his t-shirt. On it was the huge image of a white buffalo head and at the bottom the words: Sturgis, S.D. As I inched my way down the steps, the guy caught my eyes and his boyish smile peeked out at me through his furry face.

After I forced a smile, he said, "Hello there."

I looked down at the fat bike then at the brawny rider, judged him safe, and returned the greeting, "Hi, how you doing? Beautiful day for a ride."

"Yup, great to finally make it to Maine."

"So you're not from around here."

"Nope, I'm a long-haul trucker. My first time in Maine."

I teetered at the bottom step wondering if my prayer had been answered.

His openness made me feel comfortable so I jumped in and asked, "All those hours alone and all, what's that like?"

"Love it. And, I love this great country. Got no one to answer to and I like that." I took another look at the large American flag insignia on his jacket.

I asked him about his t-shirt and he boasted about participating in the motorcycle event every summer.

The white buffalo and South Dakota logo worn by a fellow solo traveler? I had my answer. I knew my trip was on.

# 27: Peaceful Mountain, Peaceful Mom

## I didn't know how to love her

Sturgis looks like the other one-hundred-year-old towns out here: unremarkable. Maybe that's because it was an afterthought, a stopover for white settlers on their way to the west coast. I don't know. The road leading out of town stretches ahead like a long ribbon that swoops left for more than a mile before delivering me back to the open plains. All of a sudden, I see a behemoth in the distance. At first it looks like a beached whale and its beauty startles me. Bear Butte. My tears and jagged breath make me pull over to the side of the road so I can collect myself. It feels like I've found something I never knew I lost, something grand and tender and intimate. As I drive closer, the small mountain begins to change. It now looks like a huge bear resting on its side alone and surrounded by miles and miles of vibrant grasslands. Suddenly, an old, half-forgotten memory seizes me. The bear-shaped mountain looks like my mother asleep in her bed.

When I was a kid, summer vacations were the best. My siblings and I got to spend our days doing pretty much whatever we wanted. Our dad always left for work real early so we kids made our own breakfasts then began our day. Our mom, as usual, was still sleeping.

One gorgeous morning when I was around eleven, something made me want to be near my mother so I went upstairs and opened the door to my parents' big, lovely bedroom. The little Catholic girl in me wondered if sneaking like that might be a venial sin. Also, I knew I had

97

to be careful not to wake her because she'd be mad. So I tiptoed past her cedar hope chest at the foot of the bed and got closer.

She was stretched out on her side and facing the wall. Her left arm was curled up across her chest and her hand hung down over her shoulder. It was her trademark sleeping posture, how I always pictured her resting. I stopped for a second and smiled because she looked so serene.

As I stood at the side of the bed, listening to her breathe, I imagined a flow of soft peaceful air moving into and out of her body. Trim and tall for her generation at 5'7", older pictures of her reminded me of the stylish 1940's pinups. When I looked at her thick, red, curly hair spread out like a headdress on her pillow, I smiled even more. She liked lacy things and I caught a glimpse of her silky nightgown draped across her freckled back. She was beautiful. It soothed me, seeing her like that, calm and trustworthy.

Being near her felt good but it also felt a little odd because in order to do that I had to sneak like this. When she was awake, I often felt nervous around her. She could be like an unexpected volcanic eruption. Confused, I didn't know how to love her.

I stepped closer, along my dad's side of the bed, bent down, then picked up the sheet, and slid under. It felt strange crawling into bed with my clothes on. I rolled to my side and faced her back then moved to the edge of the pillow so I could study her hand draped over her shoulder. She had lovely fingers; not delicate, not manly, just right. I loved being this close to her and looking at her fingers and hair and back and mostly breathing a little of the air that I knew my mother and I shared.

After a few minutes, I carefully pushed the sheet down and slid out of bed and headed to the door. I turned to look once more; my mom was still sound asleep.

I slipped in next to my mother a couple more times over that summer. She never woke up and never found out I'd been there and that was okay. I got to be close to her as she lay on her side like a grand and beautiful hibernating bear, but, sadly, like a bear, she could be unpredictable and ferocious at times.

I wish I could have talked with my mother about my confusion but it just wasn't something our family did. Decades after her death I wondered what I would have said to her if I'd had the chance. I knew writing down one's thoughts can be very healing so I decided to write a letter to her. I imagined I was twelve again and it was amazing; from the start it felt like my young self was moving my pen.

To Mom

From Regina, age 12

Dear Mom,

Our big new house is so wonderful. I really like my beautiful bedroom. Thanks for letting me choose the wallpaper and letting me have Grammy's old spool bed. I like my bed even more because it's the one you and Dad used to have.

I love everything in my room, Mom, and even if it is a little too fancy with the lace curtains and the pink bedspread you picked out, I still like it. I love my record player the most, I think. It's fun to close the door and be all by myself and play my records and sing. Paul Anka is the best!

I remember a little bit about our apartment at the corner store but not much. Our big new house feels sooo big compared to the itsy-bitsy rooms we had there. Sleeping in the same room with Lorraine and Linda was okay but it's great we all have our own rooms now. How did we ever fit our big family in that tiny apartment?

But Mom, why are you always mad at Dad? Why don't you want to go up to bed with him at night? Is it because it's not easy for you to go to sleep that early and Dad gets up early for work and that's why he goes to bed so early? Is it because us kids are so much work and you want to stay up and watch TV and smoke your cigarettes when we are all in bed and the house is quiet?

I think that Dad is sad and lonely that you never go up to bed with him when he asks you to. I wish you would try harder and go to bed with him. Maybe you are lonely too, Mom? You kinda look lonely sitting with your feet tucked under yourself on the end of the couch watching TV and not saying anything to anyone. It makes me feel a little lonely too when the TV is on and no one talks to me except when I get into a fight with Lorraine or Pat. I wish we could be happier together. All of us, Mom.

I am not mad at you, Mom. I love EVERYTHING in our new house but sometimes it just feels like it's too big for us. It's like there's too much room so we stay away from each other. I don't know. I just wish you were happier and us kids didn't fight so much and that Dad was happier when he went upstairs to bed.

I will try harder to not fight with Lorraine, Mom. Could you sit down with us sometime and tell us how to get along with each other better? We have never done that so maybe it would help. I feel awful when I am mean to her. Maybe you could punish me when I am and when all of us kids are mean to each other and not just when we do something else that makes you mad. I don't know if that would help but I hope you will try, Mom.

I love you, Mom!!!!!!

Love, Regina

# 28: Meeting the Medicine Man

## The best teachers show us our options then support us as we find our own way

Millions of years ago volcanic magma gushed to the surface. When it cooled the mound of rock weathered and eventually formed "Mato Paha," Lakota for Bear Butte. I stop the car to try to take it all in. The mountain still looks like a woman. Dappled with stunted pine and wrapped in a velvety blanket of grasses, her texture, and her shape leave me transfixed. She's a masterpiece.

I'm still a bit spellbound when my car putters down the road but I perk up near a sign: "Bear Butte National Park Visitor's Center." *There's one of those here?* I turn in and park then bounce up the steps into the tiny building. The modest space inside nearly overwhelms me. Tall, glass cabinets against the wall display what look like rare Indian artifacts. The gem of the group jumps out. It's a "ghost shirt" from the 1800s.

In the 1870s an Indian holy man, thought to be a messiah, preached that the buffalo herds and their way of life would soon return. The prophecies gave hope to those who had lost so much. He said if the white ghost shirts were worn into battle, bullets would be made harmless and many swore it to be true. This story is believed to have fueled the Wounded Knee massacre. Because the US Army was afraid the prophecy might spark another Indian rebellion, the army decided to attack first.

Maybe it's my vivid imagination or my childlike enthusiasm for Indigenous things, I don't know, but being here, a couple feet from a ghost shirt, I have a little vertigo. A couple deep breaths help me recover.

The park ranger behind the desk perks up as if he knows I'm excited. When I walk over he extends his hand and says, "Welcome to Bear Butte."

We chat about the park then I drill him with too many questions about the Butte's history but he keeps smiling and feeding me info. Finally, I ask about the camping sites.

"Are you a tourist or are you here for religious reasons?"

I almost jump out of my boots. *I'm dressed like a touristy hiker and he asks me that?*

"Oh, religious reasons," I blurt. Without one iota of hesitation he gives me a visitor's map and points to a trail leading to the religious camping area.

*Holy smoke, did that just happen?* Aflutter, I try to not sound giddy, thank him, then, as smoothly as I can, walk back to the car. For some odd reason the image of the chest-high weeds at the edge of the parking lot stays with me. *Maybe they symbolize something or maybe I just want them to.*

Once I move my car into a parking space, I notice the trailhead leading to the religious area. When I open the back, Doug bounces out and as I attach his leash, he looks up at me and, with a wag, gives his approval. Always up for an adventure, it's like he and I are following the same script.

I can hardly believe my luck because it was just this morning I read about Bear Butte. I start down the path and it feels like I'm gliding. A faint, distant drumming reminds me to step gently on this ancient path. A few minutes later the trail fans out into a large field at the mountain's base. The oblong grassy clearing is half the size of a baseball field and, scattered near the edges, are about ten small tents. Ahead of me in the distance is an imposing sight. A stately white tepee stands like a heroic lighthouse on a rocky shoreline.

I walk further into the clearing and come upon a group of people mingling inside what looks like a dining tent. A thirty-something, thin, Caucasian man with a red bandana and a blond ponytail springs out of the tent and intercepts me. He grins, "Hi, are you looking for the hiking trails?"

"No, I plan to tent here."

I was ready for some sort of rejection but without even a flinch he says, "You should go over and talk to the medicine man." He points to the tepee and a man sitting in a chair about twenty yards from us. He then digs into his shirt pocket, pulls out a cigarette, and says, "Give this to him. Tobacco is the traditional gift given to a medicine man." *Thanks, I know the drill and this coming from a White guy?*

I thank him for the cigarette, and head over to the medicine man. I'm feeling a little jittery inside, like there's a current pulling me along, and my feet are barely touching the ground. Closer to the tepee I can see him better. The medicine man's sitting on an aluminum folding chair facing the tepee and behind him is a semi-circle of short bushes. *I have to remember this iconic scene so I can return to it often.*

Even before I enter his campsite, I stretch out my hand. "Hello. My name is Regina." His hand feels dry and slight but his grip is firm and warm. I hand him my cigarette gift and he thanks me then tucks it into his shirt pocket. There are a few others standing near us. *No one's saying anything so I might as well.* "Would it be okay to camp here?"

Without looking up at me he says, "Okay." He has on dusty jeans, a long-sleeve shirt, and cowboy boots. I know his cigarette smoke is considered medicine and I think of that as I watch it drift up and cup the wide rim of his cowboy hat. Maybe in his late 70s, his skin looks sun-weathered, and his frame prematurely frail.

I feel like a fish out of water but after an uncomfortably long pause, for me, that is, I get up the nerve to ask him his name and he says, "My name is Gerald. This is my sister, Deborah, and her husband, Henry." Deborah stands like a palace guard off to Gerald's right and a little behind him. She gives me an obligatory nod and curls her mouth into a thin smile. Like a backdrop to his wife, Henry stands to her left and behind. The three of us echo the requisite nods and greetings.

With the pesky intros out of the way, it's time to get down to business. I look back at Gerald and blurt out, "I've come here from Maine following my heart." As soon as my words escape I feel like an idiot. *Your heart? You just met the man. He didn't ask, but you're telling him about your heart?*

As if my words were common ones, he says, "Many people come to this place," and he turns, looks at the Butte, and waves his arm in a slow, generous gesture of reverence, as if he's inviting me to share it.

Then like an over-inflated tire with a leak, my pride rapidly loses its power and my gut feels hollow. I remind myself that these are people of few words and this is their sacred land.

But, my childish ego bounces back. *Yes, but doesn't he know I want information, maybe a tale or two? Isn't this what medicine men do; tell stories?*

Doug stands patiently at my side and he and Gerald are at eye level. As Gerald reaches over and pats my protector's head, I gulp. Doug steps in even closer than his tail starts its slow, happy wag. *Thank god!* Doug likes him so I relax.

Anxious to get on with it, but with respect to proper protocol, I ask Gerald, "So where should I put my tent?"

"Really anywhere... Over by the tree?" He gives a sweeping, noncommittal wave towards a stunted pine, on a slight slope at the mountain's base. It's the only tree in the whole clearing.

I've sought direction from other Indigenous teachers so I'm not surprised when he gives me such a vague answer. I know the best teachers show us our options then support us as we find our own way.

Reverting into my independent "Little Regina" self, I thank Gerald, nod goodbye to Deborah and Henry then head out to find my tent site. *Well, I don't care if he **is** a medicine man; I'm not going to be told what to do.*

As I crisscross half the camping area, I stay sensitive to how my body feels in each spot. *Is this it? This place? Nope, nope, nope, doesn't feel right.* I circle back inside the large loop I've made and find myself near the solitary little pine. With a bit of a chip on my shoulder, I walk up to it then notice something familiar at the base. When I step in closer, I see it's a pink, blue, and white comforter. *Oh my gosh!* It's exactly like the one on my bed in Maine. *Well, I guess this is the spot. Good for me; see, I didn't need Gerald's help, after all.*

# 29: Stumbling Over My Ego

## Humility is not a liability

I claim my tent site, even if it's the one Gerald foretold, and then head back to the car for my gear. With Doug's leash wrapped on my wrist, I juggle bundles of camping gear as we plod along together down the footpath to the pine. I drop off the first of three loads, look out at the welcoming landscape, and smile. I wonder how long I'll stay here. My body answers. For as long as it feels right.

It's an exquisite feeling, connected to Earth like this. I can feel her subtle rustlings, what seems like her *music*. I've read that all living things, including our planet, create unique vibrations that radiate out from their center. Earth's iron core generates an electromagnetic field called the magnetosphere, which extends many miles above its surface. Single-cell organisms, with their tiny internal magnets, use the planet's magnetic field to navigate. I've watched bacteria under a microscope rush to a magnet placed at the edge of the slide. In a study to learn how creatures do this, scientists strapped tiny magnets to the heads of homing pigeons. The magnets disrupted their flight patterns home. Even humans have magnetic molecules in their brains but presently their function is unknown. I wonder if this gives some people what we call a good "sense of direction." It makes me wonder if Earth's magnetism might affect us in other ways.

The natural world is full of melodies we can't hear. I've learned that in some shamanic traditions the unique vibrations an organism emits are called its *spiritual song*. While undetectable to the human ear, technology has uncovered the "choruses" of whales, hummingbirds, plants, and even distant planets. The slowed-down recording of a chorus of crickets reveals a perfectly coordinated symphony. Place two separated heart cells in a Petri dish and each will beat according to its own rhythm. When the cells touch, though, their beats synchronize. Scientists don't understand why. Maybe their *songs* merge then coincide when they detect another's.

Thinking back on my times in meditation and in nature, I wonder if the subtle currents I felt were part of *my song*. And, I wonder if those sensations actually inform my internal compass.

On my final trip back from the car, I watch a small bird pester an eagle as it circles above the summit of the Butte. And, like that eagle, I also feel a pesky little something hell-bent on keeping me alert. *Ha! Spirit is on my tail.*

I pass the dining tent and the same white guy with the red bandana steps out into my path. With a goofy smile and in what sounds like a single breath, he says, "Hi, I'm Leo and I'm from Iowa and my family just left the encampment and I'm staying on for a couple days to help Gerald. If you want to hike up the Butte you need to ask the medicine man first because there are people doing their vision quests up there."

I introduce myself and Doug, then point to the pine tree and tell him it's my site. I doubt he hears a word I say because he's acting like a kid who just hit a home run. He gushes, "At last night's sweat lodge ceremony I was given my Native name." I know that in some Indigenous cultures, one's name can change a few times over a lifetime. Names reflect a personal trait, talent, or event. It can also come from a mystical experience. He stares at me. *Are you waiting for me to be impressed?* I've seen this kind of thing too many times: nonnatives adopting Native American traditional ways in order to elevate their sense of self. *Thank goodness I'm nothing like that.* Irritated, I don't have a response for him.

Still bug-eyed and stumbling over his words, he says, "Too bad. You just missed meeting an apprentice medicine woman and other women who gathered here last night." My response is "Oh."

I say goodbye then walk away. It takes me a while but I finally scold myself for being so snooty. I realize I was the one with the poor attitude. I assumed, because Leo was White, he was nonnative and, thus inferior to my concept of these people. He becomes a good reminder that it's not what I know but how I live my life. *Be humble, Regina, and share in another's joy.*

At the little tree, I begin picking up the mess left by the previous campers then walk back to the parking lot to dispose of the bedspread and trash. I'm disappointed that these folks litter like the rest of us. I guess we are more alike than I wanted to believe.

Doug stretches his long, dark body out on the grass in the shade of the pine. He doesn't mind being tethered and soon starts snoring. After I pitch my tent, I toss my bedding and gear inside. There's no picnic table or fire pit and that's okay because all I need are my chair, my tent, my provisions in the car, and my dog. With arms folded across my chest, I step back and admire my perfect little plot of ground. *If life could always be this simple. Pure contentment.*

Even though it's early afternoon, I'm wiped so I crawl into the tent, stretch out on a blanket, and leave the day behind. After a few deep breaths sleep washes over me like a warm, welcoming tide.

My nap done, I sit up refreshed but notice my disheveled interior. I organize my belongings to meet my aesthetic requirements. Totally smitten with this day, I peek out my south-facing back window that opens to the broad base of the Butte. My screened front door opens to the north and Gerald's majestic tepee. The Butte's small clumps of cliffs are to the west and Doug is to the east. I don't know why, but something prods me to note these directions and it makes me feel like all is in perfect order.

I'm relaxing in my chair eating lunch when a small group of people catches my attention. They're gathered at a campfire in the far eastern corner of the encampment. I take out my binoculars and spy on the scene which is a hodgepodge of blankets covering a sweat lodge, or Inipi. Their lazy campfire smoke billows up twenty feet in front of the lodge's door opening. I take a deep breath and imagine the ordained smoke is a prayer that finds me and fills my cells with humility, something I could use more of. I smile.

I sit in my chair, mind my own business, and try to write in my journal but I'm too jacked up to focus. *I'm in a real Native American encampment on consecrated land. Am I dreaming?*

Later in the afternoon, a man from the Inipi area walks over to me. He's a reedy guy with a weathered face wearing crisp, new jeans and a shirt with rolled-up sleeves. He steps into my site, squats down, extends his hand, and introduces himself with a smile. "My name is Ben." Poised on the ground a few feet away from me, he seems settled in for a stay.

He asks where I'm from and I give him the condensed version of my story. Then when I tell him I'm traveling alone, he gawks at me and says, "You're all alone?"

I smile, point over to Doug, and say, "Well, not really, Doug is with me."

Ben looks over at Doug, nods, and his smile almost seems like a relief. He asks me what I know about the Butte and I tell him the little I've read. After a long uncomfortable pause, something I'm beginning to expect, he starts telling me the Butte is a traditional place for ceremony and its significance to Aboriginals. Then, I'm not sure why, maybe he's proud of his heritage, he tells me he is Cheyenne and French.

I like the demeanor of this soft-spoken guy. I hope he visits me again because I need to connect with more people and it wouldn't hurt to improve my social skills.

After Ben leaves, it hits me again that I'm on historic land and I feel glued to my chair for a good length of time. Then like a distant observer, I halfheartedly survey the far reaches of the large meadow. At the end near the Inipi there's the sporadic movement of folks and small, puffy clouds sail overhead. Conscious of the Butte behind me, I take my time digesting Ben's words about it and remember how comfortable I felt talking with him. *I hope I'll savor and remember every conversation I have here.*

A half-hour later, I give up on my journal and stand for a good stretch. I attach Doug to his long leash and we walk to the eastern base of the Butte. It's another perfect day in the high, dry 80s and a whimsical breeze urges me to explore. I can't help but feel bubbly and a few hundred feet into my walk, it's like I'm being gently herded onto the tourist hiking trail leading to the summit.

Doug's happy, chugging along on the trail in front of me. About halfway to the top, I unhitch his leash and he gallops away like a wild mustang. Every so often he waits so I can catch up. On the few steeper grades, I have to stop to catch my breath, but overall my stamina surprises me. We're the only ones out here, except, that is, for the big doe that straddles the trail a few minutes later. She turns to survey me then glides off the trail, around a hill, and out of sight before Doug notices. This terrain is so open, I wonder how she can possibly hide from danger. I suddenly remember the fable of the gentle deer and the terrible monster and I feel small. *Humility is not a liability.*

Suddenly after what seems like too short a time, we're at the summit. A circular wood platform provides a 360-degree view of hundreds of miles of gently rolling, verdant plains. In the far distance, a dark ruffle of peaks edges the horizon: the Black Hills. I whisper, "This is amazing."

Something inside stirs me so I face each of the four directions and say a prayer of gratitude for being here. When I send prayers of love to my family and friends at home, an avalanche of emotion brings tears and my knees want to buckle. *My god, I have cried more these last few days than in the last twenty years!* After a few minutes of good, easy crying I feel better, softer, maybe stronger. *Less judgy?*

Once I collect myself, we head back down the trail. At the bottom I'm surprised we did the "hour-and-forty-five-minute hike" in a little more than an hour. My legs are a bit sore but I feel lighter, freer from my worst critic: me.

# 30: The Butte Sings

## Soft salutations to Earth's new day

Late in the afternoon I return to Sturgis for a much-needed break in this extraordinary day. Pepsi, chips, and a Snickers bar transport me back to my ordinary world.

When I'm back at Bear Butte, I notice a few guys gathered at a campfire near the base of the summit trail. After a brief respite in my tent and emboldened by Ben's friendly essence, I walk over to join them.

Three Indigenous men in jeans and cowboy shirts squat near a little fire. When I approach, their heads turn to me, their braids swing forward, and their smiles invite me to join them. I can't sit like they do so I plop down on my butt and cross my legs. After I introduce myself, their smooth, laid-back introductions come fast. One guy, Joe, tells me he's here with his wife and kids to support a friend doing his quest on the mountain. A couple minutes later two younger guys walk over, bend down, and listen in on the conversations. They remain silent then leave a few minutes later. *Boy, how to slip into and out of a crowd without any hullabaloo.* It strikes me that this would be pretty unusual in my culture: two guys walking into then out of a group and saying nothing. I realize I'm generalizing.

Such a welcoming group is my invitation to join the conversation and we talk about the smoky little fire, the good weather, and the nice trickle of people coming and going at the Butte. Then it hits me; they aren't asking *this white woman* why I'm here or who I'm with. I expect some hint of exclusion but it doesn't come. This transient community accepts me and I relax.

A short while later, I say goodbye then, during my slow walk back to the tent, I'm still puzzled. *Why did they welcome me?* I remember the family at Wounded Knee, how they didn't hesitate to let me into their home, even though once inside, I was kept at a polite distance. I wonder if their history has conditioned them to stay emotionally disengaged from us. But, then again, that might not be the case here, where folks are focused on their relationship with Earth and Spirit. Or, maybe they're just not that interested in old, boring me. After even more musing, I realize I unconsciously tap into how my body feels near people. Maybe I'm discerning their character and intentions without even intending to. As a kid, it was a real plus because I could measure the climate in our house and be prepared for any of my mom's unpredictable moods.

For supper tonight, I prepare my go-to meal of beans and rice with a side of fruit and yogurt while Doug gobbles up his smelly food. A few hours later, as the sun makes its slow slide down the backside of the Butte, I settle Doug in for the night by tying him to the small pine with his long leash. He promptly curls up on his blanket. He's usually a sound sleeper but with his sensitive nose and ears, he's my reliable alarm, too.

I remember being told a medicine woman is camping on the other side of the clearing. They said she has a wolf hybrid so while it's still light, I use my binoculars to get a good look at her. Yup, she has a BIG pup. I'm sure Doug can smell the dog but he completely ignores it and the hybrid ignores him. Maybe this hallowed land has altered the social norms of the four-legged as well as us two-legged creatures.

Burrowed inside my sleeping bag, my mind treats me to long-playing flashbacks of an incredibly rich day. As I wade through the day's amazing happenings, I want to stay there but eventually sleep pulls me in.

A few hours later, the cold courses into my sleeping bag and wakes me. I pop my head out of the tent and am startled. Far to the east and silhouetted against the magnificent night sky is the jagged, ascending contours of the Butte. And suspended within the drapery of a dark, velveteen sky are a gazillion flickering stars. Heaven's display immobilizes me at first. Then, even though retreating from a gift so amazing and rare feels ungrateful, I slide back inside my tent because it's too hard to fathom. *Why do I deserve such magic?* Soon the distant, soft drumming, sporadic easy laughter, and whispers of folks strolling near my tent lull me into a dreamy half-sleep.

A little after midnight Doug starts to bark. I can tell from the sound he's irritated and probably wants to sleep but can't with so many new sounds and smells. To spare everyone from his protests, I bring him into the tent and once I slide back into my sleeping bag, all one-hundred pounds of shedding hair stretches out next to me. Every time I move, his big tail does a slow, happy flop on the ground. I love my dog and all but sleeping with him feels weird as he's not some curled-up little guy nestled at my feet. And, with my tent pitched on a slope, I spend much of the time attempting to keep from sliding towards the door while, at the same time, trying to stay a comfortable distance from Doug's unpleasant breath.

For a long time, the muffled murmurings of distant drumming and faint, soft laughter continue. The sounds tiptoe to my tent and I invite them inside. I'm tired. But if I sleep, I know I'll miss the heartwarming songs of family.

I finally nod off but just before dawn I wake again. From the east, where I saw the stars, and about halfway up the mountain, I hear what sounds like two women singing in their native tongue. Fragile, innocent tones, only women can make, trickle down like stardust and drift into our shared clearing. Their sacred psalms waltz together in soft salutations to Earth's new day. Chills run up and down my neck and I tear up, again. Their angelic voices are the most tender sounds I have ever heard. *And I deserve this too?*

I remember Easter Sunday masses when I was a kid. Our little church would rock with joy as we sang our welcome to the return of the Light and the Resurrection. Now, in this pre-dawn hour I'm stirred by celestial voices which remind me that the sun will always return. It will always bring us a new day.

# 31: A New Kind of Medicine

## Sharing Can Benefit Everyone

The sunrise songs leave me feeling spacey so for the next two hours I slip in and out of sleep. When I finally wake up in earnest, I take my time leaving the tent, tending to Doug, and having my breakfast. A little while later I remember I need to call my daughter, Jessie. Before I left home, she said she might join me for a couple days. While I love my times with Jess, I also love my solitude here so I won't be too upset if she can't make it.

Mid-morning, before I leave camp, perky Leo, with his red bandana, stops by to say good morning. His hyper enthusiasm still annoys me so, when he asks about my night, my answer is flat. "It was fine." He's probably an okay guy but his enthusiasm feels intrusive.

On the way to the parking lot, I stop to say good morning to Joe and his two friends and he asks, "How was your night?"

"It was good but my dog started to bark so I brought him into the tent with me."

He makes a quirky face that quickly softens into a smile. "Your dog was in the tent with you?"

I'm not entirely surprised with his reaction; I'd read that, historically, dogs were important members of the tribes, serving as scouts, pack animals, and sometimes as a food source but they weren't necessarily considered pets. I say goodbye to Joe, leave him to struggle with his image of Doug in my tent, and head to Sturgis.

With only outhouses at the Butte, I plan to find a place to wash on my way into town. A decent public bathroom suffices for a good wash-up every few days. I like roughing it, free from the petty social norms of cleanliness. And Doug doesn't seem to mind.

A vintage gas station on the outskirts of Sturgis has potential so I walk in, ask for the key to the ladies' room, and cross my fingers it'll do. When I enter, the rust and mystery stains on the porcelain scare me but the toilet flushes and when I turn the handle, the faucet sputters out its cold water. I'm just happy they work. With my eyes locked on the dirty mirror, I manage a hasty cold water sponge bath then brush my teeth. Skin contact with sink, toilet, mirror, and doorknob surfaces is avoided. It's tricky but I use the sterile technique I learned working in a hospital.

A few miles from the gas station, I pull into a family-style café. After sliding into my booth a cute little waitress smiles as she takes my order. Their fresh brewed coffee and moist corn muffins take me back to my other life and for a few minutes I'm back home eating breakfast alone at Smiley's. Sitting in booths like these is a little like sitting in a church pew and I'm part of a parish family and we're sharing breakfast and life is peaceful and unremarkably good. Nourishing tasty food, an attentive waitress, and feeling safe: who could want for more?

Outside the café is a phone booth so I call Jessie. She won't be able to join me. She says it's a money issue; I think it's a husband issue but I'm relieved my solo journey is preserved. I head back to the Butte.

When Doug and I are halfway from the car to my tent, two Indigenous women approach me. They are wearing long cotton skirts and flowing blouses. Each is pushing a small child in a stroller. I slow down to meet them.

We exchange greetings and, as I expected, they're friendly. Even though they seem preoccupied, one mom asks what brought me here. Tired of telling my story, I simply say I'm on vacation. Right away she says, "My daughter is special; she has a brain problem. It's something like cerebral palsy and I bring her to Gerald for healing and after just four sessions she has gone from twenty or thirty seizures a day to less than five." Her eyes look frightened and her face fallen. A child's chronic trauma stays with a mother. I know that one well. When my son was young he had persistent, severe croup. Even though he outgrew it, the memory of his attacks, seeing him go limp and turn blue dozens of times, has stayed with me.

The two moms take turns telling me how powerful Gerald's healing gifts are and I'm awed. What I've read about these rituals and customs is fascinating. But, now, camping on this hallowed ground, hearing about their faith in Gerald and how he's helped the child in this setting, makes it seem more real.

The young mother hasn't elevated the practice to a place of lofty mysticism like many nonnatives have, including me. A jumble of ideas floods my mind. How can one marry Indigenous American healing with contemporary medicine? Years later I will see it begin: a convergence of traditional and modern healing methodologies. After my adventure here I'll work to facilitate that sacred confluence.

One of the moms asks me about my home. When I talk about Maine's lush forests, rocky coastlines, and thousands of lakes, their tired eyes sparkle. My words make it sound like a fairytale place so I smile, too. Whisked back home for a minute, my body sighs.

Deborah, Gerald's stoic sister, walks over from the tepee area and joins us. She's wearing a gray sweatshirt and faded jeans. *Not dressed how the sister of a medicine man should dress.* At first, this gray-haired woman listens in and that's fine. But Deborah grimaces a little when I mention New Age healing practices like Reiki and Polarity Therapy. "What about healing with stones or crystals? Does Gerald use them?" I ask.

Deborah glares at me, "Using crystals, any crystals, for healing is unacceptable in our tradition!"

I feel cornered like I'm suspect. I imagine she knows people who've copied their practices: cultural appropriation. For me, it's a complicated issue when it comes to healing. Mimicking in order to exploit is obviously wrong but I wonder if the merging of contemporary healing practices and traditional Indigenous practices can be made acceptable to all. I do know that sharing can benefit everyone.

After her rebuke about crystals, Deborah's irritations seem to fade and her face softens. Maybe she'd been waiting all this time to school me. She shifts gears again and tells me that she and her husband leave tomorrow for the big powwow in Rapid City. I remember the fancy woman at Wounded Knee had mentioned it, too. I turn to Deborah, smile, and say, "Maybe I'll see you there." She gives me a blank stare and is mum. Embarrassed, I feel like a naïve kid. *Hey, wait a minute. You're wearing a stupid sweatshirt and I'm embarrassed?*

Without skipping a beat, she says, "We want to invite you to eat with everyone at Gerald's later, sometime after noon." Communicating with this woman is like a car ride, at night, on a desolate curvy road where you never know what you'll meet around the bend. My empathy kicks in. *Considering what's been stolen from her people, she has a right to be protective of her heritage.*

Back near my tent, I keep watch and a little after noon I notice some folks gathered near the tepee. With his unobstructed view of me, Doug will be quiet so I can leave him at the tree as I walk over to Gerald's.

About a dozen of us gather for a traditional meal: Indian fry bread which is a batter, flattened and shaped to the size of one's palm, then deep-fried and sprinkled with sugar or honey; boiled potatoes; hard-boiled eggs for protein; and a chunky berry sauce called wojapi, made from local wild berries. The concoction of eats is simple and nourishing, like these generous people.

Leo is here and I cringe then force a smile when he walks over to me. I'm sitting in a chair so he kneels down to get eye level and says "I'm leaving today and Gerald's here alone till Sunday." That's two days from now.

I'm slow to pick up on subtle social cues but after a long pause, I say, "I'd be happy to help Gerald out."

Leo gives me two cigarettes and says, "You'll need to talk with Gerald about it."

A while later, when most folks have left, I have my opportunity. I walk over to where Gerald's seated, squat down, and ask, "Can I talk with you later?"

He looks up and with a slight smile says, "Sure, just stop by anytime." I recognize the casual cadence in his voice; it was there when he told me where to tent.

"I'll help you out if you need anything." He nods in agreement. I'm psyched. I can't wait to have him all to myself, share my personal story, and be privy to his wisdom.

# 32: The Home Across the Street

## It was paradise

I grew up in a small New Hampshire farm town in the '50s and '60s. My best friend was Barbara Johnson and her family had a farm on prime land in the Connecticut River Valley. They milked about sixty head of cattle, mostly giant, imposing black and white Holsteins. I loved hanging around their farm with its earthy scents of hay bales, molasses-coated cow feed, manure, and all the other farm scents. Barbara's parents, Elmore and Emma, and her grandparents, Percy and Julia, lived together in their hundred-year-old brick farmhouse. Barbara's parents had inherited the farm from Percy and Julia. They were a kind and close-knit family.

During summer haying season, Grandmother Julia would cook a huge meal for noontime dinner. Everyone, including the help, sometimes eight or ten of them, would gather around the over-sized, oblong kitchen table to eat. When I visited, I always got invited to join them. Sitting at the crowded table, it was fun to listen in on the good-natured ribbing and farm talk of the smiley-faced men. And I could see the sun got to them because their arms, faces, and the backs of their necks reminded me of the color of steamed lobsters.

Noontime menu was boiled potatoes, boiled onions, boiled carrots, and boiled beef, pork or a large chicken. On the table sat loaves of fresh baked bread with butter, warm homemade pies, and pitchers of raw milk and ice water. That farmer soul food delighted my heart if not my palate. I added lots of salt to bring out the flavors that hadn't been boiled away. No matter how hot the day, it was always a boiled "dinner." In New England a farmer's supper was at 5:00 which allowed for a few more daylight hours to work. My young-self left those dinners content, filled with soft, unremarkable, overcooked food and echoes of easygoing, friendly banter, always wanting more.

One summer, Barbara's dad became seriously ill. Elmore was only in his late thirties and to me had always seemed healthy. Without modern technology the doctors did exploratory surgery to determine what was wrong. They cut him open from his pelvis to the top of his chest cavity. When I heard about it, I remember thinking; *what an awful thing to do to such a good man.* The final diagnosis: he was allergic to things on the farm.

So they sold it and moved into a stately, two-story, former boarding house on the other end of town and just across the street from us. The main entrance to the house opened to a large, sunny kitchen/ dining room. It was cheery and peaceful with its sheer, lacy curtains, white trim, and walls painted the lightest blue possible without being white. Often, when I stepped inside, whiffs of fresh baked bread or simmering dinner welcomed me. The long pantry with floor-to-ceiling cupboards was off the dining area. Sometimes I'd hear Grandmother Julia in there, opening and closing cupboard doors and drawers, or sliding bowls along the wide, wooden counter tops. Julia was the family cook. Stocky and a woman of few words I never got to know her well but I trusted her and always felt welcomed.

The house was big enough for Percy and Julia to have their own living room and bedroom downstairs. Elmore and Emma had a separate living room downstairs and upstairs there were five large bedrooms. I had many sleepovers at Barbara's house along with countless boiled dinners served on the old farm table.

After Elmore recovered from surgery, he got a job working for the town maintaining roads and he seemed content. A tall slender guy, he loved to fish and hunt and he and Emma, the small, quiet, intelligent town librarian, spent many summer evenings fishing together. When I imagined the two of them, alone in their little row boat in the middle of a remote trout pond, the scene always seemed romantic, rustic but romantic. I imagined they must have discovered some sort of secret formula for good fishing and a happy relationship. I idolized Elmore and Emma's partnership and never sensed any kind of discord between them. I may have been young but, even then, I could sense conflict in a family.

Sometimes I'd visit the morning after their evening of fishing and like a great work of art, nature would be displayed on the big table. Ten speckled trout, cleaned and glistening, lay two- deep on their sides. Eight to ten inches long, they looked like streamlined mini subs. To me, their bright eyes signaled they were resigned to their fate, ready for the refrigerator, then supper's frying pan. If I found a reason to stay long enough, I'd get invited to eat. Native brook trout, fried in a dab of lard and cooked till the

116

skin just began to curl away from the tasty, pink meat was the best tasting fish I ever ate.

One of the fun things Barbara and I liked to do was go down over the bank behind my house and hunt for crayfish. The brook was loaded with them and they were easy to catch. We'd take off our shoes and socks, roll up our pants or pedal pushers, and wade into the stream being careful not to get pinched by the big ones camouflaged by the brown mossy rocks. In one smooth sweep we'd slowly lift a stone, scoop up the angry little beast waving its claws in the air then plop it in our old coffee can. Clear, clean, cool water glided all round our ankles as minnows, water bugs, and flying insects darted round us in their bustling mini maneuvers. It was paradise. Once we caught a good batch of trout bait, we'd give them to her dad who gave us five cents each.

Because I loved nature so much, oftentimes I'd sit in Elmore and Emma's living room and flip through their stacks of *Outdoor Life*, *Field and Stream*, and *Fishing* magazines. Looking at the colorful pictures of ponds, fish, animals, and the outdoors, I felt transported. One evening while I sat looking through the magazines and after Barbara had left the room for a minute, her dad came in. He walked over to my chair and stopped. My friend's towering dad looked down at me, gave me a tender smile, and said, "You're a real nature girl, aren't you?" At first I was surprised and then his words stirred something new in me. No one had ever noticed me like that before.

# 33: Fitting in is Tricky

## It's easy to absorb this delightful feel of family

After my noon meal at Gerald's, I stroll back to my campsite and it's not long before Ben, the friendly Cheyenne-French man, wanders over. He meets me with a smile then squats down near my chair to chat. He asks, "Have you done any hiking yet?"

Pointing to the far eastern end of the Butte, I say, "I took the trail over there and went up to the top. It was fun."

He stares at me and says, "That trail over there? You did it all in one afternoon?" He looks puzzled and waits for me to explain.

"I do a lot of hiking and it really wasn't much of a challenge."

"You went all the way to the top?" *Did I miss something? Either these folks are extremely out of shape, I am in better shape than I thought, I took a shorter trail, or something mysterious happened on my hike. I like mysterious.*

Before Ben leaves, Joe shows up and invites us to eat with his family later in the afternoon. His brother is coming down from his vision quest. I remember it's tradition to have a feast when a quest ends. Delighted, I accept the invitation and can't wait to join another traditional gathering.

It's time for a much-needed lazy spell so I stretch out on my sleeping bag. My journal and book play tug-of-war for my attention and I roll back and forth from one to the other. A little later I twist to stare out the door at a classic image: a grand white tepee framed by a cool blue sky and crowned with puffy white clouds. The encampment is quiet, Doug is snoozing by the pine, and I have nothing on my to-do list. All is well in my world.

Near supper time, from inside the tent, I begin my surveillance of the designated feast site. Once people start to gather, I climb outside and get ready to go. Besides sharing in on the little festivity, maybe I can eavesdrop on some vision quest chatter. Once I walk over the knoll, Doug won't be able to see me so I put him on his short leash and we walk over to the crowd.

Ten people, or so, are gathered near the campsite which is dotted with three small metal tables, a few chairs, some blankets stretched out on the ground, and four fires. Cooking tripods made of saplings stand over the fires and a big pot of some steamy food is hanging from the center.

The warm smiles and friendly hellos I get feel more than enough for me. A minute later, someone announces the food is ready. Doug, the perfect gentleman, stays positioned at my side as we all fall in line, wait our turn, then step up to the big pots of food on the tables. I fill my plate then walk over to an empty spot near a few men who're sitting on the ground. I smile when I ask if I can join them and they nod yes.

It's another traditional meal of fry bread, boiled potatoes, corn on the cob, some sort of meat stew, and chunky berry sauce. I'm guessing the stew is tasty but to me, it looks like Gravy Train and, not a big meat eater, I pass on it. Even though I'm not hungry, I want to fit in so I chow down the other starchy selections. *This is great: real food, a nice break from yogurt, corn chips, and fruit.*

Sitting on the ground with Doug lying at my side, I survey the goings-on of the group as I eat. The men huddled next to me are talking in their Indigenous language, and their frequent spurts of laughter sweeten an already inviting scene. The women seem happy buzzing about, tending to the children and the food, while sharing on-the-fly morsels of conversation. Three children, maybe seven or eight years old, bounce in and out of the adult circles laughing and running errands for their fathers. I'm positioned at the intersection of the men's and women's groups, where it's easy to absorb this delightful feel of family.

There's no talk of the quest or maybe there is but it's not in English. Even though no one asks me my name or seems to want to talk with me, I feel welcomed and grateful to be audience to such respectful chitchat laced with warm laughter. *How peaceful.*

Stretched out on the ground next to me, Doug looks relaxed but I know he's processing every bit of this scene. A cute little girl comes over and leans down to pat him and, to my horror, he snaps at her. There's no contact. The child looks surprised but undaunted. Opposite me, a big, dark-faced guy leans in close, his long, thick braid falls onto his chest, and he glares at me. "If he bites my kid I'm going to eat your dog." I attempt one of my big-eyed tentative smiles and wait for the guy to smile back but he doesn't. Embarrassed, I recoil and apologize explaining that he is protective of his space and I will keep him under control. The man listens, turns back to his food and friends, while I shrink into my naughty-little-girl self. No one else seems to have noticed what happened and, if they did, they don't react.

I believe the big guy really would eat my dog so I finish my food, thank who I guess are the hosts, and walk my scary dog back to my site. My idealistic notions about these people fade. Why do I expect so much more from them? *We're all only human.*

# 34: Laundry Lessons

## I wondered about the tales the napkins could tell

I got my first summer job in 1963 when I was almost fifteen. I worked in the laundry at the Lake Tarleton Resort and I think I got hired because my father knew the owners. The lakeside resort sat in a remote forested area a couple towns over from us. It attracted movie stars and booked comedians who also performed on the Ed Sullivan show. Town folk thought it was a summer haven for rich Jewish people from New York City. We imagined them to be glitzy, remote, and nothing like us.

My dad arranged for me to ride with two women who also worked at the laundry. I knew them from our small town and in those days everyone knew everyone else so they didn't seem like strangers to me. What I remember most about Darlene and Cheryl is how they made me feel like an equal in our three-woman team. They had young families so I imagined our $1.25/hour salary was far more important to them than to me. I was working for pocket money but, in the end, I got so much more.

On work days my alarm rang at six. Before my father dropped me off at Darlene's house, I got to have him all to myself. Everything about those mornings was glorious and sometimes I'd stick my head out the window to taste the summer's delicious dawn. Even though we didn't talk much, I loved sitting near him and listening while he sang to pop songs on the radio. With black hair, a muscular frame, and a flashy white smile, I thought he was movie-star handsome. Things were tense at home and knowing my dad was happy made me smile. He'd only made it through grade six but he was what folks called a self-made man. His successful business was solid proof of that.

121

Once we got to Darlene's, I'd get in her car then we'd pick up Cheryl. We'd make the ten-mile drive with plenty of time to arrive at work by seven. Thank goodness for the refreshing morning air because we were headed into an eight-hour sauna.

Those cool nights birthed thick banks of morning fog that covered the lower farm lands surrounding us. Sometimes it was so thick our car barely crawled. I loved it; surrounded by the mysterious mist of grounded clouds, time stopped and there was nothing beyond fog's nonexistent boundaries. It was just us three, the car, and the road we traveled. But as we climbed the hills and approached the resort, the fog thinned and the concrete, real world and all its boundaries, some physical and some social, returned. Traveling in the thick haze, I was in my most peaceful dream place where life was simple and easy to understand. We didn't care that nature slowed us on those foggy mornings. We didn't mind being reminded to pace ourselves, to take things as they come. And even the car seemed more patient, willing to just poke along on its path.

I liked our easygoing, chit-chatty rides through the steep forested hills and patchwork of farmlands. Sitting in the back seat I listened to Darlene and Cheryl tell stories about their kids and husbands.

"And then he had the nerve to ask me to get up and get him a beer! Can you imagine?"

With a child-like smile, Cheryl said, "My husband asked me to get up and get him a beer once and only once. I looked at him all serious and told him I'd be his servant when he started paying me wages."

"Where did we ever find these guys, Cheryl?"

"Well, we could've done a hell of a lot worse, right?"

"No shit, I keep telling myself that and the kids do adore him."

The talk was lively, good-natured, and I loved hearing them giggle. Every few minutes, one of them would turn back to me and ask, "What do you think, Regina?" I was used to only listening in on adult conversations and not participating so the first few times they turned to me, I got red-faced and shrugged my shoulders. After a few days, I dared to ask, "What does that mean?" or "Did that really happen?" Their responses were kind, sometimes tongue-in-cheek. I realized later, there were just some things a young girl wasn't meant to get.

For work I wore shorts, a sleeveless cotton blouse, and white Keds sneakers. Darlene and Cheryl, I guessed to be in their late twenties, wore comfortable leather shoes, and faded, cotton, sleeveless dresses. Tons of bobby pins kept their hair off their faces. Darlene and Cheryl felt like "my people."

The Lake Tarleton Inn was like Disneyland to me and our little town was like a not-so-perfect Mayberry with its fair share of gossip and hard times. The resort's main building was the largest, most elegant edifice

I'd ever seen. A magnificent example of 1920s modern architecture, the white giant dwarfed the lesser white buildings scattered over acres of manicured lawns. I was excited about my first job and it sounded simple enough: I'd fold laundry. We worked in a small, dilapidated, wooden building balanced precariously on the bank of a river. Located off the main road and a mile down the hill from the expensive real estate, the glorified shack reminded me of an old prairie barn left over from the Great Depression.

Our primary work area was in the center of the building. Its rickety, wood floor gave us grumpy backtalk when we stepped on it just right. We used four, eight-foot-long wooden tables for folding and sorting the linens. It seemed to me the four giant washers could hold more than a week's worth of my family's laundry and we were an active family of seven.

Because it was in a forest, the laundry's interior stayed dim even though it had seven windows. To let out the heat, the glass and screens had been removed and the tree-filtered daylight made only a tentative entrance. Sunlight had no choice; it had to trickle in.

My job was to fold sheets, tablecloths, and hundreds of napkins. Those linens were bleached the brightest white I'd ever seen and the giant tablecloths were heavy, probably due to their high thread count and starch. The napkins were so stiff they'd stand on their own with just a couple folds.

My mind drifted sometimes as I worked. I'd ponder what famous people dabbed their mouths or spilled their fancy drinks on them. I wondered about the tales the napkins could tell about movie stars, politicians, or just plain, rich Jewish people chatting, laughing, and telling stories like we girls did in the car. I wondered what the people up on the hill were like.

To me the linen stains represented stories: the pink circle from a pretentious beverage sipped by a woman dripping with jewelry, a brown splotch from a dropped piece of steak after a hearty laugh, and shiny yellows from melted butter on lobster. But they stood zero chance of surviving at the laundry because their destiny was extinction via a super-hot, soapy wash and bleach.

Two mangler machines sat off along the wall like tethered military K-9's. The six-foot-long steam presses had sets of rollers on the top and bottom and looked industrial grade. They would have to be. When wet linens were fed through the machines, all remnants of fine dining and frivolity got squeezed and scorched out. What emerged was spotless, white, stiff, and sterile. The mangles were uncompromising but necessary for the exorcism and they scared me so I gave them a wide berth. Because I was too young and also too frightened, Cheryl and

Darlene fed the machines wet linens from the washers. The giant steam rollers pulled the linens through and sent them out the other end hot, flat, and pressed dry. The building's average temperature was over one-hundred, sticky, deep-jungle degrees. It was probably the smell of bleach that kept the mosquitoes out.

One of my jobs was to partner with Cheryl or Darlene and do what felt like a linen-waltz of sorts: grip the long ends of a pressed sheet or tablecloth, pull and stretch it tight, marry our two corners, step forward, match the ends, glide backwards, stretch, repeat. It didn't take long for my arms to ache handling the hot, heavy cloth. Once folded, we stacked them on a table and tied them into bundles with two strips of twine. Later in the day they were sent up to the fancy big place.

I liked the physicality of the work. I liked sweating, using my muscles, and seeing the finished product. I wondered if the city people up the hill appreciated the care we put into our work. I know I did.

Cheryl said the guy who worked with us was Cuban, from New York City. His main jobs were to unload the dirty laundry from the trucks and put it into the washers. I was happy that we didn't have to handle the soiled stuff. The man had dark skin and wore tight jeans and a white t-shirt. There was something about the way he combed his black hair, slicked-back and gelled, that scared me a little. A few times, when I happened to be close enough, I stared at his tattoos, pocked face, and scarred arms glistening with sweat. Unnerved and confused, I tried to figure out what kind of person he was. I was accustomed to our pasty-white farmer guys.

Darlene and Cheryl mostly stayed clear of the man, communicating with him only when necessary. From what I could hear over the loud, dull sounds of the machines and fans, his English was sparse and choppy. I followed suit and stayed clear, too.

I'm not sure if he was harmless or not. But when he stopped stuffing dirty linens into the mouths of the washers, sometimes he'd look over at us and make a lip-smacking sound. I think he enjoyed unnerving me with a little stare or a sly smile. I pretended not to notice but what he was doing didn't feel very nice.

At the end of the day my arms ached, my feet hurt, and I was soaked with sweat. I finished the summer without complaining. It was a stable job, and I worked with some friendly, generous women. It was satisfying hands-on work and I made my own money. My parents didn't seem to notice my accomplishments but that was okay because I did and so did Cheryl and Darlene.

I was a confident young teen, but of course naïve. Looking back, I realize how Darlene and Cheryl's acceptance and guidance boosted my self-confidence. They never complained and that quality showed me how to claim my space, take pride in my work, and do my best even in a difficult work environment.

In late fall of that same summer, when the resort was closed for the season, my dad let me tag along when he went to check on some work he'd done at the inn. I couldn't wait to explore the grounds and sneak a peek into the lives of those rich city people. The thick manicured lawns were a deep green I'd not noticed before and all the buildings glowed with fresh white paint and looked perfect. When I peeked through the windows of the locked buildings, though, my heart sank. The place seemed dead inside: abandoned and lonely. I knew I was an outsider, but I would have liked it better if the wealthy people were still there, bringing life to the place.

As I sit typing this chapter, I look outside and think about the variety of people I've met and befriended over the years. Folks from here and, as we Mainers say, "from away." A picture comes to mind and on its canvas, humanity is a dynamic and colorful mixture, an amalgamation of races and cultures.

I recall how scientific phenomena have helped me understand the world, my life, and myself. When I remember the image of sunlight pouring into the laundry, I think about how the laws of physics play into essentially everything. Energy fuels nature making it dynamic: mixing, combining, and at times creating something entirely new. And here I sit trying to make sense of myself and how I fit in and what choices to make but that sunlight never hesitated. It just burst through the open laundry windows and lit up the insides. Once again, I remind myself that we're all just periodically lost humans trying to fit into our own scrambled dreams.

# 35: Lots of Wisdom for Two Cigarettes

## This is more than listening, this feels like real caring

After all the food I've eaten, I need a nap. When I wake, I poke my head out of the tent and the whole encampment looks different as most of the campers have left. And now, with Leo, Deborah, and her husband gone, Gerald is alone so it might be a good time for me to visit. I have the perfect lookout spot from my chair and, in between glances at my book, I keep watch on his site. For about twenty minutes it looks empty then Doug sits up and stares at the tepee. Two seconds later, seemingly from out of nowhere, Gerald appears. Now is a good time.

My slow amble across the grounds allows me time to settle my nerves and plan what I'll say. Wearing the same long-sleeve shirt and dusty jeans, he looks at peace parked in his chair in the shade of a blue tarp. Doug and I walk past the tepee and enter the medicine man's campsite. The ground is bare from all the people traffic.

When I ask if we can talk, he nods yes. I give him the two cigarettes then pull up a camp chair and sit down in front of him. Doug stretches out on the ground beside me. With the magnificent tepee only yards at my back, my mind wanders. *What's inside his tepee? Where's all his gear? Where does he eat and what does he sleep on?* Then I catch myself. *Regina, do you need to know this? Is this why you're here?*

When I start to talk, he looks to the far eastern end of the Butte and it seems he goes there. I tell him about the ski poles in the snowbank and my revelation when I walked into the tepee in South Dakota. I turn to look at his great white structure and am surprised when a child-like whine slips from my lips. *How the heck did I get here?* Then I begin. "I think one of the reasons I'm here is because I met a person who was my partner in some past lives and I think I'm trying to reconcile that. I have a very heavy heart because I lost her in all those lifetimes." His expression stays neutral as he listens. His generous gaze encourages me to say more. In retrospect, I realize I volunteered way too many details. I was that confused.

We share a long, but this time, comfortable, pause and, after I collect myself, I stumble on. "Do you believe in multiple lives?"

He gives me a wide smile, nods yes, and then starts. "I spent eight years overseas inside an army tank. I missed my family and cooped up inside that tank was horrible." Then after more lengthy accounts about his years in the military, he begins to talk about Mother Earth. He says to watch for birds dying for no apparent reason, to be vigilant in 1999, and to look for major planetary changes. *Why is he telling me all this? What does it have to do with me? Am I missing something?*

When he's done, there's another long pause and I assume it's my turn again. I start to talk about how I think our world needs healing and that humans can help mend it's imbalances. "As we move back and forth over the continent, we can be like needles stitching its vital web back together." For some surprising reason, I tell him I think that Wounded Knee could be the focal point for our planet's healing process. "It was there that a way of life, which included an intimate relationship with the planet, was lost." Much later I appreciate how kind he was, listening to me spout on about Wounded Knee and Earth healing, things he was far more intimately aware of than me.

He smiles then starts talking about his life in the military again. I'm intent on listening to him, but I'm confused. *How does this relate to me?*

Gerald is a bit of a mystery. *Did I expect him to judge me or question my integrity?* His chair looks like it's propping up his bent body and he smokes one cigarette after another. My heart hurts when I wonder how many more years he might have.

The confident delivery of his stories, his openness, and his patience say a lot about the man. Even though the words aren't what I expected from a medicine man, I'm sure he's a treasure to his people. Years later I found him mentioned in some books about noteworthy American Indian teachers. He's cited as an honorable tribal member, noted for his generosity and wisdom.

Slowly I began to understand. His tale was about missing our family as we follow our path and fight for positive change. I'd expected answers to my questions: facts and concrete directives. But, as I would learn, Indigenous elders use storytelling to help us understand our unique lives.

When my rambling is over and he's done, I ask if I can hike a trail on the sacred side of the mountain. It's where folks do their quests. He gives me another casual okay and points to a trail. I thank him then remind him I will help out if he needs me. Over the next day, I wait for him to signal me for help but he doesn't so I stay away. I find out afterwards I was expected to check in on him a few times that day. *I'm embarrassed, again.*

After our visit and before Doug and I head up the Butte's trail, I say a prayer. "Creator, please release from my body troubling memories and inclinations that do not serve my highest good." As usual the day is perfect and I look forward to exploring again. A few hundred feet up the barren dusty trail, I let Doug off his leash and he runs up the side of the mountain.

Every fifty feet or so, I have to stop because I feel like I've been gut-punched. But because of the healing work I've had done, I know what to do. I fan my hands over my head and down the front of my torso to flesh out things like how superior I acted with Leo and how I judged him because of his enthusiasm and white skin. I send it into the ground. Also, I release my fear of abandonment. I know I need to pray out loud so my body can hear my words. "Spirit, please help these unpleasant bits of me flow into the ground to be recycled." I have a sense of thin clouds of distortion leaving me and, like a fog, it begins to disintegrate. Then I think about Doug being overly protective of me. It can be excessive but when it comes to me protecting my children, I can relate. I ask for both Doug's and my inappropriate fears to flow into the ground.

Right when I finish, Doug circles back to join me. We hike over steep gravelly stretches of trail that test my endurance. With no trees to shade me from the strong sun, I start to bake. Ha, thank you, sun, for incinerating the junk I've released.

Near the summit I see a matted-down area used during a vision quest. It's a spot about five feet in diameter and sits off on the prairie side of the trail. It's lined with a few jagged rock outcroppings and some scraggly bushes. The woody plants are adorned with prayer bundles, tiny cotton cloths filled with tobacco. Tied to the branches are small swatches of red, blue, and yellow. These prayer flags flap in the warm breeze casting perpetual prayers into the air. *I hope that these pretty gestures comfort the poor souls stuck here for four days with no shelter, food, or water. Yikes!*

When I walk near the quest sites, I half expect to feel something but I don't. Then it dawns on me; this hike is for me. The mountain listened to my request, how I wanted to purge my body. So facing the mountain, I close my eyes, and imagine slipping deep into my center and say, "Thank you, mountain, for this beautiful hike." I hear the words flow out of me, and I know they are heard. This is more than listening; this feels like real caring.

Setting off again, I walk up the trail for about twenty minutes then feel like I'm done so I turn and head down. Once we're back at camp,

I settle Doug under his tree then crawl into my tent. My body needs a rest after my visit with Gerald and the mountain.

Late in the afternoon, I sit and snack on my usual: yogurt, corn chips, and fruit. I scan the beautiful encampment and, suddenly, realize how much lighter I feel. I truly must have left some emotional baggage on the mountain.

Early evening at the settlement brings a new wave of people. Tents get pitched, campfires built, and waves of kids flood the area with laughter. A much livelier bunch of campers has replaced the more tranquil ones. I'm glad to have had time with my more reserved neighbors.

While it's still light out and I'm in my tent reading, I peek out and see a man and a woman approaching. I watch as they set up their campsite about twenty feet from me, send their kids off to play, then crawl into their little tent. At first the loud giggles and chatter during their rambunctious lovemaking embarrass me, then I just smile. *I might have left some uptight bits of myself on the mountain.*

I've thought a lot about Gerald's stories. He had his tank experience, cooped up inside and missing his loved ones. Maybe my "tank" is my body and I've felt locked up inside, mourning for the more loving family I missed out on as a child as well as those now lost to me. Gerald did his time and left his confinement behind. Once reunited with his people, he found his calling. Maybe during my trip, unbeknownst to me, I was searching for ways to escape the confinements of my body where sad memories lingered. Maybe my true calling was ahead of me

# 36: Sage Bundles and Kindness

## A fledgling taken under the wing of its mother

On my last morning at the Butte, I want to stretch out the time I have left so before breakfast Doug and I go for a hike. The trail we take is between the large peak I climbed my first day and the smaller sacred peak I explored yesterday. Even though I've been here only two days, I'm feeling sentimental about the place.

With each step on the trail I give gratitude to this amazing land. I'm reminded of the awe I felt years ago when strolling through the majestic cathedrals in Montreal. Places of worship like that inspire me to look up with wonder as I do now.

On the trail near the summit, I find five turkey feathers, still clumped together with skin. *Hmmm, my four friends and me?* Turkey reminds us to connect with the spirit of the land and it reminds us of the importance of community. Minutes later, Doug scares up a large doe, probably the same one I saw on my first day. Deer is gentle and innocent and sees beyond people's exteriors. She sees their hearts. It hurts that my friends didn't come, but I remind myself to forgive them.

I feel grateful for the warmth and generosity of these people who welcomed me, shared their stories and songs, and challenged my inflated ego. Then, the Butte's nurturing floats me the rest of the way to the top where I once again look out over the seemingly endless plains. Like a fledgling taken under the wing of its mother, I feel cared for. This is goodbye and tears slide down my face.

To savor every last minute, my pace back down the trail is slow as is my leisurely breakfast. After that I dismantle my tent and pack up my things. I accept that this chapter of my trip is done and it helps that the encampment's energy has shifted and the semblance of community has faded. But that might just be me.

Compared to two days ago, I feel different, more confident, and energized. I know it's time to leave, but I'm still a little blue.

On my last trip moving gear to the car, I notice, again, the plethora of wild sage growing along the perimeter of the parking lot. I start to liberate a generous bunch which is used traditionally to bless a space, an article, or a person's energy field. After a small bundle of dried sage is lit on fire, it's then blown down to smoky embers and the smoke is waved over the person or article to be blessed. It's called smudging and reminds me of the smoke used in some Catholic ceremonies. I gather up a nice big bunch to take home. *Lucky me. What a find.*

After a couple minutes I look up and from the far end of the lot, a lovely Indigenous American woman approaches with her hand stretched out to shake mine. "Hello, I'm Lydia." *Wow, that's the name of my Indigenous ancestor.* She keeps eyeing my bundle of plants.

"Hi, Lydia, I'm Regina. Boy, I can't believe all the wild sage here."

She breaks into a heartfelt smile and says, "So that's what you were harvesting?"

"Yes," I say with pride.

Still grinning she says, "What you have there are weeds. Here take this batch of sage, it's very powerful because it came from the Cheyenne side of the mountain." She hands me a bundle of scrawny plants that look an awful lot like mine, but not quite. I want to crawl into a hole. But she's another kind person so the two of us giggle and I accept her bundle of the real stuff. *What a nut job you are, Regina.* We exchange names and addresses thinking we might stay in touch.

As I'm about to step into my car, an Indigenous man appears from the Cheyenne side of the lot. He's about my age, well-built, and very handsome. Red and yellow leather strips are woven into his long, thick braids and he exudes calm geniality, so right away I'm taken with him. He approaches, says hello, and then nods at my bundle of sage and comments on how powerful it is. I keep the account of how I got it to myself.

He asks, "So tell me about your travels."

"Oh, I'm rambling around the prairie, the Black Hills, and camping. It's my first time out here."

Not long into our visit he says, "I'm a Cheyenne traditional dancer at powwows. I'm from Lone Deer, Montana and attend college with a major focusing on counseling for the Sioux." *That sounds awfully interesting.*

I want to talk to him more and regret not having met him earlier. At the end of our conversation he mentions the large powwow held in

Connecticut every year. He says it's advertised as the world's largest. I definitely plan to look into it when I get home.

After we say our goodbyes, I leave for my long drive to Rapid City and the powwow. I take it slow because I'm tired, sunburned, dirty, and so saturated with memories I feel a little overwhelmed and unsteady. But, mostly I'm sad to leave this beautiful place with its sacred and historic past. I'll never forget the kind folks who welcomed me like family.

# 37: Her Win-win Situation

## It's like it's a whole new day

On a fall day in the early '90s, my coworker and friend, Gloria, and I headed to our first powwow. I'd met Gloria in a staff meeting at the school where we both taught. She was intelligent and, in her tailored outfits, she had the air of an administrator. I marveled at how she made her short, bleached-blonde hair work even with her round face and stocky body. To me, having that hair made her a bit of a maverick. But that was Gloria and she was in charge of her well-organized world. For a long time I was a little uncomfortable around her. She seemed a little too direct and confident, for a woman that is.

After a couple of years at the school, though, we became friends. It was when there was a big mystery in the town where she lived with her husband and teenage daughter. It was in the papers. Some giant animal bones were uncovered in a secluded area. The papers said they might belong to an Ice Age beast and for fear of vandalism, its location was kept secret.

Out of the blue, Gloria invited me to visit her at home. We hardly knew each other so her invitation surprised me but soon after I arrived I understood. The mystery bones were buried on her property and, since I was a biology teacher, she thought I'd be interested in seeing them.

During my short but pleasant visit, I began to see another side of Gloria: the thoughtful person and loving parent. I guessed that, like me, she donned some sort of emotional armament for school, making herself businesslike in order to get the most out of her students. Because I could relate, very slowly, I began to look past Gloria's tough exterior and appreciate her softer nature.

Gloria and I met often in town for lunch. I enjoyed our

conversations especially because we were comfortable sharing personal aspects of our lives. One day, after we finished talking about school, marriage, and kids, Gloria said something that surprised me. She told me that for fifteen years, she and her husband had been sleeping in separate rooms. As she spoke, her bright blue eyes got misty and I guessed she was hearing herself for the first time. And just like that she announced it was time to get a divorce. I didn't know what to say, if anything. Stunned, I felt like I was hearing a confession I shouldn't be privy to.

We talked at length about her marriage, and, being divorced myself, I saw some similarities between her situation and what had been mine.

After more talk, I asked her if she thought she'd marry again. Her answer was a crisp no. She said her husband was an excellent provider and a good father but there had never been much in the romance department. After she said that, she looked out the restaurant window.

I joked, "There's probably a handsome, rich guy out there waiting for you."

It was like she hadn't heard me when she faced me and said, "You know when I was a teenager I was once attracted to my teacher, a nun."

I was pretty comfortable being out at my school and felt the staff accepted my lifestyle. I looked at Gloria and hoped her statement about her crush had nothing to do with me. Often times in lesbian friendships there's a fine line that is crossed into a crush. I didn't want that to happen with us. But she looked past me, and then looked out her window again, so I relaxed.

Then she turned to me and said, "That's it. I'm going to get a divorce, get my own place, retire, and delve into my brand-new life." I had no idea how long she'd been thinking this and I didn't ask. With her enthusiasm, I doubted it had been long. It was so typical for my charge-ahead friend.

I didn't know what to say. It was like I had just witnessed a complete transformation on the other side of the table. Now, Gloria's face was softer and glowing more than I'd ever seen it.

Before climbing back into my car, she stood by the door, looked over at me then up to the sky, and said, "It's like it's a whole new day." And I knew, for her, it was.

Gloria being Gloria, she charged ahead and within a month moved into a beautiful new condo, found a wonderful group of gay women to befriend, and gave the school her retirement notice. She got her divorce in record time all while remaining a devoted mother to her teenage daughter.

Gloria called me her sponsor because I helped her become acclimated to the lesbian community. She was ecstatic with her new life and I did my best to acquaint her with gay culture and comforted her when she experienced her first broken heart. We remained good friends and supported each other.

A year or so into our friendship, we discovered we shared an interest in American Indian cultures. When I saw an ad for a powwow at a town close by, we decided to make a day of it and go. It was the first powwow for each of us.

Like chatty teenagers, Gloria and I made our way over one curvy back road after another till we found a handmade, cardboard sign on the side of the road. "Powwow Parking This Way" pointed to a farmer's field.

We climbed out of the car to the murmur of distant drumming then shared two childlike smiles. The morning sun warmed the delightful fall air as we hiked across the farm pasture towards the crowds. The day was electric.

After paying the entrance fee we walked down the midway lined with a dozen vendor booths made of poles, blankets, and blue tarps. The merchandise was mostly handmade and local with some imports: animal pelts, claws, and tooth jewelry, and exquisitely carved, wooden walking sticks.

In the distance we heard the melodic laments of Native American singing. We turned to look at each other and smiled again.

Then a couple minutes later, the crowd stilled and in synch turned to face the far end of the midway where a horse and male rider were headed in our direction. With a confident, calm pace, the horse ambled forward and I noticed how softly each hoof touched the ground. I'd never seen a horse with such a temperate gait. Everyone was quiet, staring at what seemed an illusion.

The horse was a beautiful Appaloosa with a dappled, charcoal-colored coat. The young Indigenous rider was bareback and had a single leather rein loosely tied to the horse's bottom lip. He wore beaded moccasins and buckskin-fringed leggings. On the side of his long, flowing, black hair was a single red-tailed hawk feather pointed downward.

Gloria and I couldn't look away. The handsome, charismatic horse and rider left us speechless.

Magnetized by their verve, I stood transfixed.

The pair disappeared down the other end of the midway and we followed towards the drumming. Ahead, at a large fenced-in area, a small group of people sat under a blue tarp. They were beating a large drum and singing.

A couple dozen men and women, dressed in leather leggings and dresses, stood scattered with spectators outside the ring. When I stepped closer to the drumming, chills tickled my neck and my feet felt cemented in the ground. *This is where my body wants to be.*

Because it was intertribal, anyone, even nonnatives could dance and a few did. No more than eight people danced at one time but the celebration was a lovely mix of different ages and traditions.

The MC reminded us that each dance was a prayer to Earth, her people, and Creator. And even though the day had grown a lot warmer, the dancers stayed animated and enthusiastic. They seemed "in the zone," and trance-like. The display relaxed me in a way I hadn't felt in years.

The sense of renewal I felt that day was difficult to process. Gloria said she felt something wonderful too and on the way home we tried to find words for the experience but after a few miles we just sat basking inside our memories.

Leaving the powwow and returning to my regular world gave me the contrast I needed. I knew what it felt like to be fed by the energy of a powwow. And I knew how wonderful it felt to be more engaged in my body.

Then, without warning and less than a year into her retirement, Gloria was diagnosed with cancer. The prognosis was poor. We were all shocked and frightened. Gloria acted like it was just another challenge to work through.

I offered to practice my developing healing gifts on her and went to her condo a number of times eager to flex my talents. With Gloria stretched out on her couch, I was excited to help "heal" her. But, she would look up at me and ask, "Can you turn on some Indian flute music and talk me through a nice meditation please?" So we did just that and she said she felt better even though my ego felt like I could've done so much more. Years later I understood. The most important thing I could give my friend was the sound of some kind, spirit-formed words and my caring heart.

Gloria needed a liver transplant so another woman and I organized a huge fundraiser and, together with dozens of others from the community, in just seven weeks we raised over one-hundred-thousand dollars for cancer research. We put on a big event to find a transplant donor. We knew the chances of finding a match for Gloria were minuscule but it felt good that we could do something.

Gloria had a round of chemotherapy before her first transplant but it didn't take so a second transplant was scheduled. The day before she was to go back to Boston we had lunch at her condo. After we finished eating, she stood in the middle of her kitchen, as bald as a bowling ball, and looked at me with a giggle and as spunky as ever she said, "You know, Regina, this is a win-win situation for me."

"What the heck are you talking about, Gloria?"

"If I live I can enjoy my wonderful daughter and family and friends and I'm grateful for that. But if I die, I'm okay with that too because I've had a good life and I know God has a place for me."

I was shocked and stared at her waiting for clarification but there was none. Gloria had spoken, as she so often did, to the point, period. I realize her spiritual faith and authentic lifestyle were perfect examples of the principles I aspired to live by.

My dear friend was only fifty-six when she learned she might not survive. For her funeral, she asked me to make a tape of American Indian flute music to be piped into the church. She also asked me to play my Djembe, an African style drum, along with the tape. Not a great drummer by any means, I was very uncomfortable about doing it but I knew I had to promise my friend.

Gloria died at peace surrounded by her brother and daughter.

On the day of the funeral I was a ball of nerves. I wondered what the large crowd would think of Indigenous music booming out of the speakers in a conservative Christian church.

But it worked out well, this final goodbye to my rainbow-warrior, sister, and friend. The minister, an older fellow, came up to me after and said it was the most moving service he had ever officiated.

After the funeral, I was so emotionally exhausted, I could barely stand so I decided to skip the grave-side service. When I flopped into bed and pulled the blanket up to my chest, I heard as clearly as if Gloria was at my ear, "Thank you." And that was enough.

# 38: Stupid Civilization

## How do I hold onto the peace?

The Tepee Campground is just outside Rapid City and easy to find. I get a tiny site amidst a few other tents and dozens of large campers and fifth wheels. The place is so crowded it feels like the sites overlap each other. I have returned to civilization with low expectations but, it's clean, has showers, and is well maintained. It's not Bear Butte, though.

After I set up my tent and situate my gear, I settle Doug in with water and his blanket. I eat a light lunch then crawl into my tent and in no time I drift off. An hour later I wake when something pushes down hard on my right forearm. *What the heck?* I roll over and go back to sleep. After another hour or so the same thing happens, but, to my left forearm. I'm alert enough to wonder what it is but sluggish enough to slip back to sleep. Over the years I've gotten used to things like this but they usually happen when I'm meditating or working with a healer.

The first time it happened I was with Myra and her sparkly wands. I was lying on her table when she asked me about angels. At first, I was stumped because I thought she was asking about biblical angels. When I asked her to clarify she said, "'Angels' refers to the loving celestial beings who care for you. Some are called spirit guides or entities of that kind. To me, the word 'angel' is a generic term."

I told her I hadn't thought about my angels since I was a kid. Myra said, "It doesn't matter. We all have a family of angels who support and guide us. Even if we don't believe in them, they're always there." I liked what she said so I imagined, right then, that it was true, I had my own family of angels. I especially liked the idea of family.

Myra continued with my session and, as I relaxed on my back with my eyes closed, she gently held each of my ankles in her hands. She said a prayer out loud asking for the energetic circuitry in my legs to become healthier. I felt something like a subtle electrical current move down my legs.

After a few minutes, the energy flow slowed then disappeared. I loved the reassuring feeling of my feet being held. The room was so quiet and peaceful, I could have stayed on her table a lot longer. When I opened my eyes, Myra was standing, gently holding my head in her hands. I closed my eyes. She said, "Ask your angels to come in and hold your ankles like I did. You can just think it. They will hear you."

I wasn't sure about it but I trusted her so in my mind I asked, *Please, angels, come hold my ankles and help my legs heal.* Even though Myra was at my head, I felt someone holding my ankles. Then, the faintest of prickly sensations moved down my legs.

Since then, I've experienced similar anomalies and met other folks who have, so I began to believe I was becoming more in tune with my body and, in addition, more aware of my spiritual family.

After my restorative nap in the tent, I'm eager to get on with my day. I gather up some clean clothes, bathing basics, and head off to take a shower at the campground facility. It's been a few days so when the hard-driving water pounds and soothes my tired body, it's intoxicating. For an extra few minutes, I shampoo my hair massaging out all the sweat, dirt, and tension in my scalp. I dry off, slip into crisp, fresh-smelling clothes, then look into the cracked mirror to comb out my medium-length hair. As is my norm, I'll let it dry naturally. I survey my reflection and like what I see: nice tan, bright brown eyes, and a pleasant smile.

By mid-afternoon, I'm back on the road, heading to downtown Rapid City. I see a sign for the Pioneer Museum, miss a turn, and, instead, end up at a Sioux Museum. *Providence?* The little building has some impressive prehistoric and historic collections of the Lakota people. I cruise the place reading labels and digesting the information. But, I'm tired of hurting from all these reminders of how the onslaught of pioneers devastated these Indigenous lives so, after I abbreviate my visit, I get back in the car and head to the powwow at the Civic Center.

On the way, I find a spacious city park and take Doug out for a long walk. The sirens, litter, hurried people, and chaotic atmosphere unnerve me. My transition from Bear Butte back to our contemporary world feels like a gut punch and for a second I think about hiding in my car. *How do I hold on to the peace I felt at the Butte?* I have a few hours to figure it out, the powwow starts at seven.

# 39: Captured by Drum Beats

## That's what happens when we dance, dream, and create

The Rapid City Powwow begins in two hours and even though I'm not very hungry, I want a real meal for a change. So after walking Doug, I cruise the city outskirts for a place to eat. I find a Mexican restaurant and begin fantasizing about a mouthwatering variation of my bland beans and rice. After parking the car, I give Doug his supper, then he jumps back inside and curls up. It's time to give myself a quick once-over, so I tilt the rearview mirror and stare: teeth, check; hair, check; and, thanks to Leo's influence, my red bandana sweatband, check. I'm ready to make my entrance.

A wave of cold air slams me when I open the restaurant door. Bright red tabletops and booths with glassy metal edges and legs dominate the room but the perky Mexican music livens up the place a little. I see the "Seat Yourself" sign then slide into a cherry-colored vinyl booth tucked into a quiet corner.

To start, I order a large Pepsi, then peruse the menu like a famished kid at McDonald's. Compared to what I've been eating, the menu reads like a five-star restaurant. When my two chicken burritos arrive along with a mound of corn chips, salsa, and a side of Mexican rice, I dive in. The second round is two flawlessly wrapped tortillas stuffed with delicately spiced refried beans topped with melted cheese and hot sauce. *I am in heaven. Of course, there's room for dessert.* I admire the whipped cream, nuts, and cherry on my hot fudge sundae then dig in. I think I've covered all the food groups and then some.

It's almost six o'clock when I waddle to the car then drive back into the city. I turn into the Civic Center parking lot and think about where to leave the car. I don't want Doug bothered so I park at the far corner of the lot and away from all the foot traffic closer to the entrance.

When I climb out of the car, the incessant distress calls from one siren after another jar me while the sporadic lighting gives it a spooky feel. *I'm not liking this place, not one bit.* Then the drumbeats from inside the dome remind me why I'm here and I relax.

I walk to the entrance and get quickly folded into the crowd streaming towards the Center's entrance. At first, in my head, I resist because it's like I'm following a pack. *Do I have control issues? I don't know. Probably. Well, yes.* I take a deep breath and move along with the flow amidst the cacophony of chatter and nudging bodies. Staying focused on the mesmerizing drumming, I get ushered through the entrance.

Inside, there must be a hundred vendors and more Indian artwork and crafts than I could imagine being in one place. The merchandise looks high quality too. The crowds feel friendly, the people, most of whom are Native, are chatty and excited. I maneuver through the masses to get to the booths where beaming vendors seem eager to share their knowledge or just visit with customers.

I'm like a kid in a toy store. A large black and white print of an eagle catches my eye. It has outstretched wings and is clutching poles poking out the top of a tepee. *Tepee poles.* It's titled "Eagle Dreams." I buy it, roll it up into a cardboard tube, and walk away with a bit of a swagger. *Maybe it's another good sign?* I hope.

At the end of a long row of booths, I spot a beautiful, familiar-looking painting titled, "Lakota Hills." It's of Bear Butte and though the Butte is a common theme here, I take it as another positive omen.

For a half hour or so I worm my way through the crowds then realize it's almost time for the Grand Entry. The civic center is huge, seats over seven thousand, so I have to wind my way through lots of corridors and up a half dozen flights of stairs to get to the top. I want a bird's-eye view of the Grand Entry and lucky me, when I get there, I have the place to myself.

Just when I'm about to sit down, I hear a nerve-rattling cry over the PA system. In a deep baritone voice, the Master of Ceremony bellows, "ARE YOU READY TO POWWOW?" It's a summons to the scores of drum groups and their singers set up on the perimeter of the arena floor. I'm keyed up and nervous for the start. It's a strange thought but I wonder if this might be the beginning of a new chapter in my trip.

The MC strikes again, "Let the Grand Entry begin!" The raucous rumblings of the fifty-one drums, their exuberant singers, and the shouts of thousands of people in the stands are so loud I cover my ears. I have chills. This is much more than entertainment, this is a spiritual pageant and celebration of indigenous cultures. The thunder of drums fills the stadium, fuels the crowd's excitement, and makes my skin shiver. The throaty sounds of the singers and the pride I see in these handsome people make me admire them even more.

The MC says, "Folks, look at them. Six-hundred-thirty dancers from more than a dozen different tribes lined up eight across and ready to powwow!" Veterans in military hats and carrying the American and POW flags lead. Then men carrying tribal flags and eagle staffs of various Indigenous nations complete the first six rows.

A drum group and singers sound off and dancers begin a slow, waltzing procession into the arena. Like a giant cluster of feathered bees, the dancers swarm onto the floor. Toe-heel, toe-heel, toe-heel, their mini-steps are in time with the slow, methodical drumbeats. The procession holds back, lingers, then proceeds, but just a little. The undulations are intoxicating.

The dancers' poise and restraint confound me, especially the women dancers. Their backs held straight, their bodies perfectly still, only their feet are moving. Unlike the men, they don't use face paint but hold their heads high with neutral expressions. One hand clutches a magnificent fan of eagle feathers, the other rests on a hip as they tiptoe forward. They evoke the spectacular beauty of feminine power. Each step is unremarkable but so very perfect and in unison with the others as the rows of eight sway side to side. Every few minutes a singer lets fly a high-pitched, powerful cry that breaks my hypnotic stare and rocks my bones.

They focus on each step, not on advancing. I imagine I am a dancer. And with each step, I drop further into our beloved planet and receive a blessing. Maybe that's what happens when we dance, dream, and create.

The singers continue their trilling as the dancers keep pouring into the arena. The huge mass rocks in unison, toe-heel, toe-heel to the unwavering drumbeats. War bonnets, headdresses, and staffs decorated with thousands of majestic eagle feathers sway as one.

"Grandfather" drums, some over three feet in diameter, rest on framed bases along the floor's perimeter. Small groups of men beat the drums with leather-headed drumsticks. The country's best singers and drummers are participating for prize money as well as bragging rights. Their songs vary in themes: social, war, and religious.

Traditionally only the men drum and sing. Many years ago, as tribes gathered at powwows, the singers began singing in vocables, wordless songs, so that other tribes could join in. I watch as some singers press their fingers to their throats to reach the high-pitched notes. The tantalizingly wild sounds that come out get under my skin.

Now the sea of feathers begins to look like a giant whale in an underwater ballet. The movements are slow and gliding, simple and universal. All of a sudden, I realize my face is wet with tears. *I can't believe this grandeur.*

The rows of dancers snake their way around the arena's edge in a clockwise direction till a tight spiral is formed at the center. After an hour or so, a coiled, feathered serpent covers the floor. It reminds me of Quetzalcoatl, the feathered serpent in Inca and Mayan mythology, believed by many to be an incarnation of the Christ. *Thank goodness, no one can see me standing here with a wet face and my hand on my heart.*

Once the Grand Entry is complete the MC says the opening invocation. "Please Creator, gift all nations with peace and all humans with generous hearts." He begins introducing the drum groups and singers as the dancers disperse to prepare for the dance competitions.

I watch a few dance competitions then move down closer to the drums and singers. When I get there I can't help it, the drums and singing have seduced me so next thing I know I'm standing with a group of Indigenous men near a grandfather drum. The drumming and singing are at a fever pitch and not only am I the only woman here, but I am also the only white person. For a second I feel conspicuous, then I shrug it off because the men don't seem to notice me. Maybe they're ignoring me. I don't care. I learned later the drumming areas are usually off-limits to women and white folks. And, there I stood looking like a typical tourist. I never should have intruded like that.

After a couple more songs and dances, I leave the group to find a nearby seat where spectators are supposed to sit. Relaxed, I'm ready to take in more of this magic. I especially like the war dances, performed by men with traditional leather apparel and athletic physiques. They show off their skills by using hand-held weapons and imitating prey animals. The garish colors and artificial adornments of the men's grass-dancers and the women's jingle-dancers seem out of place. The tiny tots, though, are delightful and perform with such near-perfect rhythm I'm convinced of genetic memory. The "ancients," or elders, dance too. I'm sitting near a dozen old people dressed in what looks like traditional regalia. This is truly a community event.

My favorites of the evening are the Grandmother's dance and also the Elder Men's dance. They're probably in their 80s or 90s. They keep their eyes forward with heads held high and proudly as they move in slow-motion wide circles. Their composure and pride seem to make the crowd noise soften. It's a powerful reminder of wisdom garnered from their many years.

And just when I'm getting tired and ready to leave, the strangest part of the evening happens.

Not far from my seat, on the floor, a coyote dancer catches my eye. Probably thirty, it's his fluid, muted moves that stand out most. He holds an

143

impressive wooden staff covered with the head and fur of a coyote. Half of his handsome face is painted with three, thin strips of white and black paint. He has deer antlers on his head and a deer hide swinging down the length of his back. His bare chest and legs and his animal movements get to me in a visceral way. Compared to the other more flamboyant dancers, his repertoire covers a tiny area and he's seemingly oblivious to everything else. He's mimicking a coyote: dodgy, wary, and uneasy. *The guy is content in his own reality.* If there is one dancer I'll remember from tonight, it will be him.

I remember reading that in some Indigenous American lore Coyote is known as the trickster. He teaches us about life's mysteries through trickery and humor but his lessons can be disturbing and difficult to understand. He can teach us that things are not always what they appear.

*Why has he mesmerized me?* It's not his understated regalia. I think it's something about his fluid, simple steps and arm movements, and the way he holds himself, confident but not warrior-like. He draws me in and suddenly he's the only one I see. When the dance ends, he's alone on the floor and I am glad to regain my sense of normalcy.

The powwow's still going strong, but after a couple hours I'm tired and ready to get back to Doug and my campsite. I start walking up a ramp leading outside and when I look ahead, there, leaning on his staff near the wall, is the coyote dancer. He looks calm like he's waiting for someone. But he's staring at me. Confused, I pause, look away, then turn around to see who he's looking at. There's no one there. When I glance at him, he stares back. His gaze isn't at all creepy or invasive, it just feels like I've been found. Besides that, I'm not used to this kind of intense attention, especially now having spent weeks incognito, so to speak. The female in me knows the coyote-man is not flirting. *But why is he looking at me?* And there's something about his eyes; they're saying he knows me. *But why? How is that possible?*

As I walk closer, he keeps staring then, when I get closer still, he says, "Hello." But, it's not a nice-to-meet-you hello, it's a nice-to-see-you-again hello. *And the tender energy that he exudes feels out of place in this huge dome filled with thousands of chanting voices and crazy-loud drums.* I slow down and force out a sheepish, "Hello." For some weird reason I sense he knows me and that unnerves me because I don't recognize him. Once I glide past him, I'm relieved to make my escape to the outside. *How could he know me? It's not possible, right?*

My mind's spinning as I walk back to the car. *Who was that person in coyote skins? Maybe he was an angel like Myra suggested, but not the stereotypical winged-kind, more like a spirit guide. I hope he was.* If he was, I wonder what his message is. Knowing what I know about coyote medicine, I'm probably in for a wild ride ahead.

# 40: Such a Suffocating Town

## I must be in a foreign country

It's late evening when I leave the powwow and drive back to the campground. When I see my tent, I let out a tired sigh. I can't wait to be done with this day. It's been a good one, though, with my last hike up Bear Butte, the Sioux Museum, the Powwow, and of course the curious coyote dancer. I'm on sensory overload and still full from my Mexican meal when I feed and walk Doug then settle him in the car. Now it's my turn to chill but I'm so wasted I can't even think about the Powwow. Surrounded by sudden spurts of laughter and car doors slamming, I ask my mind to quiet and, thank goodness, sleep comes quickly.

Near dawn I'm awakened. *Is that seals barking?* Too spent to care about more weirdness, I fall back to sleep.

It's mid-morning when I step out of my tent and into another gorgeous day. Remembering his long wait in the car last night, I feed Doug first then take him for an extra-long walk through the city of campers. The bustling park with its disjointed human noises makes me wilt, so I think about the Powwow. I wonder what Coyote has in store for me. I remember reading he'll stop you in your tracks and make you examine your life. *Hmmm.* I'm tempted to linger in memories of him but I know it's time to get going.

My range coffee and yogurt breakfast shift me back into my explorer mindset and, with no destination in mind, I check the map for my options. The Badlands National Park with its lunar landscape looks interesting and is only forty miles away, so I plan my route. Once I finish breakfast, I pack up the car then set out for the Sage Creek Campground located in the middle of the Badlands. It makes sense to tent there tonight and I'm excited about seeing the area's unique geological features. But then again, with its sparse vegetation, it'll probably be boring. I could use some boring for a change.

A mile away from the Rapid City campground I pass a giant aquarium. *Aha, the seals I heard last night.* Seal reminds us to pay attention to our imagination because even our craziest thoughts have an important place in our reality. *More craziness on the horizon? Great.*

According to the map, a secondary route will take me out of the city and then a remote, rural road leads to the town of Scenic near the Badlands. Once I'm beyond the city's hustle-bustle, my shoulders relax.

Thirty miles later the road takes me into hundreds of acres of dried-up grasslands. *No wonder no one's living here.* I stop to check and locate Scenic, a speck of a dot, on the map. A few miles further, I snap back in my seat when a red-tailed hawk swoops down so close I can see its eyes staring at me through the windshield. *What's your message hawk? Is something going to happen?*

Road signs have disappeared, so I need to stop and ask for directions to the campground. I drive into Scenic and its main street reminds me of an old cowboy movie set. Severely weathered buildings with western storefronts stand on either side of the dusty road: three on one side and two on the other. At the far end of the street, three banged-up cars are teetering at various angles over the edge of a ditch. There's no traffic of any kind and the hard-packed dirt road is full of potholes and quiet. *Gee whiz, I wonder if it ever rains here.*

Ahead on my right is the Longhorn Saloon. Its giant, weather-worn sign out front has big white letters scrawled on it; "Soft drinks, Cold *Bear*, Indians Allowed, and Dancing."

Next to the saloon is The Longhorn Store. It's a larger building with two big signs. One says: "Lakota Artifacts, Bead Work, and General Merchandise." The other one is five feet long and dangles high over the lengthy porch roof. Its large red letters say: "Ashes to Ashes, Dust to Dust, If we don't have It, It isn't a Must." *What a gloomy place. I must be in a foreign country.*

It appears my car is the only viable vehicle here, so parking is not an issue. I find some shade for Doug then step out onto the wide street. My insides feel strange, hollow, but I keep walking towards the least creepy place, the Longhorn Store. It's real hot and the dry air is still as are the birds if any live here. *This is a real ghost town.* All I need are a few directions. It shouldn't be a big deal.

The long porch stretches the entire front of the store and the four sun-bleached cow skulls, staged haphazardly on its floor, are not a pleasant omen. *Strange. Oh well, I'm on a mission.* I stuff my annoying fears.

My confident but fake smile, helps propel me up the steps and across the porch. I open the door and step into what looks like a giant, old garage ready for a flea market. Dark and dank, it smells of grimy antique wood and car oil. My gut tightens and I want to retreat but I force myself forward stepping into the foot hollows on the wooden floor. I can't imagine the place has had enough customers to wear down the floor like this.

I look down the far end of the store then half-whisper, half call out "Hello?" *Yikes, that sounded a little like a cry for help.*

Silence.

What I see next unnerves me even more. The merchandise and all ten counters are wrapped in some sort of thick, clear plastic. On my right, the longest counter stretches into the gloomy space at the far end of the building. *Nothing can breathe, wrapped up like this.* Suddenly I'm conscious of my own breath. But even with all this, the place feels weirdly hypnotic, like a strange dream you're curious about but at the same time want out of.

I look over the wide interior again. *Eerie there's no one here.* A few steps beyond me I see some feathers on the counter so I walk over. It's a hawk wing and it's wrapped three or four times over in clear plastic. I wonder if it's real. It looks like it. If it is, it's suffocating. I'm not even sure if this place is real. *Is this Coyote's doing?*

Then, from somewhere deeper inside the building come subtle sounds, like metal clanging. I try again, this time a little louder. "Hello?"

With a curious but cautious advance, I walk toward the sounds near the center of the building. I stop then turn to look over a chest-high room divider and see five people sitting at a 1950s kitchen table. They look ready to start a big meal.

An elderly Native American woman and man sit at one end of the table and their scraggly shirts, lined faces, and long, thinning hair fit the weary scene. Sitting on the other end of the table are two middle-aged white people: a plump woman and an obese man both in threadbare clothes. Next to them is a skinny, old, white lady in a faded house dress. The poor thing is curled up, almost sideways, in her wheelchair. The people don't seem right, or even human, certainly not like any humans I know. The scene disturbs me a lot. Maybe it has something to do with the cellophane, the skulls, the storefront, or just how lonely and lifeless the place feels. Maybe it's all of this.

The chubby white woman stays focused on her plate then starts to feed the woman in the wheelchair. Without looking up she says, "Can I help you?"

"Sorry to interrupt your lunch." I pause and look at her then at each of the others but there's no response or indication anyone heard me or even knows I'm here on the other side of the divider. They just keep looking at the massive meal covering most of the table. It looks like fried chicken and four giant platters of nondescript mashed food. *This is nothing like lunch at Bear Butte.*

I wait a minute but, still, no one looks up or acknowledges me. They're busy now passing the platters of food and helping the old lady eat.

Then I remember why I'm in here. "I was wondering if you could give me directions to the Sage Creek Campground."

And like she knew what I wanted all along, without looking up, the white woman says, "Take a left off the main street, follow that road. It's about ten miles further into the Badlands."

I look over at the obese man sitting next to her. He's chalky-white and the raised red blotches around his mouth and ears and under his chin look like some sort of creeping crud. His head's down and with a mouth full of food he says, "Yup, you'll wake up with buffalo next to your tent." Deadpan, no smile, it sounds like a cold warning. Confused and anxious to leave, I thank them, turn, and head to the door.

As I step off the porch and walk to the car, a weird thought enters my head. Although those folks were freaky, I'm amazed at the wonderful diversity in humans and for some reason I break into a grin. I remember how I judged Leo and Deborah, thinking them inferior to me. *How am I supposed to feel about them, the coyote dancer, and now the weird people inside the store?* It's all so confusing. I'm thinking Coyote's messing with me, making me question how I label people when I have no idea who they are. *Oh well. Live and let live, or something like that. I guess it couldn't hurt to be more accepting.* I remind myself that Coyote says to treasure life's richness and complexity. But, actually experiencing the doctrines can be disturbing. When our world gets topsy-turvy, Coyote prods us to be resourceful and flexible in order to survive. No big deal, I've had my share of life challenges and I'm still here.

A minute later, the thought of all the merchandise wrapped in cellophane, especially the electronics makes me cringe, big time. I wonder if the gadgets we surround ourselves with limit us in some way. What are we becoming? And with my limiting thoughts about others, what do I know of their interior landscapes and their life stories? Yup, there's probably a lot going on inside everyone.

As I near the car, I look over at the Longhorn Saloon. Two old Indigenous men are sitting on the porch with their chairs tilted back leaning against the wall. The scene looks storybook, exotic and I think about going over to check out the place but don't dare. I think I've seen enough of Scenic.

# 41: "Wicked" Lost

## Have you ever been this alone?

I leave Scenic and drive down the road leading to the Badlands and the campground. If those people in their cling-wrap world, crumbling bodies, and forgotten town were meant to shake me up, they succeeded.

Not far outside of town, I go into a rickety, little store to verify my directions. As I walk back to the car, I spy a billboard outside with notices flapping in the desert breeze. I lean in to read and one flier jumps out. "Healing of the Hoop for all Nations at Wounded Knee, July 24-28." *Wow, Wounded Knee.* I take down the info and plan to call the number later. Maybe I'll check it out on my way back East. I might be ready to go home by then.

I drive down the dusty road leading into the Badlands. I remember the brochure said Sage Creek Campground is on a buffalo reserve, then right on cue, two small buffalo herds appear in the distance. Doug pops up in the rearview mirror all wide-eyed and tense. *Please don't let this be a preview of things to come.* But after a couple of minutes, they're out of sight and he settles down.

With every mile, the terrain gets more and more inhospitable. *Remember, Regina, looks can be deceiving.*

A few miles further I'm surrounded by dozens of small, cone-topped mountains. I remember learning their wide, horizontal bands of pink and gray are rock fragments laid down by erosion thousands of years ago. It is spectacular. Surrounding them are swelling rolls of grasses that, as usual, stretch out to forever. But it's the spectacular peaks that get to me. They look like they belong on an unexplored planet. A layer of gravel and rock particulates covers the bumpy washboard road and makes for slow, aggravating progress. *Scenic, and now this moonscape, where the heck am I?*

The road takes a long, slow sweep to the right and cuts through a cluster of more pastel mountains and I imagine a runaway stagecoach could come flying round the bend. I slow down to take in the strange topography that stretches out in every direction and beyond, to parts I can't make out. Then, in my head, I imagine hearing: *"Have you ever been this alone?"* I have to stop the car and settle myself.

A short time later, I see the campground and it's not soon enough. I drive in and enter a giant cul-de-sac set in the middle of a twenty-acre, flat parcel of gravel. Scattered over the grounds are six metal chairs shaped like half a clamshell. They look like tiny spaceships, dropped and forgotten in this middle of nowhere. There are picnic tables and two outhouses, but no water or electricity hookups. The brochure boasts lots of wildlife roaming close by: buffalo, coyotes, prairie dogs, and big-horn sheep. *Hold the buffalo, but I'd like to see some big-horn sheep.*

When I look in the distance, it seems the buffalo herds are following us. I remember what the man in Scenic said and the brochure confirms it; one of their daily migration trails goes through the center of the campground. In other parts of the grasslands, I saw signs warning, "Stay in your car. Buffalo are dangerous." There are no such signs here. *Interesting...* After I circle the grounds I get out of the car to talk with an older man who's sitting with three children at a picnic table. As he and I chat, the children lean in to listen, and I watch the small approaching herd. The man sees me eyeing the bison and says, "They're young bulls, but don't worry, they're used to people." I nod but when the herd is a hundred yards away my internal alarms go off and I say a hasty goodbye, jump in my car, and leave. Doug is way too interested in these massive beasts and, besides that, their power scares me.

Buffalo teaches us not to push or force our way but to follow our path ahead. Buffalo is a symbol of strength, power, and survival. I'm not interested in testing my survival chances camping here, thank you.

The campground exit takes me onto a paved road that meanders through the rest of the Badlands. As I drive, I wonder why I don't feel connected to the land like before. I think about my times in Arizona and the exhilaration I felt surrounded by the desert's energy. But this dry land feels empty, lacking emotion. I wonder what happened on this land. My fertile imagination takes over. Later, I'll read that Crazy Horse's parents buried him out here in an unmarked grave.

Soon the park road turns back into silty gravel and my car, and the few others I meet, stir up impressive blooms of dust. My sinuses swell and I dread another infection but it's a real conundrum because if I close the windows and turn on the air conditioner, my car will overheat. So I reach into my glove compartment and take out my gauze mask, stored there for times like this, and pop it on. Now I fit right in with this eerie, extraterrestrial scene. I wonder what oncoming drivers think of me?

I start to feel like a real weirdo then it dawns on me that it's not so much about accepting my appearance but creating my own reality. My reality right now: I love my freedom, my adventure, and I don't care how I look.

Up ahead I slow down for a small herd of deer crossing the road. Later I understand how this foreshadows what is about to happen over the next few days. Deer reminds us to honor our innocence and see the good in others.

The park exit leads to a tarred road and I finally get to stash my mask. After I stop to check the map I decide to head to the town of Spearfish. I'll tent near there tonight and in the morning drive to Devils Tower which is just over the Wyoming border. I remember reading that Devils Tower is associated with some Aboriginal lore.

As I approach Spearfish, major road construction and lengthy detours bog me down then I get lost. After backtracking, I am relieved to quickly find the tourist information center. The attendant's a cheerful older woman and such a pleasant contrast to the Scenic folks. I ask her about free campsites and she says the Bear Lodge Camping Area is on the way to Devils Tower and on a secondary road in Wyoming. *Nice, free.* I'll explore Spearfish another time. I look but, the Bear Lodge campsite isn't on my maps. She seemed trustworthy, so I decide to go for it.

Back at the wheel, I can't help but think about how many times I've run across *Bear* recently. There was Bear Butte, a painting of Bear Butte at the powwow, "Cold *Bear*" sign in Scenic, Bear Lodge Campground, and now I'm heading to Devils Tower. The Lakota name for Devils Tower is Mato Tipila and translated means Bear Lodge. All the signs say "GO."

Driving for over an hour through rugged, thick forested terrain, I miss some turns. As the sun sinks behind the trees I start to get nervous. *Is this where I'm supposed to be?* Wyoming feels wild and abandoned as I drive down the empty road. Every few miles or so I pass a modest house and mini rusted signs: Pop. 51, Pop. 23, Pop. 12. I remember driving across the prairie and miss how alive I felt. I think about the coyote dancer, how he seemed completely oblivious to his surroundings, content in his own reality. *I wish I could do the same or maybe change my reality.*

Two more wrong turns on a road with no street lights amplify my anxiety. Then I finally find it. But the Bear Lodge Camping Area is just a small pull-off from the main road. When I drive in, two cars with

151

Georgia license plates drive away. An old woman with long, messy hair in raggedy clothes steps out of her van and four dogs tumble out behind her. The woman and her dinged-up van look like they've been here for a while. *Maybe she lives here.*

I drive into the one spot that's free of trash. I'm tired but determined to overcome my fears so, as I finish setting up my tent, I remind myself to stay strong like Bear, have courage, and if needed, be ferocious.

While unloading my gear I notice a man in a beat-up, stretch sedan with Wyoming plates drive into the camping area. I sense he knows this place. As he coasts past me, he looks out from his open window and gives me a menacing smile. *That's it; I'm out of here!* Devils Tower is forty miles away, it's getting darker by the minute, there are no street lights, and the dog lady and I are the only ones here. I'm thinking that Mr. Smiley-guy probably cruises this place looking for victims.

I'm shaking as I tear down my tent, throw my gear into the car, and head for Devils Tower. I remember reading that it has been a sacred site for many tribes for hundreds of years. One origin story tells that long ago, two children were playing out on the land when a gigantic grizzly charged them. They froze in place and prayed and prayed to Creator for protection. All of a sudden, the old volcanic rock beneath them pushed upward. It grew higher and higher till the children were elevated in the air and out of reach of the grizzly. But the giant grizzly was determined. He kept jumping up to the children, legs and claws stretched upward and onto the sides of the rock. To this day his huge claw marks remain along the sides of the up-thrust. The children were rescued by Eagle and returned to safety.

It's after seven and, surrounded by tall, ragged hills and forests, it'll be dark before I get there. I'll find a place to tent on the way.

My hands are locked on the steering wheel, again, as I drive through one, two, then three dark, tiny towns looking for a place to tent. But there's nothing. Bubbles of fear billow up from my midsection then spread into my chest and neck and my body actually hurts. Aside from times when my kids were acutely ill or my teenagers were MIA, I can't remember feeling so afraid, so desperate. It's difficult but I try like hell to imagine the courage of bear's essence surging through me. *I really, really need you, Bear, and now.* Ahead of me are too many miles of dark, curvy roads and seemingly vacant towns. All I want is a decent place to sleep but there's nothing and at this point, I'm not picky. All I want is to be safe.

# 42: My Darkest Night Ever

## I feel more alone than I ever have

I'm scared this gloomy road will go on forever. Bear's feminine energy reminds us to go within and to be courageous on the long path to healing ourselves. But I'm conflicted, I want Bear's help but I'm afraid because it feels like Bear's stalking me, maybe forcing me to be brave.

Right now, I have all I can do to follow my instincts, continue driving down this road, and hope for refuge. *Are my courage and faith being tested? Coyote are you in on this? I bet you are. Is this some sort of initiation?* In many shamanic traditions, initiations can lead to increased spiritual awareness. They can be real, near-death challenges, or just feel like it.

After traveling what seems like a hundred dreary miles, I feel more alone than I have ever felt in my whole life. And there's no one else to blame: not my mother, my father, my husband, or my lover, who all left. I'm the one who created this scenario and I probably should take a good hard look at it and me.

The sun sets and leaves behind a thin strip of golden glow that outlines the treetops. It looks like hope. The only other light comes from my headlights, dashboard, and a dim, shadowy sky. I've been swallowed up by a mound of brittle dark. I'm in an awful, surreal place. In some traditional cultures, Bear's hibernation reminds us to travel to the Dream Lodge, to the womb where life began and where all answers can be found. This place is as dark as dark can get.

When I drive around the next corner what I see jolts me, hard. Plunked down about a mile ahead is Devils Tower. One-thousand-feet tall and half as wide, its pale granite surface reflects just enough twilight to make it look like a cold, disturbing sculpture. It reminds me of the time

I ran out of a museum because the strange, stone sculptures moved me in such a troubling way. It felt like the memory of an old nightmare was about to surface and I had to escape.

*Was this monolith dropped here by mistake or is it a warning? Whatever the reason, it can't possibly belong here.* And there's something else. This land feels detached, apathetic about life, not welcoming like at the Butte. After I shake off some shivers of fear, I follow the road heading to the tower because there's nowhere else to go. And there's no way in hell I'm going back.

Then, about thirty yards ahead, I spot two wooden buildings set off to the side of the road with a sign, "Fort Devils Tower Campground." My dashboard says 8 p.m. when I pull off to the roadside and slink down in my seat. I lean my head back on my headrest, imagine that it knows what I've just gone through, and that comforts me. I close my eyes and after some deep breaths, bits of confidence trickle in. *Thank you, whoever helped me find this place.*

I drive into the campground's entrance. A small sign says the larger building is part office and part general store and the smaller, adjacent building has toilet and bath facilities. Further inside the grounds, I count eight campsites scrunched together in an area the size of a basketball court. Loopy strings of mini Christmas lights dangle helter-skelter at each site and a tall, wire cattle fence borders three sides of the campground. A wooden fence runs parallel to the road and forms the fourth side. It looks kinda like a big cage.

I'm leery of the place but so exhausted, I'm grateful to be anywhere that feels remotely safe. I walk into the office and a chubby teenage boy, with freckles splattered about his face and hands, barely looks up from his Nintendo Game Boy. His greasy, red hair looks like it was cut with sheep shears and his long, dirty fingernails make me squirm. I'm guessing my cheery hello probably won't work here so I just ask for a campsite then hand him my credit card. A fellow of few words and no eye contact, he runs the card for the ten-dollar fee then hands me a token and says, "It's for a free hot shower." He returns to his video game. *Creepy kid.*

When I get back into the car, Doug sits up and gives me a curious look. I forget he's sensitive to my emotions. Then his tired eyes seem to ask, *"Can we eat and sleep soon?"* I'm in luck. When I drive onto the grounds, I head to a dimly lit site set far back from the office. *That's curious, I'm the only camper.*

Well-rehearsed in setting up my tent, the limited light is not a problem. I feel bad for Doug. Even though I stop the car every two hours or so to let him stretch his legs, he's had another long day in the car. But conditions being what they are, I'm not comfortable taking him for a long stroll outside this gloomy place. We take just a few short laps through the vacant sites then I set out food and water for him. When he's finished I put him on his long leash attached to the open car. I know he understands.

Time for me to eat. Even with a dash of dried hot peppers, my go-to supper of rice and canned, black beans, salt, and pepper is still bland and pasty, but it is filling. I haven't had a meal since breakfast so all I want to do is fill my void and this combo does the trick.

Tired, cranky, and caked with Badlands dust, I start seeing wavy lines in my vision and fear a migraine's coming on. But, thank goodness, after a few minutes, it doesn't materialize. Probably because I'm completely depleted, I start feeling somewhat at peace enclosed within this funky place.

My tent is backed up near the tall wire fence and I wonder what's on the other side and how Doug might react. But right now I'm too tired to worry.

After I pack up what needs to be stowed in the car, I crawl into my tent. It's a delicious moment when I stretch out letting relief flow into every cell of me. *I made it.* Then I whisper, "Thank you for watching over me today." Soon after, I slide into a soft, delicious sleep.

A few hours later, a muffled snort then a chump, chump, chump from outside the tent wakes me. It sounds familiar so I'm not startled. Then I open my eyes because I think I can hear better that way. Fully awake I listen intently, trying to identify the sound. The smells of sweat, dry dirt, with a whiff of pine inside my tent, stir a memory of something I learned when I was a kid. When camping at night, things sound louder and closer than they actually are. And don't I know that darkness is the great magnifier.

Whatever it is, I imagine it's rubbing against the backside of my tent. It reminds me of grazing cattle. I hope I'm right and the fence between us is intact. To make sure, I unzip the door, poke my head out, and gulp. There in the milky moonlight, with Devils Tower in the background, are the outlines of the most formidable cow horns I've ever seen. It's a small herd of longhorn cattle. *Thank goodness for what I hope is a sturdy fence.* For some odd reason, Doug is quiet. After absorbing so much of my fear today, he's probably exhausted.

I fall back to sleep and, after a short while, more munching near my tent wakes me. But the sounds are different. I check outside and, where the cattle had been, see the outlines of five horses. Fully awake, I begin to worry Doug might start barking and cause a stampede or something. But when I look over at the car, there's still no movement and not a sound.

Just before sunrise, I wake again and from a distance, I hear sheep bleating. A disturbing memory from *Close Encounters of the Third Kind* slinks in. In the movie, people possessed by aliens become obsessed with traveling to Devils Tower. As they drive to the tower, they find hundreds of dead sheep covering the sides of the road. I know it was filmed near here. I might have taken the same road. Now I'm spooked even more so I make my most passionate pleas to my angels for peace and protection. It takes time but after a long while sleep finally comes again.

# 43: Finally, a Friend

## A welcomed salve to Coyote's lessons

The new day brings soft, blue sky, and warm, bashful breezes. After yesterday, this peaceful morning feels like Earth's makeup present to me and I feel rich. Thank you.

My body slumps down at the worn-out, wooden picnic table as I nurse my just-brewed cup of coffee and write in my journal. My last twenty-four hours make it easy to tap into a fast-moving river of words anxious to flood the page. A good while later I look up from my work and notice a young couple across the way. They probably checked in late last night. *Lucky them. Not.*

A few minutes later the cute duo heads over to me. They have on shabby jeans and t-shirts and their leather sandals stir up small dust clouds. They step into my site and their big smiles and firm handshakes pull me out of my morning musings. It feels good to finally find some smiles.

Ted is tall, Caucasian, bean-pole thin, and says he's just out of college. Kyra is a short, attractive woman from India with long, shiny, black hair. She doesn't say so but I assume she's just out of college, too. When I ask them about their travels, Ted gives an animated narrative of their two-month tour of the West. Kyra, with her adoring gaze fixed on her boyfriend, just smiles. Ted says it's his first time in Wyoming and it feels like home to him but they plan to settle in San Francisco in the fall. After what happened last night, I can't imagine living here. I wonder what Kyra thinks about the plan because she's just sitting there like she doesn't have an opinion. *Ugh.* This makes my skin crawl. I might be wrong but she could be one of those subservient women, always taking a back seat to her man, maybe to any man. I hate that. *Own your space and your voice, Kyra.*

Young and of course wrapped up in their own little world, I'm not surprised when they don't ask about me. But they seem like a nice couple and it's good to have some company. After their short visit, we say our goodbyes and a few minutes later I watch them from across the way pack up their gear and drive out of the campground. *I hope you two have some great adventures and settle in San Francisco, not dismal Wyoming.*

I need a lazy morning doing as little as possible. After feeding Doug, we do a few laps past the campsites, then I cook my comfort food of oatmeal with sliced apples and nuts. Sitting back at the table, I sneak a sideways peek up at the sun and smile. *You know, Sun, you abandoned me last night and for a while, I forgot something: you always return. And you did, so I forgive you for leaving me. Ha.* It dawns on me how simple things like a safe place to sleep, a faithful dog, oatmeal, and a blue sky can feel like a pot of gold.

Later in the morning, I move my chair to tree shade near the car to relax and read while Doug naps on the ground nearby. Three chapters in I look up and see a trim, fit man in his thirties walking towards me. He has rich, tan skin and two long braids swing back and forth on his tartan shirt. He looks Native. Doug barely lifts his head from his nap as the man approaches. That's a good sign.

His beautiful smile, warm hello, and handshake restore me. His name is Keith and his demeanor reminds me of the Cheyenne college man I met as I was leaving the Butte. Laid back, this guy seems comfortable in his own skin so I like him right away. We fall into easy conversation and he asks about my travels. When I start talking, I'm surprised when he leans in to hear what I'm saying. As I continue, this friendly man, sitting cross-legged on the ground, alternates between looking into my eyes and off to the horizon. *He's really listening.* I'm relieved to sense he's not working on a response to my words like most people do. Before leaving Maine, my friends and family seemed only mildly interested in my adventure. Keith's interest lifts my spirits.

He even asks about my visits to Bear Butte and Wounded Knee. And, as I hear myself speak, I become an observer, a listener to some far-fetched travels. But then it hits me. They're mine. I stir, sit higher in my seat, and hope he wants to hear more. Then I start to feel a little uncomfortable sharing all this because he's Native. I wonder what he thinks of my descriptions of what I've seen and experienced at Mission, Wounded Knee, and Wind Cave. I hope the words in my telling are respectful to his culture.

When Keith starts to talk about the geology of this area and the energy emanating from the land, I lean in closer. I think about the Lakota origin story of Devils Tower, a legend probably told for hundreds of years. I wonder if land holds the emotional signature of a story if it's told enough times. Maybe it does and it explains why ancient places of worship feel like oases of peace and hope. Even with its positive ending, I wonder if a frightening fable, like Devil's Tower, can have a disturbing effect.

We start talking about how Earth's memory might affect people and my brain soaks up every one of his words. I realize I might be romanticizing again but an insistent mental picture takes over. It's the same imagery that came to me at Bear Butte. It depicts blending the mythology of all indigenous societies with modern scientific knowledge. And with this convergence of all mythology, theology, and physics, a simple, cosmic truth is revealed. I love it when I have it all figured out, ha.

*But where did Keith come from?*

I tell him about me camping in the desert, in Arizona, in1990 and how the desert's relentless pull caused me to move there months later. Keith smiles and nods as I try to explain my strange, intimate connection with the desert, how I still cry every time I return and leave it. I don't want to tell it all, because the saga is too long and painful, but I share some of it. I talk about how Spirit was relentless in pressing me to move there with my young son. Keith's face slackens and his eyes widen when I tell him that the use of corporal punishment in schools is still legal in many states. I describe how I fought to have it outlawed in Arizona schools.

It's a lot. We've already covered so much ground and we just met but when Keith starts talking about past lives, I almost fall out of my chair. His questions invite me to join in and we share our stories and thoughts about the phenomenon. *I could talk with this guy all day.* My concept of past lives, after listening to Keith's thoughts, finds its way into a more pedestrian corner of my thinking. It's not the airy-fairy, New Age possibility I've studied for years. He explains it in an easygoing, simple way. He says recognizing someone from another lifetime just makes sense. "If the land holds memory of events, why wouldn't we?"

Years later the theory of epigenetics, would support the hypothesis of memory stored in DNA being passed from one generation to the next.

After a good long time, our conversation winds down then Keith invites me to his campsite for lunch. Later Doug and I stir up our own mini dust clouds as we stroll over to join him. We roast hot dogs over his campfire that go perfectly with chips, soda, and even more pleasant conversation. Doug stretches out and naps next to Keith. My empathic dog answers my question before I think it.

We fall into easy talk again. Past lives come up and I tell Keith about Kate, how she turned my world upside down and how her cassette

159

tape made me cry but for some strange reason, and without me knowing it, it urged me to come here. He listens and smiles and I warm to the notion that he knows and believes my story. I wonder if someone stirred his heart that way, too. He and I might be more alike than imagined, and I'm starting to feel almost comfortable in this peculiar little corner of Wyoming. Keith is a welcomed salve to Coyote's lessons.

It's just what I needed, too. It seems like weeks since I've had a long, mellow conversation with anyone. Come to think of it, I can't remember when I had the last one.

After lunch when I'm back at my site, I watch Keith climb into his truck. He flashes me a broad knowing smile, waves, then drives off and disappears like a mirage. I'd forgotten how pleasant some humans can be.

# 44: In the Devil's Shadow

## It hovers over me like a threat

It's unavoidable. I've got to freshen up, so I make a quick trip to the funky bath facility. As I brush my teeth, drag a comb through my hair, and wash my face, I plan the rest of my day. I've got to escape this skanky place and the memories of my hair-raising drive last night. I'll play tourist and visit Devils Tower which is just a short way from here. The enigmatic rock column has piqued my curiosity and, after talking with Keith, I wonder if I'll sense anything from the land.

Even from miles away, the Tower looks both troubling and alluring. Sunlight gives it a faint glow and the dozens of wide, vertical grooves make it look man-made. Then again, it looks like a giant tooth pushed up out of the ground and this bleak landscape makes it look even more unnatural. In *Close Encounters* it was where aliens landed. *Yup. It also looks like a perfect landing site for a spaceship.*

Doug jumps into the car and we strike off to play tourist. As the road moves me closer, the monolith grows taller and more and more disturbing. Then, with only a measly few acres of scrubland between us, it suddenly hovers over me like a threat. Thoughts of leaving plague me but something, maybe curiosity, maybe stubbornness, says no. These familiar feelings signal things might need to play out in order to discover something important.

It's two o'clock when I coast into the parking lot and find a shady place to park. It's sunny and the hot air is humid and still. The far end of the lot has lots of shade and is only half full so there shouldn't be a problem with foot traffic near the car. It's as if the perfect spot is always waiting for Doug.

The windows are open, the back's down, and Doug has plenty of water so I leave the car and head to the information center. But when I'm about twenty feet from the car, Doug starts barking. I turn to look and he's standing on the ground, tense and staring at me. These are warning barks, he's upset. In all the places I've left him, he's never made a fuss. I walk back to the car and pat him. "It's okay, buddy. I'll come back soon." I get him to jump back inside, cross my fingers, and walk away. But he starts barking again and this time I think I understand. He's trying to tell me, "Don't go in there." I wonder what he's sensing. Whatever it is, he doesn't like it. Even though I don't understand, I trust his instincts and once I turn and get back into the car, Doug lies down and curls up. I drive myself and my guardian away from the unsettling spot.

Last night, when I was driving on that long dark road and the Tower popped up ahead of me, it shook me up big time. I'm wondering now why I was so freaked out. Was it the movie, the scary ride from Scenic, the way it stands thrust out of the countryside, or the Indigenous legend? Could it be a combination of my experiences and memories and the memories in the land? All I know is, something is unnerving about that mercurial monster, and it seems both Doug and I feel it.

With no other plans for the day, I make an almost desperate map search for something to do because I don't want to go back to the campground. I recognize the name Sundance from another movie title. The town is thirty miles from here and I think it'll make a good escape for a couple hours.

All my windows are open and as I speed down the empty highway, it's like I'm being whisked away from a very bad dream. The road ahead courses through large expanses of hilly, rugged land. I remember reading that much of this is government-owned grazing land leased out to ranchers. After too many monotonous miles, I see in the far-off distance the rounded silhouettes of the Black Hills. Beyond them and much deeper into the horizon are what I guess are the foothills of the craggy-topped Rockies. Even from so far away, those mountain ranges look interesting and alive, a stark contrast to the drab landscape here. It could be me, it could be this land, I don't know, but the two of us just don't resonate.

As I half expected, Sundance is ordinary, with its cluster of slumping, sun-bleached buildings holding court in the center of town. The beaten-up road sign says it has a population of 1,100.

*Oh, really? Where?* I stop at a little grocery store for some snacks and as I turn to leave, I notice a rack of paperbacks on a swivel stand. The book title, *Sister of the Sioux* catches my eye so I pluck it off the stand and give it a once over. It says it's the memoir of a young teacher from New

England living with and teaching the Sioux in South Dakota in the 1880s. After I pay the clerk, I hurry down the steps to my car and can't wait to get back to camp and devour my little treasure. I love these tiny affirmations that reassure and tell me I'm heading in a good direction. A little nudge is all I need.

On my drive back to the campground, huge, angry, storm clouds form not far ahead and they look like they're headed to Devils Tower. Continuing down the road my words come out loud and insistent. "Please, Spirit, spare me another storm." Then not long after, thank goodness, someone must have listened because, by the time I arrive at the campground, the storm has deflated to a mere sputter of wind.

I'm quick to settle in my tent so I can dive into my new book. I'm swept away and become that teacher living on the prairie with the Sioux. It's a great, well-written story.

Later in the afternoon, still reading, I suddenly realize it smells like a locker room in my tent. No wonder, it's been days since I've showered. But the thought of showering in the campground's facility makes me cringe. My visits to the bathroom revealed chipped paint, wet, slimy floors, and a dirty sink. I didn't dare look in the shower. I'll have to talk to the owner about the cleanliness issue. I remember I ran into him as I left this morning and found out it's his son who checked me in last night.

When I open the office door and step inside, the chubby boy and his look-alike father are perched on stools behind the counter. The dad is huge with a beard, a puffy face, and long, blonde, scraggly hair. His wrinkled shirt has a few old stains and he barely raises his head to look at me when I walk in. I step up to the counter and say, "Hello. Wondering when you usually clean the bath facility because I'd like to take a shower." I had planned what I would say. I didn't want to sound judgmental and I'm proud of how politely the words come out. This kind of forethought is unusual for me. *Probably ought to do it more often.*

The dad gives me an indifferent gaze then looks over and grunts to his son, "You need to get to it." I stand waiting for more from him but it doesn't come.

Then I hear the boy yell, "Get him! Get him!" I glance over to where he's looking and see a little terrier dog just outside the screen door. It has what looks like a prairie dog in its mouth. The terrier is whipping the poor thing back and forth, again and again. Then it stops and using its paws and teeth it begins to shred it. The boy bursts into a fit of laughter and I am shaken at the cruelty happening right in front of me. *How do I compute this?* Without another word, I turn, step past the dog, and walk back to my site while planning a retreat to a familiar, safe place deep inside myself.

163

I wonder why I've ended up here, where everything feels dirty, including me. *Have I gone off my spiritual path?* Have I stumbled into a giant pit of anger belonging to those two guys? Now I'm pissed. Yes, anger is my go-to emotion when I or someone else is discounted or treated unfairly.

Back at my site, I take Doug out for what I hope is a very long, calming walk inside the campground. Poor Doug, I feel bad that I've exposed him to such a nasty place but he seems as happy as ever, prancing beside me with his head high and his tail wagging. As I round the corner of the campground perimeter past the office, I see a small herd of cattle grazing in the adjoining field. One of the cows is in trouble. It looks like its front leg is broken. When I get closer, I can see the break is above the knee and serious. The leg is dangling in midair. But the poor cow chugs along on its other good legs and keeps grazing. *My god. I wonder how long it's been broken and if anyone knows.* Horrified, my imagination takes me to a well-known place where no one cares and no one comes to the rescue. I am frightened for the poor creature and I realize the only thing I can do is report this to the campground owner but I'm not hopeful for the poor cow.

The last thing I want to do is go back into the office but I have to let someone know. When I tell the father, he says he'll call the rancher. *Sure, just like you'll have the bathroom cleaned.*

After our walk I sit at my picnic table, escape into my new book and try to forget all the suffering I've witnessed. After an hour or so I prepare my supper and eye the bathhouse for the improbable someone who'll show up to clean it.

It's no surprise the cleaning doesn't happen so I'll have another aromatic night in my tent. I don't mind it much but my hair is starting to stick out. Come to think of it, I fit right in here.

# 45: Dad's Best Gift

## What fairy tale years those were

After witnessing that poor injured cow, I couldn't stop thinking about it. Soon a decades-old memory, thank goodness, floods in.

—◦◦◦—

One summer morning when I was twelve, I woke to find my dad, who usually left for work at dawn, still at home. My nine-year-old sister, Linda, and I were in the kitchen eating breakfast when, with a twinkle in his eye, he told us, "Go down to the end of the field and look in the pasture." That's it, that's all he said. We looked at each other, puzzled. As a man of few words, we knew we weren't going to get anything more out of him. We finished eating then dashed out the back door and loped across the hayfield behind our house.

The sleepy morning sun suspended dabs of dew in the newborn air while night's mist lingered on the knee-high grass and wet our bare legs. Cheery, delicate meadow birds sang our excitement as we ran and giggled and bounced down the field to our surprise.

The end of our hayfield gave way to a forty-acre pasture ravine with a wide brook at the bottom. The walls of the ravine were steep, sandy, and difficult to traverse. It was our favorite place, especially for me, to fish and explore.

We raced down the field with no idea what to look for. When we got to the end we stopped at the barbed wire fence that ran along the top edge of the huge ravine. We looked to the right and without warning, a palomino mare and a chestnut colt galloped up to us. Bewildered, we looked at each other then echoed, "Whose are they?"

A few minutes later we raced back home and peppered our dad with questions. He said, "I bought them from a customer in trade for some work I did." He said he paid $400. The mare was a registered palomino and the colt's sire was a registered quarter horse so they had good bloodlines. Late the night before, he and my uncle had loaded the mare and colt into a trailer, trucked them here, and put them in the pasture.

That kind of surprise was unusual for my parents and I wasn't sure of my mother's involvement because she said nothing. I felt a little weird because Linda and I got something special and our siblings didn't but, from what I remember, it didn't seem to bother them. Even though we had some major arguments, I don't remember us kids ever being jealous of each other.

Our horses arrived with little fanfare. My dad knew I liked animals and he knew Linda liked riding a big pony owned by an old guy in town. A couple years before, I'd entered a contest popular in the day. You could win a thoroughbred by submitting a name for it. I honestly thought I had a chance of winning and I remember my father watched me fill out the form, fold it up, and put it in the envelope. I wonder if it made him realize I wanted a horse even though I hadn't asked for one outright. Bottom line, Linda and I were thrilled and too young and too inexperienced to be overwhelmed with the responsibilities of caring for two horses.

My dad had a couple of small Quonset barns moved near our house, one for hay and one for shelter. Circling them he had built a sturdy corral fence. An electric fence was installed that ran alongside a line of tall chokecherry trees extending from the barns to the forty-acre pasture ravine. It was a perfect setup; our horses had their own trail linking the corral to the pasture and they could come and go as we wanted them to. The picture of exuberance and freedom never got old. Heads held high, ears cupped forward, with sailing manes and tails, they raced up the long runway and into the corral for their evening meal.

With the help of 4-H leaders and townspeople, Linda and I became skilled at caring for our horses. We became good riders and even trained them to pull an antique buggy. Linda took over most of the training for the mare we named Missy. The chestnut colt became Red and he was mostly my charge. When Red was two, he was gelded then later we hired a man to break him in to ride. But he stayed unpredictable and more than a handful for me so Linda became his primary rider.

On many days Linda and I would saddle up and take off for the day. We'd trot side by side down quiet, dirt roads that took us to neighboring towns and race each other at a full gallop down tree-lined paths and across grassy meadows. Missy was part Arabian, spirited, and determined and she never let Red win our races even if Linda was riding him. It felt dangerous, galloping across a field astride a twelve-hundred-pound animal that could at any time stumble, fall, or run away with me. But I loved the sense of freedom exploring the beautiful farmlands of our little NH town. Mostly I loved being with my sister.

Linda loved riding more than I did. I think she loved the danger. She became a gifted, mostly self-taught rider, and she and Missy had a unique bond. Because of their deep trust in each other Linda could ride the mare bareback without a bridle, even when swimming together in the nearby Connecticut River. I looked up to my little sister and I was proud of her skills, self-confidence, and bravery.

In winter, as Linda sprinted across our field on Red, she looked like a mythical goddess kicking up white, sparkly clouds of fluff in the thigh-high snow. Ours was an amicable partnership, an unspoken contract. There was a strong bond between my sister and me. We were devoted to our horses and we shared equally in their care. When it came to Missy and Red, we never fought.

One afternoon four years after they arrived, I walked down to the end of the field to let them run to the corral. What I saw terrified me. Missy had a thick chunk of skin, the size and thickness of my sandal, hanging off the front lower part of one hind leg. Right away I guessed she had gotten tangled in some barbed wire. The skin flopped over frontward and I could see the bone. I was shaken but Missy seemed unfazed. When I opened the runway gate, she trotted down the field as if nothing was wrong. Later I guessed she must have been in shock.

Out of breath from my sprint, I caught up to the horses in the corral and yelled for Linda. She came out of the house and we stood side by side at the corral fence staring at Missy's wound. It was an awful thing to see. I went into the house to phone the vet then my mother called my father. Thank goodness they both came right away.

Our vet, Dr. Pollock, had just emigrated from Scotland. He was a kind man and I loved his hearty accent. He was extremely concerned and said he'd never seen anything like it. He conferred with my father, Linda, and me and said we had two options. We could put her down because, with the severity of the wound and the severed tendon, she probably wouldn't be able to walk on her leg again, or he could remove the large strip of flesh, reconnect the tendon, and hope scar tissue would fill in the area. He also said he worried about infection. Dr. Pollock said it would probably take months for the tissue to grow in and would require daily vet visits for a few weeks. He said it was his first time treating a wound like this. My dad did something that probably had more of a positive effect on us than anything he could have done; he left the decision up to Linda and me. We decided to treat Missy's leg. And my dad didn't hesitate. He knew vet fees would be enormous but I think he saw how responsible we'd been and knew we'd take good care of her.

Dr. Pollock removed the flap of skin and after weeks of almost daily vet visits, Missy's body generated enough scar tissue to fill in the wound. What was even more amazing, with Linda's care, Missy regained a near-normal gate. Somehow she compensated for what was missing and could not only walk but could trot and even cantor. Dr. Pollock was astonished. Missy was missing a section of a tendon that attaches bone to muscle and is responsible for springing the hoof forward when she walked. I'd often cringe when I watched Linda riding Missy after she recovered. I expected her foot to fold over on itself. The most unsettling thing was watching Missy as she and Red galloped up and down the steep banks of the ravine. But, she never faltered. Mind over matter, I guess.

Linda and I participated in horse shows in NH and nearby VT. We'd find a local farmer willing to truck our animals to the show and, as usual, my dad never hesitated to pay the tab. My sister and I, even though we were just teenagers then, handled all of the logistics and got damn good at it.

When she showed Missy, Linda almost always walked away with a blue ribbon in the conditioning and grooming category. My clever sister covered Missy's large, hairless wound with baby powder so it blended in with her white leg hair and, of course, the rest of Missy was spotless. Most judges awarded Linda extra points for the good cover-up job. The most prestigious honor in 4-H was to be selected to show at the Eastern States Exposition in Massachusetts. Only the top 4-H riders and horses in all of New England were chosen to compete and Missy and Linda were among them. My sister added another blue ribbon to the scrapbook. What fairy tale years those were.

After I went away to college, Red went to a local trainer and, after that, we lost track of him. Missy stayed with Linda, aged gracefully, and died a peaceful death at twenty-nine.

I am grateful to my father for his unwavering support of Linda and me and for our dedicated veterinarian, Dr. Pollock. Looking back on those years, I realize how our horses, especially Missy, taught us to be courageous, overlook our shortcomings, and persevere.

# 46: My Canyon Home

## This place is alive

The book, *Sister of the Sioux,* is my new best friend. It pulls me back into the 1800s when a lone unconventional teacher travels to South Dakota to help the American Indians. I stretch out the two hundred pages to make it last longer but, after an evening's marathon read, I finish then fall asleep about ten. Later in the night another pretty good storm wakes me and leaves me on edge. Not finished, it wakes me four more times over the next few hours.

Near 2 a.m., as if the storm wasn't enough, my tent feels like a hermetically sealed compartment. One minute I'm hot, then cold, hot, then cold. Blanket on, blanket off, blanket on, blanket off. These don't feel like my normal hot flashes; it's something else. The storm is on, then off, on, then off. *Yikes, everything's shifting.*

Close to four I hear a vehicle pull up so I peek out and see a truck parked near my site. The driver's door swings open and a disheveled middle-aged man and woman step out. They sit at their picnic table and start bombarding each other with screams and cusses so loud, I'm sure they wake the whole campground. An hour later they climb into their truck and leave without pitching a tent. *This place is some strange reality.* Not much sleep for me tonight.

By 7 a.m. my fretful night has taken its toll. I feel like an old dishrag but I force myself out of my sleeping bag. I definitely need to shower, so after checking on Doug, I gather up my bathing necessities and head to the facility. My mantra is: don't look, just step into the shower, bathe, step out, dry off, and leave. *And may any negative residuals of this place get washed down the drain.*

At the bathroom door I sink my "complimentary hot shower" token in the slot. With my towel and clean clothes scrunched tight to my chest, like I'm holding a newborn, I open the door and step inside. I lock the door behind me, set my things on a scarred, wooden bench, then disrobe and forget all about my intention to release negativity. *I hope my feet are immune to whatever is on this floor because in a minute I'll be barefoot.*

The floor's slippery so I move with well-thought-out steps. Hardened by soap scum, the stiff shower curtain crackles when I draw it to one side. Before stepping into the stall, I turn the handle and the showerhead coughs and sputters then spews out a slug of brown water. A minute later a thin stream of clear, tepid water squirts out, I step under it, stare straight ahead, then begin my routine. One minute I'm covered with soap and shampoo, the next, I'm a scrubbed-down, barely-rinsed body ready to flee. Even though I'm refreshed and cleaner, back at my site I use some drinking water to give my feet a good soap and water scrub. *Nasty place.*

I eat a quick breakfast then pack up the car in record time. *I'll head back to South Dakota and after that, we'll see.* Right now my goal is to put some distance between me and this awful place.

After an hour's drive, a road sign, "Welcome to South Dakota," makes me smile. But missing that familiar sensation prodding me on, I wonder if I'm lost. *Is it time to go home?* I need to stop and center myself so I find a secluded area, pull off the road, and park. After a few slow, deep breaths I close my eyes and imagine I'm flowing into my chest, my spiritual center. Once there, I listen to the peaceful parts of me and I imagine I'm looking at a beautiful sunset. After a few minutes I sense mild, warm waves welcoming me back to this land. It's good to feel safe and at home inside myself again. I remember how awful my body felt at the dirty campground and realize I'm more in tune with where my body prefers to be. It wants peace and quiet.

I ruminate for a few more minutes then open my eyes, look out the window, and grin. I'm happy the adventurer in me is back and, with my internal compass as my guide, I'm ready for what's out there waiting for me.

A few miles down the road, and right when I think about stopping for info, I look up and see an information center. After I leave the building, I feel a pull to go back to the Black Hills. I'm not sure where in the Black Hills but I'll just listen to my body. Not long after, something nudges me to take the Spearfish exit. It leads to a secondary road through the Spearfish Canyon. I inch my way along the gravel road that fishtails along the floor of the breathtaking, nineteen-mile-long canyon. The brochure says parts of the movie *Dances with Wolves* were filmed here. I think it was at the end when the main characters, both Caucasian, choose to leave the tribe and live alone out on the prairie.

Compared to the other canyons I've seen, this is by far the most secluded. I can understand why it was a good winter camp area. Surrounded by rocky cliffs and pine I feel sheltered from the bustling outside world. Puffball clouds drift about in the dark blue sky and tall grasses border the banks of a narrow brook along the road. It smells like Maine: crisp, clean, and piney. Tiny waves of joy take me back to a sweet memory of my dad and me.

—⚋—

From: Regina age 12
Dear Dad,

Last night I dreamt about the day I helped you plant the six blue spruce seedlings along the edge of the back lawn. Dad, I've always felt special to you, and I love the way you smile when you call me Genie. I knew I was your favorite and that made me happy.

It was fun to work with you, Dad, even though you didn't say much, just things like: pass the shovel, hand me that seedling, grab the hose, and give it lots of water. I noticed how you moved a little slower than you usually do, I think that was for me. I watched you when you were working at a job site. Dad, you are fast and strong. I remember I used to think you were the strongest man in our whole town.

Come to think of it, it's probably good that John or Pat were not helping us because you usually got cranky and bossy with my brothers around. I'm sorry you treated them like that, maybe it's because you didn't have a good father.

I love you, Dad, and I hope we do more projects together.
Love,
Genie

—⚋—

The spruce trees are gone but, to this day, every time I return home and crest the hill near our old house, I slow the car, crane my neck, and hope I see them. And for many years I did. They stood in a perfect line like strong-girthed monuments to my precious memory. More than a property line, they were proof of a rare, hazy-warm, time with my father.

—⚋—

Up ahead is a sign for two camping areas. Each abuts the well-groomed dirt road so I decide to take a look at both. The first one is full and the sites bump up against each other. Not for me. I drive the short distance down the road to the second area, the Timon Campground. The sites are tucked into groves of trees and the place feels friendly. It has lots of empty sites and lucky me, I find one on the edge of a pristine stream. *This place is alive.*

I scout the area some more and discover it only has toilets and water but it's rustically tranquil and clean. After I register I pull into my site, open the car door, and a large swarm of tiny, biting flies greets me. *You little guys are nothing compared to what I've been through.*

This is perfect. I never imagined such a vibrant tent site. I can't wait to explore with Doug. *I can see myself staying here for a month.* Looks like I'll be in South Dakota for a while longer.

# 47: Novembers are Cruel

## Frost had hit my mother's beautiful gladioli making them topple like dead soldiers

Spearfish Canyon is captivating on this beautiful July day. As I pitch my tent and organize my belongings, I wonder what it's like in the winter months when fierce winds howl through the canyon. Today it's easy to take my joy and security for granted. A memory wedges in and, even though I don't want it to, it takes me back almost thirty years when my young world was turned upside down.

Thanksgiving was in four days and I was home on break from college. My sister's wedding was in two weeks and between that and the holiday, our house was bursting at the seams with excitement.

We had a lot to be thankful for. My brother, John, was in the Air Force and had just returned from Vietnam with his new Filipino wife and her young daughter. Now stationed in Massachusetts, John and his family returned home on weekends. My sister Lorraine was engaged to Paul, a Green Beret just back from Vietnam, too. My siblings, Linda and Pat, both teenagers, and five-year-old Beth were all living with my mom. That was a total of ten of us in our big house and with all the comings and goings it got chaotic, but we were used to chaos. Also, it helped that we loved to party. Many evenings, with Motown music blaring, we'd have a few beers and dance and laugh amidst a steady stream of good-natured teasing. We loved our soulful music and over the years nothing changed.

My parents had divorced three years earlier but had shown signs of reconciling. With John safe at home and Lorraine's upcoming wedding, we hoped this might encourage them to get back together.

That November day in New Hampshire was not a pretty one. Temps were in the forties and a murky overcast hovered. Frost had hit my mother's beautiful gladioli making them top-heavy and toppling like dead soldiers. The roadside weeds were brown, moldy, and beyond resuscitation. It might have been a little easier on us, maybe, if there had been some sun or even slightly brighter skies. Over the years, for our family, November became the month of loss.

Mid-morning on Monday the twenty-fourth, the kitchen phone rang. It was one of my dad's employees. He said my father hadn't shown up for work. My dad loved to work and was extremely proud of his business so this made no sense to us.

I was in the kitchen with my mom, Lorraine, and Paul when the call came in. Baffled, we sat for an hour waiting for a follow-up call but none came. Finally, Paul, Lorraine, and I decided to go to my father's house to look for him. Paul drove my mom's car, Lorraine sat in the front, and I sat in the back. My dad's house was ten miles away in Ryegate, Vt.

For three years my father had been living in what he called his "little dollhouse." But, to me, there was nothing cute about it. It looked like a leftover motel unit set back from the main road with its decrepit, tiny garage nearby. Looking back now, it must have broken my dad's heart to leave his six kids and the beautiful home he'd had built for us only eleven years earlier. It's sad how long it can take before you appreciate what a parent may have endured.

It was a somber ride to Ryegate. We sat quietly for a few miles then anxiously speculated about what might have happened. Lorraine had just graduated from nursing school and guessed he might have gotten sick and couldn't get to the phone. Paul, fresh from jungle combat, sat stoically behind the wheel and said little. I sensed Paul was in military mode. Thank God he was leading us. I slumped down in the backseat, looked out the window, and watched other people's lives fly by. I became a child again.

Paul pulled into the driveway and parked facing the little house. No one spoke but I knew they didn't want to get out; I certainly didn't. Because the garage door was closed, Lorraine and Paul thought he might be in the house so they left the car and walked inside. I had the heebie-jeebies so I stayed put. Slumped down, I rested my head on the back of the seat and looked out the window. It seemed like a faint veil had dropped down in front of my face and for a couple minutes my vision got blurry. I'd never been so afraid and I couldn't even look at his house. A minute later, my vision cleared and I scanned the yard with its bare trees and the sad little garage and it didn't help me feel better. My body just wanted to stop working so I sank lower in the seat and wished so badly for them to come back so we could leave. When I looked out the window again, it seemed the sun had seized up too. A little sunshine would have been nice.

After a very long fifteen minutes or so, they came back to the car. They said he wasn't inside and everything looked normal except for the cellar. It had lots of empty wine bottles. We didn't understand this because our father didn't drink.

On the ride home we tried to make sense of the empty house and all the wine bottles but couldn't. I began to worry and, listening to my sister's nervous chatter, I knew she was worried too. Paul, our rock, took us home.

Back at our house we waited for more news. It felt like our family was on a carnival ride, spinning around and around in slow motion with no one at the controls. I heard it in our words and saw it on our faces. We suspected something bad had happened.

Paul drove back to my dad's place with Errol, another of my dad's employees. My mom, Lorraine, Pat, Linda, and I waited an hour or so in the kitchen. My little sister Beth was upstairs napping.

When the phone rang, my mom answered. It was Errol.

Her face blanched and she curled her shoulders into her chest. She pushed the phone away from her face and wept saying, "They found him. He's gone. He's in his car in the garage." A tsunami had struck our family.

All along he'd been in his garage. Thank god Lorraine and Paul didn't go in it because he'd been dead for over thirty-six hours. We found out later there was a loaded rifle in the back seat of his car and the gas tank was empty.

In the kitchen, the five of us huddled and cried. Looking back now I think it's sad to think it took something that horrific to make us embrace like that. For even though we loved each other and our times together, we weren't physically affectionate. Now we cried and cried and walked in circles and cried some more. *My poor mother, what a dreadful thing for her.* At the time, I couldn't allow for my own deepest sorrow. That would take years to surface.

After a short time my mom asked me to go tell Beth. So, like a robot with my numbed mind, I climbed the stairs then opened my sister's bedroom door. Having just woken, she turned to look at me. As was her habit, she was sucking her curled-up little pointer finger, and her big brown eyes swung back and forth searching mine. Even before I spoke, her beautiful little face looked worried.

I knelt on the floor next to her bed then scooted up close to her. With my hand on the side of her head, I began, and even before I spoke, a single tear formed in her eye. I said, "Daddy went to heaven," then that tiny tear drifted gently down her cheek. No words, no sobs, just her sad, little-girl tear. And like a frightened fawn, she stared at me then curled up into herself and kept sucking her finger.

Hours after learning of my father's death, John and his family arrived back at the house and we hugged and cried some more. And, as was typical of John, he leaped into action. He arranged the funeral plans, got an honorable discharge from the Air Force, and, at twenty-two, took over my father's business. He also became my mother's business partner and ally, and now, the patriarch of our family.

Well known and loved in our town and surrounding areas, people took my dad's death hard. The local newspaper's headline read, "Boudreault Suicide." We thought it was cold and inappropriate but at the time we were too traumatized to complain. Maybe the editor was in shock, too. I bet he was.

We trusted Mr. Strickler and his staff at the funeral home to be as compassionate and professional as usual. He knew my dad well and today I can't imagine how difficult it must have been to prepare the body of his robust, "muscle man" friend. Ironically, the funeral home was near the church where my dad's funeral would be and where my sister would marry in two weeks.

On the evening of the wake I felt like I was inside a dark cloud of hurt so dense it made it hard for me to move. I'd lost all my bearings but I knew I had to keep moving. How can a person breathe feeling such blinding dread? Our world had skidded to a screeching stop. I watched John, with his arm around my mom's frail shoulders, hold her up and urge her on. They walked into the wake and the rest of us followed. The dimly lit room was packed and there was creepy organ music moaning in the background. The dark red velvet upholstery on the furniture soaked up what little light there was. I knew my dad was up front and center in the casket but I was too afraid to look.

We inched our way into a room overflowing with grief, heavy with sorrow. As we held on to each other, we held each other up. The room had too many dark corners and its air was thick and still like right before an unexpected thunderstorm. That stupid, piped-in, organ music made me want to scream. Dad would've hated that shit. He'd have wanted upbeat new stuff, something you could sway to, like an Al Green song. When I looked over at the pained faces of folks from town, the shock in their eyes, and their drooping heads, I wanted to cry. *Healthy, spirited, popular, successful, and generous father of six, dead at forty-two.*

I sat in the front row with my mother and four siblings. My mom thought Beth was too young so she stayed at home with a babysitter. Sitting in my chair, I could sense the confusion and shock in row after row of the distressed people behind me. But my own grief was so deep I didn't know it. We were all dazed and lost in our own terrible nightmare.

One after another my siblings walked up to the open casket, knelt on a cushion, and bowed their heads. Then it was my turn. In slow motion I stood up and moved up to the casket then knelt with my rosary beads wound through my fingers and prepared to say goodbye to my father. *Dad doesn't look too bad. Strickler's did a good job. But, hold on, this isn't my father.* How could they have captured his sparkle, the way he loved life, how he loved to make people happy?

—⟋⟍—

From the time I was little, our family loved the baked bean suppers at the Methodist Church in town. When everyone finished eating, people would pester my dad to sing and do his glass trick and he always complied. He loved to perform, belting out a few verses of "Oh, Danny Boy" or "Climb Every Mountain" a cappella and always in perfect pitch with sparkling eyes and a big beautiful smile on his face. I was so proud.

For his glass trick, he'd fill three tall glasses to the very top with water. He'd lie down on his back on the hall floor then balance one glass on his forehead and one in the open palm of each outstretched arm. From there he did what I always thought was miraculous, he would bend his muscular legs sideways then hoisted himself to a standing position without using his hands. In the many times he performed, he never lost one drop of water. The bean supper audience laughed and applauded. With a big, toothy grin, my father was in his glory, having fun, and making us smile.

—⟋⟍—

At the wake, kneeling on the stool, I looked up from my rosary beads at my father's face and truly saw him. Dad was dead, and he was in that stupid box, and his skin looked like clay. I began to feel the life going on behind me, especially coming from my dad's family. At the time of my father's death, it had been years since we'd seen most of them. When my parents' relationship was strained, my dad's family, except Gram, did what many families do, they took sides. They blamed my mother for the divorce even though my mom had been religious about taking us kids up to visit my paternal grandmother and welcoming my father's sisters to live with us. Now, after all this time they finally showed up to care about him and to care about us kids. *Oh, so this is what it took for you to finally come! Where were you when Dad needed you?*

As I knelt there, a wad of grief, masked by anger, swelled inside me then began to creep up into my throat. The wad was the truth, my truth. I started to cry and it got loud fast and then it became a yell.

177

I started to stand up then turned to face his family. "What have you done to him? Why are you here? Why now?"

My two brothers rushed up and escorted me back to my seat. I was still angry, numbed, and confused but I quieted down. And we never talked about it. I imagine my Gram was there, maybe not, maybe it was just too much for her losing her favorite son like that. I don't know. Knowing Gram, I'm sure she understood my grief and outburst.

No one knows what happened to my father or why. His death certificate said "suicide caused by depression." Dr. Rand, my dad's close friend, and our family physician viewed my father's body and signed the death certificate. Years later I asked Dr. Rand if my dad could have had a heart attack. He said no, there were no signs it was a heart attack but the body signs suggested asphyxiation. My mom didn't want his body "cut up" so there was no autopsy and so no definitive answers. We were left with many questions.

Because the gas tank of my father's car was empty, his garage door shut, and he was slumped over on the driver's side of the front seat, everyone thought it was a suicide. Word had it that late on that Saturday night, just hours before he died, my dad saw his girlfriend with another man. Somebody said my father left a note on his kitchen table. I've asked family but no one wants to talk about it. I will have to go on what I know; my father passed when I was twenty-one and he died a sad, lonely, but much-loved man.

With all the challenges to our family in '69 and '70, I don't think we had a chance to grieve my father's death. That is, not until my brother Pat dropped dead suddenly twenty-five years later, almost to the day of my father's passing. My brother was only forty-three and an autopsy revealed Pat died of a brain aneurysm. He left behind his adoring wife and two young daughters. Years later my siblings and I wondered if our father planned to shoot himself but, like Pat, had an aneurysm after he started the car. We grieved long and hard for my brother, and I think I finally grieved for my father, then, too.

Now in Spearfish, hoping to find more of myself, I know I'll need to revisit those sad, sad memories again. It wasn't my plan, but the ancient memories in this land and these people are alive in me and remind me of my own life stories.

# 48: Denial Is Easy

## What are you going to do?

A month after my father's death, I went home for Christmas break. I'd been having acid indigestion off and on for a few months and the infirmary staff at UNH said I might have an ulcer so I made an appointment with our family doctor, Dr. Rand, who had delivered all of us.

I reclined on his examination table for the pelvic exam and when he was done, the good doctor stood up from his stool at the end of the table and locked eyes with me. He looked worried when he said, "Could you be pregnant?"

Startled, I lifted my head to look at him and murmured, "I don't know."

Stern for him, he repeated, "Could you be pregnant?"

Like a little slap on the face, the words jerked me into reality. I twittered, "Maybe?" At that time in my life, denial was easy. Actually, I hadn't had a normal period in months.

After I was dressed he came back into the room. We sat down on opposite sides of his desk which was a little countertop thing that swung out from the bookcase. It seemed perfect for his sunny little office. Pushing fifty, he was trim and energetic. But most of all he was caring. I couldn't imagine him sitting behind a monstrosity of a desk that created a moat between the doctor and his patient. Even though he was surprised at my condition, I didn't feel judged. He was just the kind heart I needed.

We did the math and with his exam, he estimated I was five months along. Two days later the test results confirmed I was pregnant. My tall, toned, young body had conveniently concealed five months of pregnancy.

Still numb and emotionally exhausted from my father's death, I could barely process the words. *I'm pregnant!* Now what? I phoned to tell my friend, Sandy. She and I had been friends since high school and stayed in touch after I went to college even though she'd remained in town working at her family's store. What I needed most was generous and confident support and Sandy was that. We met at her house and when she wrapped her arms around me I felt a little lighter, more alive. We sat down to work out a plan for me. After some phone detective work, Sandy located David, the father of my baby and someone we'd both gone to high school with. He was working at a resort, an hour away. That night she drove me to see him and after she dropped me off, she went home and David and I spent the night together. But the attraction and the love we'd had was gone. When I told him I was pregnant he said, "What are *you* going to do?"

Feeling gutted, I stared at him and said, "Hell, I have no idea what *I'm* going to do. My dad just died a month ago!"

In 1969 David was a young twenty and I was an even younger twenty-one. Little did I know that his new girlfriend was about two months pregnant at the time. They married and later had two more sons.

David and I grew up in the same small town and our families were extremely close. My siblings and his brother and sister were best friends and his parents were kind and respected people in the community. My family had always welcomed David and his brother's impromptu stops at our house for a visit and a snack. A popular senior class president, he was also the classic tall, dark, and handsome type. Before college, David was like a brother to me.

My sophomore year at UNH, David enrolled as a freshman but we hardly ever saw each other on campus. That winter I invited him to join my friends and me for a weekend ski trip. Saturday evening, after a long day on the slopes and some partying, we saw each other in a new light and became smitten. Back on campus we started dating and quickly fell in love. David captured my heart and for months our romance flourished. Later that spring he transferred to another school, our relationship cooled, and I was devastated. We saw each other a few times over the summer then broke up for good. It was not what I wanted. I felt shredded. I was depressed, had chronic indigestion, my grades were suffering, then a couple months later my father died.

In January of 1970, after learning I was pregnant, I returned to college to finish the semester. Final exams didn't go well. I studied as best I could for my microbiology exam but I retained little and scored a 29. I did better on my other exams but I was on the verge of flunking out.

One Sunday, with my exams done, I attended mass on campus for the first time. I'd heard the priest was young and progressive. I felt so peaceful inside the little church that I stayed after mass to talk with the priest. I wanted to know what I should do. Father Lawless's face had a warm glow as I told him the long account about my dad and being pregnant. It was a relief to tell him and when I was done, he reached over, patted my hand, and told me to pray. He said, "The answers to your questions will come. Just keep praying." I still have the letter of encouragement he sent me a month later. Knowing he was rooting for me and that I was in his prayers helped. I didn't feel so alone and I began to sense there might be a plan for me.

With the semester done, I returned home in a daze. My world had stopped rotating. I'd lost the two most important men in my life. I didn't know where to go; my life wasn't making any sense so I stopped trying to figure it out. I'd been raised Catholic and ever since childhood, talking to God in prayer was normal. Now I prayed even harder asking for guidance. I reminded myself that I was breathing for two now.

The thought of telling my mother was like an impending nightmare, I was afraid of what it would do to her. I realize now she was incredibly strong, holding it all together the way she did.

I made a plan. On Sunday morning I'd drive my mom to mass and on the way home I'd tell her. It was a moment I'll never forget: the two of us in my '53 Chevy, a tank of a car. As we rumbled home after mass, I knew it was time. My heart raced, and I felt a little lightheaded. A few miles from church I gripped my oversized steering wheel and braced myself. *I'll make this short and sweet.* I stared out the windshield, took a very deep breath, and said, "Mom, you know how I've been feeling nauseous a lot?" She didn't answer so after a long pause I said, "I'm pregnant."

I still didn't hear anything so I looked over. She was just sitting there, hands folded in her lap, shoulders hunched forward, turned away from me, and looking out her side window. She looked small sitting there in the overstuffed seat of my car. With a frozen stare, I looked ahead down the highway. *What will become of us?* When I glanced at her, again, her head was down and she was weeping softly. I don't think my mother had a hard cry left in her.

Once she stopped, she stared out her window and asked. "Who's the father?"

I said, "David." She didn't need a last name.

The air between us was as tired as the breath of a spent runner. We were exhausted so there was no discussion and no hysterics. I imagined she must have felt "gut-punched," again. Having been given up for adoption herself, I was sure some old wounds must have surfaced.

Right when we got home we sat down to tell my brother, John, the new head of the family. John and my mom's close relationship was a real asset to all of us. As we sat in the kitchen together, there was no real discussion. As they saw it, the best option was to contact Catholic Charities for help with the adoption. At that time, it was a huge disgrace to be pregnant out of wedlock and I didn't know of any unmarried girl in our area keeping her baby.

A few days later, my mother and I visited one of her married nieces. My mother asked her if I could live with her small family until I delivered. My cousin's husband said no because he didn't want his kids exposed to me in my condition. Mom was furious.

We contacted Catholic Charities in Manchester, NH and they agreed to find me a family to live with in the Manchester area. Catholic Charities would arrange and pay for my doctor visits, hospital stay, and facilitate the adoption. Now my mom, brother, and his wife Dolly knew. After a couple more weeks at home I would just disappear.

# 49: My Disappearing Act

## I sounded like a tormented cat

Catholic Charities arranged for me to live with a young couple who had a charming home on a quiet street outside of Manchester. Christi was a Realtor and Ted was a news anchor for a local TV station and they had two small children. I had my own closet-sized bedroom which worked fine for me. I would help with the kids in trade for room and board and they would take me to my doctor's appointments. It worked out well. The couple was kind, going out of their way to spend time with me and include me in their family gatherings. Their two children were delightful and easy to care for.

Years later, my sister-in-law, Dolly, said that she and my mom came to visit me but I can't remember anything about it. Sandy called often and sent me letters of encouragement. I must have sounded despondent in a letter to her because she wrote back urging me to stay positive and to remember all of the people who loved me. Ron, a college friend of David's and mine, visited me a few times. It was awkward, though, eating at a restaurant with my big belly draped in an "old lady" maternity top. But Ron didn't seem fazed. I also felt uncomfortable because he reminded me of David and our times at UNH. After a few visits we lost contact.

I was living in a new town with people I'd just met. It felt only slightly odd as well as somewhat familiar. Maybe it was reminiscent of my long hospital stay when I was young. I didn't feel lonely, I felt alone. But, as usual, I just kept chugging along.

I began praying the day I found out I was pregnant, sometimes off and on all day: "God, tell me what to do. Should I keep it or give it up? I want to do what's best for my baby." Father Lawless, his words, and my conversations with God helped. It did feel like someone was listening and there was a good plan out there. I just needed to be patient and listen for it. But many times I felt like I was adrift on a raft. Yes, I was tied up to the dock but the rope was a mile long.

After settling in with my new family, I met with Catholic Charities again and they drew up adoption papers. I told them that I intended to give up the baby and I would sign the final papers after the baby was born and the adoptive family had been found. I was just going along with that plan, I knew I had not made up my mind about the adoption.

Physically, I felt fine; my pregnancy was easy, my baby and I were healthy. My due date was June 1st.

On May ninth Christi drove me to another checkup. My doctor was nice enough and he did the usual: measured my bump, took my blood pressure, and listened to the baby's heartbeat. As he listened to my belly he looked puzzled. Then to no one in the room, he said, "I think we'll get an x-ray." Being young and unmarried I didn't ask any questions and just went along. After the x-ray, I returned to the exam room. The doctor came in and sat down, then reported, "You're going to have twins." I heard the words but they didn't compute. My brain couldn't process any more trouble. There was no further discussion. That was it. Period. He left the room.

I filed the word *twins* away somewhere deep in my muddled mind then dressed. I climbed into Christi's car and we headed home. She was a kind woman but maintained what I'd guess was a healthy detachment from what I was going through. When I told her about the twins she just nodded but when I looked over at her pretty, fresh face, she looked troubled. She didn't say it but I knew she was concerned for me and it helped. At that point, knowing she was in the car and driving me home was about all I could register. At least I had that.

When we got home I called to tell my mom and she cried. It must have been just one more layer of grief for her. For me, it was just more information and lacked any real emotional quality. Maybe that was the only way I could do it. At the time they were good qualities to have.

A little after ten that evening and only hours after my office visit, I went into labor. The pains were mild at first and I wasn't afraid. I had a job to do. In the middle of the night the contractions got harder and closer, I woke Christi and she drove me to the hospital. I was admitted and put in a ward with four other women.

For the next twelve hours my contractions were pretty mild but the following afternoon they grew stronger. I was comfortable enough to read a magazine; my period cramps had been far worse. The most painful parts involved the not-so-gentle nuns. Like little machines, they approached me, yanked the curtains closed around my bed, and announced they wanted to check "my progress." They needed to estimate the dilation of my cervix. When I hadn't progressed to their satisfaction, they used a gloved hand to stretch the opening of my vagina way beyond what was normal. It hurt so much I sounded like a tormented cat.

By early evening the nuns were exasperated with me. One of them grabbed the magazine I was reading and said, "It's time for you to get down to business!" I didn't know what she meant and I didn't dare ask. I had read a couple small books on childbirth but hadn't taken any classes and didn't have a coach or for that matter anyone to help so I was on my own. Christi and Ted knew I was in labor and I thought they must have called my family but, if they did, no one called me. I wasn't afraid, I knew I was going to have a baby, now two babies. *It's just something I have to do, right?*

Too stressed out to pray, I had only one goal in mind: get those babies born. Also, I kept wondering what "getting down to business" meant. Later that night after what seemed like a dozen excruciatingly painful examinations by the nuns, they raced me off to the delivery room, bed and all. My memory of labor ended there.

The next morning, I woke up back in bed in the ward. My doctor came in and explained that they'd injected me with Pentothol, which had put me to sleep. He said they strapped me down to the delivery table and after making an extra-large episiotomy incision, they'd pulled my baby girls out. He told me baby girl #1 was trying to be born head first with her foot up against her face. He said that had kept me from having the urge to push. Or as the nun had put it, to "get down to business." Baby girl #2 was breach and was pulled out three minutes after her sister. Both were healthy, weighing 6 lbs. 1 oz. and 5 lbs. 2 oz. It was May, 10th, Mother's Day.

Later that morning I napped in my bed, relieved the delivery part was over. I assumed I must have done a whole lot of thrashing on that table because every muscle in my body ached. Thanks to the massive incision I wouldn't be able to sit up straight for a week. The hardest part, though was I didn't see my babies. At that time, I wasn't sure what I was going to do and with no one pressuring me, I let things play out as if I was going to give them up.

I asked one nun if I should see them. She said not to if I was giving them up, so of course, I complied. At feeding time, when the newborns were brought to their moms, I held up my magazine to cover my face and tried to shut out the sounds of crying babies and cooing mothers. I shut down inside even more. I was getting good at that.

Sandy visited the next day and, to my surprise and discomfort, she brought along David. She told me she had made it a point to call him with the birth news. When David walked up to my bed, all I felt was tired and numb. He bent down and kissed me on the cheek then told me Sandy said one baby looked like me, one like him. *Why would he tell me that? Maybe he had nothing else to say.* During a very long pause, he just stood looking about the room and I had nothing to say to him either. I hadn't planned this. Then he said that someone stopped him in the hall and asked if he was Ted, the local news anchor, the father I had been living with. I answered with an "Oh." I wasn't going to give him anything more that might ease his discomfort.

Worn-out and bewildered, I continued my incessant prayers. Later I talked to a nun again about seeing my babies before I left. She scolded me, saying it was not recommended. I sat with that for a few hours then decided I'd go ahead and see them anyway. I asked for a wheelchair and, sitting cockeyed on a stack of pillows, I wheeled myself down to the nursery for a peek. Sandy was right, the smaller one, baby #2 looked like me, and the plumper one, baby #1 more like David. Even though I was leaving them behind, I was glad I saw them.

I was told the adoption papers were modified for twins and a search for a home for my babies began. I continued praying that I'd make the right decision. I was very confused. My life was on pause.

The twins stayed in the hospital for ten extra days because they were not feeding well. When I learned babies need their mothers to thrive, it broke my heart that I'd left them. But what could I do? My babies stayed with a foster family after being released from the hospital and I went back home. I planned to heal, regroup, and at some point return to college. I continued to pray for direction.

After a few weeks of resting at home, my sister, Lorraine, invited me to live with her and Paul in Nashua, NH. She helped me get a job as a nurse's aide at the hospital where she worked.

Living with Lorraine and Paul was easy and fun. During that time no one from Catholic Charities approached me.

One evening, when my twins were almost eight weeks old, Paul and I sat watching a movie at the apartment while Lorraine was at work. All of a sudden, I felt unsettled, like something was stirring outside my skin. The room felt full of static. I looked over at Paul to see if he noticed it but he was laughing at the TV. The sensations continued. It didn't scare me. I was curious but unsettled. After a few minutes I told Paul I was tired and went into my bedroom. I closed the door and flopped down on my bed, clothes and all. The whole surface of my body was gently tingling and I felt a little jittery but it wasn't unpleasant. Whatever it was felt kind. The air filling the entire room was charged like it feels right before a lightning strike. Stretched out on my back, I just went with it. My mind was still so I knew I wasn't imagining it. It was different from anything

I'd ever experienced. After an hour or so, my body felt more peaceful than it had in years. I stayed awake for the whole night and allowed myself to absorb the gift of serenity and guidance wherever it came from. Looking back now, I know it sounds fantastical but something wonderful and healing happened that night because in the morning I felt remarkably clear and free. I knew all my praying had been heard. I had my answer.

# 50: The Road Back Home

## Family provides shelter to family

Two days after my decision, my mom and her sister, Marie, picked me up in Nashua and we drove to the Catholic Charities complex in Manchester to get my babies. For the last seven weeks they'd been with a foster family. Before I left the hospital, I'd had to give them names for their birth certificates. I chose a first name for each but no middle name. I reasoned that if they got to choose their own middle names when they were older, it might make them feel a little more in charge of their lives.

When I saw my smaller twin in the nursery, the name Claire popped into my head. She looked delicate and dainty the way the name Claire sounded to me. I named her older, robust sister Jennifer. It was a popular name at the time and seemed to fit her. Before then I hadn't had any names in mind. *Why name a baby I might not keep?*

I gripped the steering wheel of my mom's car as we approached Manchester. *I'm not ready for this.* I felt like a young actor on a TV soap who hadn't been given her lines. I wondered how an unwed, new mother of two was supposed to act or even feel.

Thank goodness our meeting at Catholic Charities was slick and professional, like the transferring of a deed in a law office. I was confident about my decision but scared about being a mom. My only plan was to take my babies home to my family. The day I told my mother I'd keep my babies there was no discussion about bringing them home. Years before when my aunt's family of eight first moved from Massachusetts to New Hampshire, they'd lived with us for a year and my father's half-sisters had lived with us for a time, too. A motto for us could be: family provides shelter to family. My girls and I were welcomed and folded into the household. It was and still is a norm for us.

A nun dressed in the "penguin" uniform of the day, lead us into a large Victorian room with no windows. A more stately nun sat soldier-like behind a huge, ornate, wooden desk. Her greeting was civil enough and after we introduced ourselves, we talked about the transfer. It didn't take long. Once I signed the papers, poof, perfect timing, two glowing young nuns waltzed into the room each with a swaddled baby in her arms. The room got silent and still as if something life changing was happening. I looked at one nun then the other and each gave me a shy, encouraging smile. I felt it and relaxed just a bit. Then one nun handed a pink bundle to me and the other nun gave hers to my mom. From the looks of her pudgy face, I knew I had Jennifer. Mission accomplished but I wanted to feel more--- motherly or something. I looked down at the adorable infant in my arms. I knew she was mine, but I hated that I still felt empty, a stranger to this baby. I knew I was doing the right thing. One foot in front of the other, right? But I was seriously out of my element.

We finished the paperwork, the nuns loaded up Aunt Marie with baby things from the foster family, and we walked out to the car. I slid into the driver's seat and my mom sat next to me cradling Jennifer because we didn't have infant car seats in 1970. I stole glimpses of my baby daughter urging something more but I had only a vague sense that the tiny being belonged to me. Aunt Marie was in the back holding Claire. After we left the city, our sparse conversations soon became joyful and it was such a relief to feel a little more normal. My mom said, "Look how content darling little Jenny is and look at that blonde hair." From Aunt Marie I heard, "Claire has the most beautiful big eyes and I think she's going to have her grandma's red hair." I stared down the road ahead of me and smiled in my confusion.

Every single part of this was hard to process because I was discovering or creating a whole new part of myself. I don't know which. They were talking about my daughters. I wondered when they'd feel like mine.

Today, I wish I could remember what we talked about on that two-hour drive home. Were they mostly silent like me? Aunt Marie and my mom had been adopted, were not biologically related, and never knew their birth parents. I wonder what it was like for them to hold a baby whose mother chose to keep her. Knowing my mother, she probably shed a tear or two, but I didn't see any. I'm not sure about Aunt Marie, maybe she did too but she was more pragmatic, not as emotional as my mom. Maybe unwittingly they shared an intimate moment during the ride home. Two adopted sisters who never met their parents were helping reunite two precious infants with their mother.

I couldn't wait to get home and, once we got there, my whole family greeted us with hugs and tears of joy. This was where my girls and I belonged. It couldn't have been a better welcome and at a perfect time because my dad had died only six months earlier. I began to appreciate the solid, caring foundation my parents, even with all their flaws, had created. Growing up, my parents had never gotten the emotional nurturing owed them but they gave us what they could, what they valued: a lovely house and a rich home life.

A changing table had been added just off the kitchen, two cradles waited in the family room, and two large cribs, like parentheses, sat on each side of the bed in my mom's bedroom. She gave the twins and me her room and she moved into my sister's bedroom. She'd moved us in and moved herself out. At the time I was incapable of appreciating the gesture.

There were ten of us living in the house again. The last half-year had been rough but it was wonderful and effortless how we folded into each other's spaces and lives again. Then little by little I began to feel more like myself.

Soon after arriving home, my sister, Linda, said I should change Claire's name to Jessica because it would go better with Jennifer. Easily influenced by family and because it made sense, Claire became Jessica.

Three days after our arrival was July 4th when John and Dolly planned to celebrate their wedding anniversary with a weekend-long party and Pig Roast. Relatives and close friends were invited and, little did we know, for the next fifteen years, the "Boudreault Pig Roast" would become a gigantic family, as well as town, tradition.

The first morning of the celebration, I pictured the crowd of people who'd be showing up later. I'd been wondering how I was going to tell everyone about my twins and now I realized this was the perfect opportunity. On Saturday afternoon when the party began, I'd have my twins downstairs in their cradles in the family room and, as guests walked in, I'd lead certain relatives and close friends into the room and, "Surprise!"

As far as I determined, it worked great. When the unsuspecting guests saw the two little cradles and babies, they looked up at me confused as I smiled. After a pause then a struggle for the right words, they'd ask, "Whose are they?"

With what now seems like childlike pride, I told them, "They're mine."

Only one person asked about their father. The others probably had enough to process or maybe they felt I'd ambushed them, which I probably had. Poor social skill on my part, maybe?

It became more and more real for me every time I said, "They're mine." I didn't get any questions just surprised looks. I imagined the party crowd filled in the information gaps that they were too stunned to ask me about.

When my childhood friend, Barbara Johnson, arrived I told her I had a surprise for her then steered her into the family room. She looked at the babies, looked at me, then back to the babies.

"Whose are they?"

"They're mine," I said with a big smile.

Speechless, she looked at me in disbelief.

For a few seconds I glowed with pride. Then I told her about living in Manchester and about Catholic Charities. "Who's the father?"

I said, "David." She knew which David.

After high school and, even though we attended the same college, our friendship had fizzled as we pursued different interests and made new friends. She stretched out her arms and we hugged but I sensed we would become even more distant.

I felt unequivocally accepted by my relatives, most friends, and townspeople. The only exception was my Catholic Italian godmother. We called her Auntie Kay. She was beautiful, a stylish dresser, and when she walked into a room, she owned it. Kay and my mom were best friends, talked on the phone daily, had lunch dates, and had double-dated with my dad and Kay's husband. When I was young, I'd sleep at her fancy house and she'd treat me to gourmet meals and buy me girly-girl dresses and pretty jewelry I'd accept but didn't like much. She had a son around my age. Once when I was twelve, she, my mom, and I were eating lunch at a restaurant when Auntie Kay told me that she wanted to leave me all of her diamonds when she died. I looked over at her unimpressed and said, "I don't like diamonds that much" and took another bite of my sandwich. I thought my mother was going to kill me. I knew Auntie Kay loved me but when I was much older I knew she and I had been cast from very different molds.

When my godmother learned my mom took my twins and me in, she stopped speaking to her. I couldn't believe she was such a snob. Even though it broke her heart, my mother accepted the loss of Kay's friendship and her support for me never wavered, not once. I remember hearing gossip about them not speaking and when I asked my mom about it, she refused to say anything. I knew where my mother stood and it was with me. It was the most positive lesson she taught me. Our children learn the most from us through osmosis and by watching how we orchestrate our lives.

With all that I'd experienced, at times it was a struggle to stay present, so bonding with my daughters took time. I was super attentive and knew how to care for a baby because when Beth was born I was sixteen so I'd had lots of practice. I knew all this in my head and finally, after hours of rocking crying infants and cuddling with them in bed, I felt the bonds growing. I soon learned how to get out of bed, while barely awake, and in the dark retrieve their pacifiers from under their cribs. But when they cried out in hunger, I got nervous, and for a second felt helpless, forgetting I knew what to do. To a degree it was baby and mom boot camp for sure but within weeks, with the help of my sister-in-law and my mom, I began to feel even more like a real mother. The girls had so many people caring for them that after a while I worried they might not know who I was. I came to realize it didn't much matter since they were immersed in such an adoring family.

My easygoing, cheerful girls would readily engage with whomever was holding them. They were thriving and our family was beginning to heal. I now appreciate the timing of their birth. Just when we needed a little distraction, and more importantly, hope, they entered our lives.

# 51: Strolling Up Main Street

## There was always a smile

The Pig Roast was a raucous party and my "last hurrah" of sorts before settling into the responsibilities of motherhood. Secure in my family's dedication, I was ready to move into the next chapter of my life, whatever that was.

I don't remember everything about that first year at home but what I do remember is my mom, sisters, and sister-in-law, Dolly, were hands-on with the girls. There was always someone to help out. I was on a treadmill: eat, sleep, pitch in with housework, tend to the girls, and keep going. I liked the routine. It made me feel secure and I tried to take it minute by minute and not think about the future.

At the house we settled into an affable schedule. I'd wake most mornings to babbling and giggles coming from the cribs then I'd carry my babies into my bed, my mom's bed. Often Beth and my young niece, Gerry, would jump in for some snuggles. In those moments of tickles and laughter, I was the kind of mother I wanted to be. Life was joyful and perfect and I realized how much I loved my babies.

After our bed fun and with a precious bundle on each hip, I'd go downstairs and into the kitchen where there was always someone eating breakfast and happy to be recruited to help change and feed a twin. By three months of age, they were sleeping through the night and were great eaters. Their foster parents must have done a good job. I wish I could have thanked them.

But I still felt like something was missing. I loved my girls but I didn't have that motherly bond I hoped I would. For years I judged myself harshly until I learned bonding can take time and other moms experienced the same feeling I had. Even to this day, my heart aches to know they didn't have me those first weeks and how close I came to losing them. Now, of course, I can't imagine my life without them.

My mom gravitated towards Jessie who had red curly hair and was trimmer and more laid back than her sister. Content to stay in the background and out of her sister's spotlight, Jessie didn't walk till she was thirteen months old. I remember one day when Jessie was two. She and I were alone in my car and I turned to her in her car seat and said, "Jessie do you want to stop and get an ice cream?" She had talked very little so I expected a simple yes or no. She said, "I want chocolate ice cream and one for Jenny." I was shocked because I hadn't realized she could speak a full sentence. Jenny talked early and a lot. Jessie mostly giggled. I learned it's normal for fraternal twins to have very different personalities and skill-sets.

Dolly gravitated towards Jenny. At one year, she had blonde, spiked hair and was covered with chubby rolls so Dolly nicknamed her Buddha. I'd read that fat babies usually walk later than thin ones but gregarious Jenny walked at nine months. At two, she was hospitalized overnight with croup. The next morning when I went to the hospital to bring her home, a nurse met me with a chuckle and a smile. She told me that about midnight Jenny unzipped her croup tent, climbed down over the rails and out of her crib. She calmly walked to the nurse's station, looked up all business-like, and said, "I am looking for my mother." Even at two, she was confident and determined.

Our house was a hub of family activities and I was fine with living in the wake of the comings and goings. Some days it had what seemed like a steady stream of visitors, some expected, some not.

And there were surprises. Late one afternoon, my teenage sister, Linda, ran into my cranky, old first-grade teacher, Mrs. Harrison. She was the one who took a ruler to my legs because I couldn't manage some dance steps only months after returning home from my polio hospitalization. Another time she told me to stand up in class and tell everyone my brother was stupid. I refused and after school she put me over her lap and gave me a spanking. When I told my mom and dad about it, I never saw them so angry. They met with her and she never tried it again.

Linda had seen Mrs. Harrison in town, gushed to her about the girls, then invited her to come to the house to see them right then. With no warning, Linda bounced on home with Mrs. Harrison in tow. She strutted into the house behind my beaming sister who led her into the family room where the girls were napping. Mrs. Harrison took all of three seconds to check out the girls then left after giving me a cool glance and no goodbye. My mom and I had a talk with Linda after she left.

David lived only a few miles away. Other than Jeff, David's brother, no one in his family had acknowledged the girls. My family was bewildered because up to that time, our families had been extremely close. Their mother was so distraught when my father died, she couldn't attend his funeral.

I remember the day Jeff, all six-foot-four of him and sporting a thick arm cast, showed up unexpectedly at our house. He walked out onto the back lawn where my mom, Dolly, and I were sitting. After a brief chat, we heard my one-year olds yelling from their bedroom window, their nap time was over.

Jeff looked over at me and said, "Can I go get them?" He hadn't met them yet.

I said, "Yes," and felt a tenderness inside as I watched the lumbering young man climb the back stairs and go into the house. Jeff knew his way around inside and was quick to return with the girls.

The image is forever imprinted on my mind: that eighteen-year-old in jeans, a white t-shirt, shit-kickers, and grubby cast cradling a bubbly baby girl in each arm. He looked like he'd done it a dozen times before.

He handed the girls off to me and Dolly then asked me how the twins were doing. I told him they were doing great and we visited for a few minutes more before he left. He never came to see them or to our house again. I imagine it was just all too confusing for him.

Even though our families had been close, I guessed that David's family could not reconcile what had happened. In my conversations with townspeople, they said they didn't understand why his family was ignoring the girls and I wondered that too. Maybe it was just too complex an issue for them. But I didn't let it bother me which surprised me. Besides that, I had enough to think about just maintaining my family of three.

From the beginning I felt embraced by our town. There may have been some gossip about David and me and maybe my family hid it but I never heard anything. I wonder how much my father's tragic death had affected townsfolk. Maybe it softened their hearts making it easy to accept us.

Most days, weather permitting, I'd take my girls for a walk in their baby carriage. When they got older, there were two strollers as well as a cousin or sister to help. On the half-mile walk up Main Street we'd pass the home of my Aunt Patsy and Uncle Norman and their nine kids. With seven girls, it was my babysitter bonanza and, besides that, the family adored the twins.

After that we'd always stop at the town post office, a sturdy little building that resembled a glorified shed. Once I backed the carriage inside, Helen, the postmaster, would greet the girls with chuckles and smiles through the small, barred opening at her front counter. Then she'd come out from the back and bend down to greet her little visitors. Helen purred as she gently took one tiny hand then the other, asked me how they were doing then gave them the sugary praises and tender compliments one gives babies. When the girls could talk they named her "the lady" and asked often to visit her. I wondered if they thought Helen lived in a jail.

In the center of the village I'd wheel into Aldrich's General Store to share some baby joy. Floral-dressed, plump grandmas lit up when they saw our strollers coming. We'd pass grumpy, old grandpas, long stooped from years of farming and they'd give us a nod and a smile that tickled me. Lots of times on the way home, my favorite mechanic, Stub Fadden, would come out of his garage to give us a wave and a smile. When I was a kid he'd stop what he was doing to patch a leaky bike tire every time we needed help.

In those days when time moved slower, most people stopped to admire Jenny and Jessie and I felt their approval and delight. I'd half expected some raised eyebrows and turned-away faces but, even though some didn't say a word, there was always a smile. It never stopped surprising me and, maybe it's hyperbole, but the way my girls lightened everyone's day felt groundbreaking for our little town. I never, ever felt embarrassed about getting pregnant and keeping my babies Why should I? After all, these people got to blend my two beautiful, innocent children into their lives.

# 52: Making My Own Fire

## Is there something wrong with being alone?

I'm a little giddy as I unpack my gear and set up the tent in Spearfish. Everything about this place says welcome: the nearby canyon walls, the small, pristine stream, the neat sites, and campers who smile and nod as they walk by. Right now, even the persistent biting flies, *little bastards*, can't make me complain.

I set up camp then take Doug for a walk on the dirt road circling the campsites. After that, it doesn't take me long to choose my hot tent over the Kamikaze biters attacking me. With his thick hair, they don't seem to bother Doug, so he stretches out on the shaded ground next to the car. The air in the tent is hot and stagnant but, with my mind focused on my book, I pretend I'm in a sauna and my body is releasing bad memories from Scenic and Devils Tower. After a couple of sweaty hours and a change of clothes, I'm mellow.

In the afternoon, I drive into Spearfish to do some laundry. The beautiful upbeat town of about ten thousand is tidy, hospitable, and surprisingly modern. And its easy-to-find laundromat is modest but clean. When I dump a week's worth of dirty clothes onto the stainless steel table, the overpowering smell of mildew makes me recoil. I grab a giant armful and stuff it into the monster machine, and hope two hot-water cycles and extra soap will do the trick.

As I sit waiting for my clothes, for some reason, a long chain of plastic chairs bolted together grabs my attention. Except for their color, they're identical and, unappealing. I sit in an orange one that's so hard I need to wiggle to get comfortable. I open my book and try not to think about it.

I attempt to read but the image of the plastic chairs, shackled together creeps in. Maybe I've been alone out here for too long and now my maverick mind is thinking about people who've allowed societal expectations to limit them. I wonder if those folks fear stepping out on their unique path. I wonder if following one's own course promotes the evolution of not only the person but society. *Back to the important work, Regina, you've got laundry to do.*

After putting my clean clothes in the car Doug and I step out to explore the town. We stroll for a few blocks and come to a beautiful park that's right in the middle of the business district.

The park stretches out over a few acres of immaculate lawns bordered by a dozen drooping cottonwood trees. At the far end, a waterfall cascades down over a two-story-high exposure of smooth, granite bedrock. The water tumbles onto a big, shallow basin churning with crystalline water. The overflow gushes out into a small river running parallel to the field then disappears into a forest. I can't stop grinning. A handful of families picnic in the shade of the magnificent trees and people splash and wade near the waterfall. The cheery, human chorus takes me back to when my kids were little and the fun picnics we had. It's easy to imagine Aboriginal people spearfishing here. *I don't want to leave.*

On my drive back to camp, my daydreaming fades when I think about the preteen boys I saw earlier at camp. Before I left, the four-pack of rascals obliterated the quiet and trespassed campsite boundaries. When I'd heard Doug's warning bark and saw one of the boys swagger onto my site I yelled in my stern, teacher tone, "Hey. This is not your site. Please leave." Now, I wonder if I might have been too harsh. I wonder if I'm expecting too much from a young boy who's probably the same age as my son. *Should I just put up with their shenanigans? Maybe here in my little cocoon of an adventure, I should learn to be more tolerant of people.*

Back at camp, I sit by my own little babbling brook feeling protected by the canyon walls. I'm at peace and, as an added bonus, I have clean laundry. *Time to explore?*

After studying my map, Doug and I head out for a two-mile hike leading to the canyon's main entrance. After the last few days, it's time to play. It feels like there's a mild, spring sun up there even though it's late July. The warmed air becomes a breeze that floats and flows through the length of the canyon floor. A large creek and a few little marshes stretch out ahead of us. Doug is off-leash for most of the hike so he gets in a good run. It's just what he needs because when we return to camp, he relaxes enough to take himself off guard duty. *Note to self: Doug needs more exercise.* It might improve my disposition too.

While Doug naps, I head out in search of firewood for the evening. It's a short walk into the surrounding forest where I begin picking up dead branches and kindling. All of a sudden, and only a few yards away, a large doe confronts me with a serious stare then stomps her front feet and snorts. *Who knew deer could make such loud sounds.* She's obviously making a statement about her boundary. I don't want to challenge her so I stay put and look at her with the most nonchalant face I can muster. She makes a couple more impressive exhibitions then leaps away into the forest. Wow. All deer the I've come across have been shy and quick to escape. I guess I was trespassing in her territory.

While walking back with an armload of wood, a smiley, middle-aged man steps onto my path and says, "You found all that by yourself?" *What a stupid question.*

"Yes, I'm going to have a fire tonight."

"You need some help getting it going?"

Again, I try to be civil. "Oh, no thanks. I'm all set." *Really? Do I look that frail and helpless? If I do, that would be a first.* I think back to Bear Butte when Ben had a hard time understanding how I could hike the mountain. *What is it with people, anyway?*

My lackluster supper of a beans-and-rice combo with a can of string beans on the side is fine. After I clean my dishes in the stream, I gather kindling to start the fire. The biting-flies are so bad I put on a long-sleeve shirt. After I get the fire going the wind picks up. It's finicky but with just the right orientation, I get enough smoke to keep the flies away but not enough to choke. Nestled in my chair by the fire, I write in my journal.

After a short while, the young boys start in again. They march through the area as if they are on maneuvers. *Maybe it's just teenage hormones.* I decide to be a little more tolerant, to become an objective observer and less reactive but it's not easy for this well-seasoned classroom teacher who likes order. My tactic helps. I stick to my journal, they eventually move on, and quiet returns.

A few pages into my writing I begin thinking about being out here alone. Not just alone at this campsite but single. It's been four years since I've been in an intimate relationship. *How do I feel about that? Is there something wrong with being alone? Am I missing something here? Why is this coming up now? Really, why now? Maybe for me, intimate relationships are just too risky and the costs too high. I'm not sure. Maybe my social skills need a tune-up.*

Sometimes I think it would be nice to have someone to share my adventures with but most of the time I prefer being alone. And, I know nothing about this trip would be the same with other people along. *Well, that's settled. Case closed. Solo it is.* A little later old memories begin to stir again.

# 53: What about Chinchillas?

## I had visions of a few dozen little money-makers

After a couple months, motherhood started growing on me and I felt settled. My days were filled with baby care and family interactions. But I missed the intellectual demands of college life and I knew I had to find a way to support my small family. One day, as I flipped through the back pages of a magazine, an advertisement piqued my interest. It said you could raise chinchillas, sell their fur, and make a ton of money.

I told my mom about it and asked if she thought it was okay for me to call the number in the ad. She said yes and also agreed to let someone from the chinchilla company come to our house to talk with me about starting a business. A representative showed up a week later.

The rep was in his early thirties and as I asked questions he stayed glued to his notebook. His suit was as tired looking as his affect but he seemed harmless. We sat in the kitchen and my mother monitored our meeting while washing the same dishes over and over. We talked about his company and the basic logistics of raising chinchillas. When we finished I showed him our basement and he said it had potential because it was clean, dry, and spacious. I had visions of cages in rows down there, enough to house a few dozen little money-makers.

After the chinchilla man left, I scanned the forms and papers he'd given me, and checked the notes I'd taken. I was excited so I turned to my mom and asked, "What do you think? I could make a lot of money. Chinchilla furs are really expensive."

I reiterated pretty much what had been the rep's pitch. My mother listened like she had no opinion and, as I listened to myself ramble, it was like being in an echo chamber. That was smart of her. A chinchilla farm in the basement just wasn't practical, especially with a house full of people and two babies. My mom let me reach that decision on my own. I felt her support.

A week later, I sent a hand-written letter to the Hartz Mountain Pet Products Company about opening up a pet store. My family owned a building in town that had two vacant store fronts. I loved animals, had spent many hours as a kid helping our vet, and was a biology major in college. I was sure I had the qualifications, the experience, and the enthusiasm necessary to start up my own little business. And, with the nearest pet store over an hour away, I was confident Hartz would see it as an opportune business venture.

I was pumped. I found the address of the Hartz Mountain Co. headquarters on the package of some fish food we had at the house and sent my letter telling them about my awesome idea. I never heard back.

A couple weeks later, I read about a job opening at the Mountain Hospital in the neighboring village. It was for a nurse's aide position working in Central Supply. I didn't know what Central Supply was but I needed a job so I applied.

# 54: Blood and Guts Filled my New Classrooms

## Nothing felt alive

Things continued to fall into place for us and living in a small town helped. I got hired during my interview, probably because the hospital administrator knew my family's work ethic and our history. The job description included work in Central Supply, the ER, OR, OBS (Obstetrics), and the Medical-Surgical floor as needed. Also I had to take the EMT course.

I paid two of Aunt Patsy's daughters to babysit. They rotated days at the house helping with the girls when I worked my 3-11 p.m. shift, five days a week. One cousin would show up at five and leave at my girls' bedtime at seven and my mom and/or Dolly were always there to help. I got home at 11:30. It was a slick arrangement.

Only a short commute away, The Mountain Hospital was a single-story brick structure built in 1960. By modern standards, it was tiny and rudimentary but, with its pristine, new interior, to me it seemed ultra-modern. It also had two x-ray rooms, a morgue, two intensive care suites, and twenty med-surgical beds. Aside from the morgue, I worked wherever I was needed.

My primary assignment was Central Supply where I cleaned and sterilized trays of instruments for the other departments. On OBS, I cleaned and stocked the delivery room, helped with patients, assisted in deliveries and took care of babies in the nursery. Over time I would participate in over one hundred deliveries. I checked in and prepped patients in the ER and assisted the doctors. Unless an RN was required, I was it. A nurse gave me my best job description. She said I was a "technical surgical nurse's aide."

On my first day, a morning shift, in Central Supply I listened as Lois, my supervisor, gave me the rundown. She was short and stocky and wore a scrub dress, a matching blue cotton cap, and white nurse's shoes. Quick talking, she seemed less than thrilled having me there. After listening to her rattle off what the job required I was pretty sure I could handle it because of my science lab experience. Lois sounded like she knew her stuff and that impressed me so I started to feel excited about the position.

Later that morning Lois called me over to one of the deep, stainless steel sinks. She dipped her gloved hand into the ruddy water and pulled out a hemostat. It looked like large, thin scissors with vice grip clamps at the end and there was blood and pieces of tissue wedged in the joint. She said, "You'll need to learn the names and function for a few dozen instruments like this. A hemostat is used to clamp a blood vessel to stop bleeding. The instruments in this sink are from this morning's two surgeries. Your job is to clean them thoroughly, set them on a tray in a specific order, wrap the tray with a surgical towel, then put it in the autoclave to sterilize. Suddenly I'll show you how to work the autoclave later. It's a big responsibility. Peoples' lives are at stake so make sure the instruments are clean, in order on the right tray, and the temperature setting and timer on the autoclave are correct." *I am a college dropout and a confident person but I'd have a person's life in my hands. Are they sure about me? I'm not.*

In my first week of training, Lois had me come in early one morning to observe surgery in the OR. She told me the patient's name and I recognized it from town. The woman was going to have varicose veins stripped from her legs. I was comfortable with the idea of being an observer after having assisted our vet in dozens of surgeries and the sight of blood didn't bother me. I looked forward to watching the doctors and nurses at work. All I'd have to do is watch.

I arrived early the morning of the surgery, stepped into the nurse's locker room, and changed into what would become my standard work attire: a dull blue scrub dress, clunky but super comfortable white nurse shoes, and white pantyhose. My sleeveless, A-line dress hung just below my knees and was bland but gave me the freedom of a frock. The color and style matched the uninspiring albeit functional hospital decor and I welcomed that. It was nice to blend in for a change.

I entered the OR scrub room, put on a cap and mask, then mimicked Lois as she scrubbed her hands and arms up to her elbows. After, Lois helped me put on a surgical gown and she tied it in the back, then I put on sterile gloves. I moved my body sideways through the OR door following Lois into the operating suite.

I hoped Lois didn't hear me gasp. Three giant ceiling lamps cast a spotlight on the woman I knew from town. She was on her back on the table and a green sheet covered her torso and another covered her privates. Her bare legs were spread and each was suspended a foot above the table by an ankle strap attached to a pole. Stained orange with antiseptic, her legs and feet pointed at me. The disturbing image slammed me hard. I had to look away. Shocked and embarrassed for the woman, I side-stepped a good distance from one side of the table then backed behind an array of plastic tubing, surgical trays, IV equipment, and small motors. *My god, this is creepy.*

The windowless room wasn't just cool, it was cold. The dry air held a faint smell of alcohol and I wondered if I'd be able to take a normal breath because nothing in the room felt alive.

The surgeon and three nurses, including Lois, shuffled about as if their shoes had magnets and were controlled by a covert entity under the floor. The anesthesiologist stayed seated at the patient's head which was thankfully behind a small tent of surgical drapes. I was intrigued because, with only fragments of conversation, the team worked as a fluid unit. *Impressive.*

Then it started. The surgeon made an inch-long incision inside the poor woman's right ankle. Next, into the incision, he forced a four-foot-long wire, with a small, marble-sized metal knob at the end. He pushed it into her leg up, up, up, all the way to the top of her inner thigh where another incision had already been made. The metal knob popped out of that hole then the doctor pushed his fingers inside the incision to adjust something. After that he went back to her ankle and wrapped the other end of the wire around his hand. Whop! With a mighty yank, the entire metal wire whipped out of her ankle hole with the vein stuck at the knob like a long piece of scrunched-up wet pasta. *Yikes!* I gasped again, maybe louder, and felt woozy for a second.

Three minutes later, two nurses and the surgeon turned their attention to the other leg. When the doc started in on the other ankle, he looked up at me and said, "Tilt the lamp down here please." He pointed to the new ankle incision. *Surely, he doesn't mean me. I'm just an observer.* There were times when I wished I was petite and so, at least in my mind, inconspicuous, and maybe looking childlike.

Lois, who was standing near the IVs at the patient's head, glared at me. I reached up and grabbed the ceiling lamp's handle and aimed the beam of light on the ankle area and hoped to god I could be invisible.

Once the second leg was done, within minutes, it seemed, the patient was put on a stretcher and wheeled out and I breathed easier. Thankfully I never ran into her again. After that Lois and I went to work.

She showed me how to clean, set up, and stock the suite. She was all business, which didn't surprise me, and I liked that she expected perfection. I concentrated hard on what she showed me and was committed to memorizing the names and functions of all the equipment. My new job was an interesting challenge and I enjoyed it.

The following week I attended another early morning surgery. This time I helped Lois set up the operating room as well as clean up after. I'd gotten to know her to be a well-seasoned, intelligent nurse with a fiery disposition. She taught me a lot but I didn't enjoy working with her because she was always in a hurry and sometimes it seemed she was trying to run away from me. Later I found out she suffered from tachycardia, sudden episodes of a rapid heartbeat. It made me wonder if her frantic work pace was the cause.

When I walked into the operating suite of the second surgery, the patient's chest had been cut open exposing his beating heart. I wasn't a fainter but, I think if I had been, I surely would have dropped. Again, I wondered; should I be here? After a few minutes in the steely, sterile, and silent OR, the surgeon shouted a command, "Suction." But nothing happened, no one moved. Again he barked "Suction." This time Lois's eyes grabbed me and she snapped, "Regina, turn on the suction." *Me? Am I allowed?*

The suction machine was sitting on a stainless steel cart in front of me. Thank goodness there was only one switch so I flipped it up and the motor started. When the doctor stuck the tube into the patient's chest, I felt like I went in with it. It was like I was witnessing another intrusion into a person's sanctuary, like when the thick wire was pushed up the woman's leg. Even though the patient was asleep I had a feeling the body wasn't and years later I discovered I was right. I would learn that the body is conscious and remembers *everything*.

The white plastic attachment at the end of the tubing penetrated the chest cavity and suctioned out all sorts of thick bloody debris and at that point, the room sounded a little like a construction site.

I was a bit more relaxed than during my first surgery so after a while I stepped back a bit to observe the well-choreographed dance of the doctors and nurses. Everyone knew their parts and they followed the lead dancer, the surgeon. In 1970, in that tiny hospital, the surgeon was the family practitioner who delivered babies, admitted and cared for patients, and took turns covering the ER. Aside from major organ surgeries, there were four rural family docs who did it all and seemed competent. Except for one.

Dr. Garland was a no-nonsense gruff practitioner, what adults then called a "horse doctor." He was having a long-term affair with a young, married nurse, and from what I heard, pretty much any other woman who would have him. The gossip in town was that his wife was heavily medicated for her nerves which allowed him to carry on as he did. Someone told me that once, years ago, an older, uncircumcised man came into the ER with a bad infection in his foreskin. Dr. Garland treated him in the ER and, without anesthesia, the poor fellow got circumcised.

Months after my first day and late on a slow night, I wandered around the hospital's dark, eerily quiet halls and ended up on the morgue wing. I was curious what the morgue looked like so I pushed open the heavy door and entered what felt like a giant refrigerator. I flipped on the lights and everywhere I looked there was stainless steel: the counters along the walls, cabinets, sinks, and the large and creepy beveled table in the middle. Everything was shiny like a mirror and a strange and unsettling disinfectant smell choked out much of its breathable air. *I swear, nothing could live in here or would want to.*

After that time, if I had to walk past that dim hallway at night, I'd look straight ahead and pick up my pace. It gave me the creeps. Yes, it was cold and sterile and made me think of dead bodies but did it subconsciously trigger something deeper in me? Was I finally beginning to acknowledge how abandoned I felt all those months in Manchester, especially in the hospital? Had I been so adept at blocking my emotions that I'd sailed through my father's death and my girls' difficult birth without a normal sense of sadness and fear? I'd had to bury those feelings in order to do a good job at work, appreciate my family, and especially be a good mom. But it was just too soon and I was still too immature to survey with any depth the pain of loss and rejection. So, I avoided the morgue and the feelings trying to surface.

# 55: More than a Teacher

## It filled me with something I needed at the time: hope

Wedged at an odd angle, the bed was stuck in the door frame. Wide and as heavy as a refrigerator, I couldn't budge it. In the bed, my panicked mother-to-be was progressing fast and everyone was anxious for the doctor to arrive. Through the doorway, I could see Renee tending to another patient already in the delivery room.

Renee Garnier, RN, was seventy-five and had never married. She was wide-girthed and remarkably strong for her age. Her short, white hair was soft and sparse, a contrast to her thick-heeled, formidable nurse shoes. A full, white apron covered most of her scrub dress and, with her man's silver wristwatch pushed halfway up her arm, she commanded one's attention. Our little hospital required only one nurse on Obstetrics and Renee made sure every inch of its operation was perfect. The ward had two patient rooms with four beds each, two delivery rooms, and a nursery. If the ER was quiet, I was Renee's aide.

Stuck in the doorway that night, I was scared a baby might pop out from under the bed sheets. In my fake confident voice I called out. "Renee, can you give me a hand here?"

Ahead of me in the delivery room, she snapped, "In just a minute."

After what felt like five long minutes, I heard Renee's shoes smack the shiny hard-waxed floor as she approached. She looked like a prizefighter coming out of his corner for the next round. All I could think was, *Oh, no, she's pissed. I'm in for it now.*

She eyed the door jam and immediately saw the problem. Then, with what looked like an ordinary reflex, she muckled onto the bed's sidebar and with one great jerk freed it.

Not wanting to rile her anymore, I half-whispered, "Thanks."

She pivoted and clomped back to her patient on the delivery table. From where I stood at the doorway, I could see that mom lying on her back on the table. A long white sheet hung over her lower abdomen and thighs. She wore a white johnny, two pillows propped up her head, and her legs were up in stirrups. With every contraction, I watched the poor, exposed woman squeeze her eyes tight, grab the edges of the delivery table, and let out an ungodly moan. *Huh, she's really getting down to business.*

I wheeled my patient into the secondary delivery room and settled her on the table then Renee and I bounced back and forth between the two moms while everyone waited for the doctor. Not long after that Renee's and my patient each delivered a healthy baby.

On quiet nights at the hospital, I'd often wander onto OBS and gauge whether Renee was in the mood for a visit. When not riled up by a wailing newborn or an anxious mother in labor, she was easy to be with and I loved our chats. To me, she was a wealth of stories and wisdom.

One late night when the ward was silent and the lights down low, Renee and I sat at her nurse's station and visited. When I began talking about my father's family, she told me she remembered my second great grandparents who lived in a log cabin down on Benton Flats, where Gram grew up. She said, "Your great-great grandmother was a kind, little bit of a woman with dark hair and a round body. (Later I guessed she was talking about Lydia, my ancestor.) Your family offered travelers a meal and a place to sleep as they traveled north to Canada or south to the cities. It was the custom in those days." When I heard that, I sat back and sighed. I loved tales about my ancestors and it was nice to hear that even back then my family was generous.

Renee's stories were somewhat sparse and a few were laced with gossip, I knew that. As she talked I imagined my family's life back then, living in a log cabin, at the foot of the White Mountains, taking in travelers, and struggling against the elements. The stories made me want to know more about them and the old days. Later I wished I had recorded our conversations.

She never asked me about my immediate family and I didn't ask her about hers. I guessed she might be afraid to talk about personal things for some reason. It may have been a generational thing, some difficult life experiences, or her culture and religion, or a combination of these.

Of French Canadian descent, she was a strict Catholic and her four look-a-like siblings were unmarried too. They lived together in a large, stately home in the more modern town center nearby.

When I was young, I'd sit in the church balcony every Sunday morning before mass started and watch folks file in. I liked how I could look down from above and snoop on everyone. I remember the five white-haired, stocky siblings, three sisters with white gloves and head doilies, and two brothers in handsome gray suits, as they marched in to the front left, second row from the altar. It was their pew. During mass I looked down and studied their hair, round bodies, and most of all their stoic, unwavering postures. I wondered what kind of life Renee and her siblings had. Did they ever go on adventures, misbehave, or get dirty? Were they happy? I was just a kid with kid thoughts.

Renee and I made a good team and after a month I mastered patient-care protocol. I'd check moms into their rooms, take vitals, help them with their bathroom needs, and track their contractions. In the nursery I changed diapers, bottle-fed the babies, and rocked the criers. Tiny and finicky, the newborns made me nervous so whenever possible I left them to Renee.

She checked the laboring patients on a regular basis, monitored their dilation, prepped them with a shave of their pubic area, a common practice then, and stayed in phone contact with the doctor. Renee called the shots, even overriding the doctor's orders if she thought it benefited the patient.

If I wasn't needed elsewhere, and if OBS was quiet, I'd go into the primary delivery room, pretending I had a task to do. I liked to snoop because there was something about a super clean, well-organized space that appealed to me. Unlike the OR, the walls here seemed imbued with memories of life's most precious miracle. I could sense it and it filled me with something I didn't realize I needed at the time: hope, an existential hope.

Standing in that room with echoes of other mothers' pain, reminded me that life is dynamic, and forever unfolding, creating new territory. Those beliefs got implanted in my genetics and that familial history informed the charge-ahead person I had become.

When a patient was "cooking," or in advanced labor, I kept a close eye on her, helped Renee in the delivery room, and monitored newborns in the nursery. Every labor was different so I learned to be on my toes. It was enormously interesting and challenging and I learned how to steel my nerves, trust my intuition, and, be empathetic with some of the more hysterical moms.

Most days Renee was a comfort to the laboring patients. Most days. However, if one got under her skin, if things started moving too fast, if the newborns were restless, she could be a bear. In those times I kept my head down, remained quiet, and stayed as far away from her as I could manage. And I tried to make up for her gruffness by giving our patients extra attention.

In those days we sometimes had barefoot women, covered with garden dirt, check in, drop their underwear, if they wore any, jump into bed, and in a matter of minutes pop out their baby. Aside from a baby born in the patient's room and one nearly born in the doorway, the others arrived in the delivery room with little fanfare.

There were dashes of levity too. At the start of one shift, I checked on a woman in the early stages of labor. Soon after, I heard her screeching with each contraction. The two other patients in the room looked up at me, pleading for me to make her stop.

At one point, I asked, "Are you in a lot of pain?"

"No."

"Then why are you screaming?"

"Aren't I supposed to?"

Later that night she easily delivered a healthy baby and OBS was peaceful and quiet again.

I assisted in over one hundred healthy deliveries. At the time, I didn't realize how remarkable that was. The patient care was simple, efficient, and mostly organic. There were some interesting dynamics, though, courtesy of one doctor. He was in his forties, handsome, charismatic, with a big beer belly. At a few of his deliveries, I swore I smelled alcohol on him. Also, without failure, once we were in the delivery room and birth was imminent, he had Renee phone his wife to tell her to have a pizza waiting for him when he got home. He was distant to his patients, not like the two other doctors we worked with.

At one delivery, that same doctor brought along his salesman friend. The doc told me to help his friend put on a gown and when the friend stepped into the delivery room, the physician gave him a play-by-play commentary on the birth. Focused on her contractions, the mom was oblivious to the voyeur while Renee and I avoided looking at each other. I expected her to say something to the doc but, because I think she was so caught off guard, she said nothing. Later that night, off in a dark corner of the now quiet and mostly empty ward, the two of us ranted about the doctor's antics. As far as I know, his behavior was never reported.

Once a baby was delivered, the doctor handed the infant to me. I wrapped it in a thin blanket, put it in the bassinet, and every single time, I wiped away a tear or two from my eyes. I'd catch my breath and wonder how I got there, if I belonged. Every birth was a miracle, a real, honest-to-goodness miracle, and, for some amazing reason, I got to witness it.

On one shift, when the moon was full, Renee and I were out straight. There had been two deliveries that afternoon, there were three babies in the nursery, and three more moms were "cooking." One patient was moving right along so Renee called the doctor, prepped her, then we moved her into the primary delivery room. We situated her on the table and waited for the doctor. When he arrived, he scrubbed in and tended to the patient who was up in stirrups on the delivery table. She was having a hard time. The contractions were very strong but the baby was big and she couldn't push it out.

I went back to the ward to check on another patient and found that she was ready to transition; the head was engaged in the birth canal and she was about to deliver. I hurried back to the delivery room to tell Renee. She told me to put the mom in a wheelchair and put her in the other delivery room. I could feel my pulse in my neck.

I used a wheelchair to move the patient into the secondary delivery room then helped her up on the table. I made the mom as comfortable as possible with lots of pillows where she wanted them and lots of soft talk but she was progressing fast. I lifted the side rails on the table and stepped into the other delivery room. "Renee, she's transitioning."

She said, "Go ahead and prep her."

Gulp. *She wants me to shave her?* I'd seen her do it many times but it was one thing to observe it, and I was only an aide. *I can't be touching her privates, can I? I'll dally, maybe she'll hold that baby in and then Renee can do it.*

I found the prep tray and prepared to do the deed. I was ready to shave the poor, unsuspecting woman when, thank god, Renee bounced into the room and rescued me, us.

On OBS, we had tiny moms birth huge babies without making a peep. We had large, strapping moms birth small, slippery babies while hollering to the rafters. In all the births I attended, there was an issue just once. The mom's blood pressure was a little high so we monitored her more closely. In the end she did fine and delivered a healthy baby.

Renee and I, we were awesome together. We did good work, had some laughs, and witnessed many nighttime miracles. She taught me how to push through a dilemma, flex my weight and intelligence, in a good way, and how to shut my private life out so I could do my best work. Even today when I go to mass at home, I think of Renee and her siblings lined up in their pew like ducks in a row, beads on a rosary. I hope she is at peace and that she knows I appreciate how she trusted me.

## 56: The Families that Weren't

**You've got to keep putting yourself out there, right?**

One afternoon, when I was at work, I got paged to go to the ER. Someone had been in a fender-bender and, because I'd cared for dozens of ER patients, this was nothing out of the ordinary.

I pushed open the doors, stepped into the large room, and walked over to a stretcher. When I pulled back the curtains, I gasped. David's mother, Betsy, was lying there.

I took a giant breath and tried to collect myself. She looked like she was asleep and not wanting to startle her, I inched my way up to her head. My heart raced as I looked down at her face. Her eyes were closed, her wavy, brown hair was a mess, and she had an egg-sized bump on her forehead. *Damn, I hope the doctor gets here soon.*

I leaned in a little and looked at the docile face I'd known since childhood. *What happened to us, Betsy?*

At that very moment, she opened her eyes and they locked on mine. I stiffened. Then in a calm way that seemed practiced she said, "I dream about the babies almost every night."

I looked away from her pleading eyes and tried breathing normally again. I couldn't say anything, I hadn't imagined this moment. She turned to stare at the ceiling, and neither of us spoke. I remembered my job, thank goodness, and wiped her face clean with soap and water then gave her a cold pack for her head.

The intercom buzzed; "Renee needs your help, Regina. A nurse is coming to cover the ER." After a couple minutes I made my escape. Thank goodness for Renee and thank goodness none of Betsy's family showed up.

Over the past two years my girls and I had crossed paths with Betsy and David at town events. I never deviated from my path and marched right on through the crowd even if it meant almost brushing up against them. They'd made no attempt to communicate with me but I hadn't initiated any contact either. I was the young person dealing with this adult issue. In spite of all that, I was eager for them to know my little girls, *their* little girls. When I was much older, I wondered if I'd done the right thing. Maybe I should have called Betsy and offered to meet with her, I don't know. Sometimes there are just no rules to follow.

When my girls were two, my family encouraged me to try to get child support from David. I was less than enthusiastic about more drama. Eventually, I caved in and met with my family's attorney, filed the necessary paperwork, and set the process in motion.

David was notified but he denied he was the father. I was furious. I couldn't remember ever being that angry and was ready for a good fight. Even after the court date was set, he wouldn't budge.

On the day of the hearing my attorney and I showed up at the courthouse ready to do battle. Nervous as well as angry, I looked forward to testifying. Minutes before entering the courthouse, my attorney got word that David admitted he was the father and agreed to settle out of court. He would pay me a lump sum of money for child support and in turn I agreed not to ask for any future support.

David paid me $10,000 to cover eighteen years of child support for our two children.

It hurt knowing David was permanently out of my life. To take my mind off it I decided to start dating again. That is, if you could call double dating with my aunt and her husband on a night-skiing blind date with a sex-starved farm boy a real date. He only wanted one thing and it wasn't to shush down the slopes with me. Also, there was my neighbor's "hot" brother. I liked him a lot but he was interested in me for only a few weeks then turned to a sexy bombshell to satisfy his needs. I was more of a prude than I imagined. My double date with a slightly older guy I'd known since childhood was pathetic. I don't know who was more bored: him or me. I let two of the guys make it to first base and the other one never made it out of the batter's box. *You've got to keep putting yourself out there, right?*

Then there was the friendly, young mortician who was new in town. While I was working at the hospital, I signed up for the volunteer ambulance service and he was one of the volunteers. My mom was not happy about it because I had to stay over at the hospital one night a week when I was on call. Before that, Strickler Funeral Home had responded to emergencies with their clunky backup hearse.

Our first emergency call was fifteen bumpy miles from the hospital. Scrunched up in the back of Strickler's old tank given to the hospital, I tried calming the sick man by rubbing his forehead and offering words of comfort. "Mr. Handsome Mortician" kept asking, "How're you folks doing back there? Sorry about the ride." The chipper way he said it made me think he was more interested in me than the patient.

The next few times I saw him, he apologized for that bumpy ride. I knew he wanted to ask me out. I even daydreamed about us dating, getting married, and settling down together with my girls in the lovely, little, neighboring town. I'd be married to a well-respected mortician who was destined to own a funeral business one day. But he never got up the nerve to ask me. I wish he had. I definitely would have gone.

I found out he married his boss's daughter and eventually took over the business. Sometimes, I'd see him when he served at various funerals and he always stationed himself so he could give me a nod. It felt like another loss.

# 57: The Old Woman Spoke

## Her motherly words wrapped around me

Not far from my tent, I slump in my camp chair relaxing by the campfire. The canyon's tranquility seeps in. This feels like hallowed ground, but, like me, it probably has memories to shed. A question drifts inside my head: What am I doing here? Then a persistent something in my gut says, "Keep going." It's not the first time I've heard messages from bizarre places.

In 1988, two years after my divorce, life was demanding a lot of me. My son was a rambunctious ten-year-old and my girls were busy teenagers preparing to go to college. I was teaching a challenging science curriculum that required a great deal of creativity and preparation. We were living several miles in the woods in an unfinished house and running, of all things, a small goat farm. What helped me stay sane were ongoing counseling sessions, my friends in the women's meditation group, and my books on New Age ideas. Our group taught me to trust my instincts and to forgive myself and others for our imperfections. By studying different forms of spirituality, I recovered the close connection to Spirit that I'd had as a child and I wasn't required to follow a set of rules to feel worthy. By accepting myself, warts and all, I came to believe in a benevolent Universe that wants the best for me. I slowly began to find a new kind of peace and it required only that I be myself.

But something more was challenging me, I felt an emptiness that sometimes left me unfulfilled. Maybe I made it more difficult because I wanted to dig deep and understand on a metaphysical level what was happening to me and why. At that time it wasn't enough for me to come up with a plan then trudge through the hard times as I'd done before. This time I wanted to be more conscious of what was happening both inside and outside of me. So I read incessantly, meditated with friends, and learned from energy workers how to connect with Spirit and heal myself emotionally. I was excited as my conception of what it meant to be alive changed and I kept studying and praying to know more.

Before then, I didn't dream much but, during that time, I began having frequent and very vivid dreams. Many were so strange and full of symbolism that I couldn't wait to research what they meant. It surprised me how the dreams mirrored what was presently challenging me. Analyzing my dreams helped me connect the dots, so to speak. I got possible answers to why certain people came into my life or why I related the way I did to them. It was fascinating stuff.

My research into creativity and spirituality made me wonder where the inspiration for poets, musicians, mathematicians, and dancers comes from. *What is the source?* Could it be in dreamland, a place too ethereal to name, too illogical for the mind to perceive? I'd heard of instances where composers heard whole scores of new music and mathematicians were given math solutions while dreaming. I trusted the insights my dreams were giving me and believed the Universe was the source.

One afternoon of that fruitful year I stretched out on my bed and settled in for a quick afternoon nap. Exhausted, I fell asleep immediately but, after what felt like ten minutes, I was startled awake by a woman's voice that seemed to come from the top of my headboard. She had an Eastern European accent, maybe Turkish. Her image flashed in my mind. She looked to be in her 70s, with bold facial features, and thick black hair pulled back behind her head. She wore a big, black hat and a black dress from the early 1900s. She said, "Everything is going to be all right, honey." It was the most loving thing anyone had ever said to me. Her motherly words wrapped around me and comforted me as if I was her anxious child. I honestly felt she knew me. A split second later she was gone.

I lay there looking at the ceiling not knowing what to think. *Was that part of a dream? Was I even dreaming?* I didn't remember dreaming. *No one is going to believe what just happened.* I decided to take the vision at face value. The comforting tone and her words reassured me. It helped that about that time I was learning to listen to and trust my body's reaction to strange experiences. Even though it was outlandish, I felt like someone knew and cared about me.

—ɯ—

As I sit near my fire listening to what else the canyon has to tell me, a thin, middle-aged woman wanders over and joins me. She's attractive and has a warm smile. *I wish I could squat on the ground like that. She must be fit.* She says she's a teacher from Minnesota so right away I like her. For twelve years she's worked with the Indians at the Rosebud Reservation so they consider her family and she joins them on holidays and family celebrations. I try to hide my envy. After she leaves I feel a bit of a void, not lonely, just a bit empty.

A massive onslaught of mosquitoes invades camp so I put the fire out and let Doug join me in the tent. Thank goodness he settles down and falls asleep quickly. Even when the noisy teenagers start in, he doesn't stir and I'm too drained to be bothered by them.

An aching leg and knee keep me tossing and turning. Once I accept the fact I'm not going to sleep, I lie back, take a few deep breaths, and empty my mind. I slip into a dream-like state. Then it's like there's a 3-D screen surrounding me and playing on it are memories of Kate and me in other lifetimes.

In all of the scenes we are Indians, Kate is my wife, and I feel responsible for her death. In one lifetime our tepee burns with her inside. I am devastated because I'd left her alone. Another lifetime appears. While I am protecting our village from attack, I accidentally spear her and she dies. In each case, after she dies, I leave my people and disappear into the forest forever.

Now, in my tent, as I watch myself walking into that forest, I again feel the same sense of despair and guilt. I'm puzzled because my emotions seem both ancient and current and I don't understand why I'm feeling them now. *Did the woman who stopped by stir up something? Am I longing for a partner? Am I lonely? Maybe I'm in denial.* I often wonder if I'll ever be in a committed relationship again. I wonder if I've made myself unavailable because of the losses and near losses that have so hurt me. I whisper, "Spirit, help me to release this sadness."

Luckily through years of counseling, I've found my spunky, little-girl self still alive inside my tough exterior, still waiting for validation and love. I've discovered that acknowledging the child-like person in ourselves is key to accepting and appreciating who we are. These empowering thoughts make me feel like my body is floating off into the welcoming arms of the canyon walls. Sedated, I sink into a deep sleep.

I wake up after a couple hours because mini electrical currents are flowing through my body similar to something that happened a couple years ago when I was meditating. A healer friend who was present said my body was getting rewired. Now I ask, "Am I being healed?" I don't get an answer but soon I turn over and sleep comes again.

# 58: A Hidden Cabin in the Woods

## How to laugh at the absurdity of life

In the summer of '71, Dr. Rand approached me at the hospital to ask if I'd be interested in working at his clinic. Surprised and flattered, I met him the next day to talk about it. The position he proposed sounded a lot less stressful than my hospital job, paid more, and had better hours. I'd get home at 9 p.m. instead of 11:30 so I could be a more rested mom for my children.

As he shared his plan with me, his face lit up. He wanted to expedite the clinic's offerings by having me do preliminary microscopic analysis of patients' blood and urine. I was excited and, with my college experiences, I was confident I could handle it. I'd also take patient vitals and assist the docs with procedures. It seemed like a dream job so I agreed to take his offer and gave my two-week notice at the hospital. The only hard thing about leaving was saying good bye to Renee. I was sad leaving her but I knew I needed to keep moving forward for my little family.

Dr. Rand's office was in a clinic he owned and shared with Dr. Harriet Brown. I had assisted both physicians at the hospital and, of all the docs I worked with, they were the most competent and compassionate.

In her late fifties, Dr. Brown was a short, angular woman with white hair. She was also brilliant. She had serious, rimless glasses and a thick, white mustache I could hardly take my eyes off even after I got to know her. The mustache, as my mom would say, was "all the talk of the town." I overheard people complain that Dr. Brown was too outspoken and opinionated. She was extremely confident and, even though I didn't have words for it at the time, I thought people were upset because they couldn't pigeon-hole her into some subordinate female role. Her husband, Arthur, practiced psychotherapy out of his office at the clinic. He was tall, thin, and friendly. Soft spoken, he also seemed frail. I couldn't imagine him and Dr. Brown together "in that way." Years later I wondered if theirs was a marriage of convenience.

Every job has a hitch and for me it was Carole Morris, RN. She ran the place, including, to a degree, the doctors. Dr. Brown was the only one who ignored Carole's attempts to meddle and took as much time with her patients as she felt they needed.

Carole was in her early forties and was put together with perfection. She had a tall, well-toned body, a mouth full of gorgeous teeth, and even her hair was impressive. Come to think of it, she had the same hair as Nurse Ratched in *One Flew Over the Cuckoo's Nest*.

Quick-as-a-whip and as hypnotic as a cobra, Carole was *good*. Sometimes, as I filed folders in the office, Carole would slither up to the edge of the door jamb like a snake hugging a tree. She looked like she was in a photo shoot and, with her hip tipped into the door frame, she'd flash that smile and have her way with me. She wasn't flirting; she didn't like me. It was how she disarmed me, getting me to share personal details of my life I never intended to share.

With a coy smile she'd say, "So you have two little ones." She was clever; it was always a question that sounded like a statement.

"Yes, two little girls."

She'd flash another smile and shoot again. "So your mother takes care of them."

"Yes, along with my sister-in-law and my nieces." And she'd keep at it and I would acquiesce.

Crafty like a weasel, she dug into my business, finding her sustenance. It took me a couple weeks to recognize her trap and even longer to protect myself. Intelligent, clever, and literally fast on her feet, she also had Dr. Rand's ear and his respect.

After a few weeks at the clinic, I realized the job Dr. Rand had offered me was being systematically hijacked by Nurse Carole. The clinic was her domain and she wasn't about to let me meddle. I kept forcing the issue with her by asking to assist the doctors more and do microscope work. But she wouldn't relent and kept me busy filing folders and checking patients into the office.

On the day Dr. Rand asked me to meet with him after work, I knew I was in trouble. I had been slow to respond to Carole's whims because they kept me from doing what I was hired to do. In his kind but professional way, the good man reminded me that Carole was in charge of the entire clinic and it ran well because of her. *Okay, got it.*

My job description had been modified and clarified. I was to file records, escort patients to the examination rooms, and every so often, take vitals. *So much for a step up.*

Dr. Rand's wife, Susan, was in charge of office billing. She was small, spindly-thin, and also brilliant. Even with all her degrees, she seemed swallowed up by the tall, untidy piles of folders and papers on her huge desk. One day as I was filing folders, she and I had what I believed was a friendly chat when she inserted, "You didn't finish college? Well, nowadays, you know you can't do much without a master's degree and that seems unlikely for you now, doesn't it?" Immobilized, I had no retort. The comment hurt because she was judging my situation and me and, as far as getting a master's degree, it didn't register because I hadn't thought that far ahead. Thank goodness for my coworker Mary Ryan, RN. She and her husband were family friends and she'd known me since birth. We became fast friends and the days that dear woman and I worked together were the best.

Mary was born on an Indian reservation in North Dakota and when she was a baby, her family moved to NY. Years later she met then married her husband, Devin. A few times at the clinic, Mary lamented about the horrid conditions on some reservations in the Dakotas, "Their lives are pitiful, just horrible," she said. Twice a year she sent huge bundles of clothes to the Rosebud.

Mary had three children, two daughters and a son, but her life had been tragic. One daughter, two years older than me, was born mentally challenged and was a constant worry for her. As far as I know, after she graduated from high school she got a job allowing her to support herself. Her other daughter was two years younger than me. Creative and intelligent, she became a successful entrepreneur. Mary's son, Devin Jr., was in my first grade class and died when he was seven.

I remember that morning in 1955. We were in our classroom and we knew Devin had died. Our teacher, Mrs. Harrison, told two of the boys to empty Devin's desk. I watched from my seat at the back of the room as the boys put his things in a big paper bag then set it on the wooden floor by the classroom door. I wondered where the bag would end up. Mrs. Harrison didn't talk about Devin at all.

Devin's desk was in the middle aisle, third row from the front. Now, it sat up there, empty and alone. It was hard to not look at it. At recess, we still played marbles in the dimpled dirt of the schoolyard where later the buses would come to take some of the kids home. I always walked home but I remember watching my classmates clamber up the bus steps and thought about Devin. *He'll never get to ride the bus again.*

The previous day, little Devin had been playing in the old barn across the road from his house when Mary called him home for supper.

Just as Devin started to cross the road, a car came up over the hill and hit him. He died instantly. Mary was leaning out her front door. She saw everything.

The driver of the car was the father of a girl in our class. Even though I was young, I sensed how that terrible thing shocked everyone. To me it seemed like an insidious gloom had invaded our town. We were stunned but in those days people didn't talk to children about loss like that. Mostly adults tried to protect us from it. I wonder, now, how the other children in town were affected.

—︎𝕞︎—

Mary was 5'7" and trim. Her black hair was graying but her soft, brown eyes were childlike. She was my mom's age but a lot younger. Even though she was very intelligent, at times, she seemed a bit spacey but that may have helped her move on and have a good life with her husband and two daughters after "Little Devin's" death.

At work, Mary and I were simpatico. We formed an alliance. We complained about Carol's antics and shared clinic gossip while trying to comply with the doctors' needs. Most importantly, we laughed a lot.

When the clinic got crazy busy and chaotic, Mary would walk over, lean in to me, and with a serious stare, say, "So, did you hear about the weather in Chile?" Those words got me every time. I'd crack up then we'd duck behind the office desk to hide our faces and shaking bodies from patients in the waiting room.

Some days Mary seemed to be teetering on the edge of emotional disaster, other days she'd escape into comic release. She had a way of making the drama and the chaos in the office seem imaginary. That kind of mindset may have kept her sane. But every time she talked about her son, whom she called Little Devin, her eyes showed her brutal sorrow and I wanted to give her something to help but mostly I wanted her to stop talking about him. Now that I was a mother, I couldn't imagine losing a child.

I visited Mary at her country home a few times. It was a beautiful early 19th century white cape that sat at the top of that fateful hill. It was surrounded by stately ancient maples and oaks, old orchards, and hay fields.

Once inside her house, Mary insisted I say hello to each of her nine cats as she hoisted each to greet me. Then we'd head out back to her little cabin. I followed as she chirped about a tree she loved, her cats' antics, and funny stories about her husband. We crossed the colonial lawns invaded by furry coats of moss, and made our way through the long-standing apple orchard infiltrated with blackberry bushes and opportunistic saplings. Once we made it over a couple of crumbling stone walls, we arrived. Mary's cabin resembled the old shadow of a child's playhouse. It was too tired to stand upright so it leaned heavily to one side and was too fragile to enter. Her cabin seemed a place rather than a structure. But it was her place, the spot I imagined she'd visit to try and stay sane. She did it for her two daughters, her husband, and her cats. Mary adored her cats, I think as much as her humans.

My dear friend showed me how to laugh at the absurdity of life and bend with the challenges we're given. Maybe the most important thing I learned happened when she walked me to her place in the woods where nature called her to find comfort. Mary seemed lighter and younger at her cabin. Her face shone. Though I didn't have the words at the time, I felt something when I was there too. It was nature's mothering. When I think of Mary, I miss her a lot, and I remember how it felt to be that close to nature and to feel that safe with someone.

# 59: Time to Jump

## It was a huge boost to my confidence

When the clinic wasn't too busy, Dr. Brown encouraged me to assist her in treating patients. She was tough and thorough, and I respected her intelligence. A number of times after work we had long conversations in her office. When she was in medical school decades earlier, she was the only woman in her class. Even back then she must have been quite the stand out.

In the summer of '72, I learned about a new program at Dartmouth College, only twenty miles from home. It was the groundbreaking Physician's Assistant Program. I did some research and found it resembled what I'd hoped to be doing at the clinic and then some. It was the precursor of the modern-day Nurse Practitioner and Physician's Assistant Program.

One night when Dr. Brown and I were working late, I told her about the new PA program at Dartmouth. Immediately, she offered to write a letter of recommendation for me if I was serious about applying. I was blown away. It was a huge boost to my confidence.

A couple weeks later I mailed my application, college transcript, and letters of recommendation from Dr. Rand, Dr. Brown, and my former hospital supervisor. I thought I had a good shot at being accepted. A month later, I got my reply. The college explained that I was highly qualified for their first class but there was one problem. They didn't understand how I could participate in their program with two children. I was turned down because I was a mother.

It began to hit me. I might end up living out my whole life here, in my small town, as a single mom working at a job that didn't challenge me and was going nowhere. I reviewed my options and none were exciting. After a couple weeks of feeling sorry for myself I had no new ideas so I made a call that would change the trajectory of my life. I called the admissions office at UNH and asked about readmission.

It happened fast. I was connected to someone in the office and began to tell her my story. "I've completed 2 ½ years as a biology major. I want to return as a second semester junior, and oh, with my two-year-old daughters."

The young-sounding woman said, "There's a new program here at the University. A bill introduced by Governor Peterson was passed to help parents who want to go to college. The state will pay for all your expenses."

"What?"

"Yes, it was passed by the state legislature a few years ago. You can go to college for free."

"Wow, what do I need to do to get on board?"

"Well first thing, you'll have to go on welfare."

"Oh, I don't know, I'm not comfortable being on welfare."

She yelled, "Well then, what the fuck are you going to do?"

Once I caught my breath, I understood her point and settled down. It was time to stop what my mom called "pussy-footing-around." *Either I jump or stay put.* I jumped.

# 60: My Next Best Step

## Our new life was about to begin

Once I hung up the phone, I realized the person was right. What was I going to do? The sheltering gates of complacency had opened and it was time to leave my predictable life. Later, I'd realize it was all in perfect order.

With the money I earned working, I was able to take care of my girls' needs and pay my mom something every week. My mother cosigned a loan and, with the child support money, I bought a new Chevy Vega station wagon. Dull gray and absent any sleek curves or lines, it was the unsexiest vehicle I'd ever seen. But, it had a great radio and ample room for my girls so it was my jewel. After driving home from work, I'd park in the driveway, savor the new-car smells, and sway to songs like "Papa Was a Rolling Stone" by The Temptations on the radio. The soulful rhythms and my safe solitude were like a tonic. Transported back a few years, I felt like a kid again. I needed that before walking into the house and facing my mother.

It was pretty much the same *every* night. I'd go into the living room and she'd be sitting curled up at the end of the couch watching Johnny Carson. Her pack of Winstons, an ashtray, and a small glass of Southern Comfort on ice waited for her on the end table. I'd step closer and say, "Hi, Mom. How were the girls?" Without looking away from the TV, she'd answer, "They were fine." I wished I was still in my car.

Because my mom was unpredictable, I needed to be cautious. Naive and hurting, too, I wasn't sensitive to her grief and her emotional health issues. At least, I hope that's why she didn't talk to me. But, being immature, I began to think I'd done something wrong and deserved her iciness. As I look back now, I realize she was barely keeping herself together. Even with all she'd gone through, she'd made room for our whole family. She'd lost her true love, so she curled herself up on the end of the couch and clung to a life with her "cigs," whiskey, and Johnny Carson.

—ɯ—

Late summer of 1972 I reapplied to UNH and even though my GPA was terrible, they reinstated me, conditionally. I was ecstatic. Next, I applied for Aid to Families with Dependent Children (AFDC) and was approved. I hated the idea of being on Welfare but knew it was only temporary and a means to an end. After that, all I needed to do was sign up for classes, find an apartment, and move in with my 2 ½ year-olds.

On a day off from work, I drove two and a half hours to the Durham campus. At the admissions office I signed up for classes then checked the bulletin boards at the student union for apartments and found something.

The tiny, three-room apartment was in the old mill town of Newmarket and just a few miles from campus. It was on the ground floor of an old colonial home where the owners lived. As I opened the apartment door, a train rumbled by only fifty feet from the house making the walls rattle. But the young owners were nice and the rent was doable so I took it.

*There, done.* Everything was coming together. All I had to do was finish my job at the clinic, gather things at home, and relocate. I didn't have much: clothes, stereo, TV, and my antique rocking chair. I hoped my mom would give me a couple mattresses, some sheets, and blankets. That was all we needed. I knew it was going to be great.

Thank goodness my mother saw the big picture. On moving day, she and Beth followed me in her car that was filled with things I needed but hadn't thought of: silverware, dishes, bath linens, and a bureau.

I was beyond happy. We had our own place and our new life was about to begin. But, when my mother saw the apartment, she cried because she thought we'd moved into the slums. I didn't understand.

The apartment bedroom was cozy. Our three twin mattresses covered every inch of the floor and, to get to her bed on the far wall, Jessie had to crawl over the other two.

The efficient living room had just enough space for the TV, stereo, and my rocking chair. After we were settled, I built a ramp that extended out the living room window to the fenced-in yard so my girls could go outside on their own. We had a slick setup.

Our kitchen and bathroom were tiny but they worked out fine. The faded wallpaper and linoleum floors probably added to my mother's dismay but, to me, they looked clean enough.

I think my mom tried to be happy for us but she didn't understand what a huge step into my new life this was. After my dad died, I think she stopped dreaming.

Months later my mother called to say she and Auntie Kay were going to visit Kay's son, a student on campus. It surprised me that she and Auntie Kay were talking again. She said they wanted to meet me for lunch so we set a time to meet at my apartment. When the day came, I waited and waited in the apartment with my car in my driveway but they never showed up. The next day I called my mom and she told me they drove to my apartment but my car wasn't there so they thought I was gone. I was definitely home, she had my number and could have called but she didn't. I was heartbroken. Seems my snotty godmother had gotten to her again. *What happened, Mom?*

—⟋⟍—

The first night in our new apartment felt like a sleep-over with the three of us lying side by side in our cozy bedroom. I was so excited about the next day and our new life, I hardly slept. We had our own place and now some big adventures ahead of us. I just knew it. *Thank you, God, for taking care of us and making this happen. And, thank you, Mom.*

In the morning and for many mornings after, I'd drive my girls to The Little People's Center, a daycare I had checked out weeks before. It was on campus and staffed mostly by hippie-type students and parents. Welfare paid for daycare as well as our medical expenses and rent. We also got monthly surplus food from the federal government. It was difficult to register why I was getting all this assistance but I appreciated it. Since my dad's death I felt like I was riding a merry-go-round and with each revolution and within arm's length, an exciting opportunity appeared. All I had to do was go for it.

Raised in our rich and loving home environment, my kids were happy, intelligent, and inquisitive. I couldn't wait to introduce them to daycare and show them off. I knew it would be a perfect fit.

The Little People's Center was located on the edge of campus and housed in the spacious rooms of a church basement. About twenty children were enrolled. On my first visit, mild earthy smells of watercolor paints, peanut butter, clay, and the powdery scent of diapered babies flooded the air. Alive with squeals of laughter and chatter, a half dozen toddlers darted about the large central room like a swarm of foraging butterflies.

When we walked in on their first day, a tall lanky guy with glasses greeted us. His long black beard hung onto his chest like a man-sized bib. He had a buzz cut, spoke in slow motion, and was oblivious to the two little giggly ones wrapped on each of his legs. My girls, especially Jessie would grow to love this guy's easygoing ways. Brian was a Ph.D. physics student.

Then a beautiful, blonde-headed child scooted past me. I saw the dress and thought it was a girl but it was a little boy. His mother, Janice, was tall with long, beautiful brunette hair and was the day care's director. An intelligent and charitable woman in her mid-twenties, she was ahead of her time. She encouraged her son to wear whatever he wanted. No one else seemed fazed but at the time, I wondered about it. What did it mean about him? What effect might it have? I was confused. It was never an issue with the other children so I let it go. It took some time for the staff's easygoing liberal ways to rub off on me.

Bonnie was a round, motherly, young woman and second in charge. A Quaker, her values of community, nonviolence, and sharing dominated the daycare culture. Everyone loved Bonnie, especially my shy, docile Jessie.

A week later I met Sharon, a tall, heavyset African American university student. Her son attended daycare and she was its music teacher. She and Jenny bonded when Sharon recognized Jenny was a gifted singer. Sharon and I would become good friends.

There was a reading room at daycare and when children wanted to read, they'd knock on the room's door and someone would read with them or teach them to read. By the time they were only three and a half, Jessie and Jenny were reading.

Mats covered the nap room floor where the children had daily quiet time. In the spacious kitchen, staff rotated as cooks and served nutritious, rather bland, mostly vegetarian meals. The artistic masterpieces plastering the art room walls were evidence of creative mayhem and aesthetic freedom.

If children misbehaved, they were sent to time-out, a little windowed room off the kitchen. Precocious Jenny got to know it well. It was used to pause the behavior for a short few minutes and the staff stayed calm and business-like when time-out was needed. The no-shaming protocol impressed me.

The Little People's Center's environment and programs were unbelievably rich. The confident children were inquisitive and at times a handful. After volunteering a few times, I appreciated the staff's patience and commitment even more. Each day everyone but the babies went on a field trip to the ocean, woodland parks, campus horse barns, libraries, or greenhouses.

The state of New Hampshire provided all this so we could get a good education in order to support ourselves and our children. I could hardly believe it.

# 61: Exams and Cheerios

## What if I am a loser?

It was a perfect setup. We'd wake, get dressed, eat breakfast together, then I'd drop the girls off at daycare and I'd go to class. Jenny and Jessie were two-and-a-half, easygoing, and cooperative so it usually came together without a hitch.

However, one morning, when I was almost set to leave, I couldn't find my car keys. I looked everywhere in the apartment with no luck. I then gently interrogated my two likely suspects. "Girls, Mom can't find her car keys. Have you seen them?" Sporting grape juice mustaches, they looked up from their bowls of Cheerios and smiled at me. There was not a word. Something seemed fishy. I stood in the middle of the kitchen and visualized the morning in rewind then went to everything I'd touched. By the time I got to the box of Cheerios, I was frantic, time was fleeting, and I was going to be late to class. I tore open the box top, drove my hand into the Os, and Bingo. I shouted, "Yay." Grinning, the two co-conspirators clapped their hands and giggled. I smiled too but was too frantic to laugh. I suspected impish Jenny was the mastermind and, with her doe-eyes, Jessie was probably an innocent bystander.

After they finished eating, I herded my cherubs out the door and into the backseat of my Vega wagon and headed to daycare then campus.

It was great having the whole day to myself if I needed it. But there were a couple times I took advantage of daycare and spent the afternoon with friends or meeting guys. I had some growing up to do. But when I was with my girls, I was fully engaged with them and, as some friends have suggested, to the point of being overly attentive.

In order to take full advantage of the state's generosity, I always signed up for at least four classes per semester. On my first semester back one of my classes was Plant Physiology. A nature lover, I was psyched but nervous having been out of school for almost three years. I wondered if my brain still worked well enough, to say nothing about carving out ample time with my girls.

My plant physiology professor was in his thirties and a real gem. He was easy to understand, kind, and generous with students. I met with him a few days before the first exam to go over my notes and to talk about my nervousness. He leaned in a little as he listened then smiled and said. "I think you'll do fine and your notes are excellent." His words were reassuring so I started to relax a little.

Even though I was prepared, on exam day I was a bundle of nerves. But once I started, I was relieved that most of the material was familiar. A couple days later the professor strolled down the classroom aisles handing back our exams. In our class of fifteen, he knew everyone's name. My heart was pounding hard; I wanted to see my grade but I didn't dare look. *What if I failed? What if coming back was a stupid idea? What if Susan Rand was right and I am a loser?*

I watched as he fingered the next exam in the stack he was holding. He read the name then looked over at me and pushed it my way. I took a deep breath then looked down at the 90 circled in red ink and the word "Congrats!" He stood at my desk for a couple extra seconds then gave me a smile and a nod before passing back the other exams. *I made it. I can do this.*

Over the following semesters I was consistently on the Dean's List. My professors were great, available for help, and allowed me to take an exam late if one of my girls was sick. But there were two exceptions.

My entomology professor was tall, bony, and stooped forward with gangling arms like a praying mantis. I met with him after missing an exam because Jessie had been sick the night before. The creep tried to shame me. "Why do you think you should be favored over the other students? It was your choice to have a child so you need to deal with the consequences." *Why would I be ashamed of my girls? Who the hell does he think he is?* He gave me an extension anyway and I didn't let his words bother me much because he didn't know my story.

My chemistry professor was a real piece of work, too. Students in our class called him "Mr. Perfect." He had the perfect job as department chair, was top dog in a perfect Christian church on campus, had a perfect family of four, and lived in a perfect house. (Every time I drove by it, I was tempted to get out and move a lawn ornament or leave some litter.)

He flaunted his flawless grooming and would waltz into class without a briefcase or notes and with his back to us, he'd spend the next hour "talking to the chalkboard" while covering it with lengthy chemical equations. He never entertained a single student question and when he finished, he just turned and left. The twerp made me squirm.

I prayed I'd make it through my two semesters of chemistry without having to meet with him. No luck. I skipped one exam to stay home with a very sick little Jenny. When I met with the professor the next day I told him what happened. Then his interrogation began. He asked me one question after another, digging into my personal life and, it seemed, like my other professor, tried to shame me. It didn't work. Even though I was tired, I remained confident in my decision to take care of my child, skip the exam, and to take my chances with him.

"So what do you plan to do once you graduate?" he asked.

"Maybe teach," I said.

"I want you to remember this when, in the future, a student of yours asks for an extension."

*You fool, Mr. Perfect, I will remember this and your cold heart.*

On days when one of my girls wasn't up to going to daycare but not ill, I'd take her to class with me. I'd stuff a thick pad of paper and some crayons in my backpack and we'd march off to class together. In the lecture theater of a couple hundred students, my small sidekick would sit quietly coloring. Of course, Jenny kept looking up intent on listening to the lecturer while Jessie focused more on her coloring. I think oftentimes they asked to come because they missed me and what a treat it was for both of us to have each other all to ourselves for the day. Raised in a big family and now in daycare, my girls were even more easygoing. What precious memories we were making

After a month or so, I was feeling like a real student again. Thanks to my medical jobs and mothering experiences, I was more confident, focused, and organized because I had to be. Having matured, my comprehension and retention of class material had improved. Also, with the state paying for almost everything, I felt a responsibility to do well. Every day I appreciated the opportunity I'd been given.

# 62: Dreaming in the Key of Make-up

## You can contain yourself,
## box yourself up inside a feel-safe place

I wake up with a start, forgetting I'm inside my tent in the canyon. My strange dream reminds me of a plucky TV commercial that grabs my attention and entices me to believe its message. In it there was a small, transparent, plastic box stuffed with cotton balls, half of them soaked in Cover Girl makeup, half untouched. I'm not sure why the dream woke me but I'm intrigued and want to make sense of it. Stretched out on my back with my flashlight wedged between my neck and shoulder, the words stream into my journal as if I'm in another dream. "You can contain yourself, box yourself up inside a feel-safe place. You can masquerade as something you're not but you know who you are." Therefore, I have two questions. Do I want to live contained and disguised? Do I want to limit myself in order to feel safe?

Once the words stop coming, I settle down and listen to my body. And, like when you know what a loved one is thinking, I hear my body. *Even though your mind may not understand, take up all the space you have been granted in this life.* I whisper, "I promise to listen to and trust the wisdom of my body." Soon sleep returns.

In a short couple of years, listening to the wisdom of my body would become even more important.

After a few hours I wake again. *It's freakin' cold tonight.* Even in my sleeping bag and wearing a shirt, two sweaters, sweat pants, jeans, and covered with a blanket, I'm still shivering. At 2 a.m. I have to pee. Cold and grumpy, I take a deep breath, yank back my covers, squirm out of my sleeping bag, and poke my head outside. The sky's black canvas is aglow with countless flickering gemstones. *A magical gift just for me.* I wiggle my way upright and walk a few paces to the backside of my tent. *Love the facilities and thank goodness it's too cold for mosquitoes.* Mission accomplished and my chill gone, I linger absorbing this night's sacred sleep. As I tilt my head and pan the sky, heaven's breadth reminds me there truly are no limits.

I wiggle back inside my sleeping bag then look over at Doug who's sound asleep. I pull up my blanket and drift off then just after sunrise I wake again and something peculiar comes over me. I look over at Doug and realize how much I love him. It feels weird though because he knows all my imperfections and he still loves me.

As I lie next to Doug, I feel a stream of affection pouring out of me and into him. It makes me a little uncomfortable but I let the flow continue then start to cry at the thought of losing him. I reach over and pat him then with his eyes still closed, he stretches out his front paw, touches my arm, and flops his tail on the ground.

For a few minutes, I wonder about this soul-connection thing; it feels important. Also, I'm beginning to think this kind of intimacy probably requires something; I have to stay emotionally open and share myself. *So much to think about, so much to understand.* Finally, I fall into a long undisturbed sleep.

At 8 a.m. I'm up and energized. After a quick breakfast, Doug and I set out on another hike. The Upper Rim Rock Trail is a five-mile loop and, lucky me, the trailhead is near my site. It says it's moderately difficult and has a well-maintained dirt path that zigzags up to the canyon bluffs. I want to get some good shots of Doug and the landscapes, so I decide to take along my camera and tripod.

We're gifted again with mild temps, soft, blue skies, and a lenient sun. The trail snakes before us and connects with small adjoining canyons. It's like I'm walking through an earth science picture book; sporadic cliffs jut out amidst tiny, half-hidden caves and stands of pine, aspen, and birch dapple the walls. On the canyon floor, wavy rushes outline a wide, shallow brook and above me, noisy birds pluck snacks from the air. I bend down and clear away the reeds at the brook's edge and spot a small school of huge trout hovering in the pure, icy stream. Probably intoxicated by the sun's warm rays penetrating their silky, smooth bodies they're untroubled by my spying. *What a great place to spearfish, haha.*

Doug is off-leash most of our hike and as usual dashes about like a colt but circles back often. Near the four-mile mark, I arrive at a flat, wide section of the canyon floor covered with shorter grass. I'm pretty sure this is where they filmed the Native's encampment scenes in *Dances With Wolves.* Wow.

It's 1:30 when we arrive back at the trailhead and I can't believe it's been five hours. *You can just leave me here. I enjoyed the prairie and all but this is the best. I guess when it comes to Earth, I am a fickle lover.* It dawns on me that, on my hike, I was so entranced by the beauty of this land that even though I brought my camera I never used it. Come to think of it, I suppose people can miss a lot if they spend too much time behind a camera with just a narrow focus on their surroundings. Because I didn't use it I stayed more immersed in my whole environment.

Back at camp, after a rest and some reading time, I head back to Spearfish for groceries. Tastefully located on the edge of the canyon's waterfalls, with everything so convenient and understated, it's a peaceful town. *I wonder what it's like to live here. There you go, dreaming again, Regina. You've got a job, three kids, and a big house back in Maine.*

Driving back to camp I realize I haven't seen any hawks for days. I miss my messenger friends. Also, it's been unusually quiet with very little wind and the rambunctious boys have left camp. *Is this "the calm before the storm"?*

# 63: At the Chicken Coop

## My bland worldview was changing fast

Things had fallen into place for my girls and me but sometimes I felt lonely. I tried not thinking about it and focused on all the positives in my life but when that didn't work, I'd stroll into DWHE, a campus organization founded by women a few years earlier. It stood for Disadvantaged Women for Higher Education and we called it "Dwaa-hee." It supported single mothers, and one father, in college and was a gathering place for about twenty others in a similar situation as me.

Its offices were in a refurbished chicken coop near the center of campus. Its large central room was lined on one wall with a row of cloudy windows. Along another two walls were a hodgepodge of tattered, overstuffed chairs and sagging sofas. There was also a tiny room where we could make free long-distance phone calls using the WATTS line. It was a busy place.

At one end of the big room was a clothes-swap table and it was covered with messy mounds of used kids' clothing. I never had to buy outfits for my girls and I discovered it took only one wash cycle to remove the musty coop smells from the garments. On a table near the bathroom door a giant aluminum coffee pot heated water for instant coffee and tea. But the collage of chipped and stained coffee mugs was a bit too iffy for me. Everything about DWHE was about re-purposing, maybe even us moms.

After a short visit and usually without speaking to anyone, I'd leave feeling a whole lot better. The vigor of the DWHE women filled my emptiness. I still felt a little lonely but I didn't feel alone and it helped me think I was doing okay.

DWHE was a driving force for women's rights, especially in higher education. The women were far more intelligent and definitely more radical than me. They were feminists, a philosophy that both confused and unnerved me. Maybe it was because I was just beginning to find my new role in society and now they were telling me I had it all wrong. The heated discussions at DWHE about discrimination against women, people of color, and the poor made me nervous. The issues were foreign to me and also I didn't know where the women would go with their outrage. *Won't their anger alienate people? Wasn't it counterproductive?*

It was hard to identify with everything about DWHE so I became a fringe member. But it was reassuring to know those women supported me. I think they knew and believed in my potential even before I did.

One day while I was studying in the college library, the front edge of my desk abutted the front of another desk where a woman my age was hunched over her notes. She was slim and attractive with long, dark blond hair. After a half hour or so, we struck up a conversation. She told me she was a single mom with a toddler in the Little People's Center and was also in DWHE. Our conversation blossomed after we realized we lived a short distance from each other in Newmarket. She told me her nickname was Buffy.

We became instant friends. She introduced me to other DWHE moms like Sarah who had been married in Africa to a Somali man and got a camel as a wedding gift, and Carol whose son was conceived when she was raped. Another woman, Pam, was in her early twenties and friends with Buffy. She wasn't a mom but she blended in perfectly with our group and we became friends, too. At the time I didn't question why she hung out with us but many years later I learned Pam had given birth just before me but had given up her baby. I didn't want to imagine her heartache.

My small, rather bland world view was changing fast. Soon my twins and I became part of a clan of six moms and their kids. We were all dedicated students with interesting histories. We shared babysitting duties, evening meals, birthday celebrations, afternoons at the beach, and weekend trips. This was my new family.

# 64: A More Erotic Dance

## I might have blushed

"Hey, wanna go to a party?" Buffy asked. "Aah, sure." I said. She warned me, "It might be a little rough." A little rough. What did that mean? I had no clue.

My life had become predictable, maybe a little too predictable. I hadn't had a night out in months so I got a friend to babysit my girls and drove to the party.

Buffy's directions made it easy to find the aged apartment building in the middle of the old mill town. I parked my car at the curb then stepped out into the damp night air. Ahead of me, the long rows of three-story buildings looked like they belonged in a spooky Hawthorne tale. My heart quickened. *Please make this the place.*

The building number was right so I opened the door and entered an enclosed foyer with a long staircase. As I climbed the steps, funky, bass beats wafted down from the top and bounced back and forth off the staircase walls. The muffled, primal throbs pulled me to the top.

I was nervous about what might be inside but, after three hard knocks, Buffy opened the door and welcomed me with a big smile. That helped. Stopped in the doorway I looked through the kitchen and into the living room which was bursting with music and laughter. I stepped inside and closed the door. My life was about to change, big time.

I couldn't stop looking at the couple dancing in the living room. Gently bumping into each other, they were tap, tap, tapping each other's bodies to the Motown beats. *Is this what Buffy warned me about?* I might have blushed. *It does seem a little rough.*

I recognized the tall, handsome guy from the college newspaper. He was an African American basketball star and he was doing "The Bump" with a sultry, red haired, white girl. With each beat, he bent down, then, with his hip, or arm, or thigh, he gently tapped her hip, arm, or thigh and she reciprocated in perfect rhythm. As I stood visiting with Buffy I kept being drawn into their exhibition. I wasn't used to seeing a white woman dance with a Black man. It was beautifully tender but the prudish me recoiled. *Too sexual, too suggestive.*

I struggled to concentrate on Buffy's words because the music and dancing were far more interesting. After a few minutes she lead me into the living room and introduced me to a few of her friends. The room was overflowing with the cheerful chatter and raucous laughter of about fifteen people and I felt welcomed. I noticed a couple of white women and men but what held my attention were the African American men with their Afros, brightly colored shirts, and tight bell-bottom pants. Other than on TV, I'd never seen guys dressed like that. *Flashy.*

The music continued to pulse through the sweet-smelling haze of pot and uninhibited laughter. I felt invited into the mirth evident on everyone's face. It, all of it, even the new and alluring dark faces intrigued me.

I found a chair so I could sit and watch the dancing. For some reason, the gyrations began to feel familiar and after a few minutes, I was aware of my body in a way I hadn't been before. I'd always loved music and I liked to dance but this was different. I could feel the rhythm in my midsection and my hips. I didn't need my ears to sync up with the beat; my body knew the score so I "listened" with it. The awareness snuck up on me and I felt freer and more alive.

Buffy's party was nothing like the fraternity parties my freshman year in college. The goal at those parties was to drink a lot of beer, dance, and maybe find a boyfriend. My first one was a blind date at the agriculture fraternity with a guy named Howard, a name I would never forget. At first he seemed nice enough but there definitely were no sparks. We spent the first part of the evening trying to make conversation, drinking beer, and watching couples dance to clunky country-western music. Later that night, sitting next to him, I turned to say something and gasped. Howard, who obviously had had too much beer, had taken out his false teeth and set them on the back of his chair. It was bizarre, disgusting, and I was in shock. Needless to say, I left the party and steered clear of the "Agi' guys,

At Buffy's, everyone was engaged in the music, the dance, and, it seemed, the simple joy of being together. And it surprised me that when I got up to dance, I felt inconspicuous, like I blended in and that felt fun and familiar and beautiful. *This is my kind of music, my kind of party.*

I would come to realize it was the unbridled laughter, the unabashed affection for each other, and the soulful, hip-swaying music that made it feel so wonderful. This different culture captivated me.

# 65: Free-range Kids

## Freedom to explore

My first spring back at college, I heard about Forest Park. It was the on-campus family housing for married grad students and anyone with kids. Anyone.

The handsome little development had long rows of two-story condos surrounded by pine trees. The brick buildings were organized into eight blocks of six. The second floor apartments opened to a deck and most bottom floor apartments opened to swing sets and slides. The clean, well maintained grounds had paved walkways that branched out through the neighborhood. On my first visit the wild stream of little bikers and packs of galloping kids bowled me over making me smile. *This is the perfect place for us.* And it abutted DWHE.

For a few months I'd been wanting to move closer to campus and once again, I lucked out. An apartment opened up in July. It was perfect: on the ground floor, at the end of a row of units, and next to the parking lot. A couple weeks later, A1 Forest Park became our new address.

Our place had a roomy living room, two good-sized bedrooms, a small bathroom, and a mini kitchen that opened to a playground near a grove of pines. The apartment was sunny and freshly painted.

The bedroom walls were white and I was told I could paint them. I wanted my girls to feel like it was their very own room so I bought some watercolor paints and brushes. I pushed their beds to the center of the bedroom and handed them brushes and jars of paint. I said, "That wall near your bed is your wall and you can paint whatever you want on it." Arms crossed, standing at the doorway, I smiled, proud of my clever idea. But, I realized I was a lot more excited than they were. They looked so tiny next to the twelve-foot long wall and just three minutes later they were done. Each masterpiece covered a square foot of wall. I hadn't realized how small a three-year-old's world is.

Early every morning the Little People's Center van came to Forest Park to pick up the children. I still have memories of rainy days when I dressed them in small plastic garbage bags instead of rain coats. I sent them off with the driver who had a smile on his face and was in his own large plastic bag. We had enough money for food and essentials and I was learning to be frugal, so real raincoats seemed unnecessary when trash bags worked and were all the style at day care.

Surrounded by single moms, their kids, and married grad students, Forest Park was idyllic. It was a place where children could run out the door and safely roam the park in kid clusters or alone. Jessie liked hanging out with her little girlfriends playing on the slides and swings. Jenny hung out with the slightly older boys and many times ventured off alone knocking on doors and inviting herself into people's apartments. With so much freedom to explore and a large extended family, of sorts, I was reminded of the best parts of my own childhood.

# 66: Another of Life's Landslides

## Damn you, gravity!

The tent's ceiling is drip, drip, dripping onto my hand. It's early. My god, it was cold again last night. My sluggish eyes open and struggle to focus. Condensation, like a thin layer of fleece, coats the tent walls and water drops slide down, collide with others, and grow. Fat ones sled down the tent shell, pick up speed, and ram into even more. Some hit the ceiling seam, are too heavy to contain themselves, and free-fall, landing on my hand.

Water molecules behave like tiny magnets. They have a static charge on their surface that pulls them together and they touch. I'm captivated by this mini physics phenomenon playing out near me. *Because our bodies also have a static charge, could our bodies be attracted to other bodies? If so, does it affect or change us? And does gravity, a curious force for sure, play a role in this?*

Pervasive dampness motivates me to get up at seven. Last night's cold makes for some stiff muscles and a slow-motion start this morning. After I tend to Doug and hang my blankets and sleeping bag on tree branches, I start to perk up when I remember the two hikers who stopped by last evening. They recommended I try the Crow Peak trail that's named after a long-ago battle between the Sioux and Crow. It's weird, well, more accurately, I'm weird. Since I've decided I have some sort of kinship with the Sioux, I'm happy to hear they were victorious.

On my map, the Crow Peak trail looks doable: not far from camp, and not too challenging. To clear my foggy brain, I walk a few paces over to the stream and splash cold water on my face. As I towel-dry, I look down on what's probably melt water from a glacier high in the Rockies.

Gravity has pulled it many hundreds of miles to this spot to sustain us. I hope it remains pristine.

My zany mind thinks that if I scurry around this chilly morning, I can rush into the warmer parts of the day. So, after a light breakfast, Doug and I get in the car and head to the Crow Peak trailhead. I've stuffed some raisins, an apple, nuts, and corn chips in my backpack along with a gallon of water, mostly for Doug. It's cool and sunny now but I remember it gets hot fast.

I drive slowly on the twenty-mile trip trying to stretch out my time in the warm, dry car. When we get close to the trailhead, the dirt road ahead is well groomed which for some odd reason, comforts me. Dense clusters of familiar pine, aspen, and birch stand guard on the sides like starchy soldiers lining a tunnel. Wedges of sunlight cut through the canopies dabbing the road with light. It reminds me of the forests in NH.

The single car parked at the trailhead is a good sign. *Maybe I'll have the trail to myself.* Once we're out of the car, I snap on Doug's leash and we start out. He senses I want to take it slow and goes easy. After walking for a couple minutes, I look up, smile, and try to absorb all the aliveness of this land. It feels like good medicine.

The gravel trail is well-maintained and bordered by splashes of hardwoods and pine. Sunlight charges through the foliage shifting their greens to muted shades of yellow. It's a beautiful medley of conifer needles and wind-fluttered leaves. A short way down the trail, familiar sounds whisk me back to Maine again. A rowdy gang of chickadees swoops down and perches on a nearby limb. Hyperactive and curious, they bob and tilt their heads to study me and I can't help but chuckle. Then some unfamiliar little singers with hollow voices and high-pitched notes remind me I'm noticed.

I have a little spring in my step now and let Doug run ahead on the trail but keep his leash handy, just in case. My brisk pace pulls me out of my morning slump and I roll, wide awake, into mid-morning. But forty-five minutes later my throat tightens and I have to stop. The trail ahead is covered by a massive landslide. It's at least thirty feet across and composed of six-to-ten-inch chunks of jagged rock. *So much for my dreamy morning hike. I wish there was someone here to keep an eye on me.* I look out over the rubble hoping for a safe place to cross. My heart is racing and I feel awful small. The possibility of tumbling down hundreds of feet of rock shards, crashing at the bottom, never to be found is real. *You've been frightened like this before. You know what to do.* I won't pretend to be a superhero. I'll just shift into a well-used gear. A friend once called that gear the "warrior gear." I think it's the place we go to when we need to put fear aside in order to make it through.

It would be easy to turn around, walk back to the car, and find another trail to hike. But, here again, I feel that familiar nudge, that subtle encouragement to take on the challenge and maybe learn something.

*There would be a warning sign if this place was hazardous, right?* I haven't met anyone all morning so I sputter aloud, "Please, angels, help me get across." The "cassette tape" in my head sputters back, *Be careful, test your footing first, and don't look around for Doug. He'll manage.*

I test the chunky path but even with careful, well-thought-out steps, the loose rocks slide over each other and I can almost feel them gliding down the slope, just like those drops of water in my tent. *Damn you, gravity.* And with each slow-motion step I think, *Who would find me if I fall?* My rational and intuitive self are in a fretful battle as I move. Then something strong and daring inside me says, *What's the worst that could happen?* I'm thinking broken bones, concussion, bloody limbs, things like that. I decide to just go for it.

When I do go, I move in a slow-motion glide. I am more frightened than I was in the storm but I know, for some cockeyed reason, I must do this. When I get to the other side, I bend over with my hands on my knees and, finally, after a couple minutes, breathe normally again. But my triumphant feeling fades when I see Doug standing back on the other side. He looks up and I'm scared to call him but I do and he prances over the perilous path like it was nothing. Watching him I'm not as proud of myself as I was a minute ago.

As we continue up the trail we have to cross five more giant landslides. But it gets easier because I've progressed. I'm no longer paralyzed by the fear of falling and not being found. I'm walking a little more upright, with more confidence. The crossing was a full-body experience, not just a change in the way I think. It's like during the prairie storm when I let go and trusted in fate. It reminds me of how helpless and alone I felt when my parents got divorced.

From: adult Regina
Dear Dad,

When you and Mom got divorced, I felt like I got hit by a bulldozer. I'm sure it was horrible for you too, but I imagine in a different way. I remember that after you moved out, you came to visit us kids, every few weeks. It was so sad to see you walk into the house, go into the living room, and sit down on what used to be your recliner. Dad, you just sat there, looked at the TV, didn't talk to us kids or Mom, and nobody talked to you. We ignored you and you ignored us. That heartbreaking picture is fixed in my mind. I know you didn't do it because you were mad at us; I know you did it because you didn't know how to talk to us. Also, we didn't know how to talk to you. We just never communicated much. To this day, I can picture you in your recliner and I feel bad for you and sad for myself because every young girl needs her father to talk to her.

I hope, wherever you are, you are at peace and enjoying lots of long conversations with our family. I am doing my best to improve my communication skills with my own children and the rest of our family. It's hard work and sometimes scary to make myself vulnerable but that's what I need to do to really listen to my children and at the same time hear what my own heart wants to say. Thanks, Dad, for staying with us for as long as you could.

I love you, Dad,
Regina

—⁂—

As I expected, the day heats up fast. Off-leash and on rodent pursuit, Doug looks the happiest he's been since leaving Maine. Every so often, to slow him down, I leash him. After a couple miles he's panting at a good clip so I stop often and coax him to drink water. A half mile from the top, I call him to me and I panic. He's panting so hard his tongue is dark red and hanging out the side of his mouth. I persuade him to walk beside me but he moves in slow motion. Back a mile or so on the trail, I was concerned about him and wondered if I should stop but I wanted to go on. *Maybe I should have turned around. Am I being selfish?*

Closer to the top, I stop six more times so he can rest. *I wish he could have ignored the squirrels and walked beside me like a "regular" dog.* Three college-age hikers meet us on their way down from the summit. We exchange greetings and gush about the beautiful canyon and their cheerful zest revive him for a bit.

Thank goodness, about twenty minutes later, we finally reach the summit. I scout the area and find a shady spot where Doug and I can rest. He stretches out his long, hot body over the cool ground and I fill his water bowl then set it near his head. He's not interested. I try not to worry. *Maybe he just needs to rest.*

I sit on the ground and take in another spectacular panorama. The brochure says you can see seventy miles into the distance. When I start to focus, there, directly across from me, many miles away, is Bear Butte. I relax and don't feel so nervous or alone.

Now that I think about it, my endurance is pretty damn good. So after only a few minutes of rest, I'm ready to start down. Unfortunately, when I stand up, my legs and one knee hurt a lot. I remember last night when I sank into my body and it felt like I got some healing. I wonder if it'll work here.

I sit back down then talk silently to my achy muscles. I imagine that my legs and knee receive my thoughts of comfort and appreciation for the hike today. After a couple minutes the pain is almost gone. I'm not that surprised.

As I lean back and stretch out on the ground next to Doug, the surface of my skin starts to tingle. It's a delicate sensation, something I could have easily missed or ignored if I wasn't here and hadn't just asked for healing. I can feel the life force of this place. The trees and the rocks are shimmering with delicate vibrations, like a little magnetic force of aliveness and for a second it feels like there are no boundaries to anything around me. I think of the drops of water in my tent and how they merged. Maybe that's what's supposed to happen with humans, and trees, and rocks. We're supposed to feel that kind of connection. *Boy, I wish I felt like this at the landslide.*

I want to remember to not over-plan my life but dance along with it. I want to remember to allow for life's twists and turns and landslides along my trails. I need to be patient in growing myself, stay alert, and opportunities will show up at just the right time.

Doug and I start back down the trail and, thank goodness, he looks better. Then it's my turn to mope. Sadness in the form of old memories that most parents can identify with, fill my chest. I slow down and cry about being a less-than-perfect parent. A few steps further, I whisper to each of my children and ask them to forgive me for my shortcomings. *Where is this coming from? Is it my guilt for not turning around for Doug?* Then I remember it's futile to ask these kinds of questions, especially on *this* trip. I think about a couple instances with my children that I feel bad about. Then I send a ray of love to them, say I'm sorry and when I do, I cry so hard I can hardly see the trail. But thank goodness, after that, I feel clearer and just keep walking.

A little further, I think about my four friends who had planned to join me. I speak out loud asking them to forgive me for any of my transgressions and as I continue down from the peak, I send my sorrows about them into the sun. After a couple minutes my body does feel lighter. I wonder if my kids and friends can sense my apologies. I hope they can. When I get back home I will, at some point, make amends with each person.

I start thinking about the little water landslide inside my tent this morning. The dampness didn't seem like a mistake and the drops seemed totally fine with the fall. Hmmm, they surrendered, to gravity. *What if I throw in the towel, wave the white flag, surrender too?* The idea doesn't feel like a death wish. It's more like an appeal to my overbearing mindset. If I surrender to the Universe's plan, I can release my regrets and disappointments. *And that sounds like freedom. Well, there you go lady, ha, ha.*

For the next few miles, I'm feeling serene and agile but Doug is still sluggish. The brochure is wrong because it says it's a five-mile intermediate hike. I find out later it's over eight miles with sections rated as strenuous. I stop often to rest him and encourage him to drink but he takes little. When we finally get to the parking lot, he is so disoriented he doesn't even recognize the car. Now I'm scared. I know I have to cool him down fast.

There's a small stream not far down the entrance road. When I pull in, I coax him out of the car and into the stream, I pour water over his back. He perks up a bit but he's still awfully groggy. It suddenly hits me and I feel stupid. He has heat exhaustion. I try not to overreact but I am a ball of nerves just like I used to get when my kids got sick. *Doug could die.* I check my map and am relieved to see there's a lake nearby. I don't know what the speed limit is on this back road but I'm sure I deserve a ticket. After a few minutes I see the sign for Iron Creek Lake. *Thank you, God.*

From the car I can see that the sandy beach is packed with people. But I'm so scared it's easy to block out proper decorum as I lead my hundred-pound Shepherd over the sand, past startled bathers, and into the thigh-deep water. *Sorry, people, but my dog needs saving.* The swimmers around us are not amused. I get some dirty looks and they give us a wide berth but I block it out, too.

Doug has a nice, long, cool swim and, thank goodness, within ten minutes or so he's back to his easy-going self. As my leashed dog and I make our way out of the water and up through the mob of sunbathers, Doug pauses a few times to shake himself dry. I smile and make a mental calculation: we made absolutely no fans here today.

# 67: The Music of Diversity

## 'Tis the gift to be free

I loved my classes at UNH: molecular biology, vertebrate physiology, and pretty much anything involving biochemistry. My grades were great, but most importantly, we were happy.

Weekday mornings I'd send my girls off to daycare then spend the rest of the day in class, studying, doing errands, or socializing. On the weekends we'd do fun things with the other moms and kids. I was content and not looking for more.

One winter afternoon after I'd finished my classes, I scooted over to day care to pick up my kids. Sitting in the center of the activity room was a cluster of what the staff called "little people." On the periphery of the bunch were Theresa and Ben, her toddler. Theresa had a beautiful Afro and a dazzling smile. She was directing an ensemble of free-spirited singers and musicians playing well-loved, wooden flutes, xylophones, tambourines, and tiny drums. At Theresa's command, the ever-morphing mound of kids erupted into disjointed rhythms and rambling melodies. The children were sitting on stubby chairs just like the one Theresa teetered on. She wore a short, denim skirt and blue tights that hugged her long, thick legs. Her face told how much she loved children.

To outsiders it may have sounded like a cacophony of missed notes and syncopation but to me and, I think, to other moms and staff, it was the simple truth and then some. I recognized the melody of the daycare's anthem which I'd heard often. It was the old Shaker song, "Simple Gifts,"written in 1848:

"'Tis the gift to be simple, 'tis the gift to be free
'Tis the gift to come down where we ought to be,
And when we find ourselves in the place just right,
'Twill be in the valley of love and delight."

247

Theresa was a gifted pianist, gifted but a little bit quirky. Once, at a small campus concert, she showed up in her denim miniskirt, tights, and perfectly shaped Afro. She was scheduled to play a classical piece on the baby grand for the crowd of two hundred. Her playing was beautiful as she meandered through the score and flipped through the sheet music propped up on the piano. But near the end of the piece she stopped, swiveled on the piano bench, faced the audience, and said, "I lost the last page of the piece so I can't finish." Then without another word, she picked up her sheet music and walked off the stage.

A stunned silence filled the room. Then one, two, three clapped, and finally, the rest of us joined in. That was Theresa, gifted, generous, and just a little eccentric.

I stood at daycare that day and enjoyed a couple more songs. More mothers arrived, the musicians dispersed, and moms began culling their kids from the pack. The giggles and shrieks of the runaways almost drowned out the tired pleadings of the moms. With each capture, hugs and kisses ensued and the room settled as the herd of little people dwindled.

Jessie and Jenny were drawn to Theresa. I loved watching Jenny, with her chubby cheeks and bowl-cut, blond hair, belt out a song for her. Reticent Jessie had curly, ginger hair and I couldn't help but giggle listening to her tell us long elaborate stories about her finger paintings.

I snagged my two girls, bagged their artwork, then put on their boots and jackets. Theresa walked over and said, "Hey, a friend of mine is having a party Saturday night. Do you want to go?"

"Oh, thanks, Theresa. I'm not sure. I'll get back to you."

My girls and I headed out to the parking lot and I drove us back to our perfect little apartment in Forest Park. We settled into another of our typical evenings: a little kid TV, supper, baths, story, bed, and my study time. Then Theresa's invitation began to gnaw at me. *A party? Did I want to go? Should I?*

I thought about it for a couple days then decided I needed a night out and began asking around for a babysitter. Although I had a lot of friends in the park, it was sometimes hard to find a sitter because some left for the weekend and others had their own plans.

Someone gave me the name of a married woman from India who lived in the grad student block. I called and we agreed to meet at her apartment to talk. I knocked on her door and it opened to a beautiful, tan-skinned woman in colorful, traditional Indian attire. As we talked, I told her about myself and my three-year-old girls. I found her charming. She agreed to babysit and I knew she'd work out fine. I wasn't so sure about the party, but after meeting the lovely babysitter, I knew I'd follow through and go.

On the night of the party Theresa came to my apartment in her signature denim mini skirt, black tights, and snowmobile boots. She was a large woman and her down parka, zipped up to just below her big breasts, made her look even bulkier.

A few minutes later there was another knock at our door. Jenny ran to open it and in glided the babysitter. Her headscarf framed her pretty face while wings of bright, silky garments trailed behind her. It was cold outside but a thin jacket and layers of fluid material were all she wore.

I invited her in and introduced her to Theresa. Jenny, then Jessie stood toe-to-toe with the lovely lady and made their visual inspection. They tilted up their heads and she looked down at them. Jenny blurted, "What's that big red dot on your head for?"

I sucked in what felt like a gallon of air and thought I should say something but I couldn't think of anything.

The woman looked down with a kind smile then said "I wear the red bindi to show that I am married." I knew that babysitter would do just fine.

It wasn't the first time I was shocked by what one of my girls said and it wouldn't be the last. On our way to the party, I entertained Teresa with a few of their antics. Gregarious and observant, they were quick to pick up on a situation. With Jessie, it usually happened in the company of family. My mom and Jessie had a special bond. Once, while driving my car, I looked over to see Jessie studying the skin on my mom's arm. Looking up lovingly, Jessie volunteered, "Grandma, your skin is too big for you." I wanted to laugh but I pretended not to hear. Even in her forties, my mother was overly sensitive about her looks.

Another time I noticed Jessie studying the broken veins on my mother's legs. Jessie smiled and as proud as could be, said, "Grandma, your legs look like a road map." My mother raised her eyebrows and looked down at Jessie with a bewildered look but said nothing. Knowing my mom's dread of getting old, I'm sure it stung. *Oops.*

But to my embarrassment, Jenny's announcements were much more public. Proud of her discoveries, she was eager to share them with the world. One day when we were living in Newmarket, we went to the little town laundromat. After I lugged in the dirty laundry and got things started, from behind me I heard Jenny. "Mom, look. This lady has really long hair all over her legs. It's real. Come look!" A ways from me and near the entrance, my two little darlings had cornered a poor woman and were staring at her legs. She just looked at me, pleading to be rescued. I raced over, grabbed their little hands, and marched them outside. I explained, as best I could to three-year-olds, the importance of keeping their observations about the appearance of others to themselves. Jessie, quiet and reserved, didn't need the lecture. For Jenny it would to be a lifelong challenge.

Theresa and I laughed all the way to the party

# 68: And, a Yellow Firebird, Too

## This small-town white girl was confused

It was a short drive to the party and for the rest of the night Theresa and I stood together, sipped beer, and visited, mostly with each other. The crowd was largely white students and the hum of the party was just that, a hum, a dull hum. No boisterous laughter, just the drone of overly familiar pop tunes, clumps of intense conversation, and sporadic, platonic dancing that bored me. I didn't know anyone but I danced a few times and I noticed Theresa dancing in her snowmobile boots.

This uneventful and forgettable gathering was definitely not Buffy's rough party. I didn't care to engage in idle conversation and the crowd was just not that interesting for either of us so we left early. When I stepped into my apartment I was nervous about what the babysitter would say but her report was good. *Thank you, Lord.*

The next day was Sunday and it started out the way I liked my Sundays to go, with no real plans, little classwork, and lots of time to putter the day away with my girls.

In early afternoon there was a knock at the door. I opened it and was jolted. A tall, trim, and handsome African American man wearing a leather jacket and dress pants stood beaming down at me.

"Hello, my name is Larry. I saw you at the party last night."

My mouth dropped. *Who is this guy?*

"When I saw your beautiful smile, I knew I had to meet you. When you left, I followed you home to see where you lived. I hope you don't mind. I'd like to take you out."

*All that in one breath? And of all the nerve...*

I wasn't sure how I felt about that. Either my guy-radar was malfunctioning and/or his boldness bewildered me. But he seemed harmless.

When he told me he was in the Air Force and stationed at Pease Air Force Base in nearby Portsmouth, I relaxed, a little. He didn't ask anything about me and I assumed he knew I was a student. Stunned, I said yes to a date, gave him my phone number and we set a time when he'd pick me up the following Saturday night.

After he left I stood looking at the closed door. I didn't even know his last name. What was I thinking? It did feel good to be pursued by such a handsome guy though.

It was a long week. Larry and my impulsive acceptance were in the back of my mind. I hadn't been on a real date in months so it was time.

It felt like forever since I'd had a real boyfriend even though the summer before I'd had a fling with a Georgetown University law student. But it wasn't like we dated, we just did things together. Dan was in my chemistry class and with his olive complexion and long, black hair, he was stand-out handsome. I couldn't believe he chose me over all the other young women gaga over him, and I noticed there were a bunch.

Dan was outdoorsy and pragmatic. In his downtime he read the Congressional Record and also got to have me on the side while the Watergate hearings blared on my TV. We had a fun summer scuba diving, hiking, and taking my girls to the local parks. My heart broke at summer's end when he went back to DC. Even though he'd made it clear ours was only a summer romance, it still hurt.

Saturday date night arrived, Theresa came to babysit, and punctual Larry knocked on my door. When I opened it, he stepped in, beaming. He had on a preppy sweater with a button-down shirt collar, new fitted jeans, and fine leather dress boots. Had I expected something a little more ghetto? Was he trying to fit in with my lifestyle? This small town, white girl was confused.

Theresa perked up when she saw him. It was obvious she thought he was hot because all of a sudden she got chatty. I chuckled under my breath.

Jenny and Jessie bounded out of their bedroom in their pajamas and, again, stood toe-to-toe with our visitor. As I introduced them to him, he looked down, smiled, and seemed unfazed that I had kids.

Then it happened, abruptly, and from Jenny, of course. "You smell like diapers!" I wanted to hide.

Larry chuckled, Theresa shifted in her seat, and I pretended to have heard nothing then turned to get my coat from the closet.

He did smell of cologne, but diapers? It dawned on me later that new diapers at daycare had a powdery smell. That's what she meant.

After I kissed my girls goodnight, we headed to the parking lot. I looked up and there, sticking out like a carnival ride and parked in a row of dull, slush-covered clunkers was his brand new buttercup yellow Pontiac Firebird. It was sexy hot, and its long, sleek body evoked confident power and machismo. It was inanimate, but I pictured it as having a swagger that was palpable. Larry opened the door for me and I slid across the soft, white, leather seat into the welcoming, warm interior. *The flashy car, the gorgeous guy; do I belong here?* But as I sat in that foreign environment the purr of R&B love songs and smell of sandalwood air freshener stopped the hitch in my breathing. I felt safe.

Accompanied by easy, light conversation, Larry and I headed to Portsmouth to catch a movie. When we arrived, we didn't recognize any of the four movies playing so we randomly chose *The Stepford Wives*.

The movie's about a group of successful men who form a gated community with the intention of turning their wives into ideal, compliant servants who will eventually become robots. I groaned along with the audience as the plot played out and the women became slaves. Larry stayed silent.

After the movie we stopped at a diner for a bite to eat. I was beginning to like this soft-spoken, well-mannered guy, and I wanted to know more about him.

Inside we found a booth, placed our order, and began the first of what would become many long, easy-going conversations. Larry started to tell me about himself.

He grew up poor in the inner city of Washington, DC. For dinner some nights there was only one cupcake to be shared among five people. Now he was an Air Force MP and proud at having escaped that life. Larry beamed when he talked about his work and his dream of getting stationed at Andrews Air Force Base in DC to work alongside government big shots.

When it was my turn, I began to tell about myself then, suddenly, from the other end of the near-empty restaurant came a woman's high-pitched scream. We both twisted in our seats to look. A middle-aged man was sitting on a chair at a table. Opposite him on the floor was a woman on her back with her legs up in the air laughing hysterically.

Larry and I raced over and helped the woman to her feet. The man tried to tell us what happened but amidst their laughter, he couldn't get it out. He finally said his wife went to sit in a chair she thought was at the table but there wasn't one. He cracked up again telling us and the four of us doubled over remembering her scream and seeing her on the floor with her waving legs.

When a waitress came over to help, she got caught up in our hysterics, too. Larry and I went back to our table but every few minutes the couple started in again and we couldn't help it, we did too.

When the laughter subsided, I told him about me. He gave me all his attention and that surprised me. I began to like him even more. But I was puzzled by something he said. When I brought up the absurdity of the movie's premise, women molded into the perfect wives, he turned and looked at me, confused, and said, "So what's the big deal?"

I chuckled inside, brushed it off, and answered, "Oh, it's nothing." Surely he was pulling my leg. I imagined what my DWHE moms would say about the movie and it wasn't pretty.

# 69: Bingo, Blush, and Boston

## Another of life's mysteries

I think I was lonely but, because my life was full, I didn't realize it. The affection of the DWHE moms then Larry's attention revived me, grew my confidence, and I began to trust myself more. It's interesting how good relationships can do that.

On our second date Larry took me to the Air Force Base to play Bingo. After he parked the car we walked to what looked like an old airplane hangar. When he opened the entrance door his eyes lit up and he smiled at me. *Bingo couldn't be that exciting, could it?* I followed him inside, curious about his attraction to the game. With his stylish lifestyle and all, I wondered if this was a joke.

The interior was a half-acre of long, church-supper-type tables and rickety, metal chairs. A few hundred people, mostly middle-aged women, sat poised to play while clouds of cigarette smoke spiraled upward then disappeared into the hanger's vast atmosphere. Their eyes flashed back and forth, then up and down over their cards. Like a synchronized flock of birds, they paused and waited for the next number. When it came, with heads down, and card chips in hand the scanning resumed. Concentration was key. It was serious business.

Larry led me to our seats. I scooted my chair up close to him but I felt awkward, out of place next to a Black man surrounded by all those white women. When he laid out his cards, he arched his back, picked up his Bingo chips, and started to scan, too. He looked right at home. After a couple of less-than-riveting games, he leaned over beaming. "We can come to play every week if you want to."

I gulped my surprise then half-whispered, "That would be nice."

So my handsome MP date, with a hot car, liked playing Bingo with a bunch of older women? *Who is this guy?*

On the drive back to my apartment, Larry asked if I wanted to go to a party in Boston the following Saturday. *Bingo, then a Boston party?* I had a vision of me, a farm girl with this city guy I barely knew, partying in Boston. I wondered what I was getting myself into.

He must have sensed my hesitation because he said, "I've spent a lot of time in that city so I know my way around and, with what's in my glove compartment you'll be fine."

I shot a look at him expecting a sly smile but he nodded at the glove compartment so I opened it. Cushioned on a stack of neatly folded paper napkins and illuminated by the compartment light was the biggest handgun I'd ever seen. It looked dangerous. I was falling for him.

With his good looks and, of course, his flashy car, my girlfriends were gaga about Larry and it seemed my status in the group had been elevated. I liked the new attention even though I knew it had little to do with me.

My friend Celeste, a DWHE mom, was about my size but she was a smart dresser and far more worldly than me. I was good with jeans, sweaters, and sneakers. Celeste heard about my Boston date and decided I should "dress to kill" for the party. I trusted her and seeing fashion was not my forte, I agreed to go along. It was a big mistake.

The night of the party, with my girls at a friend's house, Celeste and Theresa showed up early to do my makeover. They put me in heels, a swishy dress that hung just below my knees, and Celeste's mink stole which perched precariously on my shoulders. They curled and hair-sprayed my medium-length hair, put on eyeliner, and painted my cheeks and lips. It all felt foreign but I trusted my friends and got posh.

When I heard Larry's knock at the door I was scared. *What would he think of my outfit, my efforts to fit in at the party?* I opened the door and my fine-looking date stood smiling. He was dressed in black: leather jacket, turtle neck, dress pants, and dress boots. And as usual, he smelled wonderful. He bent down and gave me a peck on the cheek but made no mention of my outfit. After a few minutes of chatter with my enamored friends, we left for the party.

I was relieved to be sitting in the dark car, hiding what I was beginning to regard as "my stupid getup." I remember the ride into the city. I remember the ride home too, but I have no memory of the party. It remains a mystery to this day. I wonder if I smoked some pot laced with a hallucinogen. It was 1974 before there were date drugs, I think, and I'm sure Larry wouldn't have done anything like that. Also, I was perfectly fine after. Nothing about my body felt amiss so I chalked it up as a very weird and embarrassing night out and left it at that.

Years later, I told a counselor friend about that night. He asked me if I'd ever "blacked out" before or if I had any family history of that sort of thing. I told him no but the question shocked me because it hadn't been an unsettling experience. It was just a curiosity. But after ruminating about it for a long time I still couldn't make sense of it. At one point I wondered if someone at the party slipped something into my drink and Larry found out. Maybe he never talked to me about it because he felt responsible and embarrassed for taking me there.

I've read books and attended seminars on the workings of the mind, how it helps us understand our experiences. I learned, in some instances, when the mind can't draw a logical conclusion for why something is happening, it can make up a story or erase the memory altogether. The mind is limited in its comprehension of reality, whatever reality is. For some reason those three hours vanished so in the end it seems I filed it under "another of life's mysteries." But I still cringe wondering how my outfit went over at the party. And, poor Larry.

That night, and with my kids gone, Larry and I spent our first night together at my apartment. It was tender and wonderful. I knew it was more than a physical attraction for us which made it even more romantic.

He dazzled me and, besides that, I loved that he was attracted to me. I loved the attention. But, I was beginning to notice differences in our values and life goals.

Larry liked predictability. Our twice-a-week routine became Bingo or movies, dinner at my place, and romance. I was afraid to ask why we didn't attend another party and a few weeks later he said, "You probably think I might be embarrassed to take you to a party." I looked at him pretending I had no idea what he was talking about. *Well, yes, dressed like that, I'd be embarrassed to take me to a party, too.* The poor guy must have freaked out when he opened my door that night. He said nothing specific, though and it was never brought up again.

Our next movie date was *Young Frankenstein* with Mel Brooks whom I loved, I was psyched. Theresa was happy to babysit as she had a bit of a crush on Larry and took every opportunity to see him. I didn't blame her and was amused.

On movie night Theresa's parents watched her son so she could babysit my girls. After I put them to bed, Theresa said, "I've got a present for you, some weed. It's strong so you'll need only one hit. It'll make watching the movie even more fun."

I'd had pot only once before, as far as I can remember that is, and it was not fun. At a party during my sophomore year, I took a couple hits from a friend's joint. After a short time, I felt so disoriented I retired to my friend's bedroom for the duration of the party. Stretched out on his bed, I hallucinated for the remainder of the night. In my delusion I saw and experienced the workings of every organ in my body, and in color no less. Part of me was calm and I found it interesting to be able to see my insides. But, after a few hours, I got scared when I saw myself jumping out of the third-story window. After that I avoided pot, that is, until Theresa offered me some.

I didn't think it through and took one hit, finished dressing, and when Larry arrived, we left for the movie. Once again I remember the drive to the movie. I remember the drive home but nothing in between. *Damn it. I wanted to see that movie.* I don't remember talking with Larry about it either and I wonder if I'd laughed in all the right places. Normal for me, I was just going along for the ride and now another three hours of my life were lost.

# 70: Chocolate Ice Cream and White Leather

## His kiss told me he loved me

Later that spring, on a Saturday morning, I helped my kids into the back seat of Larry's car and we headed north for a weekend with my family. I looked forward to traveling together and I knew the girls liked Larry. If they didn't, I certainly would have heard about it. I loved listening to him joke about Jenny's antics and Jessie's charming ways. As we left campus he popped a favorite tune into the car's tape deck and, as usual, with his beautiful voice, he sang along and kept turning to smile at me. This guy was singing to me and it felt strange and wonderful. I didn't know it at the time, but the words to "Family Affair" by Sly and the Family Stone were prophetic. It's a song about creating a new family, one with children who have distinctly different personalities, and it foreshadowed the challenges Larry and I would face in our relationship.

As we traveled north, I pictured us as a family unit, sort of. In the car like that, and even though our relationship was relatively new and seemed a little foreign, I felt secure.

I had told my family about Larry so they were anxious to meet him. We were in love and I was excited to show him off. *How could they not like him?*

We left the seacoast area and I was curious about Larry's reaction to the rural countryside. He seemed unfazed and not especially interested in the changing landscape. But he was obviously happy singing or humming to one song after another.

It was more than a two-hour drive home, a long one for the girls, so we stopped a few times to let the them get out and unwind. They did pretty well until I had the bright idea of stopping for ice cream. The girls were quiet in the back working on their chocolate cones. Five minutes after we got back on the road, I heard, "Moooom. I need a napkin."

I didn't look back, just opened the glove compartment, and pulled out a bunch of napkins from under the .45.

When I turned to pass them back, I realized it was too late. Their little faces, hands, and legs as well as the white leather seat were splotched with chocolate ice cream.

I took a deep breath, then said, "Larry we need to pull over."

He nodded, turned off the music, and parked us on the side of the country road. I opened my door, and dashed back to clean up the disaster.

I was worried about his reaction to the mess but he didn't say a word or even make a face. He just kept handing me napkins as I attempted to quell the avalanche of melting ice cream flowing through little fingers and onto the seat. *What a great guy. What a freakin' relief.*

Bringing a boyfriend home to meet my mom was nothing new. Dan and I had visited the summer before but, in my mind, it was less complicated because he was white. Now as we rode along I started thinking about what happened my freshman year of college. I'd brought two guy friends home to visit, one of whom was Somalian, one Panamanian. We arrived late in the evening and after sitting and visiting, we watched some TV while my mother stayed busy and out of sight. With all our spare rooms, I expected my friends would sleep at our house. But when I asked my mom which rooms to use she said, "Oh, Beverly said your friends can sleep at her house." My mother had arranged for them to sleep at her friend's house. I didn't understand but without questioning her I drove them to Beverly's and, thank goodness, my friends seemed oblivious to my confusion.

Early the next morning I phoned to tell them I'd go pick them up. Christian, my Panamanian friend, said, "No thanks. We'll walk." Right away I knew what they were up to. They wanted to make a statement after what my mom pulled and they definitely did. They took their sweet time walking the mile-long stretch down the main street to our house. I heard that for weeks after, my tall, Art Garfunkel look-a-like friend wearing a sarape and my Black, skateboarding buddy, Abraham, were the talk of the town. When I heard that, I was embarrassed and didn't understand the issue. When I talked to my two friends about it, they said it was easy to spot that kind of subtle prejudice. Come to think of it, 1968 was just before Woodstock, long hair, and hippies. It makes sense that they'd have shaken things up a bit. As well they should have.

I made us breakfast at my mom's house and afterwards I drove them around showing off the farmlands and back roads I loved so much. But the best part of the visit was when we walked down to our pasture ravine behind the house, the place with the beautiful stream and many of my childhood memories. Once we came to the water we hardly talked, just sat down near the brook's sandy shore absorbing nature's beauty. It was one of those perfect early fall days when everything agrees to be in perfect harmony. As Christian and I sat on a log a few feet from the water, he smiled as he pointed to our friend and whispered, "Look at how he squats and cups his hands in prayer over the water before drinking. And look, when he drinks he's like a fine gazelle." That image is something I will never forget: my friend bent down at the stream, giving thanks to the water. He looked like African nobility.

When Larry, the girls, and I, arrived at my mother's house, my family welcomed us with a meal fit for a holiday feast. Along with John, Dolly, Gerry, my mom, and Beth, we celebrated into the evening, drinking and dancing to the latest disco tunes. We had a blast, especially Dolly who loved to dance and appreciated Larry's prowess on the dance floor. I scored big with my family.

My mom surprised me even more when she allowed Larry and me to sleep together; at least she didn't make any overt objections. Overall, she seemed to like Larry well enough so I relaxed. The next day everyone reveled in the afterglow of our fun night and later in the afternoon we made an uneventful trip back to Durham.

A couple weeks later we went home again and it started off like a replay of our first visit, but I was not prepared for what happened at the end of the weekend.

Before our Sunday afternoon departure Larry said his goodbyes then he and the girls headed for the car. My mom leaned in to me, held my arms, and looked into my eyes. She said, "Don't bring him home again. He's just too dark."

*What did she just say?* It didn't register. We'd had such a great time, everyone liked Larry, and I knew he liked them. It looked to me like everything was working fine.

Shocked, I barely spoke on the ride back to campus. My mind was spinning as I tried to make sense of something that didn't make sense. *Why would Mom say that?*

We had been brought up to accept everyone, but we had grown up with some conservative '50s values and with next to no contact with people of color. Dolly was Filipino, loved by everyone, and it was never an issue. *What is Mom afraid of?*

On the ride home Larry was quiet, too. Later he told me he had suspected that my mom disapproved of us. I imagined he'd had too many experiences with racism. I hurt for him but I also felt adrift and it was because of my mother. I wasn't mad at her but I was confused and sad about what she said.

261

Days later, I noticed Larry was pulling away from me. There were fewer and fewer phone calls, and no more dates. I tried calling him at work but he was always out. He just disappeared. The old raw wounds from losing my dad and David surfaced and I was desperate not to be left behind, again.

I wanted to lure him back, to have him explain why he left, even though I knew why. After a couple weeks of tormented days and night, I was worn out so I surrendered. I accepted that it was over but I hurt. *I'm tired of hurting, God.*

A few weeks later I was sitting at a table with a friend at a dance club when Larry walked over and, without a word, bent down, and kissed my cheek. It took some time but I began to understand. He knew we wouldn't work because our cultures, our back stories, and our dreams for the future were too different. His kiss told me he loved me, anyway, so I began to accept that. But, it took a long time.

# 71: My Naked Realities

## After that I stood a little bit taller

By the time I get back to camp, Doug has recovered from over-heating, thank goodness. I have a late lunch, rest for a while, then take a drive to check out the area surrounding Spearfish.

"Cheyenne Crossing" is a general store sitting on the outskirts of the canyon. Its log cabin design fits perfectly with the surrounding thick forest. Inside is a large selection of packaged food, hiking needs, Indigenous crafts, and peculiar, cheap trinkets that don't belong here. I'm not big on shopping but it's fun to mill through the kitschy mercantile. It's been a while.

I notice a payphone on the wall near the door then search my backpack for my note with info about the powwow at Wounded Knee. I'd written it when I was in Scenic. I dial the numbers then a few rings later a young woman answers.

"Hello, my name's Regina. I'm calling to get more information about the powwow at Wounded Knee."

She sounds happy I called. "Yes, okay, well, I can help you. Also, there's going to be a buffalo killed here two days before that. You're welcome to come. There will be teachings from elders, traditional dancing, and a pipe ceremony."

"Oh, thanks for the invitation. I'm not sure I can make it but thanks." It all sounds great except the buffalo killing. It's not my cup of tea and, besides that, with Doug and all, it would be a nightmare.

She tells me the number to call if I change my mind and I write it down. "My name is Rochelle or Rocky. The 2nd Annual Healing of the Hoop is July 24-28 and that's when the powwow is happening. It's open to anyone. Even people from Europe attend and you can tent on the property. We're expecting a large crowd and there will be a lot going on." I ask where exactly it'll be held and she says, "It'll be located on my property which is one mile east of the Wounded Knee church. The property has two tepees in the yard." It's the house where I took shelter. *What are the chances?*

"Was it your house I visited during a storm a couple weeks ago?" She says she isn't sure. I guess if it was hers, I didn't leave as big an impression as I feared. She repeats that the main gathering will be on the 24th. "I'd like to attend but I'm not sure when I'll head back east. Again, thanks for the invitation." A big crowd of people and all that drumming and singing would probably push Doug over the edge. *What an opportunity though. Maybe another time.*

After I hang up, I get back in the car and sit for a few minutes wondering what to do next. Feeling frumpy and sweaty, I take out my map and decide to drive into the nearby town of Leads to look for a public showering facility and maybe even a car wash. We'll see what's available.

The brochure says Leads is an old mining town with a population of about 3,000. As I approach the town I'm surrounded by gloomy old mining gorges but the city center is quaint and attractive. *Sometimes you need to pass through the ugly to find the beauty.*

As I drive down the main street I keep my eyes peeled for a place to bathe. *I might be pushing my luck here.* I don't even know what a public bathhouse would look like or even if they exist anymore. But again, good fortune is with me and after making only one trip up the main drag, I see a YMCA sign. I park in a cool, shady spot then head into the building to ask about showers. *Voila.* Their women's locker room is open to the public. I head back to the car to get some clean clothes and bathing needs. I can't remember ever being this excited about showering.

After I undress in the locker room I give myself a once-over in the wide, full-length mirror. *Boy, I have quite the tan, that is, my legs, arms, and face do.* I like what I see though: a healthy and happy body.

My excitement fades a little when I walk into the shower room. It's just one large open space with eight shower heads circling the walls and aimed at a single central drain.

I'm happy to have the place to myself, and it looks and smells clean, not like at slimy Devil's

Tower. Stepping onto the damp, cool, cement floor makes me shiver a little. *Damn, I wish I had some flip-flops.* I turn the shower knob and the water begins to pound my tired body and, in no time it feels like jello. I imagine my muscles are getting the best revitalizing massage possible. After this morning's nerve-wracking hike over the rockslides, my body begins to relax.

A few minutes later, I have company. Two very overweight women in their 70s walk into the room, smile, say hi, and I smile back. At first I feel self-conscious, unaccustomed to being naked in public. *Maybe I'm not happy with my body after all?* I focus on the feeling of embarrassment then get bored with my shame and decide to let it go. I have that choice. I can choose how I feel. *Good to remember that.*

One afternoon, two days ago at the campground, I suddenly had to pee, badly. I knew I couldn't make it to the bathhouse so I scampered to the backside of my tent, pulled down my shorts, and assumed the familiar female pose. All was going as I'd hoped till I looked up and saw a pickup truck filled front and back with young guys. They were scouting the scenery as they cruised up the main road. To my horror, the scenery included me behind my tent, bent over with my butt sticking out, and mid-stream. I couldn't stop. I realized I had three choices: I could stand up, let pee run down my legs and make a run for the tent, I could stuff toilet paper into my underwear then limp to the other side of the tent and hide, or I could imagine I was in an alternate reality where there was no truck of onlookers and finish my business in peace. I chose the latter. I decided the truck was a figment of someone else's reality, not mine. It worked. I kept my head down as I heard the truck continue slowly down the road and I finished my business in peace. After that I walked back to the front side of my tent and stood a little bit taller in my dry underwear.

It's been a couple long days since I showered so I decide to enjoy, well, actually luxuriate in it, and savor every drop of pleasure. And it helps that the ladies don't know me and, after their polite hellos, they continue their giggling and we ignore each other.

When I walk out of the YMCA, I see I'm parked across the street from a car wash. Convenient. My Subaru gets a much-needed shower, too.

After the car wash I realize I'm starved. My starchy lightweight suppers are starting to get old so I treat myself to a burger at a take-out place. It's delicious but afterwards my stomach feels like I've consumed a boulder.

Back at camp I stretch out in my tent and think about my physical body. I whisper a thank you to it for getting me here and enabling me to have so many wonderful adventures. *Boy, being this clean makes me feel super young.*

It's probably going to be another cold night. I'll try leaving Doug in the car because I need to stretch out in the tent. Squeaky clean, alone, and unattached to anything or anyone right now is heaven

# 72: Swimming in Synchronicities

## It was time to think about what to do next

In the spring of '74 my girls, almost four, were thriving and happy and I was set to graduate. My mom sent me a lovely card and inside she wrote she was proud of me. It was the first time she ever acknowledged my academic achievements. More importantly, I was pretty proud of myself. I'd earned a BA in biology and I looked forward to relaxing for a few weeks.

One day when my twins were at daycare, I took a walk on campus to try and take it all in. There was nothing on my horizon, our horizon. I felt like a single woman but I wasn't, actually; I was a mom and it was time to think about what I'd do next. Should I find a job or stay in school and get another degree? Part of me felt like a naive twenty-five-year-old while a different part trusted there was yet another plan for me so I needed to get ready to roll into my next adventure. That is, once I decided what it would be.

Grad school had crossed my mind so after I'd finished my class exams, I took the four-hour Graduate Record Exam. Having taken so many natural science and chemistry classes, my score on the biology section was phenomenal but my verbal scores, as usual, were pathetic. I loved biochemistry so I considered getting a master's in that field but, when I talked to my advisor about it, he said I didn't stand a chance. He cited my low verbal test scores and said the biochem field was too competitive. I left his office, undeterred. I never did like the guy. Next stop was my favorite biochemistry professor, a kind man and a great teacher. After listening to me, he recommended I spend some time exploring the department. I was encouraged.

The biochem department was in the basement of the University's science complex. As I walked down the stairs and into the long main hallway, my steps kinda echoed on the hard tile floor. If air could be cranky then this air was. It seemed stiff and so dry it made me think about my next breath. Industrial wooden doors with small wired windows lined the corridor and the silence made the place feel hollow like living things didn't belong there.

I thought I might as well investigate the place so I picked a door, turned the thick, metal handle, and entered. The large room had no windows and was chock full of exotic glassware, stainless steel ventilation hoods, and lab machines set on black counters and tabletops. It was like I'd stepped onto the floor of a small industry.

I walked across the hall then into a computer room where a half dozen machines were consuming boxes of accordion-shaped paper and spitting out yards of data sheets on their other end. Data in, data out. I felt like I was inside a giant robot. In another room and half hidden inside cubicles, sat preoccupied people reading. A low, determined machine hum dominated the still air. Biochemistry: the study of the chemistry of living things. I wasn't sure whether to frown or chuckle. I couldn't wait to leave the half-dead department.

A single-story brick building sat near the edge of campus. It looked substantial but unappealing. It was the kind of building you might pass dozens of times but forget was there. I'd heard it was an insecticide research company.

My two entomology classes were pretty interesting, so when I learned the company had a job opening I made an appointment to visit. A worker greeted me at the door and took me on a tour, a very brief tour, then left me to roam alone. The building had an office and two rooms filled with dozens of big basins containing large grasshopper-type insects. There were thousands of them. Sacrifices for the good of humankind, the poor little imprisoned things would never get to live out their potential. It hit me how awful it would be to be caged and limited. For a brief minute, I felt like I was at a dead-end too, so I left the building and walked home.

Summer classes were imminent. I had my degree, had taken my GRE, but nothing called to me. I wasn't anxious, I was just wondering what was next. I remembered my father's grandmother telling me, *"You'll make a good teacher you know."* Along with that, she promised to leave me her fine leather briefcase when she died. I asked about it after she passed but the family knew nothing about it. Still, her words stayed with me.

After rejecting biochemistry and the bug-killing business, I spent some time wandering the historic campus enjoying its old ivy-covered brick buildings. Summer classes hadn't started so it was pretty deserted

267

and I liked that. It felt like I had it all to myself.

I loved being a student. I remembered my days dashing to classes, enjoying outings with my girls on the rambling commons, and sprawling under a stately maple or oak pretending to study while checking out the cute guys.

One day before summer classes started, I found myself outside the Education Department building. It was one of the original, three-story brick beauties the college was famous for. When I walked up the granite stairs to the entrance, something gently led me to the second floor. It was my first time inside.

At the top of the stairway, I stepped out onto the ancient wood floor and it gave way just a little. I looked to my right down the long hallway then swung to my left. At the end of the hall was a tall, red-haired man in a stylish suit. He recognized me first.

"Regina? Regina Boudreault? Is that you?"

Surprised, I replied, "Yes." We were the only ones there.

We walked towards each other and I realized the handsome thirty-something man was Charlie Ashley, from my hometown. He was a Dean in the Education Department and had a reputation for being authentic and kind.

He smiled as we shook hands then asked, "So what brings you here?"

"Well, I'm just wandering around campus. I've finished my undergraduate degree and I'm exploring what I might do next."

His face lit up and he asked, "So have you considered teaching?"

Sheepishly I replied, "I've thought about it a little."

It was like I'd stepped into a whirlwind. Right away he began talking about the exclusive new program in the Ed. Dept. called the "Masters in the Art of Teaching."

His eyes danced as he said, "It's a two-year master's program which includes course work, a summer program teaching high school students, a week of personal development camping in the White Mountains, then a year's internship teaching in a town in southern New Hampshire or Maine. He emphasized that only the "cream of the crop" were accepted into the program. I just stood there trying to digest his monologue.

When I heard, "cream of the crop," I listened politely with only mild interest thinking I most definitely was not in that category. Then he said, "What do you think? Shall we take a look at your records?"

I thought I might as well humor the guy so I said okay.

Charlie showed me into his huge, sunny office and I sat down in a chair opposite his ornate oak desk. He left the room to make some phone calls and locate my records.

A short time later he returned, sat down, then looked up from his folder of notes. "Mmmm, your GPA is good, not great but solid. You have an extensive science background and your GRE science scores are excellent but your verbal scores, well, not so hot."

I wanted to sink deeper into my chair. "Yes, I've never been good with standard achievement tests but I loved the science section. Even though it took four hours, it was a lot of fun."

Charlie smiled, and as I told him about my science classes, he sat more erect. He nodded and I sensed he noticed my enthusiasm.

Then he said, "Listen, I knew your dad and I know your family's work ethic. If you like, I can see if there's an opening in the MAT program. Maybe we can get you in."

In what felt like slow motion I nodded my head and said, "Oh, okay, great, thanks."

He excused himself, got up from his desk, and left the room. Bewildered, I sat there looking around his gorgeous, library-like office wondering what was happening.

After a few minutes Dr. Charlie returned. He walked to his side of the desk, tipped the papers he was holding towards me, then sat down in his chair. He looked up with a smile and said, "There was one spot left. You're in."

I felt a whoosh inside my chest. *What just happened?* I stared at him, "I'm in?"

"Yes. You're all set to go."

He handed me a folder with MAT program info, pointed out the names of the two professors in charge, and told me to connect with them as soon as possible because the summer program started in a week. *A week?*

If there is such a thing as emotional vertigo, I had it. A half hour earlier I'd been wandering aimlessly on campus, then I stumbled into this building and just happened to cross paths with Charlie. It was like a magic key had miraculously found my next lock and it opened, again. I was in. I was not sure what it entailed but it felt as if I had leaped into my next chapter. And this time the jump was effortless.

# 73: Take that Spiderwoman!

## I'd trained my shoulders to droop
## so I could conceal my strength

Halfway up the cliff, my foot found another fissure then my arm stretched to its limit and found my next best grip. Everything else disappeared: my harness, the rope to the person belaying on top, and the team of climbers cheering me on from below. My underside hugged the craggy hundred-foot granite wall and, even attached to the rope, I felt alone and exposed. I know now that trust was the issue, trusting in myself. It was another solo trek.

I'd arrived. It had taken some juggling but I'd made it. We were eighteen student teachers in the MAT summer program. For the next week we'd live together in a sparse Appalachian Mountain Trail hut in the White Mountains of NH. The week would consist of daily group-encounter circles, skits, hiking, rock-climbing, and sharing of our personal talents like song, dance, and massage. For some there would be skinny-dipping in cold mountain streams and joining our counselor as he got naked and led an avalanche of students streaking down a trail. It was the '70s and remnants of Woodstock lived on.

Early in that week we were bused to Cathedral Ledge for our day of rock-climbing. It was a perfect summer's day with a sapphire sky and giddy breezes that kept mosquitoes at bay. We lumbered in a line up the short trail to a small clearing at the foot of the ledge. Rascally red squirrels chided us intruders and chickadees, harbingers of joy, lightened the space and our challenge.

I panned the faces of my companions as the two climbing instructors dished out directions. I could feel it and see it in their childlike faces. The shared excitement and anticipation of the climb had already bonded us.

On the bus ride over I'd heard it was the first climb for most. Half of the group were women and I guessed we had varying degrees of athleticism. I wondered how the shorter, girly-girl women would do. I thought I was, by far, the most adept.

I also wondered who'd volunteer to go first. It was obvious to me: the wide-shouldered guy, the thin, wiry, runner fellow, and the compact jock girl. I guessed right. They scaled the wall easily and were met with hugs and little cheers from the few at the top. I joined the group at the bottom encouraging each new climber.

What followed was a mix of successes. One rugged, farmer-type guy, got red-faced as he squirmed and tugged at the rock edges trying to muscle his way up. Tears tumbled down the face of a spindly, young woman in short-shorts as she tried one, two, three, then four times to muster the courage to start her climb. She quit then promised us she'd try again later. I could feel the group's optimism for her. A young man with curly, ginger hair, wide calves, and broad shoulders got halfway up, lost his nerve, and stalled. He yelled to go down and the rope slowly slackened and lowered him to the base. On the ground he paused, acted oblivious to the group's supportive words, then started up again. He made a smooth and rapid climb to the top and was greeted with the loudest cheering yet. They certainly pulled for him.

The waiting line at the base dwindled until I suddenly realized I was up next. No longer just a cheerleader, it was my turn in the spotlight on the edge of the rock face.

I was tall and strong with excellent stamina. I was in good shape, I thought.

I tightened my helmet as the climbing instructor helped me with my harness, lacing his technical advice with kind words of encouragement. I walked to the base of the cliff and heard my small cheering section mumbling something that sounded like support but I was too nervous to process it. At the cliff, I reached up and found a crevice, and then with my other hand, I found another. I wedged my foot into a gap a few feet off the ground, pushed up, and found another for my other foot. I inched my way up and the harness rope in front inched along with me. It loosened then tightened thanks to the belayer on top.

That landscape of sharp-edged cracks and small, weathered protrusions was the terrain of my newest journey. I had no desire to look up or down. What commanded my attention was the glorious, languid pause after each advance. It was my progress, no matter how small, that fed me. My calculated stretch, the muscle flex of leg then arm, arm then leg, a spontaneous, original dance, repeated again and again. I wore a t-shirt, cotton shorts, and hiking sneakers but I felt naked. My body, flattened against its challenge, felt oblivious to my mind which was begging for any safe port. My only interest was the next foot crevice or finger hold. Life's journey.

Now on that spot on the cliff, opportunities to progress had vanished. I was secure and stable but the next foothold was too high and the handholds looked out of reach. My shoulders and my chest trembled with fatigue. I was stuck, alone, and scared.

Muffled voices trickled into my head. They were talking to me, telling me this and that but the sounds made no sense. Hanging on the side of that rock face, I knew I'd have to do it alone, something I understood. *What good were their words, anyway? I'm stranded. Words can't save me. Words don't have that kind of power.* I knew it was going to take something physical.

Something else hit me. I wasn't going to let anyone rescue me, and I knew I wasn't going to quit. I was not a quitter. I looked up to the closest handholds but they were way up past my reach. And again, more reality sank in. I shivered, feeling like "just a girl." But thank goodness the thought lasted only a second.

Then I began to sense a reserve in my body, especially in my muscles. A reserve I'd never acknowledged, had never dared to draw on before. "Too tall, too strong for a girl," was the message I'd heard when I was young. I'd trained my shoulders to droop so I could keep my secret, conceal my strength.

*Enough, this is foolish, I'm getting out of here.* And with that, I looked down and twisted each foot in its perch. They felt secure, I was stable. With both arms stretched up to those unreachable handholds, I called on all my arm and shoulder muscles to lengthen. I began to feel strong partners inside me come alive, areas I had ignored for years, maybe forever. I extended one hand then the other and grabbed hold of the shallow lip of a horizontal outcropping. Then I had second thoughts. Did I dare do this, show how strong I was?

*Going for it!* With both arms and hands engaged, like I was doing a chin-up, I pulled my body up beyond its impasse. I used my raw strength; I had to. After that, one foot then the other found a new perch. I not only advanced, I was advanced.

A self-imposed barrier, an internal limitation, was exposed then dissolved. Springs of energy bubbled up my spine and flowed through my chest. There became more of my body and me and it felt wonderful. From there, it was an easy climb to the top where hugs and tired grins greeted me.

That night, after supper at the mountain cabin, we broke out into small groups to share our experiences on the climb. Our group began and everyone listened with polite interest. Each account was followed with a question or two and encouraging words of support. Even though it sometimes sounded a bit too enthusiastic, I liked that the group of student teachers truly listened to each other.

I couldn't wait for my turn. I knew my experience was phenomenal so I waited to go last. And after hearing everyone else, I was sure mine would wow the group.

When I began, the group was as attentive as usual. They smiled and nodded in the right places. I said how at one point I was stopped, I couldn't advance, and had stayed stuck. I told how I was afraid to show my upper body and core strength.

"I was afraid of being too strong." Tears floated down my cheeks and I discharged a spontaneous little cough. At that moment I was alone in the room and my younger self was talking to me. I quickly composed myself and looked at the others. They just looked at me and said nothing. I waited what felt like a long minute, and still there were no comments just half-smiles and faces pointed in my direction. They might have been embarrassed with my honesty but I also wondered if they just didn't understand what a powerful experience it was.

It never crossed my mind that they said nothing because they thought I'd exaggerated. After all I'd experienced, I knew I processed experiences differently, maybe more deeply than most. And as usual, I wondered if it was me or if they were off the mark as they stood up and quietly funneled away from our circle and into the other rooms.

It was the cliff's flaws and its "unreachable" hand knobs that offered me a chance to commit to my progress and make it to the top. And like my sharing that night, it was another opportunity to grow.

I'd followed something. No, I got caught up in something, was seduced, then traveled with it. That thing and I made it to a new height. Then another challenge presented itself so I levered myself, stretched higher, sometimes laterally, but overall my trajectory was to the whispered goal I heard somewhere deep inside of me. That goal had yet to organize itself and find its way into my mind but I trusted the promise of success and so I climbed.

# 74: Big Boulders and Tiny Penises

## I liked these future educators who enjoyed being in nature

On day two of the MAT summer program, the whole group did a daylong hike. We took the strenuous nine-mile trail that connects the summits of Lafayette, Lincoln, and Little Haystack Mountains in the Presidential Range. The day was sunny and mild, a perfect day to hike.

At the top of Mount Lafayette, elevation 5,200 feet, I sat alone on a small boulder. It was good to rest and have some water after the tough climb. My body felt drained and I scolded myself for not bringing more snacks. Thanks to a cloudless sky the view was breathtaking. I'd read that on clear days it's sometimes possible to see the ocean over a hundred miles away. I believed it.

The rest of the gravel trail stretched out past me and onto the bare, bedrock tops of Lincoln and Little Haystack. It was something to see: a two-mile-long strip connecting three bare summits then disappearing over the side. I was in an alpine zone, where harsh, temperamental conditions made it a suitable home for mostly stubby bushes, lichen, and hardy rodents. And scavengers, there are always scavengers waiting for easy leftovers. As I rested I wondered what it cost the creatures who lived there. Their struggle to find food and shelter must be exhausting. I couldn't imagine calling that place home.

Perched so high above where I'd come from, I couldn't take it all in. Part of a group of like-minded people, I felt free. But I sat alone and studied the trail charging out in front of me and wondered if I could trust it, disappearing as it did over the side of that distant peak. Although the trip came together effortlessly, with friends caring for my girls and all, I still wondered what I had committed to.

After a short rest, I stood and began again. I followed the path to the next summit, then the next, and then trekked down the other side. The trail was inundated with exposed, giant, tree roots, up-thrusts of weather-beaten bedrock, and magnificent, moss-covered boulders. It was a typical White Mountain Forest track: slow, twisty, and steep. When someone up ahead yelled the base was close by, I could feel my body loosen with relief. I was proud of myself and maybe just a little cocky. I'd completed the rigorous hike unscathed,

Near the bottom, I stopped and turned to watch the last few in our group bounce down the trail amid yippees and laughter. The trail ahead faded away into a large spray of round boulders of every size and in the middle of it was a stream emptying into a voluptuous pool. I knew about mountain water like that, it was pure but frigid.

On the bus, before our hike, Sarah, James, and I had talked it up. They were laid-back students and easy to be with. We ended up hiking parts of the trail together then at the bottom the three of us walked towards everyone gathered near the pool. When we got close to the group, I froze. All fifteen of them were naked, skinny dipping in broad daylight.

I knew I couldn't just stand there staring, so I headed to the far side of the pool. And as I made my way, I looked straight ahead and hoped I didn't seem like a snob for not joining in. Then I saw Ed, another naked student, approaching me. Unfazed, he stepped up and greeted me as if he had pants on. Wide-eyed and embarrassed, I tried not to look, but I couldn't help notice his privates were in retreat mode, so to speak. I'd never seen a penis disappear like that. Friendly Ed was super chatty but I was a ball of nerves. He introduced himself then we talked about the beautiful day and the great hike. He said that descending the steep slopes bothered his knee a lot. I listened, empathized as best I could under the circumstances with most of my attention going into squelching my embarrassment and keeping my eyes at a polite angle. I wanted to look at his knee but I was afraid to go down there.

I caught sight of the now naked James and Sarah. They stepped into the pool like they were stepping into a bathtub. *Oh jeez, what do I do now? I so do not fit in here.* Luckily I spotted a large boulder at the far side of the pool so I began my escape. I climbed up on the rock, plunked myself down, then pretended to study the tree canopies, the beautiful stream, and the miniature plants covering the forest floor, in case anyone cared what I was doing. I wondered if Dr. Charlie had made a mistake because, at that moment, I felt like the odd-man-out.

At the cabin, later that night, and after another hardy dinner, everyone regrouped. As was routine, we sat at the long, pine-slab tables and shared our experiences from the day. It was fun to hear all the stories of challenge, camaraderie, and childish fun. I liked these future educators who appreciated being in nature and, from what I overheard, embraced frugal lifestyles. After that, we trickled off into groups of three or four to chat and relax. I followed Sarah and James as they climbed the rustic stairs into the spacious loft which loomed halfway over the large dining area.

I found a spot, rolled out my sleeping bag, and collapsed for a much-needed quiet evening. I think the faint scent of aged wood and the muted amber from antique kerosene lights on the tables below had a calming effect on everyone. The soft chatter sprinkled with giggles made me feel at peace.

Sarah was lying on a sleeping bag next to me and James was sitting bent over her head giving her a face massage. The day had been fun and invigorating but I was exhausted. After a short time I started to feel dizzy, then cold, and I began to tremble. I thought I might be dehydrated after the long hike. *So much for being in great shape.*

As I listened to my companions' whispered recounts of their day, I began to tremble even more. Then I got scared. From my physiology classes, I remembered that too much exercise can deplete your electrolytes enough to be serious. I popped up my head and told Sarah and James I felt sick. They gave me a nod but they didn't seem concerned. I wasn't sure they heard me right. Maybe I was just too ill to even ask for help in the right way.

James finished with Sarah and asked if I wanted a massage. Still stretched out on my back, I mumbled, "Yes." James sat crossed-legged at my head and began to massage my face. Slow, thoughtful fingers delicately kneaded my skin and asked it to relax. It felt wonderful. I told him again I felt sick. He told me to drink some water and offered me his canteen and I drank. His massage soothed and comforted me. At the end he bent down and lightly kissed my forehead. It felt a little weird but not invasive, maybe because I was so sick.

My trembling persisted, my heartbeat became erratic, and my breathing got shallow. The long hike had definitely depleted my reserves so I didn't have the strength or sense to make the others listen to me. It took me a long time to get to sleep and when I did, it was spotty. I ached all over and felt feverish and a bit delirious. It was like being in a bad dream.

When I woke in the morning, I could hardly move. My body felt as if it had been pummeled like a prize fighter's. After a short time I hobbled down the loft stairs to the breakfast table, relieved it wasn't my turn to cook. Soon James and Sarah joined me. They didn't even ask how I felt but I was just grateful to be upright and almost normal again.

As we talked over our breakfast of lumpy oatmeal, fried eggs, burnt toast, and coffee, I noticed freckle-faced, spunky Sarah seemed captivated with James. And from the confident way she carried herself, I surmised she was used to getting what she wanted. She could have him. James was kind, well-read, and intelligent but, with his scraggly hair, bushy beard, and pale skin, he wasn't my type. But, as he sat on the other side of the table, I sensed his interest in me and it made me uneasy. Besides not being my type, I was still getting over Larry.

Over the next two days and out of curiosity, I watched Sarah who watched James who I could feel watching me. Everyone liked James and maybe that was the problem; he was too nice, too predictable. Anyway, what I did enjoy was the fact that he favored me over a little, intellectual beauty. By supper time, on the second day, Sarah stopped seeking James's attention, her cutesy smile disappeared, and she was not happy. I hid my boastful grin. I hadn't tried to win but it felt good to be desired.

Our two professors asked us to decide what we wanted to do for the last two days of the program. We had the option of staying at the cabin and taking more day hikes or doing an overnight hike in the mountains. Once our professors finished talking, the room bubbled up with loud conversation as we sought out people to spend the remaining time with. James, another student named Karen, and naked guy, Ed, and I had hit it off, so we decided to do an overnight hike together.

We planned to do about twelve miles each day and tent one night. We'd take only a few provisions, fish the streams for trout, and pick berries and other edibles found along the trail. We were psyched.

# 75: Bumbling Beau

## I gave him a snarky smile

The Zealand Falls trail, all twenty-five miles of it, was the spectacular beauty I'd come to expect that week. With only moderate inclines, it was an easy trek alongside wide mountain streams and through shadowy tunnels of mature pine and oak. The vibrant forest was flush with razzing red squirrels, thin flocks of giddy birds, and a bashful breeze. The trickle of intermittent sunlight and the subtle, damp fragrance of life renewing itself, revived me. Being that deep in nature was part of my best dream.

That first day of our two-day hike unfolded exquisitely and I felt strong and excited to be hiking with three other nature lovers.

We had packed granola and tea for the morning and for dinner rice to go along with the trout we'd catch. In one of the large group session, we were told to write on a piece of paper something we had a passion for. I had written "fishing" on mine and, when James shared the same word, I decided to give the guy a chance, as just a friend. It did help that James brought his fishing rod along on our hike.

We each carried a backpack, a camp dish and cup, and a few personal items. In addition, James and Ed each lugged a tent. Before heading out, it was understood James and I would share one tent and Ed and Karen the other. We didn't discuss the possible ramifications and I wasn't excited about the prospect, but I was willing to go along with the group. For me it wasn't complicated, I liked these people and, after all I'd gone through over the last few years, it would be easier to just go with the flow. But, maybe I was still recovering from the other night's illness and from my breakup with Larry. I didn't know. How can a person know anything for sure? It just felt nice to be with some kind souls and that made it easy to comply.

Ed was married but not to Karen. Their sleeping together didn't seem scandalous but I was just a little bit uncomfortable, for them, that is. And, I gave little thought to what sleeping with James might involve. There we were, the four of us, unburdened by society's rules and bonded by our academic journey and presently, our hike. We were unconstrained and I was living in the moment.

We hiked about fifteen miles then stopped to set up camp near a wide, shallow river. I was tired but the background murmur of rushing water, the smell of tangy pine, and the cool shade revived me. Pine needle carpeting cushioned the ground near the river bank where we cleared away branches, rocks, and roots. After we pitched our tents a good ways from each other, we gathered a dozen or so grapefruit-sized stones from the river bank and stacked them in a circle for our fire. Stretched out on some blankets near the pit we settled into easy conversation. That dreamy part of our rich day was perfect.

After a time, the river called to me. *A river like that has to be fished.* I asked James if I could use his fishing rod then stood up and began my preparations. I scouted shady areas in the forest looking for bait in the cool, damp soil underneath crumbling logs. The worms were thin and undersized compared to what I would have liked, but a worm is a worm and I knew if trout were hungry they'd strike most anything that wiggled. I found a half dozen little guys, stuffed them in the pocket of my shorts, and, with the fly rod in hand, I set out to catch supper.

That stretch of the river reminded me of the Ammonoosuc River back home. Ammonoosuc is Abenaki for "small, narrow fishing place." It was in that river that I first learned to swim when my dad carefully dropped me into the water then stood guard till I bobbed to the surface and, eventually, figured out how to dog paddle. It was how we all learned. I knew the Ammonoosuc's origin was in these mountains and this river had the same crystal-clear water, bony banks, and bottom.

With judiciously placed steps and careful attention to my balance, I explored the shoreline. Sometimes I slid and other times I stepped over the rocks and boulders covering every inch of the wide banks. I kept an eye out for a good place to cast from, and on the other side, a fishing hole where dinner waited. My easygoing search reminded me of something. If I let my life unfold without urgency and little hesitation, I'll feel the guidance towards a good destination.

Soon, among the half-submerged mounds of pale, smooth rocks, I saw what looked like a good spot to stand. Near the opposite bank was a place that looked promising. It seemed deep enough because the river's

279

current slowed after water cascaded down into it. It was a perfect location for a trout to rest and wait for a meal to tumble in.

I stabilized my footing then reached into my pocket for a "volunteer" and skewered the poor thing onto my hook. I pulled out a few yards of line from my reel then flicked my rod's tip towards the trout's hideaway on the other side. I smiled as I watched the magic. My line flew through the pure mountain air then skipped across the water's surface and landed on my target. With its perfect weight, the hook and worm rested on the water's surface for a second then fell through. I imagined my worm doing a zig-zag drift to the bottom where the insistent current tumbled hook and bait over the gravelly bottom, escorting it slowly downstream.

Once the current tightened my line, I reeled it in to within a couple feet of the rod's tip. Then I pulled out enough line from the reel to hit my target, wagged my rod out from my side and behind, and sent the bait and line to the water once more. Again, and again it sailed and I watched and smiled, and was entranced. I breathed in all of those enchanting moments. Every single one of them.

While fingering the line, held tenderly between my thumb and index finger, I waited for it to signal an interest, a nose butt, or maybe a nibble. It was beautiful: the dance of the rod and the line; the gurgling water, tumbling over the rocks, being pulled and pushed forever and always racing downstream; the sun, beginning its slide to the forest's edge, sending winks of light to float on the water's surface.

I cast again and again into the mystery where my gift waited. I fingered the line, alert for any signal. Then, after a few casts, I felt it but it was barely discernible. I knew it was a nibble because I was part of the river and its rhythm.

The line quivered in my fingertips then something tugged hard. I gave the rod a sharp sideways snap. "Got one," I yelled to my friends and it felt like a good one.

Out of the corner of my eye, I saw James jump up and race towards me, slip-sliding and stumbling over the river rocks.

"Great job. Give him some line, no, not too much. Keep your line tense," James offered.

But, I was doing fine. I'd fished all my life. This was not a big deal. As he got closer with his unsolicited help, he slid on a wet rock, dove into my rod, and made it fly into the water.

"Lost him," I barked after being tipped sideways and almost tumbling into the water myself. Pissed, I regained my footing, waded into the water, and retrieved the rod.

James turned to look at me then broke into nervous laughter, "Oh, sorry 'bout that."

I couldn't help myself, I gave him a snarky smile, then tried my best to be civil. I thanked him for trying to help then gathered myself, reached into my pocket for a worm, and got back to work. It seemed James thought I needed to be rescued.

Thank goodness he returned to the campsite, leaving me alone in my piece of heaven. After a half hour or so, three, 8-10 inchers found their way to my hook. I headed back to camp relaxed and proud I'd done my part for the group. *We'll eat well tonight.*

Dinner was brown rice cooked to perfection in river water over an open fire. We roasted the trout on sticks and their pink meat was so tasty it reminded me of dinners with my childhood friends. For dessert we had raspberries and blackberries picked along the trail. The beautiful river, the fire, my new friends, and nature's simple sustenance made it one of the most memorable meals I'd ever eaten.

I hadn't thought much about sharing James's tent. I wasn't a prude but I wasn't attracted to him either. That evening he gave me another great massage but it didn't change the lukewarm feelings I had for him. After some awkward romance, and before falling asleep, I began thinking of fate. I sensed an invisible force, like the current moving a river to the sea, had brought me to the MAT program and the week in the mountains. Unbeknownst to me, at that time, doors were going to open to an even richer life.

# 76: Water, Water, Everywhere

## Turns out it wasn't about my destination

Temps in Spearfish Canyon last night were mild so I don't stir till 8 a.m. Even after yesterday's hike, when I crawl out of the tent my body feels damn good. I head over to Doug who's in the car. "Good morning, big boy. Are you ready for your walk?" He wags his whole body but, when we start out, he moves a little slower than normal. Residuals from getting dehydrated, I assume.

Back at our site, Doug gets his breakfast then I head to the stream behind my tent. Kneeling on the bank, I cup my hands together then scoop up some feisty, chilled water and splash my face awake. Hey. Where's my quart of yogurt? Last night I set it in the stream to cool then put some rocks on it and now it's gone. There are no signs of a struggle, no footprints, no apologetic note, nothing. Oh, well. This intruder is happy to make a contribution to wildlife and it could have been a lot worse. At one of the other campgrounds, there were some serious car troubles when porcupines chewed through brake lines leaving campers stranded.

Porcupine teaches us about innocence. It's a good reminder. Like all young children, I was myopic in my vision of the world. What interested me most was close-up and new. Maybe that's why having an intimate relationship with nature was easy. Back then I felt small but safe in creation and I wanted to know how life worked. I've learned we not only have to look at the big picture but we need to study small things and small spaces because that's where life lives.

I walk back to my tent and start thinking about my phone call to Kate yesterday. We're planning a woman's canoe trip and I wanted to know if it was still on. She'd said it was and sounded awfully excited to hear from me. After the call I'd gone to my tent to read and relax but I was restless. Hearing her voice left me antsy and even a little annoyed with myself because I'd interrupted my no-drama life out here. I realized I don't know what I want.

On this gorgeous morning, as I sit at my picnic table, wordless thoughts or maybe feelings-- sometimes it's hard to tell the difference-- float around inside me. But like a cryptic new melody haunting a musician or a phrase plaguing a poet, it begs expression. Get on with your journey.

Hunched over my coffee and oatmeal, I don't care if someone hears me, I need to hear me, so I say out loud. "I release all my inappropriate expectations of others. I release all beliefs that make me socially inept and frightened of intimacy." I choose the best words I can but, again, it's hard to name things I scarcely understand.

I open up my trail map and the words "Eagle Cliff Trail" jump out. I like the name. It's not far from here and is a moderate hike. At 10:30 we're in the car headed to the trailhead.

A few miles from the canyon I see a road sign for Rough Lock Waterfalls so I turn off to investigate. Only twenty yards from the road, the secluded spot is deserted and tidy. Lovely cottonwood and a few pine trees line the riverbanks. When I step out of the car, I immediately feel it. The air is effervescent. It's like I've stepped into a natural spritzer. Near the small waterfalls, my skin's prickly and I feel a little dreamy watching the water race by then tumble over half-submerged boulders. The water slams into rocks then into more water and ions, charged particles, are released into the air. My body's jazzed making me even more excited about my hike.

I arrive at the pull-off leading to the Eagle Cliff Trail at eleven. It's at least 85 degrees and the hottest part of the day is still a couple hours away. I know hiking at this hour is a little risky but I'm eager to trek again and maybe learn more about myself. I remember porcupine's teaching says to be innocent. I wonder if that includes being less critical of myself.

I've brought along my medicine bundle and some turkey feathers from Maine. They replaced my rosary beads and Catholic missal years ago. Inside the bundle are a rose quartz crystal and two tiny felt bags: one with tobacco and one with cornmeal. Everything is wrapped together in red flannel, considered a respectful way to carry prayer objects. Rose quartz is believed to resonate with our hearts and over the years I've carried it in my pocket to remind me to be at peace. The tobacco and cornmeal are gratitude offerings to give Earth. The turkey feathers represent the "give-away" in some spiritual traditions. Turkey teaches us to give away with an open heart knowing that we will always have what we most need. I wonder if turkey's "give away" involves unwanted personality traits which I have my share of. I remind myself that, even though the gifts in my medicine bundle may seem trivial to others, every gift is significant. I think the act of giving is the real gift.

At the car I load my backpack with a plastic gallon of water and my medicine bundle, leash Doug, and head towards the main trail. It might be the heat, I don't know, but I walk back to the car, dig around in my clothes satchel, then put on my red bandana. Maybe Leo's zeal at Bear Butte has rubbed off on me? Nope, it's just a hiker's headband. And this feels right. It's just me being me.

A short distance in I notice lots of cow patties. It's not a good sign, especially with Doug along, so we go back to the car and I drive a mile further up the road to another trailhead leading to Eagle Cliff. This place seems even more deserted with no signs of humans or cattle. These locations are not the usual recreation parks, they're more like pasturelands. I have my backpack with the precious water and this time I carry my medicine bundle in one hand. I'm curious as to why it's the first time I've taken it out. It must want to come.

As I poke along, the sun seems hell-bent on baking me. It's got to be over ninety degrees and rising. There's no breeze so I stop often to drink and rest under the few pines near the trail. The terrain is totally different from yesterday's forests at Crow Peak. This trail flows down the center of a dry, grassy valley then meanders up a slight slope, and continues three miles in-country. This pastureland is owned by the federal government, leased to ranchers, and open to the public for recreational use.

Tall pines dot the first mile of the trail, and further up the valley, there are small, dense stands of impressive spruce. I stop to enjoy their rugged beauty and an extra tall spruce with a disfigured top grabs my attention. It's a little spooky because it looks just like the one in a dream I had seven years ago. It was when I was studying various forms of spirituality. I'd read that dreaming of a disfigured evergreen was a sign the person was finishing an important phase in their emotional development. Huh. I wonder what's getting completed.

A few water holes, muddied by dirt, hoof prints, probably cow manure, pepper the easygoing trail. Doug is staying cool as he gets to drink and swim all he wants. It's fun to watch him galloping like a mustang and I'm happy I don't need to share my water.

I hike four connecting trails before coming to the Eagle Cliff Trail. With the sun's intensity and the high temps, I guzzle mega amounts of water. Doug is panting but not like yesterday, thank goodness.

After two more miles on the main trail, I come to another broad U-shaped valley lined with even taller spruce trees. I continue halfway to the end then stop. I still feel the gentle buzz from the river and now sense there's no need to go further. Ahead on my left a small cliff juts out. It's about forty feet high and, like a compelling piece of artwork, it calls to me. It's on the southwest side of the trail and projects northeast. Again, I'm puzzled because I'm aware of compass directions. Also, for some reason, I know it's time for me to stop.

Doug reads my mind and leads the way as we exit the trail and bushwhack our way up to the backside of the cliff to the top. When he gallops to the very edge of the outcropping, I almost have a heart attack. But, he stops just in time. I don't want him to misstep so I tiptoe to the edge and snap on his leash. I tie him to a nearby little tree and he lies down in its shade.

It might be the heat but perched on this little precipice I still feel the waterfall's energy. It feels like I'm retracing steps in a dream.

Then without thinking, it feels like my body has something to say. I step closer to the edge, stretch out my arms, and let the words form. I'm facing home. I'm relieved to be alone because I have no idea what I am doing but when I hear the words I say, they feel like good ones, peaceful ones.

I'm still listening to my body when I pour some water into my hands then move them like in a slow waltz. I lift them up to the heavens and say, "Thank you for bringing me here." Then, with a deep sense of gratitude, I let the water drizzle back to the ground. My body feels lighter and lighter and it feels like it might dissolve into a faint mist. My knees start to buckle and I begin to teeter. I'm scared of falling off the cliff but I manage to right myself.

I flashback to when I was a kid. At mass I wanted to know what secret things the priest, with his back to us, was doing at the altar. I loved the ceremony but felt excluded from the ritual's blessings and mysteries. With my impromptu little cliff ceremony, I get to create my own and it feels powerful.

This is all spontaneous, but I know it's part of a plan or maybe an opportunity. And most importantly, I know I'm right where I ought to be and that feels wonderful.

I open the two small bags in my medicine bundle then drop pinches of tobacco and cornmeal on the ground. I ask that humans be connected again to the good spirits of this land. Caught off guard by the deep sadness in my gut, I start to cry. I know the source is the heartaches experienced by the first people and this land holds that sorrow.

Intense grief rushes up through me and my breathing gets ragged. Now I feel powerless. It reminds me of when I gave birth to my son. It was natural and fast and near the end, all I could do was breathe along with the contractions. When you're in labor, for a time you go out of your mind. Right now, I'm probably not in my right mind and maybe in a small way I am giving birth to something new in me.

Even though I feel much too insignificant to be saying and doing all this, I know there's still more to say. "Thank you, hawk, and all the animal spirits who have traveled with me. Please help me to release into the sun, all my negative emotions, especially related to family and friends. Thank you, Creator, for this journey and please help me in my small efforts to heal our globe's human web. Please help me to love myself."

At the very edge of the cliff I start to teeter again and feel so light that I fear falling. I remind myself to concentrate on staying put.

I finish my prayers then prop up my medicine bundle and feathers in a small pile of rocks near the cliff's edge. I face them northeast and say goodbye to them. Maybe it's because my words and gestures seem so trivial, even silly, but right now I'm just not sure of anything. All I know is our planet is hurting and it needs our prayers. Maybe we can begin the healing by honoring the good inside ourselves and others and by taking bold steps to help all communities.

It feels done now so, in slow motion, I unhitch Doug and we head down the backside of the cliff then onto the main trail. And even with the heat and my tears, my pace is good. About halfway back to the car, a Wildlife Ranger drives up beside me in his pickup truck. He gives me a friendly hello then asks about my hike, where I'm heading, and if I have enough water. I fill him in, tell him I'm all set and am heading back to my car. When I tell him where I'm from, he goes on and on telling me how much he loves Maine. He says there is a shorter trail back to the trailhead so I thank him and take it. I find out later that he may have saved me from significant danger.

As I continue, I talk out loud naming old disappointments and hurts inside me, the ones making me judgmental and quick to anger. But the sad feelings just keep bubbling up and out which catches me by surprise. I'm happy to let them go but I didn't realize there were so many. After a mile or so, I settle back down into my new lighter, more peaceful self. Even my stride is different, a little crisper, and happier. I know there's more in me to discover and heal. Christ, there's always more. But I feel like a brand new chapter may have begun.

Back at the car I check my map. The little cliff I was on was not Eagle Cliff. Turns out it probably wasn't about the destination, it was about my journey.

# 77: Purging the Nasties

## I'm feeling pretty goofy

Doug and I make it back to the car, hot and wasted after our Eagle Cliff hike. My car reeks of cow poop and one dirty, sweat-covered hiker.

I start the car and head back onto Rt. 85 then the campground. A few miles out, I spot a hurried, little river running alongside the road. Its pull-off area is empty so I drive in and park. I put Doug on his leash, grab his water bowl, and inch my way down the steep slide of bedrock that ends at the water. With one hand holding the leash and the other out straight to balance, I step, slip, step, and slip some more on the smooth, wet granite. I have to do this because Doug and I need more than just a ritualistic wash.

What I see ahead of me is intriguing. Mini whitecaps are everywhere and the sunlight reflecting off their crests makes the spray sparkle. Tiny waves roll up in unbridled exuberance, pause, then fall back in to rise again. It makes me think about the momentum in our lives. Maybe it's the interruptions that form its magic and beauty. Blessed are our disruptions. Simple... Not simple.

I know I've been given gifts of water today: my morning visit at the brook, the effervescent river before my hike, the water saving Doug and me from blistering heat, and the water at my cliff ceremony. And now the chaotic commotion ahead that's challenging me to give it a go and jump into the turmoil.

From where I stand, the crystal-clear water looks about waist deep. I step in and shiver from its cold. Doug hesitates to go in but, with a little persuasion, he drops his head, tucks his tail, and relents. I scoop up copious amounts of water with his dish and pour it over his nasty-smelling body. As I rinse off the mud etc., I watch it drift away and the biologist in me wonders where it'll end up. In my attempt to honor the ecosystem, after the fact, I imagine the muck is feeding little organisms downstream.

When we're done and back near the car, Doug gives a few massive shakes, hops back into the car and curls up for his much-needed nap. My boy covered a lot of ground today.

It's my turn now so I scan the area. There's only me and, so far, there's no pickup truck full of peeping toms. I grab some clean shorts and a t-shirt from the car then climb back onto the slippery bedrock and creep down to the water. Just in case I have visitors, I plan to disrobe underwater. With one hand clutching clean clothes stretched high over my head, I wade in. Navigating the bony riverbed is tricky but it feels like the rivers back home. You have to love muscle memory.

The coldest water I've ever waded in rises up to my hips. I've gotta make it quick so I submerge my torso then my head. "Yow." After one more check for visitors, I pull off my t-shirt then submerge again, bra and all. When I surface, I pull on my clean t-shirt then peel off my wet shorts and underwear. I stumble, and nearly fall headfirst into the river. Naked from the waist down, I hurry as best I can back to the car, then wiggle my wet body into dry shorts. *I'm feeling pretty goofy right now.*

Cold but revived, it feels like more than dirt and sweat got washed away. On my hike I'd asked that hurtful memories and belief systems be released. I wonder if this might be a baptism or absolution of sorts. I don't think I need to name what I feel so I whisper, "Thank you, water, for your blessings today."

I feel like a new woman when I climb back into the car. And, surprise, surprise, the car smells a whole lot better. I drive out of the pull-off and notice a sign I'd missed before. It says: "No swimming or bathing. This river is a source of municipal drinking water." Oops. It's a good reminder to be observant and also mindful of where we discard our crap, physical and emotional.

I backtrack down route 85 to the Cheyenne Crossing store, the one I stopped at yesterday. It's a perfect time for a much-needed snack and after the hike I definitely need more grounding. The store is tucked in a dense pine forest and has lots of shady places to park. I check on Doug who's curled up and sound asleep. Relaxed, finally, I head to the store.

The contemporary exterior is weathered wood and the long porch in front has well-worn steps leading to the front door. The lighting inside is a little dingy and the rough-cut boards on the walls are dark and dusty. Hanging from the ultra-high ceiling is a haphazard weave of giant, ancient cobwebs. *I wonder what memories they hold?* Even so, for some reason it feels welcoming. Maybe it's just the newly refreshed me.

The man behind the counter gives me a nod and a cordial hello. After I check out the chips and soda selection, I head to the counter to pay up and maybe get a visit.

He's handsome, maybe in his forties. A red bandana, like mine, holds back his long hair and bristly whiskers cover his chops. He starts first, asks about my camping and the places I've visited. I give him a short overview of my last two weeks and he listens intently. I like how our chat is going. "I just finished a nice hike on the Eagle Cliff trail."

He makes change for my purchase then looks up and with an impish smile asks, "Did you see the big Brahma bull up there? Yesterday, he treed two hikers!"

My chest tightens, my pulse gallops, and all I can get out is, "Nope, didn't see him."

I thank him for the chat then like a robot with my gaze fixed on nothing in particular, I walk to my car, slide into my seat, and close the door. His words conjure up terrifying images of Doug trying to ward-off the bull while protecting me and getting pulverized in the fracas. I imagine myself, beyond scared, running to find a tree to hide behind. It's a terrifying scenario.

Minutes later my breathing ekes back to normal but my skin's clammy, as if I'd had a hot flash. Closed off inside the protective bubble of my car, once again, I'm safe from the unpredictable world. *Shit. What the hell am I doing out here?*

# 78: A Date with Nightcrawlers

## It was like a spooky fairy tale

When my week in the White Mountains was over, I picked up my girls from a friend's house and we headed home to Forest Park. With most of the summer ahead of us, I looked forward to outings with my DWHE friends and our kids. Even with that, I was a little on edge. I wondered about my new classes and how I'd juggle getting decent grades with being a good mom.

It was fun and effortless for James and me to remain friends. Often when our classes and teaching responsibilities were done for the day, we went fishing. He taught me how to tie flies, cast for striped bass at the seashore, and hunt for forgotten freshwater ponds. I wasn't looking for a boyfriend but what I got was a generous and dependable friend who shared my love of education and the outdoors. Also, at that point in my life, I was emotionally tired so I welcomed the intimacy and his devotion to me.

One afternoon while we were leaving the Ed building, James looked down at the lawn and said, "Look at all those worm castings!" There were dozens and dozens of tiny dirt piles, residuals of worm digestion. "This place is loaded with nightcrawlers." He was giddy, like a kid who'd found a treasure. He suggested we come back at night to harvest some fishing bait. It wasn't a promise of Bingo at the base or a ride in a sexy car but it was something so I agreed.

The following evening was a perfect time for our mission. I sat my daughters down in our apartment and explained we were going on an adventure, a hunt outside in the dark. My wide-eyed, rambunctious four-year-olds were excited and peppered me with a stream of questions. I wanted them to be surprised so I just said we were going for a walk to find some worms. James busied himself locating flashlights buried somewhere inside our not-so-tidy cars. When he hurried back into the apartment, he looked like a big, disheveled kid, and as amped as my girls.

The four of us left the apartment and walked towards campus only a few minutes away. We each had a flashlight and an old tin can. It was nine o'clock and late for my kids. Summer's humid air had cooled so condensation coated everything, perfect conditions for the hunt. I smelled hints of damp soil and scant traces of musty other things, untraceable, impermanent things. It was like walking into a children's spooky fairy tale.

As we made our way to campus, Jess and Jen bounced along oblivious to what I noticed. Huge, looming trees cast creepy shadows across dimly lit walkways and onto old brick buildings and, like a mother bear, I kept a close watch over my little ones. Waving their flashlight streams my two were thrilled at their ability to command the dark. *My brave little adventurers.*

The evening was perfect for worm romance. I remembered when my young siblings and I, flashlights in hand, would scavenge lawns and cow pastures hunting for nightcrawlers. I fantasized, now, about being a four-year-old, up way past my bedtime on an adventure, exploring like this in the dark with my mother. I wished my mom had joined us kids but I know it wasn't her thing to get down in the dirt with us.

We trooped down the campus sidewalks then on to the lawns near the Ed building. With the place all to ourselves, we tucked our cans in our pockets or, in the girl's case, set them on the ground, and we began.

Stooped over, I illuminated the grass looking for signs of any auburn, tube-like irregularity. The best technique for success was to bend close to the target then slowly sneak up on our blind, love-sick prey when they emerged from their holes to mate. Some of them zipped back inside even before we could make a stab at them. I wasn't sure if they sensed the light or our movement but, with slow-motion advances then a quick snatch, I remembered how to grab hold of one, sometimes two intertwined. If locked in mating, they were thick with worm slime and hardly reacted to their capture. But the single ones were fast and felt like thin tubes of thick muscle in my hand; it made me squirm. I pretended it was just a rubber worm, shoved it into the can, and continued my hunt.

With flashlights in hand, Jessie and Jenny were having a ball scooting on their knees. The dark, slimy business didn't faze them a bit and it tickled me hearing their squeals and shouts of triumph.

"Mom, look, I got one!"

"Mom, look they're hugging each other. I got two at once!"

My siblings would have been as proud of them as I was.

James was laid back but helpful. He showed the girls how to spot a worm and grab it, then he complimented them on a catch. James scored big points with their mother that night.

We were surrounded by what seemed like hundreds of worms so after just twenty minutes or so our cans were filled enough and the novelty had worn off. Our hands were covered with mud and goop, so I showed my girls how to wipe their hands back and forth on the grass, like painting with a brush. It was only minimally effective so with filthy hands, fingernails caked with dirt, and two sets of little muddied knees we headed back to the apartment for baths and showers. For a time it felt like we were a real family.

One sunny day after our classes were done, James and I set out to fish for bass in a most unlikely place. It was a small, shaded pond on the edge of campus near the center of town. A serene beauty of a spot, it was surrounded by a thick, conifer forest so was easily overlooked. We'd found a jewel hidden right under the nose of the University. It was also home to a pair of mated swans.

We cast our lines onto the pond's glassy surface and, as our bait sank, we both got hits. In unison we reeled in good-sized largemouth bass. The spot was idyllic and, to top it off, I got to share it with someone as enthusiastic about fishing as I was. *In some cultures, swan can signal that the one you're with is a soulmate. Some soulmates are lovers for life, some shake us up so we can release Karma.* Was James my soulmate?

Our peace was short lived. The two swans, creating barely a wake, glided towards us like a pair of white, stealth destroyers. Charmed by their beauty and tameness, I commented to James, "This place is amazing!" I barely got the words out when, with 6-foot wingspans, they half flew, half ran on the water and attacked. They sounded like ungodly shrieking horns. *Swan also warns us that things might not be what they appear.*

Terrified, I scooped up my rod and tackle box as did James. Side by side, like a sorry-ass mated pair, we bolted down the road and away from the pond. The screeching swans with their long, stretched-out necks and flapping wings were close behind. I had no idea I could run that fast. It seemed like we ran a mile with our assailants in hot pursuit. Good God, I was frightened.

Finally, after a hundred yards or so they gave up and we stopped, bent over our knees, and tried to catch our breath. We were so shocked and embarrassed at being naive that we looked at each other and started laughing. As we checked our gear, I kept giggling, pretending to recover from my trauma but it actually took days. We never fished that spot again.

# 79: Our Family of Four

## The ugly duckling deserves to be loved

On many nights after a day at the beach or fishing, James stayed for dinner with us. That was how our dating began and it was fun, like having a best friend who was also my boyfriend. He'd graduated from a prestigious Ivy League school and was a student of Eastern healing arts. His credentials intrigued and impressed me.

We'd had some romance in the mountains and I didn't see it going any further, but James did though. Back on campus he wined and dined me, well more like, he wooed me with fishing trips, great massages, and spicy Asian dishes. I found our heady conversations about Eastern spirituality and assorted philosophies both outlandish and interesting. He did most of the talking.

One afternoon, after a few weeks of dating, James showed up unexpectedly at my apartment. I heard his knock and when I opened the door, he stood there with a somber face. He pivoted so I could see the curb where his muddy sedan was parked. The front and back seats were filled with boxes. I looked at the car then at James, wondering what was going on. He said, "All of my worldly possessions are in my car." He looked lost and I could feel the dead-air space between us but I didn't know what to say. I knew he'd been living with a friend in southern NH but I had no clue what had happened. He told me later that he and his friend had had a falling-out so he'd packed up and left.

He didn't move or speak, just stood there looking at me and I felt pressured. "You can stay with us if you want."

He smiled, hugged me, and moved in. That is, he and his over-sized English spaniel, Aslan, moved in. Jenny and Jessie were delighted to have a dog in the house and the dog tolerated them to a point but he never warmed up to me. When James and I were in bed, the dog kept jumping in between us. He was ill mannered and headstrong and, being a purebred, I think he'd had a lot of common sense bred out of him. But the dog and I had something in common: our dislike for each other.

Most everything in our lives was falling into an easy-going routine that included some intermittent adventures. With his laid-back personality, my girls and James hit it off so it was easy for me to welcome him into our lives. James was so compromising there was no drama, *ever*, in our relationship.

A month or so after he moved in, I took James home to meet my family. My mother gave him her ultimate stamp of approval. As we were saying our good-byes and heading out the door she planted a quick kiss on his cheek. It was weird and the disturbing image has stayed with me to this day. I think my mom liked that James came from a wealthy family but more importantly, she was relieved he was white.

Two years later, in 1976, James and I married and a couple years after that our son, Jake, was born. By 1981 we both had teaching jobs and, along with some financial gifts from his grandmother, we bought 51 acres of remote land in southern Maine and began building our earth-bermed home. With help from only a couple others, we built most of it ourselves. It was demanding work, especially with three kids, but we camped out at the site for the whole summer and made our dream come true.

Two years later we were living in a house that still had some dirt floors and unfinished interior and exterior sections. Jessie and Jenny were entering the brutal teenage years and I was teaching full time. Jake had been hospitalized thirteen times with severe croup and I was in a constant state of anxiety fearing for our son's life. After Jake had to be intubated and spent a week in Boston in the ICU, I grew more and more emotionally distant. James fell from the roof and sustained a terrible leg fracture and spent a month in the hospital. Every day after work I visited him while the kids waited in the car. After six months at home James was fully recovered but he told me he didn't want to finish the house. It felt like a gut punch.

I was pissed at James and embarrassed because I had believed in his dedication to our project and our family. His refusal to finish the house was probably the beginning of our end. Dinner time at the house had become a sad scene. He'd sit alone, usually reading, at the end of my family's long dining room table while the kids and I sat at the other end. Unfortunately, even though he was devoted to our son, that scenario played out every night. The children chose to sit with me. The memory still breaks my heart. I wondered where all the fun and spontaneity had gone. What happened to those two people running from the swans with fishing poles in their hands? Swan teaches us to look within ourselves and, after a time, I would begin to forgive myself for my flaws. The ugly duckling inside me deserved to be acknowledged and loved and ultimately set free.

For three long years, though, we went to marriage counseling. Mickie was a fresh-out-of-college young counselor who loved her job. She helped us delve into our messed up histories but, boy, did we give her three years of craziness.

Determined to try and save our marriage, James and I were unwavering, attending our grueling sessions, sometimes twice a week. When we got on a roll, we'd ramble on, voicing childhood stories and current gripes oftentimes forgetting Mickie was in the room. Sometimes we'd carry on for two or three hours. She helped us a lot but she was single, had no children, and grew up in NYC. We were in our late thirties, had been together for ten years, had three children, and were homesteaders. We made an interesting trio.

One day, after attending a family wedding, I finally accepted that our marriage was over. James had driven to the wedding alone while the kids rode with me. At the reception, the kids sat with me and James sat at a different table. When we got home, I looked at him and said, "We're done, aren't we." He agreed. It ended as it had begun, with very little fanfare. James packed up his personal things and left with his dog.

At times the divorce proceedings were emotionally charged and difficult, which is normal, but we got through them and I know it helped us both. In the divorce agreement, I got the house and land and became the sole support of our son and my daughters. James would help with our son's medical bills and Jake would spend every other weekend and most of the summer with him. In the beginning James's relationship with my girls had been a close one but by the time they were teens their relationship had disintegrated.

Our family story continued; Jenny and Jessie had been abandoned by their birth father and now their stepfather. And, another important relationship in my life came to an end.

# 80: Tickleneck Thunder

## Like a spring being tightened over time, it will eventually break

In 1988 my ten-year-old son, Jake, and I drove to Tickleneck Pond in Vermont for a family reunion. Most of my immediate family, my three sisters, my brother, Pat, Gram, and a dozen or so nieces, nephews, and some aunts attended.

It was a beautiful, warm summer's day and everybody was having a great time swimming and boating. Happy chitchat and the usual joking ensued while some of us picnicked under the huge tent the family had rented. It was great to see so many had shown up.

Later that afternoon, I sat under the tent visiting with my sisters, Lorraine and Linda. As usual, we began talking about our mother who had died ten years earlier. And as was typical, my sisters carried most of the conversation because I usually blended into the background during family discussions since my memories of our mother differed from theirs. They began to expound on my mom's difficult childhood, how being raised by her mean mother had shaped her. I started to get frustrated because they'd left out the most critical parts: on many occasions, our mom was irrational and abusive to us. My sisters' words seemed insufficient but it could have been their attempt at explaining away their own hurt. At the very least, their words were ambiguous.

On that day, under the tent, it seemed like my sisters were excusing the mistreatment and dismissing the pain she'd inflicted on us and especially on me. Being discounted, again, hurt big time.

On the surface, with a beautiful house, lots of pets, and any material thing we wanted, life looked damn good to the outsider, and in some ways it was. But missing was tenderness and unequivocal love from our mother. How could they forget all the times she chased us through the house with a fly swatter or lashed out at us with a slap? She had a sadistic side too. Did they forget how she'd smile and ask, "Is that hot?' after taking a hot spoon from her teacup and putting it on our hand? I wondered if they could remember a single "I love you," or hug, or pat on the back from her. To say nothing about what she made them endure because they wet the bed.

The harmful effects of chronic emotional neglect and trauma are cumulative. Like a spring being tightened more and more, over time it will eventually break.

—⁂—

In 1979 my mom was critically ill. She'd often said that her biggest fear was she would go in for surgery and they would open her up and find her full of cancer. That's exactly what happened.

She had a couple surgeries and a series of chemotherapy treatments but it was a losing battle; it was terminal. My sister, Lorraine, a nurse, helped to guide her treatments and hospitalizations. Near the end, I didn't want to visit her because Lorraine had told me she was almost unrecognizable and incoherent from the medication. I was petrified of seeing her like that. Also, to be honest, I didn't know what I'd say to her. She was my mom and I loved her but, after all the hurtful ways she had treated us, I was afraid of her too. I did go to the hospital, but only once, and, on the drive, memories surfaced of our relationship. I remembered how after I graduated from college, for some inexplicable reasons, my relationship with my mother became stranger. It seems she had issues that she projected onto me and it didn't help that I had no allies within the family.

On the morning of my marriage to James, I got ready in my old bedroom at my mom's house. As I was stepping into my pale pink wedding dress, I was surprised to see my mom come into my room. I warmed at the thought we'd have one of those mother-daughter keepsake moments. As we embraced, she began to weep so I rested my chin on her shoulder and patted her back while she cried. I thought she was happy for me.

But then she whimpered, "I wish your father was here. I miss him so much." So that was it. She was crying for herself and they weren't happy tears for me. It hit me hard. I pulled away and said, "I miss him too, Mom." I realized I couldn't expect anything more from her.

We finished dressing for my wedding, went downstairs, gathered our things, and headed to church. There was no "I'm so happy for you, Regina," no "I love you." She never did congratulate me; there was nothing.

My whole family, especially my mom, liked James a lot. But my mother's strange behavior towards me was becoming more and more noticeable and hurtful.

It was insidious how she singled me out then tried making me feel responsible for the actions of others. One year James and I hosted a huge family Thanksgiving at our house in southern NH. Some of my siblings, their kids, and their partners planned to spend the night. The afternoon before the big day some of the guys smoked pot in our living room. I was in the kitchen with my mom and sisters when she said, "I can't believe you're allowing pot in your house." I was unaware they were smoking and her attack hurt and also bewildered me especially since she never confronted them.

My sister Linda and her boyfriend, Andy, had been living together for years. Thanksgiving morning my mom said, "I can't believe you allowed Linda and Andy to sleep together with your little sister, Beth, in the next room." She never chastised Linda; it was me. I was again caught off guard and shocked. I felt numb. And even though some family heard her vilifying me, no one talked about it, let alone defended me. Maybe that was when I became the family scapegoat. To say the least, I began feeling disoriented within the family ranks.

The last time I talked to my mother was when Jake was four months old and we all stayed over at her house. I was exhausted from what seemed like around-the-clock nursing and worries about Jake who had already had a bout of croup even at that young age. My mom heard James and me talking about our romantic life. He wanted more intimacy and I told him I was just too tired. My mother appeared at the corner of the room and yelled at me. "I'd like to slap you across the face." Stunned, I couldn't believe she'd said that. My response to James must have hit a nerve, a raw one that reminded her of the times she refused to go to bed with my dad.

It had become the norm: my mother would blurt out a putdown, I'd be shocked but take it in, and no one, not even my husband, who'd heard it, said anything.

As I approached my mom's hospital room when she was dying, I peeked in and got a glimpse of an emaciated body sitting up in bed. Her eyes were closed, her wig was misplaced on her bald head, and there were tons of tubes sticking out of her. It was a scene from a terrible nightmare. I backed away then skulked down the hallway and left not having the guts to say goodbye. My disturbed mother died alone two nights later.

At her funeral I was dry-eyed till I saw one of my mom's friends crying. That's when I cried, a little, and not for my mother but for her friend's pain. I was numb and, honestly, almost relieved to think my confusing nightmare was over.

A couple weeks later, while riding in the car with my sister, Linda, I began talking about my mom's furniture, some of our family treasures, and how I envisioned which siblings would enjoy getting certain pieces. Sheepishly, my sister looked over at me and said, "No one told you?"

"Told me what?"

"You're not getting any of Mom's things."

I turn and stared at her. She looked straight ahead but I saw tears in the corner of her eye.

Linda told me my mother had changed her will when she was in the hospital. My brother, John, had tried to talk her out of it but she insisted. My mom had singled me out, stating that I was not to get any of her possessions. I would only get a relatively small financial sum. I stopped feeling anything.

My mother had remarried after my dad died but divorced a year later. Mom had also named her ex-husband, a very decent man, in the will. She left him one dollar. To this day none of my siblings has ever mentioned the will; at least it has never been brought up around me. I began to feel more and more separated from them.

For years I had pushed hurtful incidents involving my mom deep inside but this was the biggest one. It's ironic because family is so very important to me. I sometimes wonder what my siblings think about what she did to me and her ex but I'm not stupid enough to bring it up.

Until that day at Tickleneck, ten years after her death, the will was never mentioned. If the roles had been reversed, I would have talked to them, showed my support, and discussed the will. And it wasn't about not getting the family items or a bigger piece of the inheritance. It was being excluded and never, except for Linda's announcement in the car, talking to me about it. But, thankfully I got my chance at the reunion.

Sitting under the big tent and a few minutes into my sisters' narrative, their words began to fan embers of hurt inside me. It felt like an impending volcanic eruption needed to happen and from somewhere I heard, *It's time to get it out, time to have my say.* It felt like I was being given a rare opportunity to have my say, to tell my family how I felt.

Sitting at the picnic table I looked at my two sisters and in a normal tone, I began. "Do you know how it felt to be left out of Mom's will and have no one, not one person, say anything to me about it? Do you know how horrible I felt?" I probably looked angry but mostly I felt strong and energized to be releasing for the first time my long-suppressed feelings.

"Do you know how I felt and did anyone even care?" At first my sisters just listened, probably in shock. Then, like I needed to be scolded, they began wagging their fingers at me, saying I had it all wrong and how they pitied Mom. When I heard that, my words got louder and as I had learned from therapy, I kept to "I feel" statements. They started to shout saying I had no right to say this now and then they started to cry. But I didn't care because for the first time in my life I felt detached and courageous enough to stand up to my family and my reality.

Everyone in the tent was staring at us, mostly at me. The folks inside and outside were super quiet then some began to leave. Once I finished my rant, my brother, Pat, approached me with tears running down his face. He looked me in the eyes, hugged me, and said he was sorry. His attention surprised me and made me feel a little stronger.

Then my Gram walked over to me. She grabbed both my arms, pulled me close to her, and gave me her trademark show of affection: a firm kiss on the mouth. Like a force to be reckoned with, she stood in front of me, stared into my eyes, smiled, and said, "You've got to get it out. Good for you, you have got to get it out." One time I had asked her how she survived all those years of abuse from her second husband. She told me that when it got really bad, she'd go into the barn and scream at the top of her lungs. In that horrible environment that's what she did to stay sane enough to care for her nine children.

Gram was my angel that day and not just figuratively. I felt like her strong heart and spirit were sent to help me stand up, have my say, and release my anguish. It was almost like she'd been inserted into my drama. She hadn't known about the will until that day.

I hadn't planned it but in my gut, I knew I'd been given an opportunity and I might not get another. Thankfully I was brave enough or foolish enough to go for it.

Soon after, most everyone left the gathering and I got into my car for the long drive home. I realized that during the commotion I'd lost track of Jake so I looked over at him sitting next to me; he seemed okay. He glanced at me and said, "Mom that was awesome!" It made me smile. A few minutes later he looked over at me again and said, "Mom, I don't know if you should have done that." I smiled once more and kept driving.

For the next few hours driving back to Maine, my mind replayed my outburst, over and over again. *Should I have done that? My body signaled a definite YES. Absolutely.*

I think my mom's will and how it was handled cemented my place in the family even more and I began to feel a little less-than. It felt like my mom got in her last shot. The next morning it came to me; in order for me to reclaim self-respect, I'd had to tell my story. And I felt lighter for having done it.

# 81: Shit Gets Real

## What erupted was like a gunshot

During one of the many individual sessions with my counselor, Mickie, we started talking about my relationship with my deceased mother. She asked, "If your mother was in the room right now, what would you want to say to her?"

The thought was terrifying, like inviting a grizzly bear into the room. I froze for a few seconds then uttered, "Oh, it would be way too scary to have her here." Mickie looked confused.

"What if she was in the other room?"

"Nope, I couldn't do that." My whole body started to tremble.

"How about the other end of town?"

"Too close."

"What about California?"

My mind was on idle and seemed to shut down; it was my body that spoke up, "Nope, it's just too close."

Finally, after suggesting the moon and closer planets Mickie said, "Jupiter?"

"Yes, I could handle that." That is, my body felt safe with that.

Wide-eyed and puzzled, Mickie leaned forward in her chair. I tried to curl back into mine and distance myself from her questions. I wanted to speak up but at that moment I felt like a little speck of a thing and so completely exposed, a slight breeze could have whisked me into oblivion.

Mickie's suggestion that my mother could be in the room was terrifying and as real as anything I had ever experienced. It was more real because I felt the pent-up fear in every cell of my body. Over the years I'd built a protective wall around my heart. I panicked because if she showed up, the wall would crumble and I'd be left raw and vulnerable to her shaming. I sank deeper and deeper into the safety of my abdomen. At that moment I became *little Regina* again and I was petrified of what she'd say or do next.

Mickie asked, "With your mother on Jupiter, what do you want to say to her?"

Knots in my gut began to twist and turn. It was a decade's old accumulation of confusion and fear. Then spontaneously, a giant tangle of old wounds surfaced and like a gunshot, an unfiltered wad of hurt catapulted out of me. They were words I'd never thought before.

"I want to piss on her grave!"

*Who said that? Where did that come from?*

Two seconds later, I knew. It came from my young self, the one who had kept yearning for my mother's warmth. Stoked by fear and confusion, the pressures inside me had silently grown over the years. Eventually my fear and sadness turned to rage.

My anguish was freed. It had finally surfaced. Right away I felt lighter but my old friend, self-judgment, jumped on board and embarrassment sank me deeper into the couch and left me feeling small again.

Red-faced Mickie leaned back in her chair, the chair she'd almost toppled a minute ago, and pretended to take notes but I knew she was just gathering herself. The flood gates had opened; my confession to myself had been made.

I began telling Mickie more about my mom and me and how I'd needed words of love and physical affection from her but never got them. Trying to make sense of years of her dysfunction was tremendously confusing and painful. But as difficult and awkward as it was, I was determined to continue. I thought three years of counseling would heal me and my relationship with my mother. Little did I know it would take more than one lifetime.

# 82: The Little Girl in Me

## I follow the road I'm on

Come morning I have to say goodbye to Spearfish Canyon. It feels like I'm leaving a newfound friend but with nothing more to explore, I know it's time to go. I pace myself stretching out my morning rituals in order to savor every last second here. But eventually, I pack up, drive down the gravel road, and follow the long creek to the canyon's end. My heart sinks; I hate endings. Then a subtle restlessness nudges me to continue and I follow the road I'm on.

My hundred-mile drive through the most mountainous parts of the Black Hills is a sunny and hot one. The paved roads are narrow with few shoulders and hardly any pull-offs. Traffic's not bumper to bumper but close to it as tourists slow down and take in the many spectacular panoramas. Driving through the Needles, with its tall granite spikes, takes me back to my first day tenting. I remember young Jay, from the campground, telling me he hoped to motorcycle through these majestic spires one day. I hope his dream comes true and, as the mother of a teenage boy, I hope he drives carefully.

I wind my way through long stretches of steep uphill and downhill grades when, out of the blue, Doug, makes an ear-shattering bark that jars every one of my nerves. I look in my rear-view mirror and see terror in his eyes. He's barking at me. Oblivious to the line of cars behind, I slam on my brakes and slide to a cockeyed stop in the road. There should have been a pile-up but I get away with only a half dozen screaming horns and angry stares as cars swerve around me.

I jump out, ignore the commotion, and bolt to the back. When I open the hatch Doug leaps out onto the side of the road and squats. Poor guy has the runs; it must be from the nasty water holes on yesterday's hike. Seems we're both doing some purging. He looks okay, just a little sluggish when he jumps back into the car.

He makes me stop three more times and each time it's after a car-rattling bark. Being the gentleman he is, he leaves no sign of his distress in the car.

My route takes me even higher into the Hills and soon clouds roll in bringing some welcomed relief from the heat. After a while, nature calls so I pull over onto the sandy shoulder, open the front and back doors on the passenger side for privacy. When I finish, I turn and realize I'm standing on the edge of an obscure lookout point. I step closer to the rim to take it all in. Then I see it. Many miles away and illuminated — again by a single shaft of sunlight — is the Crazy Horse Monument. For some reason, it seems dreamlike, like a silent companion is following me.

I keep driving for miles without checking a map until I see signs for Elk Mountain Park, a part of the Wind Cave National Park. Surrounded again by thousands of acres of wild prairie, it feels like a homecoming so I stop to take it in. It's the delicate beauty of brown grasses swaying like rolls on a sleepy ocean that gets to me, again. *Thank you, coy breezes.* I gaze out over the land and for a minute imagine I live here in a nomadic existence. The replicated scene stretches out in all directions and far beyond what I can actually see or imagine. I love how the land seems to invite me to visit. *Oh, I will.*

Nevertheless, after a few minutes, in this "big sky" country, I feel exposed. I might be missing the security of the canyon. It's beautiful here, but maybe getting too familiar; the newness is wearing off. I miss my child-like excitement.

The campground is just a short drive ahead. It's a large peaceful area with a spacious layout of sites and there are only a few campers. After choosing my site I register at the office then set up my tent and gear. Doug and I take a long walk down the well-groomed road then I settle him in the car and within two minutes, after what he's gone through, he's asleep. I'm ready for a rest, too, so I stretch out in my tent and begin to recover from our hair-raising ride through the Black Hills.

Twenty peaceful minutes later I hear Doug whimpering. I pop my head outside and see him dancing on the ground then jumping in and out of the back of the car. I race over to him and as I do, I feel things crawling up my legs. Crowds of little, biting critters are zooming up my bare legs and heading up my thighs. We must be on a giant anthill.

I swipe them off my legs and feet with my hands then dash off to help Doug. I unhitch him from the car then we trot the short distance to the entrance road. I tie him to a tree and use my hands to wipe the pests from his fur. Thank goodness it works.

I dread going back to get my stuff but after a giant breath, I sprint back to it. I yank up my tent, stakes and all, crumble them up with contents inside, and throw the whole thing into the car. I drive over to get Doug then scout around to find a better site.

I find a vacant one not far down the road so I drive there and check it out. No ants. I leave the car and Doug there to claim it and walk to the office to make it legal. Back at the car I settle Doug in, set up my tent again, and crawl in for a break.

Later in the afternoon, after a good rest, I sit in my chair to read. I'm on a gently-sloped parcel that stretches to the park's cul-de-sac and extensive prairie. A refreshing wind brushes up against me as I set my book in my lap and soak up the serenity. I close my eyes and drift off into a bit of a daze. After a few minutes, I read a couple more pages then look up at the Hills on the horizon and sigh. *Peace.*

Twenty more minutes of pure contentment are ruined when I notice a man in a campsite about thirty-yards downslope from me. He's looking in my direction so I twist around in my chair to check if there's something of interest behind me. Nope, just prairie. He's staring at me. Maybe I've been alone out here for too long. Maybe I'm paranoid. *Maybe I'm becoming a hermit.* I have the same creepy feeling I had at the turn-off going to Devil's Tower. I want to scream, "Stop looking at me, you weirdo!" I feel invaded.

I struggle for a few minutes with my internal drama then feel pissed so I walk over to Doug, put him on his leash, and we walk down the road away from the creep. One extra-long walk later, we return and I hitch Doug back to the car. Thank goodness, when I look up, the guy is gone.

I'm still rattled a half-hour later so I decide to go into Hot Springs only eleven miles away. I need an escape and some solace would be nice. My escape is an easygoing car ride and my solace is ice cream.

Near the outskirts of town, I find a tiny, no-frills place. The faded blue wood siding and pink window frames match the scallop trim along the roof edges. The hints of bright colors and the garish architecture make me think of a children's fairy tale and it lifts my spirits. Cherished things, even if they lose their luster, can still inspire.

As it's handed to me, my two-stories-high mint chocolate chip cone begins its slow drip down the sides. Sweet, cold, and smooth, with just a little crunch, it's wonderful medicine for my tired, edgy soul. My tongue works fast, first smoothing the ragged ridges of the melting sides then licking bottom to top forming a point before I flatten the top. My work ends with a crunchy demolition as I chomp through the bottom of the cone searching out the last and, actually, most satisfying remnants of my treat. This is exactly what I needed after the long, hot drive from Spearfish, Doug's emergencies, the ants, and the creepy voyeur.

The ride back to camp is pleasant but I'm tired and I think about going home. *Maybe tomorrow I'll know if it's time.* I probably just need a rest after yesterday's Eagle Cliff hike.

In the cool evening, I stretch out in my tent and am ready for sleep when an onslaught of hot flashes hits me and my body begins to vibrate. It feels familiar, so I just let it happen. Then my ultimate dream comes to mind: I want to become a healer and create a healing center. A second later I hear coyotes howling in the distance. I remember that coyote will come and disrupt our plans if we feel undeserving. I tell myself to trust that, if my dreams are right for me, I don't have to worry about logistics; it's my enthusiasm that will make it happen. Wow, creating a healing center might be my next big adventure. *How long has this dream been percolating?*

I remember our ant invasion. Ants teach us not to make mountains out of anthills. They remind us to be patient as we create and work for the good of the community. *It must be why ant visited today.*

Before nodding off to sleep, I'm feeling hot and sweaty so I stretch out on my left side on top of my sleeping bag. My insides feel like they're calming, softening. I think about parts of me that needed to be tough in order to protect myself and my children. But right now, I feel a warm tenderness melting those parts, hardened for way too long. It's a new sensation and, at first, confusing because it leaves me feeling vulnerable and uneasy. But because I'm in a meditative sort of state, I slowly begin to accept it. I realize, that in order to attract new adventures into my life, I must be open and, to a degree, unguarded. Also, I need to love myself more, well, maybe even, for the first time.

When the healing stops flowing, I turn over on my other side and can hear a child crying—I realize it's me.

# 83: Doug vs the Buffalo

**I've got to escape this calamity.**

At 6:30 a.m. I roll over and face the gray, translucent wall of my sunlit tent. Ugh, wake up? Not yet. I close my eyes, wiggle back under my blanket, hide from the humid, morning air, and escape into dreamland.

After a short sleep, nature calls so I begrudgingly climb outside, stretch up to the brand new sun, then walk over to check on Doug. He's about as listless as I am and barely lifts his head. Thank goodness he's over the runs.

I think I should be "up-and-at-'em" this morning, so I make my usual breakfast: coffee, oatmeal, nuts, and yogurt. Sitting at the picnic table feels like a chore but I shovel in breakfast because it's part of this Virgo's morning routine.

Even after coffee I'm still lethargic so, when I finish eating, I unhitch Doug and we take a walk through the park. I'm hoping it'll energize me and improve my mood but it doesn't. We're both dragging. Something doesn't feel right. *Where's my zip and curiosity? Maybe a shower will help? Oops, no showers here.*

In the shade near my tent I sit in my chair then open up *Buffalo Woman Comes Singing*, my faithful friend. The book is comforting as it echoes the many challenges I've encountered trying to heal myself from the inside out.

At about 10:00 I feel so out of it that I go back to bed and for the next few hours I waft in and out of consciousness. My brain's adrift, lost in a fog. Inside my oven-of-a-tent, I'm sweating and burning up.

My emotional exhaustion makes me so agitated I can't sleep. *I am so very tired of everything.* After a short time I try going with it, try staying present without knowing what's happening. I try releasing any expectations, even about the very next minute but, even though I keep working at it, nothing changes, and I feel so out of it I honestly don't care what happens to me.

It's probably hours later when I head to the campground bathroom which is only a few hundred feet down the road. When I come out of it, I try to remember being inside it but I can't. *Where am I? What's happening to my mind, my body?* I wonder if my body's tired from yesterday's Eagle Cliff hike but that doesn't seem right.

After another hour or so I eat some leftover chips and candy and begin to feel better. I might be romanticizing but I wonder if my body's going through some type of shift in preparation for becoming a healer. Maybe I needed this quiet morning to allow these changes to occur. It's probably one of those happenings a person just can't ever fully understand.

And something else is bothering me; Doug and I are surrounded by buffalo that are grazing just outside the park fencing. They're a good distance away but the beasts are huge...calm but huge. *I'd love to see one up close.* They make me think about something I read in my book where the author talked about being a spiritual warrior with a heavy razor-sharp sword. She said it's a metaphor for wielding one's power for the benefit of others, having a no-nonsense attitude, and having self-esteem. *I need to continue working on this.* I think about my four friends who bowed out of this trip. I'm still confused as to why they did it but I promise myself that I'll talk with each of them about it when I get home. Even though I'm scared to speak up for myself, I know I need to. If I muster up my warrior courage to confront them, I'll make it happen. It's part of an assignment I give myself: to do a better job honoring and sharing my feelings, in an appropriate fashion, that is. Also, I'm excited to tell them about my adventures.

After another hour or so I'm feeling much better so I decide to go for a ride. I'm thinking I'll be directed to a destination. After driving for just a few miles, I suddenly feel a hand resting on my right shoulder. I can feel its weight and its outline and it feels like an adult man's hand. I'm a little shaken so I look back to see who's there. *No one.* Then for some reason, I put my left hand on that same spot. Maybe it's to make sure a hand isn't still there? I'm a little freaked out but mostly it seems like affirmation that I'm not alone. It dawns on me that I've become less unnerved with this kind of anomaly.

A few miles later, I end up on the Wildlife Loop in Custer State Park. It's a beautiful eighteen-mile, super slow drive through rolling hills and flat grasslands and more steadfast pine clusters. It's lovely but seems too familiar and I fantasize about the thick, green forests of Maine.

Near the end of the Wildlife Loop and just a short ways ahead, a small buffalo herd is ambling across the road. I follow the cars in front of me and inch my vehicle through the herd. Some beasts are almost as big as my car. Suddenly Doug begins barking and the car starts rocking side to side as he knocks the car sides trying to get at them. I'm terrified. His angry barking is bone chilling. I imagine the carnage these beasts could inflict and it's like being in another nightmare.

Not far ahead on the road is an even larger herd heading our way. I pull over to the side of the road behind a few other cars as the herd continues in our direction. I remember the signs warning people not to approach the buffalo because it's rutting season and the aggressive bulls are very dangerous. I've got to escape this calamity so I crank my wheel, and ever so slowly do a U-turn in the middle of the road. I check my rear view mirror and see another herd filling the road behind me.

The noise inside my car is now beyond jarring as I white-knuckle the steering wheel and pray for this to end. I ease my car down the road while pretending to be brave and finally make my escape. I wonder if the hand I felt was a spirit helping me through this. *And to think, just minutes earlier I'd felt cheated out of seeing herds up close.*

On my drive through the rest of the loop, I see at least six more herds with at least two hundred head in each along with lots of antelope, wild burros, and two elk. It's definitely a day for herd animals, ones who thrive in a community. I like the concept: family living close to each other physically and emotionally. But then, I've always been a dreamer.

On my way back to camp, for some reason, I start thinking about the Pine Ridge Reservation. Maybe I'll go there tomorrow. I remember reading that Lake Side Camping is right on the reservation. This makes me feel good. I'll be traveling to Wounded Knee, then probably home to Maine. I feel ready; I'm tired.

I'm also tired of my different combinations of rice, beans, and potatoes for dinner and oatmeal for breakfast. Maybe tomorrow I'll go out for breakfast and I'll have home fries, scrambled eggs, toast, and bacon. My mouth waters. I've eaten out only twice since camping. I don't count my junk food splurges.

After my four-hour cruise on the Wildlife Loop, I arrive back at the campground and am happy to see it's now deserted. I climb out of the car, look up, and whisper, "Thank you for this peaceful land, the constant, gentle breeze, and the sunny, comfortable temps." This place is heavenly and I have it all to myself.

By 6:30 p.m. I think I've eaten my very last dinner of beans and potato for a while. I'm feeling a whole lot better than I did this morning. I'm awake. *Did I get some buffalo medicine today or what?*

Later in the evening tears fill my eyes, lots of them, when I write in my journal: "*I am preparing to leave the Wind Cave area today. Wind Cave is only one mile down the road. I remember the spirits I saw there and how I first learned about the cave when I visited the Rosebud Reservation. I know that something happened to me when I was there but I don't know what it was. I think it's something internal. I might not need to know but, I trust it's something good.*"

After journaling I get my book out and read that Buffalo might be asking us to use our energy to help others. I start thinking again about my four friends back home and how we formed a group that turned into a healing circle. It helped us learn to meditate, understand more about the spiritual realm, and ourselves. I'm trying hard to let go of the idea that our circle might dissolve after I return home. Maybe it's run it's course. Maybe it's time for each of us to go our separate ways and develop our spiritual selves as we choose. *Endings are so hard*

# 84: Childish Fantasies

## Many of these folks are struggling

On my drive back to Hot Springs, all I can think about is my yummy breakfast ahead. I'll stop at the first decent-looking place I see. A modest little diner just off the road catches my eye so I park in some shade. I take a booth along a row of windows. It smells like coffee and bacon and the service is fast and friendly but it's unquestionably the worst meal I've ever eaten. It's difficult to screw up your basic breakfast and I'm pissed but hungry enough to eat the slimy eggs, mushy home fries, and the burnt bacon and toast. I scan the bustling room searching for signs of disorder, disgruntled staff or customers but there are none. And it's way overpriced. So much for my fantasy breakfast.

I get back on the road and remember that today I'm leaving the Black Hills. I'm leaving more than the geography. The land gifted me experiences that challenged me to grow and I'm sad to leave. I bet it'll take a long time to understand what happened to me here.

But for now, it's sunny with comfortable temps and I realize I've taken for granted the near-perfect weather these last couple of weeks.

I coast down another runway that reaches into the horizon. My destination's unclear, but I trust my inner compass so heading east feels right. I remind myself I'll be going home soon.

It's time to check my options so I stop the car. The brochure says there's a public camping area on the Pine Ridge reservation. I'm psyched. Maybe I'll camp there tonight. But when I drive onto the campground, an angry dog charges my car and the grounds are disheveled so I leave. More of my romantic notions about reservation life evaporate. I have to face the fact that many of these folks are struggling.

I drive into the town center of Pine Ridge and an unusually large building stands out among the others. The big sign says it's the Red Cloud Indian School and when I drive closer I see that the main doors are open. With only a couple cars in the parking lot, I decide to go in and explore.

I head down a long hallway of cinder block walls leading to the gymnasium. All the doors and windows are open so the hallway acts like a breezeway. Robust currents of fresh air rush in diluting the familiar, dankish school smells. It's summer break and the place has a familiar feel to it, abandoned and empty except for old memories. I remember going in to tidy up my classroom after the school year had ended. I had conflicted feelings: excited about my new freedom but lonely too. I missed the built-in social time with students and staff. Now that I think about it, it's another of my internal conflicts; I relish being alone but need the affirmation of others. Paintings and matted photographs hang on the gym walls, others rest on the floor leaning against it. I'm not an artist but some look like high-end, expensive pieces.

The gym paint is faded, the windows are cloudy, and the torn basketball nets hang lopsided from the hoops. I'm disappointed and feel let down. Let down? This is about you? Then I remind myself this isn't a tourist attraction, it's a community where students might lack what I probably take for granted.

I want to think the kids who come here have a decent shot at a good life. Maybe I'm investing more into my visit than I should but even the murals are chipped and dingy. That bothers me too. But who am I to judge. I know very little about this town and these people. Their lives could be rich in spiritual tradition, love, and hope, exactly what I'm looking for.

After circling the gym I see more stacks of extra-large photographs on the floor, leaning against the wall. They depict brutal scenes of the Wounded Knee massacre: frozen, mangled bodies, some lying in the snow, some dumped into a pit with hundreds of other souls. It's the first time I've seen most of the pictures and I hope I never see them again. The massacre seems even more real and grotesque now.

How does a community live with such traumatic memories? I remember that trauma inflicted on parents can be passed, via DNA, to their children. I stop for a second and think about carrying the suffering of a parent as well as our own. It's just too much so I stop thinking. Here in the gym, surrounded by images of the terrible past as well as their hopes for the future, I might understand a fraction more about this community. And I just have to believe that they're holding on.

As I leave the building, I remember something from the brochure. The tomb of the Lakota chief, Red Cloud, is nearby, so I decide to visit it before driving on to Wounded Knee. Red Cloud is remembered for convincing his band to give up their way of life and live as wards of the US Government on the Pine Ridge reservation. He was a controversial figure. Some hated that he gave in to the army and some respected him for taking care of his people. Who is to say what's true. By nature, so much of history is subjective.

Red Cloud's tomb is a rectangular above-ground cement vault. It's located in a cemetery filled with the gravestones of dozens of Indian scouts and school-age children. During the 1800s and into the middle 1900s, the US government took Indigenous children from their parents and put them in Christian boarding schools. It was an attempt to assimilate them into the Euro-American culture. Punished for speaking their own language and practicing their religion, they also suffered terrible abuses at the hands of the priests and nuns and many died before seeing their family again. My depressing discovery is made worse by the overgrown burial grounds. Trauma and loss of family can gum up everything, every single part of a person. I think I understand a little more.

Immersion into more of Pine Ridge's history leaves me despondent so I can't wait to leave. Deep down, the little girl in me hoped the settlement would feel like I imagined it was two hundred years ago before the army and white settlers came. Now, only a fraction of the true history of these people is in books written mostly by white people who have shifted and shaped history to suit their superiority. Damn!

I continue to struggle to integrate the reality of reservation life with my idealist notions of how I want it to be. I wonder why this is so important to me. Maybe it's related to my dream of having the perfect family. Maybe it's because I resonate with American Indian spirituality and their reverence for the Earth. Maybe we do live multiple lives and, in one of mine, I lived here. I suppose it could be one or all of these.

Leaving Pine Ridge is a relief and, with every mile, I'm more relaxed. My drive to Wounded Knee is a long but easy one. When I arrive, I ride down past the monument then continue by the house where I took shelter. Two camping trailers are parked near the little blue home and I guess that they belong to folks going to the "Healing of the Hoop" starting in two days. I remember the word hoop refers to how life moves in a circle and how all living things are connected within that circle or hoop. The concept of interrelationship and dependency resonates deeply with me. I want to try and remember that my family includes everyone I meet.

I'm curious about the settlement of Porcupine which is a few miles beyond the blue house so I keep driving. But the road is terribly rutted so I turn back. When I pass the blue house once more, there are more campers in the driveway. Again, I get the feeling that it's definitely not a good place for Doug and me.

When I leave Wounded Knee, it feels like it's time to go home. I drive east towards the town of Kadoka and hope to find a campsite for the night. Once I'm on the main highway, I whisper, "Spirit, show me a sign so I know I'm doing the right thing." One second later a huge red-tailed hawk swoops down in front of me then perches on a fence post near the side of the road. I drive a short way past it, pull over, and check him out with my binoculars. He's staring at me. After a minute or so he takes off and flies towards me. Only a few yards away he veers up and tips his wings and sunlight shines through his beautiful, red tail feathers. It's the only hawk I've seen since I drove into Wounded Knee two weeks ago. I smile knowing I'm on the right track.

The eighty-mile drive across the prairie to Kadoka is another long, hot one and this time feels monotonous. Once I arrive, I stop at three different campgrounds: no dogs allowed in the first one, another one is a hole, but the next one looks good. It allows dogs, has a shower, and is only $5 per night. Boy, did I luck out.

It's nothing fancy. My site's just big enough for my tent and a picnic table and I can barely squeeze my car in a few feet from the tent.

Once I settle in, I walk to the bathhouse for a much-needed shower. It's a dirty little stall that adjoins the office area. After I undress and step in, I turn on the water and hear people talking. It sounds like they're right in the room with me. I look up and realize there's no top to the shower stall. It's wide open to the office. I can hear every conversation as if I'm in that room. Well, I sort of am in the room. I hear, "Them dirty Indians, always coming in for a $5 shower. Wish they'd get their own damn plumbing." It takes me all of two minutes to finish up then rush, still damp, back to my site. I don't even bother combing my hair. Who the hell cares about my hair in this dump.

A few minutes later and a little drier, I remember I'm out of groceries so I drive to the little settlement just down the road. The feel of the town is as bizarre as the people in the office. When I walk out of the store, the wind must have shifted because the most god-awful smell hits me. There's got to be a stockyard nearby and even with my strong stomach, I want to retch.

I drive back to my site hoping I'm escaping the bad air but when I open my car door the smell has followed me and now I have some company, lots of company. There are swarms of giant, bright-green, grasshoppers everywhere. By the time I crawl into the tent, my campsite is covered with them: flying, springing, and munching on any available vegetation. I plan to just stay inside the tent till they move along. Well, they don't. Even from inside I see hundreds landing then leaping off my tent walls. I can hear them fluttering in the air and hitting the sides. I'm in a bible movie and God has cast out a cloud of punishing locusts. I peek out at Doug and my poor pup is in a frenzy, bouncing about trying to escape the plague.

Sometimes Grasshopper can show us that our fears have to do with the fact that "no one else has done it this way." It urges us to trust our instincts and our unique rhythms to know when to make our best moves. Sometimes grasshopper shows up if we are afraid to make the leap. Grasshopper always leaps up or forward.

And, with that thought, I know what I have to do. I've had enough; I'm done here. I immediately pack up and at 7:00 p.m. we're headed to Maine.

I'm elated at having escaped but also at having completed something. I don't know what it is but it's done and I feel more energized than I've felt in days. I'm headed to Sioux Falls, South Dakota then three days later I'll be home. I know my life will be different when I get back but for now, all is well inside this car, this body, and my heart.

# 85: Stay Safe or Sail?

## I can create my own reality

After a long, disturbing day I'm happy to leave Kadoka. And as I drive down the last strip of prairie, I think about the previous three weeks and the great distances I've traveled both on land and internally. I followed delicate vibrations of Earth and my inner compass. And by living simply I became more sensitive to my body and now I want to become even more fully engaged in it. It's not clear how it will look but I know this is how I want to navigate the rest of my life.

It's near sundown now and I know it was a good decision to leave. All my windows are open and the warm air bolsters me. I flash back to sailing off the coast of Maine. It was exhilarating but sometimes the wind was so strong and the boat tipped so much, I thought we'd capsize. The challenge was to keep the boat in sync with the currents, both water and air. So we watched the sails for signs that we needed to tack.

My friend, Gary, captain of the thirty-footer, impressed me. He knew every inch of the vessel and, depending on the conditions, he made it waltz or jitterbug on the water. Experienced and intuitive, he knew the dance and, even when the seas were choppy, he kept us safe and on course.

Gary is a confidant guy and a life-long friend. For many decades I've watched him delve into, what I'd label as one high-risk hobby after another: hang gliders, prop planes, gliders, biplanes, and jets. He started as a logging contractor became a corporate pilot, and recently was a successful tuna fisherman. A fitting motto for Gary might be: "There's a whole world to explore. Keep trying new things, interesting things, and especially, try them if it's dangerous."

In the fall of 1998, for my fiftieth birthday party, Gary and his wife, my dear friend, Linda, flew down from their home in northern NH to southern Maine in their yellow, antique biplane. Gary navigated by sight following the familiar roads. I asked him, "What do you do if it's cloudy?" He smiled and said, "Then I'd do whatever I can."

The afternoon after my birthday party, I drove my friends to the tiny municipal airport for their flight home. I got out of the car and walked over to say goodbye when Gary told me to jump in the plane. I sucked in a breath and probably looked shocked. He and Linda flashed big smiles and I tried on a smile too. I said, "Really?" I was scared but I knew I had to do it.

While Linda settled into her fold-up chair and her newest book, Gary and I walked to the beautiful, yellow craft. Poised like a sprinter, with its head tipped towards the sky, the beast looked poised to take off. Gary guided me as I stepped up onto the wing then slid into the front open cockpit. I sat down on a small, dinged-up bench then buckled a thin, cotton strap across my lap to hold me in. I put on a leather aviator hat and goggles then looked for a parachute but there wasn't one. I felt like I was sitting in an empty wooden barrel. It's probably good that my friends sprang this on me because I had no time to get frightened, just moderately nervous.

Gary climbed into his cockpit behind me. Earlier I had peeked at his controls: a foot pedal and a single stick-lever. That was it. A minute later the big plane roared then started to move. As we taxied down the bumpy runway, ready to take off, I told myself, I had a choice; I could be afraid and miss out on this amazing experience or I could imagine I was one small part of this big, beautiful "bird."

It was as loud as a train and, showing its age, trembled hard all over. But, after what seemed too long a takeoff, we gained speed then finally lifted off into the brisk, autumn air. For some strange reason, the deafening noise and mighty rush of air on my face made me feel a vital part of that creature. In that moment thoughts and ego evaporated. Fully engaged in my flight I was no longer an earthling. I became my journey. We did a gradual climb rising into the clear sky and over the glistening ocean. The day was made for it. We tipped left and began to drift over miles of salt marshes sliced with serpentine waterways. Then we cruised over rocky beaches. It was exhilarating and breathtaking and the relentless thrust of air fanned tears across my face. Fear and regret found no home in me as I rode that simple vehicle above our gorgeous, glorious planet. And I did feel I was part of that plane. What a gift: to fly free in the in-between space between heaven and Earth. I was reminded that, at any time, I can create my own reality and be there again. I can be grounded by fear or, untethered, I can fly.

Why not soar?

317

# 86: My Red Bandana

## It represents me not being afraid to be me.

While driving back to Maine, I call ahead each morning to reserve a motel room for that night. On my first night, it's late evening when I get to Sioux Falls. After weeks of camping, sleeping in a bed feels weird and the room artificial. I miss being curled up inside my tent, relishing the cool, clean night air and the company of crickets. But Doug flops down on the carpet and quickly falls asleep. He's probably relieved he doesn't have insects and furry critters to contend with. Tomorrow night I'll be in Portage, IL, then Buffalo, NY, then home.

My trip is uneventful and restorative. I've always loved driving. The closer I get to Maine the more excited I am. I've missed my kids and I can't wait to tell my meditation group about my trip. Right now, the thought of being home with absolutely nothing to do and no place to explore sounds wonderful.

I arrive home, call my kids, then after that, pretty much all I do is rest and unwind for the next few days. I'd forgotten how much I love my house and it's so good to be back. With all my hiking the last couple weeks, I feel like a real adventurer and I'm still wearing a red bandana. I'm starting to realize it represents me not being afraid to be me. But initially I thought about Bear Butte and Leo's bandana and how annoyed I was, thinking he was trying to look Indian. At home now, I feel like a bubbly teenager on gradation day and, steeped in the afterglow of my journey, I want to preserve it. It's a bit of a hippie look, and new for me, but people in town pay no attention. I do feel a puzzled vibe from some friends and family but all that matters is how it reminds me of my joy living on the prairie.

A week after my return and even though they know, through common friends, that I'm back, none of my four friends has called me. To clear things up, I know I'll have to initiate a visit before I get to tell them about my trip. But first, I want to know why they decided not to go.

I call each friend and set a time to talk to her individually. With my new-found confidence, calling isn't as difficult as I'd thought it would be.

I meet with each on different days: April, Karen, Jo, and lastly, Paula. When we meet, I remember how excited we'd all been talking about our trip. I can't wait to tell them everything. Grinning like a kid on Christmas morning, I'm primed to jump into my tales. *I hope I don't come across too "out there."* But it's hard not to be jazzed up after what I've experienced.

I meet with April, then Karen, and then Jo. We greet each other with a hug and pleasantries about our homes and pets. I ask, in a curious and courteous manner, why they didn't join me. Each friend gives me a vague excuse: it just wasn't good timing or they didn't want to leave their house or dogs. I know them well enough to know they aren't telling me the whole story but I don't want to press them and make them upset with me. After their response, I pause for a short time and wait for them to ask about my trip. The silence that follows confuses and hurts me. It's a shock when I realize they're not interested. So after that, I say goodbye and walk back to the car. But, as I drive away, I feel proud that I had the courage to ask them why they didn't go. Confronting a friend, actually anyone, who may have hurt my feelings, is torturous. It feels like I'm facing my imperfections.

*Living with people isn't easy and it looks like my sense of self-worth could use some reinforcement.*

It's a sunny day when I visit Paula, so we head out back to sit on her deck. My sunglasses and deep tan add to my confidence and I love my healthy, toned body. To some people it might not be a big deal, but, for me asking for clarification, from a strong woman like Paula, takes courage. Over the years I'd worked closely with her, learning about energy healing and spirituality. She's a healer and counselor so I expect that she, of all people, will appreciate my experiences. Well, I'm in for a shock. I skip asking about why she didn't come along because I already know. I remembered her saying, "So you don't want to ride in the car with me" after the meditation where I saw Doug and me alone in the car going to the Black Hills. On the deck I'm animated telling her about my trip but because she isn't wearing sunglasses, I get the full force of her stare. She says, "Why are you bragging?"

Shocked and embarrassed, I stop talking, stand up, then slowly make my way back to my car. I drive home, confused and upset. *Was I bragging? I don't think I was.* I couldn't wait to share my delight with my friend but now I feel like a naughty child, chastised by an unhinged mother. *I must have done something wrong. But what?* This humiliating memory stays with me. Paula and I never speak again.

For years I stayed confused about why I felt so hurt about Paula. However, when I told my sage friend, Jan, what happened, she assured me it was very normal for me to be excited sharing my adventure. She said true friends enjoy sharing in our joy. Jan's words helped but I still felt like an overly sensitive, naive kid. It would take me a long time to understand, then believe what Jan said. She even suggested that Paula might have been jealous of me. Who knows, but today, I don't care.

I've always felt it's important to have a healthy sense of pride. Growing up we were taught to be proud of our accomplishments. If we did good work, we took credit for it. Period. Life's not a competition. It's a classroom where we have opportunities to grow ourselves, enjoy our achievements, and, be cheerleaders for others.

Even though I was saddened by the loss of these friendships, I knew many of my experiences on the prairie had been deeply personal and could have only happened if I was alone. I came back even more independent. My life challenges enriched me, and eventually made me feel freer. My emotional and spiritual evolution is, aside from my spiritual guides, mostly a solitary one and I am fine with that.

My life was changing big time and it felt like I was outgrowing the former me. I knew I didn't want to keep my ex-husband's name or my maiden name. I wanted my own. One day, sitting with a friend talking about a name change, she said, "Where is your spiritual center?" I said, "In my heart." She asked, "What feels both the most powerful and most vulnerable place in you?" I said, "My heart." And so it became Strongheart. The name resonates with a quality way beyond my reach but reminds me to keep stretching and growing.

A year after my trip I sat in a packed courtroom waiting for the judge to call me up to his bench to legally change my last name. I handed him the document and after he read and signed it, he looked up at me, smiled, and said, "Strongheart. Great name."

And, gradually it dawned on me; it was homage to my Gram who had the strongest heart of anyone I know.

# 87: Her Last Kiss

## An angel deserves white

One day in November, a year after my trip west, my brother called to tell me that Gram was in the hospital. Her heart was failing and she wasn't expected to last long so I drove to my hometown to see her. For years, Gram's pet cockatiel was her only companion. After it died, I asked if she would get another. "I'll never have another pet. I'm tired of things dying," she said. It made me think, for the very first time, how my father's sudden death must have shattered her.

I was relieved Gram had a private room in our tiny hospital and that she wasn't hooked up to any devices, not even an IV. She looked peaceful, lying on her back with a bright white sheet pulled up to her chest and her head cushioned on a generous white pillow. Her hands, folded into each other, rested on top of her midsection. They still looked strong.

She appeared to be napping. As I walked up to the bed, I stopped to count her breaths and was relieved her respiration rate was normal. Someone had combed her short white hair and pulled it back into some nice, neat waves. *This is my lovely Gram, swaddled in white.* An angel always comes with this much white.

I bent over, patted her hands, and whispered, "Hi Gram. How are you feeling?" She didn't answer or stir which felt strange to me. I was in denial about my dear grandmother dying. Over the years, whenever we met, her eyes would light up, she'd give a broad smile, then grab me and give me a quick, hard kiss on the mouth. Even though it shocked me, I'd smile because I could feel her love. *Gram, this is so not you, lying here all quiet.*

I pulled up a chair and sat for what felt like an hour but I know was less. Alone in that tiny, near-empty hospital, the quiet was unnerving. *Should I talk to her? Will she hear me, and what do I say?* I felt like I was in some sort of in-between reality.

After a long uncomfortable spell, I knew it was time to leave. It was my last visit with my dear grandmother, my cheerleader, and my rock. I stood up then bent down to kiss her on the forehead. As I got near, Gram whipped open her eyes, stared at me for two seconds, then pulled me down and landed her signature firm kiss on my lips. I almost gasped out loud; it was like she'd returned from the dead. *OMG, Gram.* Then in smooth slow motion, she let me go, folded her hands on her stomach again, and sank back into her pillow and sleep.

I recovered, then in a bit of a daze, I said, "Goodbye Gram. I love you." Then my avalanche of tears and rumblings of sorrow caught me off guard as I stumbled down the hall, out of the hospital, and into my car.

A few days later, after most of her large family and friends got to trickle in for a visit, Gram's strong heart rested, and I knew I had lost my champion.

# 88: My X-Ray Vision

## A blessed instrument for healing

One day not long after my trip, a friend phoned me. We chatted for a bit then she said, "I fell, twisted my ankle, and..." Before she finished her sentence, in my mind's-eye, I saw what looked like an x-ray of her ankle. The once misaligned bones were highlighted in fuzzy grays.

Without thinking, I said, "It's just a sprain, nothing too serious." She said, "How do you know?"

"I just have a feeling about it." I thought it was an adequate response. But, the spontaneous image of her ankle was striking and something that had never happened to me before. With so many mystical experiences "under my belt," it was noteworthy and interesting but it didn't rattle me enough to want to tell anyone about it.

Days later the friend called and confirmed what I'd seen. She had a bad sprain but nothing was broken. I was surprised and found it curious that both my description and prognosis were accurate. My life had been a wild long roller coaster ride of self-discovery with many crazy metaphysical events so I really didn't give it much attention.

Weeks later I got a letter in the mail from my daughter, Jennifer. It seemed odd because she lived in a neighboring town and we talked often on the phone. I stood in my dining room, opened the letter, and began to read; "Mom, Ted's father is going in for an x-ray tomorrow." Ted was her boyfriend.

Right when I read the first sentence, something pushed me back into my rocking chair and in my mind's eye flashed a picture of the man's large intestine. It looked like the whole left side of his colon was stuffed full with a black substance. I began to weep out loud with sorrow for a man I'd never even met.

After a minute my crying let up so I wiped my eyes and continued reading the letter. "They think it might be serious. Mom, can you pray for him? We are all so scared it might be cancer."

I regained my composure then called Jennifer. When I told her what I'd seen, she thanked me and said she'd call me when the x-ray results came back. Being pushed into the chair startled me but, for some strange reason, seeing his insides didn't. This kind of imagery was beginning to feel almost normal.

For the rest of the day I wondered about the man and the scientist in me wanted to find a name for what I'd been able to do. So I dove into my self-help books, rereading sections on intuitive healers and various therapeutic techniques. I also called a practitioner friend to get her opinion and she suggested it could be a skill I might want to develop.

Later that day, I settled into my recliner to meditate and maybe get some answers on my own. Everything I'd been doing helped put my body at ease but I still had questions. *Why did I see his intestine? What does this mean? Why me?*

Two days later, Jennifer called with the results of the x-ray. She said, "Mom, they think he has cancer. There's a huge black mass in his intestines."

"Oh no, how awful. Can I ask, what part of his intestines?"

"On his left side. They said it looks like the whole left side of his intestine is full of cancer."

I shared what I had seen and she said the x-ray image sounded identical. Then something, I didn't know what, prompted me to say, "I think he's going to be okay." I hoped my words comforted Jennifer and after a short chat we said goodbye. The man had surgery and decades later is still healthy.

For years, with the help of research, therapists, and energy healers, I'd been on a mini crusade to purge my body of negative memory and belief systems that limited my spiritual development. I began to like the person I was becoming: more generous, confident, and compassionate. To my daily prayers I added, *I want to live to my highest spiritual potential,* and my prayers were being answered. My continued efforts were helping me heal physically and emotionally. It was as if places inside me were being prepared for something new and important.

When these strange events began I was hesitant and insecure at first but I slowly began to accept that I'd been given a gift. I had the ability to scan a person's body, even from a distance, and get images which I could interpret. Trusting my intuition, I was able to sense health problems and ways to help. I was becoming a medical intuitive.

In the following months I worked with healer friends who helped me understand and make use of another ability: moving energy through my body. With their guidance and the help of other brave friends serving as guinea pigs, I practiced. I'd put my hands on a person and a slight force, which I understood originated from the Universe, moved through me then into them.

It dawned on me that my body was operating like a step-down transformer; it would download large amounts of energy then transform it into the appropriate quality for the person receiving it. I discovered it also worked at a distance; I could send it to someone at a different location. To me, it was like prayer in motion, a way to share vibrations of peace and good health, and is one of the many ways Spirit can speak to us. I wondered how my experiences out west prepared me for this.

At another time, while meditating with friends and unbeknownst to me, they watched as my chakra centers (the body has seven spiritual energy centers) were being modified. One friend said the rewiring left my circuitry in a very unusual configuration that was not normal. When I asked her about it, she told me it had something to do with my developing gifts. This revision of my spiritual centers probably enhanced my ability to help people.

I wondered if I should take a class, get some formal training for an accepted healing modality but every time I seriously considered it, my gut gave me a resounding NO. So I continued to study books, work with healers, practice on friends, and pray for guidance. I also began to delve into a variety of traditional healing techniques.

Through the late 1990s, I meditated while listening to Aboriginal drums and singing. At home, I danced to the songs and sank deep into my body, and connected with Earth in a deep meditative way. It caused me to release some deep-seated sorrow and fear. Sometimes, I got flashes of a friend's struggles or emotional injuries and I often sensed some of the raw feelings they had experienced. It was not planned or pleasant but it seemed to be part of my schooling; I was being challenged to stay detached from others but with compassion. This became the philosophical foundation of my healing work. Caring for someone while maintaining healthy detachment. I called it compassionate objectivity.

At one point I realized that I had a strong urge to put my hands on people. At the time this was unusual for "stand-offish" me. I asked a healer friend, Amy, to guide me. Another friend, Wendy, was brave enough to let me practice on her. What happened was remarkable. Amy guided me as I'd put my hands on Wendy who was lying on the massage table. I focused on staying peaceful and relaxed. With my hands in place, Amy told me she "saw" a current of light flow through my body, out my hands, and into Wendy. She said it was powerful but I was only focused on helping and had no sense of anything else. This technique and medical intuition became my standard healing methodologies.

When I think back to how these gifts were revealed, I recall being on Myra's massage table and the shock on her face when I said, "Why do I have to drag this big body around?" It turned out that the human body is not only a precious repository of memory and wisdom, it's also a blessed instrument that can be used for conducting healing. So, housed in my wonderfully resilient body, I navigate my life and try to help others.

# 89: St. Peter's Hand

## It feels as normal as if I'm riding in a car

I'm excited about my next adventure: building a healing center. I hope to offer the spiritual traditions of various cultures, forest retreats, and classes for developing one's own healing gifts. It will host traditional elders who'll teach about honoring the Earth, each other, and ourselves. The center will be located on sacred land and all I need to do is to find it.

One summer afternoon, while taking a break from the day's chores, I stretch out on my oversized recliner with my two new kittens curled up together on my lap. Their melodic purring and the warm sun pouring through the window make me drowsy.

A little weak from an earlier massage, I lapse quickly into semi-consciousness. Then, almost immediately, on my right, I sense the hazy figure of a man. I'm curious but wary. *Do I want this? Is this real?* After some internal questioning, I sense the being is friendly.

He's a big-knuckled, husky man with rounded features. His mostly bald head has only thin white hair and he is wearing a white toga. Right away Saint Peter's name comes to mind and that feels right even though he doesn't look like pictures of him I've seen in books. But I trust my intuition and don't care about his name. What's important is how he makes me feel. With a tender, knowing smile, he extends his broad left hand to me. I feel like I'm in an awake dream. The experience feels right, not occultist or extravagant, just, kind of normal for me. I give him my hand and when we float off together, it feels as normal as if I'm riding in my car.

We stop near a tunnel opening in the ground and for some reason, I can see deep below the crust. The tunnel's length is shaped like a corkscrew and it slopes gradually downward to the dark, grayish center of the Earth.

In my listless state, I start to feel Earth communicating with me like it did on the prairie so it seems normal and easy to accept. Suddenly, a powerful knowing comes over me. It's like I am being "told," that I will be shown the location for the healing center. The directions will be vibrations that I'll feel in my body. *This seems all so familiar.*

Through some sort of telepathy St. Peter asks me to join him. When we approach the opening of the tunnel and I look down, my belly quivers.

Time disappears as we drift side-by-side down the hole. The dark humus walls, rich in organic matter, smell dank. It seems newly excavated and is a little too dark and damp for me. When we reach the bottom, we float out into the colossal space of Earth's center. What looks to be only a half-mile away and suspended in midair, is a huge army-green rectangular building. It is the size of about ten football fields, has no windows, and resembles a shoe box with an overlapping lid. *This could be a scene from "Star Wars."* The science teacher in me is amazed and in my gut, for some curious reason, it all makes perfect sense. I so want to know more about the surreal panorama before me.

I stand gawking as if contemplating an abstract painting. Then suddenly it all becomes clear and I understand. I know, not in my mind but in my body, the building in Earth's center contains all the information for the workings of our planet and its inhabitants. No words, data, or images are conveyed to me. It is the truth, as accepted as the color red, a perfectly shaped snowflake, or a mother's love for her baby. To describe things like these, words are useless. What I get is an internal knowing and it is everything I need. I'm at peace with the aberration so I relax.

Time is still impalpable but while I have Earth's attention, I silently ask for help with a few things: some sacred, some relationship issues, and some monetary. Simply asking for help floods me with more peace and confidence than I've ever known. It's wonderful. I then ask for continued healing of my imperfections and guidance on my new quest. I am "told" to start looking for land for the healing center in three years, in 2003.

I sense it's time to leave and as we drift to the surface, I notice the tunnel has been lined with the glistening interiors of alabaster shells. *That was thoughtful.* Someone knew the dark tunnel had unnerved me.

My strange experience ends right then. My kittens are still in my lap purring and the sun is still shining down on me. *Damn, what a trip.*

I know I have something important to do so during a meditation a few days later I ask, "Where is the healing center's location?" Right away a large, wispy cloud of hope and creativity washes through me giving me chills and I see the image of the center's main building. It's a simple design with a large central peak, and a steep, sloped roof. When I close my eyes and ask again for its location, I see a map with a large shaded sphere extending a little northeast of Portland, Maine.

My new adventure is to create *a* healing center, not, *Regina's* healing center. It will be built for the benefit of all who are searching for a higher connection to Earth, Spirit, and themselves. I know I'll have to do the legwork necessary to find the land and build it but it seems easier because it isn't about me. When I try to make more sense of it all, I remember the spirits at Wind Cave and on Mt. Agamenticus and how I'd understood and believed their wordless communications. Being inside Earth, I had no questions about why I was there because all the answers had already been given so everything inside and outside of me felt perfectly satisfied. But now, I wonder how I might pass on to others what I have learned.

Spirit's message, *You'll be guided to the land,* is the song that begins resonating inside me. I can't stop thinking about the land that's waiting to be discovered. When I tell friends who'll listen, they say my face lights up and my eyes sparkle. I'm ten years old again, listening to Nature's invitation and ready to walk down to the pasture with my fishing rod and bait.

Every time I close my eyes, I can see the map given to me by my spirit guides. I'm sure the land is somewhere north of Portland and all I need to do is track it down. And the high I'm feeling is familiar; I'm back in the Black Hills, climbing to the top of an outcropping, excited about what I'll discover. With the help of my inner compass, I'm sure I'll find it.

By the summer of 2002, I'm ready. Doug jumps into the back of the car and before we head out, I sit and slip into my internal navigation mode. But this feels different, the pull to go is missing but I ignore that and head out. Once I reach an area I'd seen on my mental map, I'm confused because I feel no connections to the land. It takes me a couple more trips to realize I've started my search a year too early.

In early summer of 2003, I start my search again. I help Doug, who's thirteen and has bad hips, into the car. I look up in the rear view mirror and see him staring at me with those big brown eyes, graying muzzle, and wagging tail. He's still game for our adventures.

After a short prayer I settle into my quiet place. I have unwavering trust I'll be guided to the land. As I drive, I stay focused on my body's sensations and less on the physical world. I'm like a kid on a treasure hunt but I have an advantage. I have an otherworldly coach or two. *There's nothing else I want to be doing.*

With school out for the summer and my kids old enough to be on their own, I can search pretty much at will. I always head a little northeast of Portland then alter my direction depending on what I sense. At times it feels like someone's helping me steer.

Ten miles beyond Portland, I drive through unfamiliar rural areas, some vibrant, some a little dreary. There are hundreds of acres of thriving farm lands. Other parcels of land are beautiful but feel unsettled like a confused child. The tangled energy reminds me of Mt. Harney in the Black Hills, where Black Elk had his vision. The land there, and maybe here, has not been honored. I drive into tiny, colonial towns struggling to keep their character and others that've lost their souls to gentrification. I say a prayer for peace and leave it with the land and its people.

# 90: Farewell, My Friend

## He treated me like I was more than good enough

A few weeks after beginning my land search again, I get a phone call from my intuitive daughter, Jessica. "Mom, Doug was in my dreams last night. Over and over he kept saying to tell you he's ready to go."

At first I don't understand. *What does she mean he's "ready to go"?* My poor boy's hips had gotten much worse over the last six months and he'd lost control of his bowels so he had to sleep in the basement. Even though the space was clean and warm and he had a big mattress to rest on, it made me sad to see him relegated to that. Sure, now I have to lift him into the back of the car but once he got in there he was his puppy self again. It's much easier to focus on my search and not his suffering.

After Jessie's call, I admit to myself that it's time. I call the vet and make an appointment for Doug to be put down in two days. I call my three kids and invite them to see Doug once more. Jessica can't make it but Jake and Jen come to the house to say goodbye. I'm happy they have the opportunity, especially Jake who was only twelve when we got Doug.

The day comes and a dear friend offers to go with me to the vet's. I thank her and say I'll be okay. Doug and I have spent so many hours traveling in the car together, it's only fitting he should have his last trip alone with me. I'm confident I can give him a good sendoff, the comfortable easy transition he deserves after thirteen and a half years of adventures and devotion to me. It's easy to transform into my robotic-like self that I know so well. It's a reflex; it's how I handle trauma.

I help him out of the car and for the last time I attach his leash. He looks up into my eyes and wags his tail. *Thank god he doesn't know.* We walk into the waiting room and I sit down and prepare myself to go in

331

the examination room when it's time. I'm totally divorced from the whole situation. I just can't be here and in my body.

After a short wait, the vet tech opens the door and she waves me into a little room. I walk my boy inside, hand off the leash, then, as she starts to close the door, I grab the door handle and run wailing through the waiting room and out to my car. It is my loudest crying ever. My heart and chest feel torn apart and bleeding with grief. I am losing my best friend, my protector, the one willing to wait in the background, ask for little, devote himself to my safety, and revel in our adventures. He loved our travels, to Arizona and South Dakota and I just know he understood everything I was doing. I feel eviscerated. My love for him and his love for me is exposed and, for the very first time, I really feel it. And, what do I do? I run away. I'm so distraught I'm not sure how I manage to drive home. When I pull into the driveway and look at the big, deluxe doghouse I'd built him, I fold my arms around myself and cry and cry and cry. *This hurts too much. Thank you for being my friend, big boy. I love you. And even with all my rough edges, thank you for loving me. I wish I had been better.*

I spend the rest of the day and night in a haze of tears, paralyzed with grief. Doug had required so little of me and he happily would have given me so much more. *Why didn't I appreciate that till now?* The next morning, I start to judge myself, thinking I could have been more attentive and pampered him more. It feels like an old pattern, thinking I'm never good enough. But then I realize that's exactly what he taught me. He treated me like I was more than good enough. *And, he loved me, didn't he.*

The staff at the vet's office are just lovely. They call me the next day to ask how I am and it helps. I'd made plans to have Doug cremated so they also want to let me know I can pick up his ashes in two weeks. A couple days later a card from them arrives in the mail. On the front is a photo, taken from the back, of a teenage boy sitting with his arm around a German Shepherd. The boy could be Jake and of course, the dog looks just like Doug. They had never met my son and didn't know I even had a son. My knees begin to buckle. Inside they'd written kind words saying how they know how much I loved him and what a good life he'd had. It brings on another fit of weeping. Later I slide the card into my folder with my children's old artwork.

Earlier in the Spring I had watched a pair of finches building a tiny nest high in a corner of my old shed. For a few weeks I monitored the comings and goings of the parents hoping they'd raise a healthy brood. When the activity ceased and the nest was empty I took it down and smiled. The outer surface was a charming weave of dried grasses with cloth threads, and its soft center was full of Doug's hair. I still have the nest and to this day, it feels like Doug never left.

# 91: Office Pumps and Hiking Boots

## I'm tumbling along towards everything

I love my search for the land. It reminds me of roaming the plains and I feel as free as a released kite. Then after a few weeks of surveying, I ask my guides to help narrow down the search. It's funny because right after I ask, I close my eyes and see a revised map. There's a much smaller shaded area ballooning out even more northeast of Portland.

In 2003 sightings of bald eagles in southern Maine are unusual but I see one most days of my land search. When I get on I-295 N in Portland, I start noticing hawks, all told, at least six. In the town of Brunswick, where two tidal rivers converge, bald eagles show up. I spot four today. *This has to be a sign I'm close.*

Eagle reminds us to soar above our ordinary life. But first we'll be challenged to risk it all in order to grow ourselves and cut the tethers that keep us safe.

On my third trip to the Brunswick area, I decide to consult a realtor. So, without an appointment I walk into a Real Estate office in Topsham just over the bridge from Brunswick. It's in a repurposed old paper mill perched high on the granite banks of the Androscoggin River. When I step into the office and a bald eagle swoops a mere twenty feet outside the window, my heart does a little swoop too.

Lucky for me, the owner, Pricilla, is in. I take a seat in her gorgeous space with its floor-to-ceiling windows that offer breathtaking views spanning miles down the river. *I could camp out in here for a month.* Middle-aged and attractive, Pricilla is friendly and professional but what I appreciate most is her sincerity. Right away we get down to business. I tell her I'm looking for a secluded lot, possibly with a house, about ten acres, maybe with a brook, and in this general area. I say I'll have to sell my Hollis home before I can purchase land. As I rattle off more details, she takes copious notes and when we're done, she says she'll be in touch. A couple days later she calls and says she has three properties to show me. A realtor for decades and a trusted community leader, I'm confident she'll be able help me. *It's all coming together.*

We meet at her office and I get into her car, excited to see what she has to show me. We travel to a rural location in a neighboring town but after a half-hour searching, she can't find the property. Obviously frustrated, she says it's never happened to her before. The second property is a parcel with a run-down trailer on it. The land seems okay but it's definitely not for me. The third listing is a fifty-acre lot on an unmaintained dirt road in Topsham so we head there.

Pricilla's high-end sedan bounces up the rutted dirt road leading to the remote lot. The last half mile cuts through a dense conifer forest speckled with thin hardwood groves. This land's energy feels alive but almost like it's hibernating.

She pulls into the entrance to an old logging yard and says the land had been harvested about five decades earlier. Then it happens. I open the car door and right when I put my foot onto the ground, I feel it. I step out onto the belt of smooth bedrock road and I feel something I haven't felt in a very long time: I'm home. I turn to Pricilla, "This is it."

Amused, she turns to me. "What do you mean? This is it? You haven't even seen it."

"I don't know how I know, I just do."

We walk down the old moss-covered logging road. Its center is a thin, patted-down path, probably a wildlife route. We inch our way for another forty yards into the hemlock and pine forest and I can't stop smiling. *How can a forest feel this alive?* I am sure this vibrant land is greeting us. When long tree branches and downed limbs obstruct the trail, we turn and head back to the car. At her office we peruse the specs of the lot, discuss the sale, and agree to meet again soon and walk further onto the property. She says her business partner, Donna, will join us next time.

A couple days later the three of us drive up the bumpy, dirt road to the land. Ready for a good trek, I'm wearing my brother, Pat's, safari hat and my hiking boots. To my surprise the two ladies have on flowery, summer dresses and dainty, little office pumps. Pricilla leads, Donna follows, then me. We meander along the old trails on another perfect summer's day. At one point not far into our hike Donna stops, turns back, and looks at me. She says, "It's like there are eyes looking at us and saying they found us." For a moment I freeze and feel a giant shiver. *How could she know?* I smile at her and we walk on.

After a good, short hike, we head back to the car and when I walk into their office, two bald eagles glide side by side past the windows. The three of us begin sifting through the hurdles associated with making the purchase. Having bought and sold property before, I know there's always a lot to it and my list of needs before I can move is a bit longer than most. I have to sell my house in Hollis, purchase the land, have a new house built, locate a temporary place to live, and get a new job. Like being inside a giant rolling wave, I'm tumbling along towards everything I want and all I have to do is keep moving with it. And for some reason I'm not one bit worried.

And like magic, it all comes together. In early August I sell my Hollis home for a very good price, make an offer on the land, and have it accepted. I get an interview for a teaching position in Topsham and am hired on the spot. Pricilla manages a local rental and arranges for me to stay there while my son-in-law builds my house. Then to top it off, because people associated with the land sale are pulling for me, a neighbor abutting the parcel has the property line moved and the seller and realtor absorb $10,000 in unforeseen fees. Construction begins in early spring of 2004 and I move into my new home in early August of that same year. My quest is over. I've found the magical piece of land that was waiting to be rediscovered.

# Epilogue: Home at Forest Circles

## Singing a new beginning

Fancy's whispered meows wake me early. She wants her breakfast and waits politely at my bedroom door. She's a pretty little calico and we two introverts make good roommates. We like to come and go as we please. But unlike her two predecessors, Fancy's not a hunter. She's friends with the countless red squirrels, chickadees, and rabbits near our house. Curious, she gets close but doesn't physically engage. *Hmmm, sounds familiar.*

I'm tempted to feed Fancy then go back to bed but I know I'd miss this luscious summer morning. Next to May, June, and January, August is my favorite month in Maine. I lie between two open, screened windows and listen to the forest waking. Troupes of melodic buzzing, squeaks, and chirps flood the air. I think back to my first morning on the prairie, tenting by the pond, the air electric with life and singing a new beginning. Twenty-five years later, I'm in my cedar shingle cape surrounded by hundreds of acres of woodlands. The forest, only twenty feet from my window allows me to eavesdrop on all kinds of daytime and nocturnal escapades. It's like camping. I couldn't have found, or I should say, I couldn't have been guided to a more perfect spot.

I finally get out of bed and feed Fancy. The open-concept design makes my roomy kitchen, living, and dining areas flow into each other. There's also a loft, bedroom, healing room, and utility room. My primary heat source is a wood stove and its stucco chimney stretches up in the middle of the house to the cathedral ceiling. With so many windows, and set so deep into the forest, everywhere I look, all I see are trees. And even after a string of long winter days inside, I'm content.

I open the sliding glass door and step onto my generous deck. The chatter-filled woods draw me into my favorite part of the day. The trees whir, *Come and visit.* But it's early yet and I've got my routine so I go inside to make breakfast.

Back on the deck, I stretch out on my lounge with my coffee and bowl of oatmeal embellished with honey, sunflower seeds, and wild blueberries from the land. My binoculars sit ready on a nearby table but huge clusters of mint, black-eyed Susans, and wildflowers surrounding the deck draw me in. Legions of foraging wasps, bees, and butterflies make the blossoms shimmer as I lean back, sip my coffee, and pretend I'm one of them. Life is enigmatic and interesting and exciting. It really is.

The sun's still hiding behind the trees giving me a couple more hours of shade. Fancy meows to come out so I slide open the screen door. She hops out then scurries under the deck to scout for evidence of chipmunk and rabbit friends and not-so-friendly nocturnal trespassers.

This day will require little of me so I can sit for as long as I want as life cavorts around me. *Feeling invisible is the best.* Today, I'm off: no healing sessions, health fairs, or classes to teach. No one's coming for a forest retreat and there are no programs to host. I can't remember how the name of my business, Forest Circles, came to be. It could have been from brainstorming with a friend or from a daydream, I'm not sure. And, does it matter? All I know is it fits perfectly. It's where circles of people gather in this mystical forest.

I focus my binoculars on the feeder hanging from a nearby tree. The mated pair of rose-breasted grosbeaks brought along their fledgling this time. A small gang of chickadees, like tiny masked bandits, dart in and pluck sunflower seeds from the feeder, and below them, a chestnut red squirrel stakes claim to the dropped seeds. On the deck, a downy woodpecker, with its red beret, hangs upside down on the suet feeder stabbing at the fat-coated kernels. An iridescent dragonfly lands on my arm: *magic abounds.* Then, from high above, I hear a screech. I'm not sure if it's an eagle or a hawk. Then I remember it's too early in the day to see eagles so I think it's a hawk. About one o'clock, once the sun's heat has created enough thermals, I often see eagles spiraling up and southwest towards the ocean tributaries. I focus my binoculars on the shadow of that soaring bird, and, as it turns away, I see its beautiful red tail. Dreamy mornings like this, surrounded by such vibrant Nature, make it hard for me to leave home. Some people have told me that, as they drive up the dirt road to my house, they feel an energy shift. I'm not surprised. I recall times in '96 when I noticed something similar while exploring the Eagle Cliff trail and Spearfish Canyon. It's like drifting into a peaceful space that has no borders.

Another memory stirs as I look at the other end of the deck. When Jessie's daughter, Grace, was six, she'd sit perched there in her tiny chair and practice casting with her little fishing rod. It amazed me how focused and accurate she was. She's a lot like her grandma and the memory makes me smile.

A little while later, I'm antsy. Fancy's occupied for the morning and it's still cool, so it's a good time for a stroll. I put on my red bandana and tears well-up as I remember Doug and I hiking in the Black Hills. *It's been a long trek but I've finally come home, to myself.* I grab my walking stick from the kitchen. It's a gift from some men in recovery who spent a weekend here. I've tied bells near the top so I don't inadvertently spook a bear. I step down the deck steps then walk towards the other end of the house and to the "magic rock." When I was scouting with little Grace and her dad for a place to build my house, we discovered a huge flat area of exposed bedrock. I told her dad, my contractor, I wanted this to be right outside my bedroom window. And it came to pass.

Over the years, as I explored this parcel of land, I began to understand how diverse it is. The giant swamp ferns and, rare for Maine, tupelo trees make it unique. A kaleidoscope of pale green lichen and kelly green mosses carpet acre after acre. Thick stands of mixed softwood mottled with hardwood cover most of it. Everywhere I look, I can see long, weather-worn tabletops of bedrock and they're still making their way to the surface.

The first time I climbed onto one of these massive up-thrusts, it was like climbing onto the back of a whale. And as I looked for places to insert my feet and knobs to grab, it reminded me of scaling Cathedral Ledge in the White Mts. When I stood on top of the "whale," twenty feet above my forest's primordial, fern-filled pond, it was like I had ascended another Bear Butte and I knew that more adventures awaited me. At that moment, Earth again recognized me and in a familiar way communicated through the bedrock. *This is it, this is your home.* Standing on the back of this sentient thing I wept because I felt welcomed.

Whale signals we have found our destiny as encoded in our DNA. We have returned to our beginning. By giving voice to our essence, we, like whale, show uniqueness.

On his first walk on the forest trails, a shaman friend told me he sensed a tearing in the land. Later I told him my research revealed that the land was on the Norumbaga Fault Line. Turns out he was right because eons ago the European Continent collided with North America and Maine. As it tore away, part of Northern Europe's crust remained. Some of this land once lived in Europe.

There are round boulders on the bedrock near my bedroom. They make a good place to sit and when I look up at the soft blue sky, a flashback makes me chuckle. About ten years ago twenty men in a rehab program spent a weekend tenting with their counselors in the forest. A few of the men told me they'd been jailed off and on for most of their lives. That weekend program was one of my most memorable at Forest Circles. The counselors and I had worked out a trade where the men would spend time clearing deadwood from the forest in trade for camping. The guys were wonderful and I enjoyed our many delightful conversations. One morning, a couple of the men greeted me near the deck. "Regina, what's with the big rock over there?"

"Well, we call it 'the magic rock' because some folks can feel something when they stand on it." With impish smiles, they asked if they could try and I nodded yes.

"If you stand up straight near the middle, close your eyes, and spread your arms something might happen," I said.

They positioned themselves on the rock and closed their eyes and I stepped back to watch. About thirty seconds later one of them yelled, "Jeeesuuus Christ! What is that?" Then the other guy began to laugh saying he felt something too. I explained, "The Earth shoots healing energy up into whoever invites it." They just smiled, shook their heads, and walked back into the woods and their work. I giggled.

One of the many gifts the men gave me was this walking stick. They engraved it with a thank-you and their names. Every time I use it, I remember their stories. Hard, tragic stories but I also remember how much I enjoyed their honesty and seeing their boyish joy working in the woods. One man said it was the best day he'd had in thirty years. I remember thinking these men need good physical work to rebuild healthy self-esteem and maybe their lives.

I step off the magic rock, into the forest, and onto the old logging trail. Swatches of mosses and delicate, tiny plants speckle the path. Other sections are strewn with pine needles and oak and maple leaves. Every few years I remove the ferns and small trees rooting in the path so it looks cared for. Yet, the forest is crisscrossed with lots of old trails I've yet to explore.

One step, then another, my staff pounds the ground and bells ring: step, jingle, step, jingle repeat. I think of my friend, Oscar whose birth name is Ogugua, which means comforter. He is a high priest and chief from West Africa. His ancient metal staff has bells, too. With his traditional regalia, including a tall, ancient mask and ankle bells, he blessed my house and the land with his ceremonies. Raised in both Christian and an aboriginal religion, his New Moon Ceremonies at Forest Circles have raised a lot of eyebrows but healed even more.

His programs lasted up to eight hours ending late into the night. Sometimes coyotes serenaded us as we sat in chairs circling the fire pit's raging flames. With all my outside lights off, it was pitch black except for the fire. Oscar had told us not to speak until the ritual was over because it helped him stay in an altered state.

Settled in, sitting near the fire, I knew what was coming but the new participants didn't. From outside, around the other side of my darkened house, came sleigh bell sounds, blunt thuds, then jingles. In excruciatingly slow motion for us fast-paced Westerners, the sounds grew louder and closer. I knew he'd be wearing one of his stunning wooden masks, some of which are hundreds of years old. I didn't know which one, though. I knew the magnificent mask would startle some people and in his tradition, it was meant to. "The Mask" is believed to be imbued with a spirit. When a tribe's values went astray, "The Mask" ceremony jolted people, reminding them of good behavior.

I loved watching the faces as the imposing figure of a seven-foot-tall decrepit old man emerged from the veil of darkness then limped into the fire's light. He moved with the pace of an arthritic centenarian. Impatient, I was as fidgety as the others. But that's one lesson we were charged to learn: slow down, listen to our bodies, and trust our hearts.

The first time I saw Oscar was at a Mask Ceremony in a neighboring town. He was wearing beautiful, traditional West African regalia and a black mahogany mask. It had a human face. When he approached me, I got confused and uneasy because the mask's deep, hollowed-out eyes were as dark as night. After he moved past me, I pulled back to scan the others in the crowd. Their faces radiated reverence. When I looked back at Oscar, I didn't look at the mask, I focused on his whole being; dressed in layers of flowing fabrics, he swayed to the drum beats, and stopped to bless each person with foreign words and a wave of his wand. I reminded myself to see with my heart and not just my brain. My insides told me the mask and the person inside were not only safe, they were good.

That night at my place, "The Mask" chanted, swayed, and blessed the fire with his elephant-tail wand. He waved it through the flames and got so close I panicked thinking he'd catch on fire. But Oscar was in an altered state and not entirely human. Later, when I'd tell him how I worried about him catching on fire he'd smile and say, "The flames are not dangerous."

"The Mask" stood before each person. He shuffled and swayed some more, and chanted a personal blessing while waving his wand above the person's head and body. When that part was done, and it took a long, long time, he shuffled back to the other side of the house, entered, and removed his regalia. Afterwards, he joined us at the fire and cheerfully answered questions about what happened. His serious answers were laced with jokes and mischievous comments. I'm grateful to have such a valued family friend, mentor, and confidante.

Today, on this cheery morning I'm back on the trail and walking up a gentle incline. At the top is a giant high-bush blueberry plant, one of dozens scattered on the land. This large clearing extends deep into the forest and its thick, spongy mosses make me think it might offer a magic carpet ride. Surrounded by stately pines, it's been the site of many smaller workshops like "Making Native American-style Flutes," and "Peruvian Despacho Ceremonies" which honors the generosity and the life force of Pachamama (Mother Earth). This is the spot where my young friend, Jackie, did her very first "Crystal Bowls" workshop. One at a time, she tapped then swirled her wooden dowel on the rim of each different bowl sending beautiful vibrations into our bodies. Another friend, Ken is a student of South American shamanic traditions. His drumming and spirit-journeying circles held at the fire pit are always uplifting and inspirational.

I meander further along the main trail and the unusual diversity of small plants makes me think of my dear friend, Ray, a farmer, Maine Guide, and spiritual teacher. A slow talker with a thick Maine accent, he's quite the contrast to Oscar. On one of his nature-walk programs here, we identified edible and medicinal native plants while he led us to the far side of the land. We climbed a tall rounded ledge and sat listening to his teachings. He showed us how to quiet our minds so we can hear our inner realities. The words from this kindhearted man are always simple but profound. We ended the day with our traditional potluck and a real sense of community. Ray is another mentor and beloved friend.

A short way further down the trail is a small valley I named Owl Ravine. It's half the length of a football field with a tiny seasonal brook on the bottom. The abundance of stately pines and hemlock hold off the sun making it shady. Though I've never seen one there, I imagine owls would like it. Chuckling, I recall the day a friend and I found a pair of men's boxers on a boulder in that spot. At first, I was baffled then I remembered it was where a guy had done his solo retreat. An experienced outdoorsman, he was also deeply spiritual. For three days he fasted, consumed just water, and used only a blanket on a mossy spot for a bed. At the end of his last day we met to talk, something I offer to help folks process their experiences. He said that one night the mosquitoes got so bad he took off all his clothes and smeared himself with mud. In the morning he walked out of the forest and down the dirt road to wash off in a stream. I laughed wondering what the neighbors must have thought seeing a mud-covered creature walking past their house.

The forest comes more alive when people visit and especially if they do a retreat. For them it's a time to reconnect with their inner selves, Earth, and Spirit. Some use a tent, some only a sleeping bag, and some sleep on just a bed of moss. One man sat against a tree for the night. I ask that they leave all electronics behind and I give them a small shovel for bathroom needs. During their retreat, I "hold space" for them meaning I stay close to home and keep them in my thoughts. I am available to talk about their time in the forest before and when they're done.

The trail flows up a longer incline then moves into a shady section dense with pine. At the crest of the hill is a wide sunny area. It's a patchwork of frosty-looking lichen and cobblestones of vibrant, fuzzy mosses. Only in community can they thrive.

Years ago, Amanda set her tent near here. We'd met at a New Moon Ceremony and soon became friends. I did healing sessions with her, helping her heal from her abusive past. Her stories of personal trauma were horrific. It was hard to imagine that my lovely friend had suffered so. But Amanda was a rock and, though she struggled, she always saw the bright side of life.

Serious about freeing herself from her past, she did three, three-day solo retreats near this spot. The most memorable, and they were all significant, was when a moose woke her late at night. She told me she heard it snorting and pawing near her tent and was terrorized. In the morning, she guessed her tent was set too close to the moose's nighttime route. She moved her tent a short distance away but the angry moose returned and she had another nearly sleepless night. In the morning she moved her tent again but this time much farther away. That night something bizarre woke her so she unzipped her tent and looked out. In the distance, where the moose had been, the whole forest was lit up from behind as if by floodlights. What she said next didn't surprise me. She said she crawled back into her tent, thanked the Universe for the breathtaking lights, and slept dreaming of Moose.

The next morning, we sat on my deck and talked for hours about her time in the woods and especially about the moose and the mysterious forest lights. Amanda told me the lights were the Universe's way of saying. "You are valued and being cared for. You are also lovable." Because of the abuse she had suffered, the words touched her deeply and we both cried. At one point I read from my book, "Moose shows up and snorts to remind us to feel joy in our accomplishments and to be proud of our renewed sense of self. It's something we've fought hard for and won. Bellow your joy!"

Amanda wrote a not-so-short report about her meeting moose and gave me permission to share it. Tears come quickly when I think of her sparkle, generosity, and bravery. In her early fifties, she died of cancer in 2014 after dedicating her life to helping the less fortunate through her art and community actions.

Often times I think of Amanda when friends and I hold "The Grandmother's Circle" at Forest Circles. Women aged 20 to 80 gather to support each other and share wisdom through personal stories, art, and spiritual wisdom. Amanda would have loved these circles.

After a half-hour I'm ready to head back. When I approach the house I pass the sweat lodge frame and it takes me back to 2012 when I began hosting programs taught by a Native American physician from the area. An accomplished author and international teacher, his focus is mostly on healing through storytelling and Indigenous lore. One cool fall day, ten of us gathered saplings from the forest to build the Inipi frame. Since then he's led a number of ceremonies here offering powerful opportunities to heal.

A little further down the path, I stumble on a root and almost tumble. Melissa comes to mind. I'd been here for a few years when she called me from Nova Scotia. She'd seen my website online and wanted to talk with me about her relationship issues. Of course, I said yes but I was puzzled as to why she'd come all the way to Maine for help.

It was winter, a rough snowy one. The day she visited the sky was gray, the sun subdued. When I saw her giant pickup come up the driveway I was curious and when the door swung open and a six-foot-something husky woman climbed out, I was even more curious. She had on one-piece Carhartt work coveralls, snowmobile boots, and a knit beanie. I'd never seen such a strapping woman.

Melissa, with her childish smile, came inside then we sat in the living room sipping tea. As she began telling me about herself, her kind and gentle mannerisms made me instantly like her. She said she was confused and sensed some big life changes were coming. Then she began telling me about her abusive partner. He made her pull, by hand, sleds full of cordwood a half-mile to the house every day. I listened as she told her troubling narrative of feeling locked in a relationship and a lifestyle that left her feeling empty. I had expected her to complain about the work but it was her feelings of emptiness that hurt her. As I do with my clients, I listened with both my ears and my body. And in its own unique and subtle way, her body spoke to me and I heard and began to understand Melissa's confusion and sorrow.

After a long and convoluted conversation, I followed my instincts and suggested we go for a walk in the forest. The snow was almost to my knees so I strapped on snowshoes. I offered some to Melissa but she declined saying she was used to hauling wood in even deeper snow. She followed my tracks and, with her big frame and experience, I was sure she could handle it. Something bizarre happened, though. As she followed me along the trail, she kept falling. She didn't trip, or feel dizzy, but, at least five times, she fell. Puzzled, she lamented that she'd never had this problem before.

Before leaving my house Melissa had told me about her fondness for trees and how she loved communicating with them. Since childhood, they'd been her treasured companions and conversations with them helped keep her sane. She told me she'd been looking forward to visiting this part of Maine and its trees but as we ventured further into the forest, she got quieter and her head hung down. We stopped on the trail and with a puzzled look she said, "None of them are talking to me." I felt bad. It was more rejection for this poor, dear woman.

After a good hour, we headed home. Halfway back, while she led the way, we walked past a large old pine tree that I'd never truly notice before. But today it drew my attention so I stopped and kept looking at it for a few seconds. I wasn't reaching out to it but it began communicating with me. It was a diffuse kind of language that only my intuition understood. It was information for Melissa so I stored it inside me for sharing with her later. This tree communication was a first for me.

Back at the house we sat in the living room sipping more tea and talked about our walk. She wondered, out loud, why she kept falling. After a bit I finally told her about the pine tree.

I told her what the tree told me: she could break loose from the jail she was living in and find herself again. Spirit was trying to shake her up, make her trip and fall to the ground. The tree was saying to take control of her life. It was time to honor the wonderful woman she was, create a life that would bring her joy, and surround herself with what she loves.

Some people want a healer/teacher to fix them or tell them what to do. I don't do that. I offer my insights, some options to try, and encourage them to go to their spiritual heart center to find direction and answers. I told Melissa I would pray for her and support her. She drove all the way down here trusting a tree would help her and it did, not exactly as she thought it would, but it did. I told her to trust herself, listen to her beautiful heart, and stay connected with the little girl who lives forever inside her. It was all up to her.

In the spring, Melissa moved to NY to be closer to friends. She and I stayed in touch for a year or so. In her last email, she said she was happy, surrounded by good people, and learning more and more about communication with trees.

The summer sun is peeking through the tree line as I walk the last bit of the trail. From where I stand my little house looks like it's always belonged here. Three times during the first year here, I was jolted awake at exactly 3:00 a.m. by three bangs on the front of the house. It was loud, like a giant's forearm slamming against my home. I sat up in bed wondering what it was and also why I wasn't freaked out. It had disturbed my sleep but for some odd reason, I wasn't afraid. After a few minutes I fell back into a peaceful sleep.

When I asked my friend, Oscar about it, he never raised an eyebrow and just said, "Oh, that's the forest spirits. They want some attention. Set out some fruit for them." I waited expecting him to giggle or even smile but he was serious. That afternoon I put an apple and some grapes out near my compost pile. I was never awakened again. *There are so many invisible worlds.*

I often find little treasures along the trail and this morning it's a pure white piece of quartzite. I decide to take it back to the house and set it on the windowsill in my healing room. It's believed that quartzite helps people stay anchored in their physical bodies. It's a perfect stone for the healing work I offer. In our modern, data-driven world it's easy to abandon our bodies and live mostly in our minds.

Not all folks who book a private session with me go into the healing room. Some want just conversation along with a medical intuitive or past-life reading. I've found that the body holds memories of past lifetimes and, in the right setting, will share them. Before my clients arrive, I say a prayer that I will help by sensing relevant information. Once their bodies begin sharing information with me, I ask one question after another related to what I sense. It helps them to figure out what's bothering them. Having a fresh look, from a different angle can make a world of difference.

One former client stands out as she resembles many. Katrina requested a comprehensive healing session so after a two-hour conversation and intuitive reading sitting in my living room, we went into the healing room. It's a sunny room adorned with multicultural artwork and nature treasures from my travels. Katrina lay on her back on my massage table and I sat close by in a chair. Out loud I said, "I welcome all the highest guides and angels who wish to be part of this healing. May Katrina receive the highest level of healing that's appropriate for her at this time."

From that point on I was mostly an observer then, near the end, an energy conductor. I began to see a shadowy image above Katrina's belly. Her eyes stayed closed as I asked if she saw anything in that area. Even though I gave her no details, she described what I saw. I asked what the image meant to her, how it made her feel. That's when *her* work began. I waited to sense the questions I should ask her, questions that would take her deep into her body and her resilient child-like self.

The general outline for each healing session is similar but the content is remarkably different. Always interesting, the sessions are somewhat client directed, and sometimes life changing. The way I understand it, I'm the navigator and the client is the pilot of her body's energy. Katrina had access to the gauges and so had the capability of changing course. I know it's trust in my spirit guides and compassion for my client that help make it happen. It's a blessed time to leave my ego behind and be part of the up-welling of restorative energy.

Katrina sounded drugged when she responded to my question about what she saw on her abdomen. For me, it was proof that she was completely relaxed. There's something about the vibes of the forest and the healing room that helps it happen spontaneously. Next, I "heard" questions to ask her that would help take her to places in her body needing attention. I didn't "see" much of anything inside her body after that. Once she surveyed her body and gave it what it needed, I asked her to go to her heart area to find her little-girl self. I asked her to describe the little girl to me. It didn't take long. Katrina described herself as a five-year-old wearing a sparkly red skirt. She said she was a tap dancer. I asked her to ask the little one if she would help her. The little one said yes. After a long pause, I asked, "Where is little Katrina now?"

She said, "Oh, she's on my liver."

As is normal, I don't see the child so I asked, "What's she doing?"

"Oh, she's tapping out all the junk and hurt feelings in there. She's sending it to the light." We both smiled.

As the minutes went by, I continued to ask where the little one was, what she was doing, then waited for my next question to come through. Finally, I felt a nudge to stand up then put my hands, sometimes just fingertips on certain parts of her body where energy was needed. All of my attention was on my hands and where they felt they wanted to go. Sometimes imagery of an injury came up and I asked about it and my hands lingered there sending it some love.

When Katrina said the tap dancer was done dancing inside her, I told her to tell the child to go to her heart. I saw only parts of what came next. Katrina said the little dancer twirled and tapped with a fury. As she spun, sparkles flew off to all parts of Katrina's torso. It was a dance of peace and self-love.

When the dancing stopped, I asked Katrina to imagine that her swirling heart was growing, swelling in size. I told her to ask it to fill her chest, then her body, then the room, and maybe the whole house. We took our time with that part. Some clients have expanded out into the galaxy. It's a shamanic experience that's directed by their angels and guides. All that while I sit focused on the central core of my own body and keep my mind blank. I am not privy to seeing their journey but I do ask about it later.

After a couple minutes and when it felt right, I asked Katrina to very slowly come back to this house, this room, and then into her body. We sat in silence for a short time then I reminded her, if it felt right, to ask her little-child self to stay inside her heart and help her to evolve and heal.

We took our time before going back to the living room then we talked about the session. I answered questions and reminded her about what she said she saw. The most important question I asked was, "How did it feel to be in your heart, and to have it be that big, and then to travel?" I reminded her that same feeling would always center her and fill her with peace and courage any time she needed it. In addition, I suggested she stay in communication with her little-girl self as she has great wisdom and healing abilities.

After I've set the quartzite down in the healing room, I close the door and walk into the dining area. I run my hand over the long pine table my folks purchased back in 1958. I feel the dents and cracks and this scarred old friend takes me back to family times, both joyful and strained. A friend that also reminds me of the pain I had to shed before I could find peace in order to help others. I think of us wild kids and my dad and especially my mom sitting around it while each of us did our best to find a way to enjoy our lives. Years later when my siblings and I got together, sometimes the "pissy sheets" story would come up. We'd laugh recounting how our mother fumed when Linda poked her finger through the sheet. They would laugh more than me, then after a couple more beers we'd hug and leave each to our own memories.

Above all, I think of my mother, how challenged she was sometimes to love us when she'd had no parent to model that behavior. I can understand how she probably feared intimacy when it could lead to pregnancy, and how she held herself together even when the whole town knew my dad was cheating on her. Finally, I forgive her for her weaknesses.

It took decades of self-examination, therapy, and spiritual development to begin to understand my mother. And now after six long years of struggle and internal torment while writing this book, I can admit to forgiving her for her missteps and for taking me out of her will. Even though it hurt at the time, I now choose to remember all the ways she helped and supported my daughters and me. It's a relief to be able to say I love my mom.

I walk into the kitchen, step up to the sink, and look out into the forest. Eight years after his death, I was finally strong enough to scatter Doug's ashes. A dog represents loyalty and Doug was the epitome of loyal. To honor him I chose a spot a short distance from my kitchen windows, in a sunny stand of hemlock and pine. At least a dozen times a day I look into the forest where he rests on his very own bed of pine needles and keeps his eyes on me, waiting for our next adventure.